"THIS IS BERLIN"

ALSO BY WILLIAM L. SHIRER

NON-FICTION

Berlin Diary

End of a Berlin Diary

Midcentury Journey

The Challenge of Scandinavia

The Collapse of the Third Republic

The Rise and Fall of the Third Reich

*Love and Hatred: The Stormy
Marriage of Leo and Sonya Tolstoy*

FICTION

The Traitor

Stranger Come Home

The Consul's Wife

"THIS IS BERLIN"

RADIO BROADCASTS FROM NAZI GERMANY

WILLIAM L. SHIRER
INTRODUCTION BY JOHN KEEGAN

THE OVERLOOK PRESS
WOODSTOCK • NEW YORK

First published in the United States in 1999 by
The Overlook Press, Peter Mayer Publishers, Inc.
Lewis Hollow Road
Woodstock, New York 12498
www.overlookpress.com

Library of Congress Catalog-in-Publication Data

Shirer, William L. (William Lawrence), 1904–1993
"This is Berlin" : radio broadcasts from Nazi Germany / William L. Shirer ;
edited by Noel Rae ; preface by John Keegan : introduction by Inga Shirer Dean.
p.   cm.
Includes index.
1. World War, 1939–1945.   I. Rae, Noel (Noel Martin Douglas)
II. Title.
D743.9.S512   1999
940.53--dc21   99-37201

ISBN 0-87951-719-0 (hardcover)

Manufactured in the United States of America

1 3 5 7 9 8 6 4 2

Contents

Illustrations

INTRODUCTION

John Keegan

William L. Shirer was, when he died in 1993, two months short of his ninetieth birthday, one of the most famous journalists in the world. His best known achievement was his monumental book, *The Rise and Fall of the Third Reich* (1959), one of the most successful works of contemporary history published in this century, though his fame had already been made by his *Berlin Diary*. Both were based on the years he spent as a *Chicago Tribune* and later Columbia Broadcasting System (CBS) reporter in the German capital before Hitler's seizure of power and during the first seven years of the Nazi era.

Shirer, the individual, remarkable figure though he was, ought properly be seen, however, in the context of the generation to which he belonged, that generation of self-confident, fact-seeking, radical Americans who left the young United States to bring their fellow-countrymen the truth, as they perceived it, of events in the Old World and in the rest of the globe which belonged to or depended upon it. Theodore White was such an American, so was Virginia Cowles, so was Ed Murrow, whose relationship with Shirer was to be a decisive influence on his life. They established, long before Tom Wolfe coined the phrase, the New Journalism. John Reed had been a precursor. Reed, author of *Ten Days that Shook the World*, was, however, too partisan to be counted among the true band of American pioneers, while Hemingway was too solipsistic. He confused the reportage of great events with personal adventure and resolved that dilemma only in novel form. White, Cowles, Murrow, and Shirer showed themselves to be true New Journalists in their impartiality, their eschewal of self-dramatization, their whole-hearted resistance to censorship, their suspicion of news management, their determination to see for themselves, and their passion for the truth.

It is significant that Shirer, like Hemingway, was a Chicagoan, and of almost the same generation. The capital of the Middle West was, in the years before the Great War in which both men grew up, a fountainhead of American energy and independence, detached from the Europeanism of the East Coast and proud to represent the free-thinking, undeferential spirit of the great republic's heartland. That heartland thought the Old World and much of what it stood for – the persistence of a hierarchy of classes, the ethos of imperialism, the code of conformity, the repression of individual enterprise – a society ripe for exposure.

Spain, during the Spanish Civil War, was the theater in which the New Journalists first practiced their mission – though Theodore White was already at work in corrupt old China, and Virginia Cowles in the shaky Versailles states of Central and Southern Europe. It was the rise of Nazism, however, which gave the American missionaries their great chance. Shirer was foremost among them. He had already, before Hitler's appointment as Reichschancellor in 1933, cut his European teeth, working for the *Chicago Tribune* and other newspapers in several European countries and acquiring fluency in French and German.

Germany was to be the key to his success as a journalist. In 1937, once again out of a job, a familiar interruption in the careers of expatriate American journalists in the Depression years, he met Ed Murrow, an established CBS newsman, in Berlin. Murrow, later to become the authentic voice of America from blitzed London, got him hired on the spot. When Murrow returned to Britain, Shirer became the principal CBS European correspondent, based first in Vienna, then in Berlin. In 1938 he began the series of broadcasts, most of them introduced by a crisp "This is Berlin," which was to make him famous across America.

Berlin, in 1938, was a city which the Nazis had brought wholly under their control; its government was Nazified, as was that of the German Reich, and so was its journalism. The Enlightenment (Propaganda) Ministry directed by Dr. Josef Goebbels dictated the content of all German newspapers and broadcasts and laid a heavy hand on the output of the foreign press also. In September 1939, when war with Poland broke out, and almost immediately with France and Britain as well, Shirer's broadcasts became subject to strict Nazi censorship. He felt the strongest obligation to tell such truth as the censorship system allowed him to report. He managed to evade its interference to some extent by establishing friendly relations with some of the censors, who at first were "reasonable" and "friendly." Later, as the war became more serious, he resorted to what he called "careful writing" and the use of American colloquialisms to evade the censor's blue pencil. By September 1940, when the Germans had already lost the Battle of Britain, and so the chance to invade Britain across the English Channel, he recognized that his ability to circumvent censorship had gone. In December, when the Battle of Britain had finished, the German invasion fleet had been dispersed and Berlin was under regular, though ineffective, attack by Bomber Command, an attack he was not permitted to witness or effectively report, he decided that his journalistic role no longer had value, and he decided to return to the United States. "The Gestapo accuses me of working for the American intelligence service," he told his superiors. It was the fitting authentication of his integrity during his Berlin years.

What had he reported? The impression these transcripts of his Berlin broadcasts most clearly conveys is of his immersion in contemporary German life. The Germany he knew in 1939 was not enthused by the prospect of war. The memory of defeat in 1918, and of the hardships of the Allied blockade that preceded and followed it, until the forced signature of the Versailles Treaty, were too strong for ordinary Germans to take any pleasure in a return to hostilities with France and Britain. Hence his repeated descriptions of the impact of an imposed war economy on the Berliner: ration cards, even for meals in restaurants, and clothes rationing so severe that the purchase of stockings or socks meant forgoing warm outerwear. Shirer congratulates himself that he had bought a new winter overcoat just before the outbreak of war on September 1, 1939. War brought blackout also, but British bombing raids, even when they started in the autumn of 1940, did little damage. Alarms drove Berliners to cellars by night but the morning showed at most the odd crater or isolated burnt-out building. War, on the home front, was an affair of newspaper headlines, not of hardship or danger.

The German press and radio, both wholly controlled by the Propaganda Ministry, conveyed a highly sanitized version of events to the German public. There was much execration of the British, less of the French, and Winston Churchill, the *Lügenlord* (Lord of Lies), was regularly vilified even before he had become Prime Minister. In the joint broadcast he made with his mentor, Ed Murrow, in Amsterdam on January 18, 1940, Shirer told of a German people oppressed by the fear of another 1918. "Every day it's hammered into them that they have only two alternatives: either to win the war, in which case they will have a bright future, or to lose the war, in which case, their present leaders assure them, there will be such a peace as will make Versailles look like an ideal instrument of justice and fair dealing." Versailles remained to all Germans shorthand for a settlement of the world that left Germany not only defeated but impoverished, diminished and humiliated. Hitler had risen to power on his promises to reverse the Versailles Treaty. No German could face a repetition, let alone something worse.

Shirer was able to breathe freely only on his rare escapes from Germany to neutral territory, Holland until May 10, 1940, otherwise to Switzerland. Even then he had to be circumspect in his reporting, which was heard in Berlin, lest his press credentials were withdrawn. When he returned to Berlin the cloud of censorship and controlled news descended again, engulfing and muffling him throughout one of the most dramatic summers of modern history. By the winter he had had enough. He had already sent his wife and daughter home. In December 1940, he told the head of CBS News that his "usefulness in Germany is over." Almost all other independent American correspondents in Germany had been expelled and, though his own relations with German officialdom remained "correct," and with the German radio and army even "friendly," it was the Gestapo that was the real power and, as mentioned above, it had accused him of "working for the American intelligence service." Europe, he said, "is completely dominated by Germany," and "it is no longer possible to do even faintly objective broadcasts." Accordingly, he had decided to leave and stay away. "There is no continent of Europe to go back to for my kind of reporting."

Americans of Shirer's sort would return, and would revive the directness and integrity of his "kind of reporting," but they would come with the Allied armies of liberation. Between 1941 and 1944, the style of "This is Berlin" would disappear from the airwaves of occupied Europe, leaving Americans with no listening-post inside Hitler's empire. Europeans themselves, starved of anything but the untruths served to them by Goebbels' Enlightenment Ministry, would risk imprisonment for a few mouthfuls of truth illegally picked up from the lifeline of the BBC. *"This is Berlin"* will remind its readers, complacent as they may have become in a multi-media world, of how stifling it is to live under a controlled press and how essential to life and happiness is the output of free speech.

Kilmington, England
July 1999

PREFACE

Inga Shirer Dean

My father was always astonished by his life. That he had come from placid small-town Iowa to Kabul, Ur, Babylon, Delhi, Paris, Vienna, Berlin during two of the most turbulent decades in modern history, never ceased to amaze him. Nor did the quirks of fate that had brought him there. He told us stories of traveling through the mountain passes of Afghanistan, of marching beside Gandhi in India, of watching the frightening theater of the Nuremberg rallies, of the thick dark night of a Berlin wartime blackout and the whine of falling bombs, of mountains and rivers and paintings and cafés. The stories sailed like kites above the landscape of the midwestern childhood that always seemed so much a part of him, despite all he had seen and learned in a lifetime away.

"I was born in the horse and buggy age," he would frequently point out, happily reciting lists of inventions and conveniences of daily life we children took for granted. And it was true that the America of his childhood had only just passed into a new century and was still largely agrarian, gas-lit, and horse-drawn. He was born months before the birth of the hemophiliac son of the Tsar, more than a decade before revolution brought Communism to Russia, and lived to see the Soviet empire dissolve. On the mantelpiece in his house in the Berkshire Hills where he spent the last twenty-five years of his life, there was a piece of the Berlin Wall a friend had brought him.

My grandfather, a U.S. attorney in Chicago with a growing reputation as a trial lawyer and national political prospects, died in 1913 when my father was nine. My grandmother had little choice but to sell the Chicago house and return to a circumscribed small-town life with her parents in Cedar Rapids, Iowa. As children, my sister and I would roll our eyes as my father started yet another story about delivering newspapers at dawn and selling eggs to help with family finances. But behind these stories was a profound sadness at the early loss of a father he revered, a loss that had banished his family from a world that seemed, in the quiet of a prairie night, exciting, promising, and distant.

My father was a great believer in luck. "Being in the right place at the right time," he told us often, was what made a great journalistic career. That was part of it for him: in 1925 he had gone to Europe with a college

1

friend and, immediately smitten by Paris, tried to find a newspaper job. Though he had worked for a Cedar Rapids daily since high school, he realized his small-town background seemed pallid next to the more urbane Ivy Leaguers who were flocking to Paris in the twenties. After a summer of vigorous sightseeing nothing had materialized from either of the Paris newspapers to which he had applied. Packed and ready to bid Paris farewell, he found a note from the *Chicago Tribune* under his door offering him a job. It was a job on the copy desk and paid $15 a week, even then and even in Paris hardly a living wage. He accepted immediately. And so the course of his life was altered forever and for the next twenty years he found "the right place."

Nine years later, fluent now in German and French and with a working knowledge of Spanish and Italian, he had reported from Austria, Italy, France, Germany, Eastern Europe, the Balkans, Afghanistan, India, and the Middle East. He had married a Viennese photographer, and in 1933 they pooled their money to spend a sabbatical year in Spain where he worked on a novel about India, and with my mother got to know his neighbor Andres Segovia, read, swam, hiked, and entertained visiting friends. In 1934, with their funds dwindling, my parents returned to Paris where my father took a job on the copy desk of the Paris *Herald*, a great come-down for the young foreign correspondent, but it was the best he could do. He watched the developments in Berlin, writing in his diary at the end of June, 1934, "Wish I could get a post in Berlin. It's a story I'd like to cover." Less than two months later his old friend Arno Dosch-Fleurot offered him a job in Berlin with Universal Service, one of Hearst's two wire services. He eagerly accepted and moved to the German capital where he would chronicle the rise of Adolf Hitler and the Nazi party.

Three years later he lost his job again. For the third time in five years he had been fired, and it would not be the last. This time it was because Hearst decided to fold Universal Service which was losing money. My father's relief at being offered a job on the other Hearst wire service, INS, was short-lived. Before the month was out, on an August night while he was working on a dispatch at the office, he received a wire on the ticker that gave him two weeks' notice. In another of those moments of "luck" that so marked his career, a telegram from Edward R. Murrow arrived at the same time. My father had not taken notice of it, had with his typical unflappable if occasionally disheartened calm, finished his dispatch and gone for a walk, "a little depressed" as he noted in his diary that night. Returning to his office he noticed the wire:

WILL YOU HAVE DINNER WITH ME AT THE ADLON FRIDAY NIGHT? MURROW, COLUMBIA BROADCASTING.

With his wife Tess expecting a baby, jobless, feeling like a failure and old at thirty-three, he probably regarded Murrow's invitation to dinner more hopefully than he would later admit, though radio was a medium he had paid little attention to, and Murrow's name was only vaguely familiar.

The rapport between the two men was instantaneous. They had both left small-town America and felt immediately at home in the capitals of Europe. They shared the same liberal politics, the same moral perspective. That evening was the beginning of the closest friendship my father ever had, one born of respect, affection, and trust, nurtured by the intensity of the work and the times.

Ed Murrow, my father would later discover, had to fight to get him hired. Murrow, who at the time had no newspaper experience, wanted a reporter knowledgeable about Europe, fluent in its languages, with contacts and sources. Yet there was the question of the voice. Unlike Murrow's deep voice and elegant phrasing, my father's intonation was flat, his timbre reedy. Murrow must have also heard it and known he would probably have to go to bat to get this reporter hired. The test, in a small and dusty room in the Post and Telegraph office in Berlin was a comedy of errors. The CBS Berlin representative who would introduce him on the air, had to race back to a café where she had dined to retrieve her script and only returned moments before the broadcast. My father could not reach the microphone and, advised to point his head upward, his voice strangled into a squeak. Seconds before air time he pushed some packing boxes under the mike, had the engineer help him up and then sat, with legs dangling, knowing that his job depended not so much on what he said, but how he sounded saying it.

New York was not impressed. But he was saved by Murrow's insistence. His job would be to arrange broadcasts and to recruit other reporters to speak on the air. In fact neither Murrow nor my father was expected to speak on the air, and it was not until the Nazis marched into Austria the following February that either man was allowed to broadcast.

In 1938 radio was considered a vehicle for entertainment and light news. A few years earlier *Editor and Publisher* had asserted that radio "can only skim the news . . . with some news bulletins and a few routine reports such as a smattering of stock quotations, grain and produce reports, weather, sporting results and . . . key-hole gossip reporting." Radio news had begun in 1920 but as the decade closed commentators like H. V. Kaltenborn and Lowell Thomas were exceptions to the rule of radio, providing little more than headline news.

Still, while Europe headed to war, with Hitler increasingly governing the course of events, the balance of programming remained entertainment of varying quality, often in quest of cultural "understanding" as in its presentation of Bulgarian children's choirs and tulip festivals in Holland. In 1930 news broadcasting from Europe started with coverage of the Five-Power conference in London but because of the time difference and the edict against recording, the broadcasts went on the air at hours most Americans were asleep. Yet, radio's ability to effect a distinctive sort of news, projecting a sense of intimacy and immediacy that was not possible on the printed page, was becoming apparent.

The potential of radio had not escaped the Nazis. Propaganda chief Josef Goebbels already understood the power of radio to persuade, inform, and misinform. Shortly after Hitler came to power in 1933, Goebbels and his new Ministry for Public Enlightenment and Propaganda built a bureaucracy that controlled every aspect of broadcasting from transmitters to personnel. "What press has been in the 19th century, radio will be for the 20th," he announced. Inexpensive radios were made available to Germans, loudspeakers broadcast on streets and into restaurants and cafés. By the time Germany went to war, there were often zealous wardens in place to see to it that everyone stopped to listen to broadcasts, the most important introduced by portentous music, announcers, and periods of silence. No waiter could serve, nor diner eat during those bulletins.

Murrow's vision of the future of broadcast journalism and the excitement that lay ahead for these two young Americans who had so quickly formed a bond, must have been remarkably inspiring. My father, who never had much taste for popular culture, seemed excessively eager about doing his job. He wrote Murrow in December with a proposal for a program on Tyrolean zither music and dances:

> one of those kind where they slap themselves all over, you know, and make a lot of noise . . . This really ought to have 30 minutes instead of 15, if you could get the time.

He was still awkward, feeling his way. When he was putting together one of Columbia's beloved children's choir broadcasts he wrote Ed:

> do you keep the kids in the studio during the broadcast all the time? . . . They wouldn't gum things up, would they, crowd around the mike, and talk all at once?

Somewhat wiser, Murrow replied: "re kids: the difficulty will be to get ONE to talk!"

They could laugh at the business. "Please contact vaudeville agencies ascertain whether any parrot available willing talk microphonely," Murrow cabled my father in December 1937. Did the parrot have to be

4

English-speaking? my father queried. "German parrot okay," Murrow replied.

Separating entertainment and news would come later. A long cable from my father to CBS in December 1938, nine months after Hitler marched into Austria, describes a possible Christmas toy broadcast from Lausanne which "features exhibition toy boxes and musical toys."

Though radio historians credit the Anschluss broadcasts in March of 1938 as being the turning point for radio news, days before the brewing Austrian crisis climaxed in the Nazi takeover of the country, with the birth of his first child imminent, my father was called to Bulgaria to broadcast yet another children's choir. My birth, which occurred during his absence, turned out to be very difficult, leaving my mother dangerously ill for weeks.

During the critical month of March my father was rushing back and forth to the hospital to visit my mother whose health was not improving, gathering the story which was moving chaotically fast, and trying to get on the radio to broadcast. Austria was the most demanding story of my father's career. As Hitler's troops marched into Vienna and took over Austrian radio, he was unable to get on the air. NBC, which had signed special contracts with most state-owned radio systems in Europe had, as usual, better luck.

My father anxiously tried to get hold of Ed, who was in Warsaw, but repeated attempts failed. Finally Ed's call from Poland came through. "Fly to London, why don't you?" said Murrow. "You can get there by tomorrow evening and give the first uncensored eyewitness account." Ed would come to Vienna to maintain Columbia's coverage there. My father managed to get a plane to Berlin, then to London.

From New York the next day Columbia's news director Paul White ordered a "European roundup." The Roundup, which is now the pattern for television news broadcasting, with segments relayed from different spots where news is breaking, was fairly new to radio. It had been tried before but not with news, and even with months to make the arrangements there were frequent breakdowns in transmission and timing. This time there were only eight hours to get it organized. It did not help that this was Sunday afternoon and many of the people Columbia wanted for the program were out of town. But, my father wrote in his diary that night, "the more I thought about it, the simpler it became." He and Ed knew American newspaper correspondents in every capital as well as the directors and chief engineers of various European broadcasting facilities. Murrow would arrange the Berlin and Vienna end, explaining to my father how the entire job could be done technically. Where there were no short-wave transmitters available, phone lines would have to be

5

used. Rome was a problem, but the correspondent could dictate his story to New York. Cues from New York to start speaking sometimes could not be heard and so the reporter would just have to start and finish at exactly the times appointed. Cables on times, permissions, frequencies went back and forth.

It worked, with no cues missed, no technical glitches. In that "half hour radio came into its own as a full-fledged news medium," writes Alexander Kendrick in his book *Prime Time*. His sentiments were shared. The British magazine *Cavalcade* lauded the "spot relays from European capitals plus expert commentaries by students of foreign affairs" that kept America informed. "Fortunate are those Britons who have receivers which bring in the Columbia broadcasts."

Mixed with the excitement of the new venture and developing friendship was the reality of living in Nazi Germany. My father wrote in his diary at the time he joined Murrow that the Nazis and their war preparations

> hang over all our lives, like a dark, brooding cloud that never clears.
> Often we have tried to segregate ourselves from it all. We have found
> three refuges: ourselves, our books . . . our friends . . . the lakes and
> woods around Berlin.

When my parents agreed my mother should move to Switzerland in 1938 shortly after my birth, he missed her. For the next two and a half years my mother ran the CBS office in Geneva, from where she could communicate with New York by telephone and cable without fear of Nazi eavesdropping, and relay messages to and from my father in Berlin. He looked forward to the brief sojourns in Switzerland with us, escaping the increasing darkness of Germany.

He disliked Nazi Berlin as much as he loved Paris. Though he lived in comfort at the Adlon Hotel, the telephones were bugged, the rooms surreptitiously searched, and the staff were generally believed to be Gestapo informers. There was evidence everywhere of increasingly virulent anti-Semitism: in the smashed windows of Kristall Nacht, the signs in parks forbidding Jews to sit on the benches, the crude cartoons in the papers. Howard K. Smith, who was also in Berlin at the time, has written of the "hermetically sealed atmosphere, the awful fit of depression each of us fell into with periodic regularity," which came to be known in the press community as the Berlin Blues.

For a radio reporter there were special frustrations. There were the crucial broadcasts that never got through. Weather and sun spots could interfere, lines could go down or be unavailable, unfriendly countries could block transmissions, but in Germany and the countries it

6

conquered, censorship was the radio reporter's primary concern. In its bureaucratic set-up, the Germans decreed that broadcasts had to be submitted to the Propaganda Ministry, Foreign Office, and High Command, in contrast to the print journalists whose cables were not censored, though the ever-present threat of banishment or worse was in itself a form of censorship. My father, broadcasting in late evening because of the time difference, would bring his script in about an hour before air time. The three censors would sit around a table and read the broadcasts carefully. My father's frustrations with the censors rankled all his life. Once when I told him rather blithely that one of the censors, an ardent Nazi when my father knew him in Berlin, had surfaced at Harvard where I was a student at the time, he did not find it at all amusing. Instead he was outraged and exploded in anger, something I rarely saw him do and never forgot.

In trying to get past the censors he would often employ idiomatic English since most Germans spoke England's version of the language, as well as a dry, ironic humor and a certain ingenuous tone. Trying to show that British Prime Minister Chamberlain was backing Hitler against Czechoslovakia he said:

> one thing is certain: Mr. Chamberlain will certainly get a warm welcome at Godesberg. In fact I get the impression in Berlin tonight that Mr. Chamberlain is a pretty popular figure around here.

Describing a newsreel that had been privately shown to correspondents after the invasion of Poland his last two sentences were:

> I mention a second thing in that newsreel that interested me. It was a series of shots showing Polish Jews with long beards and long black coats working on the road gangs in Poland.

Those techniques sometimes failed because one of the censors frequently at that table had lived in the States a long time. It was best to give them something to cut, he would tell us, and hope they would let other things go by.

In the increasing isolation of the German capital, as his words went off into the darkness, he often was not sure if people would understand. The frequent calls, letters, and cables he and Murrow had exchanged before Germany went to war with England, were no longer possible. Censorship grew more rigorous: sometimes most of his broadcast was censored. Words such as "alleged," "claimed," "asserted" could not be used in conjunction with any official statement as they cast doubt on its veracity. The word "Nazi" was forbidden because censors were aware that it

7

sounded like "nasty." National Socialist was the correct term. By late 1939 he was having an edgy exchange of cables with CBS news director Paul White in New York, that outlined my father's feelings about not going on the air with an eviscerated script. After what must have been a reprimand from White, my father cabled, in the abbreviated language of the telegram:

WHITE: APPRECIATE YOUR EMBARRASSMENT BUT EYE CANNOT GO ON WHEN UNALLOWED SAY ANYTHING AFTER FIGHTING CENSOR ALL EVENING PREVIOUS TWO SCRIPTS. DECLINED GO ON ANY MORE. WITH CENSORSHIP STRICT AND OFFICIAL NEWS OBVIOUSLY HIDING ALL UNPLEASANTNESSES THINK WE OVERPLAYING BERLIN. SHIRER.

and again:

WHITE: DONT UNDERSTAND YOUR ATTITUDE SINCE FAILURE TALK DUE FACT CUTS MADE BY CENSOR RENDERED SCRIPT UN-INTELLIGIBLE IMPOSSIBLE ME GIVE ONLY OFFICIAL PROPAGANDA ITEM. PLEASE CABLE TESS TEXT ANY MESSAGE RECEIVED YESTERDAY EXHERE OTHER THAN FROM ME. SUSPECT FUNNY BUSINESS. SHIRER.

In December 1940, my father left Berlin. He had a serious case of the Berlin Blues and for some time had been feeling that his days were numbered in Germany. He always told us that he feared he would be accused of being a spy and end up in jail. Several reporters suffered that fate, including United Press reporter Richard C. Hottelet who was jailed on trumped-up charges. Howard K. Smith remembered that it took "devotion and sheer luck to stay in the country and refuse to play the Nazi game."

My mother and I had left Geneva in October, and after a rather harrowing trip through occupied France en route to Lisbon, were living in New York, so the relief and retreat she had offered in Switzerland were gone. My father missed the close contact with Murrow. They got together once more in Europe: a week in Portugal, where Ed came to see my father off. He would write in his diary as his boat steamed out of Lisbon on December 13, 1940:

all day both of us depressed at leaving, for we have worked together very closely, Ed and I, during the last three turbulent years over here and a bond grew that was very real, a kind you make only a few times in your life, and somehow, absurdly no doubt, sentimentally

8

perhaps, we had a presentiment that the fortunes of war, maybe just a little bomb, would make this reunion the last.

Though it was not to be their last meeting, the relationship soon faltered and, shortly after the war, ruptured bitterly. It was then that my father was fired by CBS, and he blamed Murrow who had become a CBS vice president. It was a rupture that Ed tried to heal shortly before his death in 1964 by inviting my parents to his farm in Pawling, New York. It had been a painful break for both families: my mother and Janet Murrow were also very fond of each other, and she was my sister's godmother. My father would always say that we can never know another person completely, and sometimes we know them quite incompletely, and his refusal to accept Ed's olive branch baffles me to this day. Though the afternoon was pleasant on the surface as they chatted about old times and old friends, when Ed took my reluctant father off for a ride around the property in his jeep, sweating from the pain of his cancer, my father determinedly kept the conversation light. Ed, whom he had loved, now so clearly near death, was plainly trying to discuss what had happened and heal the breach between them. My father, with his disingenuous chatter, would not let him. When I asked him about it again not long before his death two months short of his ninetieth birthday, his face tensed with grim determination. He was not going to let Ed bring it up, he said. Even though he was dying? I asked. That's right he said firmly, ending the conversation.

My father spent his last twenty-five years in the Berkshire Hills of western Massachusetts. Perhaps it was a return to the simpler life of a small town that he had known as a boy, but he never saw it that way. He had come to find country life better for a writer, and after his career in radio ended in the fifties, he had started spending more and more time at our farm in northwestern Connecticut. He found New York distracting, too many friends to lunch and dine with, too much theater and music to tempt him away from his desk. He often said, and I think came to believe, that being fired from CBS was a blessing. It gave him a chance for an entirely different second act, of which there were supposed to be none in America.

In the last three decades of his long life he became the writer he had always wanted to be. Not, as he had once hoped, of great works of the imagination on the scale of his beloved French and Russian nineteenth-century novelists, but as an historian of the events he had witnessed, deepening his knowledge with years of research in archives and libraries. Outwardly, in his later years, he seemed the amiable, populist midwesterner of his heritage, walking around the small New England village where he made his home, sporting a red woolen gnome hat and old blue parka during the long winters, or jeans and straw hat while working in his large vegetable garden on summer afternoons.

But in his twenties and thirties he had been far from this tranquil village. He was learning about the immensity of the human spirit from Mahatma Gandhi and of the enormous evil that could destroy it from Adolf Hitler. He saw the great country of Beethoven, Luther, Goethe, and Schiller, of his own paternal forebears, lose its soul and conscience. He learned, as he frequently said, how thin and brittle the veneer of civilization can be. What had happened, and why, was the question he asked over and over and spent the rest of his life trying to answer.

Lenox, Massachusetts
December 1998

PROLOGUE

Shirer CBS London March 12, 1938

[This report on the Anschluss was Shirer's first major news broadcast. It was made from London, the newly-installed Nazis having refused him access to the Vienna radio station. A few days earlier he had been in Ljubljana, Yugoslavia, arranging for a broadcast by a chorus of coal-miners' children for Columbia's School of the Air. On his return to Vienna, he found that Chancellor Schuschnigg had defied Hitler by suddenly ordering a plebiscite that asked: "Are you for an independent, social, Christian, German, united Austria?"]

Well, it all happened very quickly in Vienna last night. I have just arrived by air from Vienna, after an all-day flight by way of Prague, Dresden, Berlin and Amsterdam. The regular planes to London from Vienna were very crowded; I couldn't get a seat.

When I returned to Vienna yesterday from Yugoslavia, I found a fair lot of tension. Some called it election fever. As you know, Dr. Schuschnigg, the Austrian chancellor, had suddenly called a plebiscite for Sunday. Hitler and the Nazis had been demanding one for years – and there it was. But this time it was evident that the Nazis did not like it. "Why?" I asked them; and they said that in the form it was, and in the way it was suddenly sprung, it was unfair. They agreed with everyone else in Vienna that Dr. Schuschnigg would probably win it.

As I made my way yesterday morning from the station to my home, I found the Vienna streets littered with millions of electioneering leaflets, calling on the populace to vote for Schuschnigg and Austrian independence. Men were throwing them out of trucks, wagons, carts, knapsacks and airplanes. When I reached home I noticed a radio van parked at a nearby corner. Its loudspeaker was blaring away selections from Dr. Schuschnigg's latest speeches, and urging listeners to vote for him. Right behind the van was a bus full of police. That struck a friend I was with as a bit funny. He wondered if the government was getting a bit uncertain about things.

Neither of us knew of Hitler's ultimatum. That was about 10 a.m.

11

yesterday. Along before noon I walked down towards the center of town. Here and there small groups of high school boys were loitering about shouting "Heil Hitler!" and raising their arms in salute. And there were a lot of policemen about, politely keeping the youngsters circulating.

I went into a café and there met two friends. We encountered some Austrian newspapermen who reported that the Nazis had just broken the windows of the monarchists' offices, and that the monarchists, a legion working for the return of Otto of Hapsburg, were a bit frightened. But no one in the café seemed unduly nervous. We still had the impression, I must admit, that the plebiscite would be held peacefully. We heard the radio announce the call-out of army reserves to keep order. We know now that that was Dr. Schuschnigg's first answer to Hitler's ultimatum; but at that time we thought it would help insure a peaceful election.

At noon I left the café and strolled down the street to the Opera, the center of town. There I found a couple of hundred socialists gathered. They were raising their hands in a clenched-fist salute. And answering them with a fascist salute was a crowd of about the same number of Nazis standing in front of the German tourist bureau across the street. In this bureau hung a full-length picture of Hitler.

Nothing much happened at the Opera then, so the police dispersed both groups. I went from there to the former imperial palace, and noted that the courtyard was full of trucks loaded with workers. Their cars were decorated with Schuschnigg posters. And they were shouting against the Nazis and for the government. I then made a quick tour of the workers' district – nothing exciting. I mention these things because a few hours later, you remember, Dr. Schuschnigg in his dramatic farewell message over the radio declared that the news brought from Germany concerning what had been caused by the workers, the shedding of blood, etc., were lies from A to Z, as he put it.

I'm here reporting what I saw, not giving my personal opinions. I saw no disorders in Vienna provoked by the workers. But when I arrived in Berlin this noon I found that the newspapers were appearing in flaming headlines about violent red disorders – as they put it – in Vienna. And I have here before me the front page of Chancellor Hitler's own newspaper, the focus of attention this morning. Its banner headline reads: GERMAN-AUSTRIA SAVED FROM CHAOS.

People here in London keep asking me who were the Nazis from Berlin who superintended last night's remarkable turn of events. Well, there were conflicting reports in both Vienna and Berlin; but early this morning we were officially informed in Vienna that Rudolph Hess, Hitler's deputy and right-hand man, had arrived during the evening and gone straight to the Chancellery.

Austria's resistance to Nazi socialism actually collapsed at 6.15 p.m.

12

yesterday, March 11, when it was announced on the radio that the plebiscite had been indefinitely postponed.

In the streets you could feel the consternation among the workers. Many had been armed and placed around the railroad stations and public buildings. When that radio announcement came over the loudspeakers, they melted away and stole home as best they could. On the other hand, it was the signal for the Nazis to come out and capture the streets of the capital.

And yet, as late as 6 p.m. the picture had been quite different. I was walking across a large square just a block from the Opera as two lone policemen were driving a crowd of 500 Nazis off the square without the slightest difficulty. A half hour later you would not have recognized Vienna as being the same city.

With the announcement that the plebiscite was off, the Nazis suddenly poured by tens of thousands into the old inner city. They were a curious crowd. I have never seen anything like it in twelve years in Europe and the East. They were certainly delirious with excitement and joy, and yet they were good-natured. They seemed to get a particular kick out of saluting and yelling "Heil Hitler!" And yet there were none of those assaults against foreigners like myself who did not join in the saluting or the yelling, such as you saw in Germany in 1933. The crowds really got warmed up with enthusiasm after Dr. Schuschnigg's farewell speech. They seemed to like especially his request that there should be no resistance to in-marching German troops.

At 10 p.m., as nearly as I can remember, I got carried around with the crowd up Vienna's main shopping thoroughfare. I noticed then that the police had entirely gone over. Young girls pinned flowers on their coats, and young men fastened red Swastika arm-bands on their sleeves. Hundreds of police were carried around with the crowd, just as I was. I also noticed for the first time that hundreds of young men had miraculously sprouted brown S.A. uniforms and black S.S. uniforms – you could smell the moth-balls.

I sensed that the crowd this time had a definite objective. And it had. In a few minutes it had poured into the small square opposite the Fatherland-front headquarters. A few ringleaders quickly tore down the government election posters and the Fatherland-front banners, and hoisted the Nazi hooked cross amid deafening cheers from their followers.

Next, the main part of the crowd made its way triumphantly to the federal Chancellery, where Metternich once pulled his strings, and where in July, 1934, as you know, Dollfuss was murdered. When the crowd first approached, I was told, six soldiers on guard closed the gates, the same gates through which the Nazis drove in their 1934 putsch. But by the time

I got there they were opened again. I immediately felt that the Nazis were beginning to get the thing organized. Lights were playing on the facade of the old building. Pretty soon a radio van drew up and began broadcasting the scene over the Austrian radio station. They began to rig up a microphone on the balcony.

At first the crowd proceeded to tear down every Fatherland-front sign in sight. Next door to the Chancellery a new building was under construction, and on top of this was a huge banner displaying the Fatherland-front insignia. Twenty Nazis immediately stormed up the scaffolding and tore it down. A Swastika flag was soon in its place.

And then I saw a strange sight: Twenty men bent down, formed a pyramid, and a little man – I suppose he was picked for his weight – scampered over a lot of huge shoulders and, clutching a huge Swastika flag, climbed to the balcony of the Chancellery.

About midnight they got a microphone rigged up on the balcony and it was from there that the official announcements were made to the crowd (it must have numbered one hundred thousand by now) and, through the radio, to the whole country.

At 1.30 a.m. we saw a Nazi leader come out on the balcony. He was greeted with delirious cheering. When it had died down he stepped up to the microphone and announced a new cabinet list – composed, I believe, of Nazis with one exception. A cold drizzle fanned by a sharp wind now set in, and quickly turned to snow. The crowd started to break up. As there are no street cars or buses in Vienna after midnight, they walked to their homes. By 2 a.m. there were few policemen to be seen in the streets. Instead, the Nazis in civilian clothes and with fixed bayonets were keeping order. By 3 a.m. the streets were fairly quiet.

This morning when I flew away from Vienna at 9 a.m. it looked like any German city in the Reich – red, white and black Swastika flags hung from the balconies of most of the homes. And in the streets people raised their hands in Nazi salute, and greeted each other with "Heil Hitler!" Arriving in Berlin three hours later I hardly realized I was in another country. It was the same picture, the same flag, the same ritual. And they were yelling the same slogan – "One Reich, one people, one leader". That's what they got. And very quickly, too.

THE BROADCASTS

Berlin September 19, 1938

[By the time of the Munich Crisis, Shirer had left Vienna and shifted his base to Berlin.]

Hello America. This is Berlin calling.

Germany, like the rest of Europe, is waiting on Prague tonight.

But if I judge the temper of the people in the street right – and I've talked with many of them since flying up here from Prague this morning – they are waiting with a sense of relief.

Whereas three weeks ago when I was last here – or even a week ago – the people were wondering what could be in store for them, tonight they seem sure of one thing. That there will be no war.

"Isn't it wonderful," I've been told a hundred times today by scores of people who did not hide their sense of relief. "Isn't it wonderful. There's to be no war. We're going to have peace."

And today as the news came in that Britain and France – Britain and France, mind you – had agreed on a settlement which would hand over most of the Sudetenland to this country, the sense of elation among the people you saw about was very marked.

Not only National Socialist Party members, but others. They all felt that Chancellor Hitler had brought them undoubtedly the greatest victory of his career.

"And mind you," a German newspaperman said to me tonight. "It's a bloodless victory."

That's a feeling that's very deep in the minds of these people here tonight. That Chancellor Hitler appears to have achieved what he wanted without bloodshed.

"Like the occupation of the Rhine. Like the Anschluss with Austria. Done peacefully, without war." I've heard those phrases from a dozen people in the course of today.

None here that I've talked to today seems to doubt for a single moment that the Czechs will accept the Franco-British proposals.

Last night in Prague – and this morning, just before I left, talking with

15

Czechs, I wasn't so sure. But tonight in Prague may be a different story. I have no definite last minute information. It is a very grave decision they're taking in Prague. But, as I said, here in Berlin the Germans seem to think that it can only be acceptance. The ordinary little man doesn't seem to think it can be anything else. And he's glad.

As a matter of fact, it appears that even yesterday people here made up their minds that there would be no war. Friends of mine tell me that thousands – it was a lovely warm, summer-like day – drove down in their cars to the Sudeten frontier, and picnicked while they gazed over the frontier at the lovely, blue Sudeten mountains.

And while the people in the Berlin streets going home to work tonight seemed relieved and pleased with the turn of events, the excitement on the Sudeten frontier – especially among the Sudetens who've come over to this side – was at a feverish pitch.

I sat most of this evening at the side of a loudspeaker, listening to the broadcast of a great Sudeten mass-meeting at Dresden tonight where thousands crowded into a great hall went literally mad with excitement.

It was really indescribable.

I happened to be stationed in this country at the moment of Chancellor Hitler's first two great achievements. The tearing up of Versailles in 1935 when he proclaimed conscription and set out to build up the modern German army.

I thought I had seen the peak of mass enthusiasm that day.

A year later when he reoccupied the Rhineland I went up and down the Rhine, and the enthusiasm, as the troops marched in, was even greater. Unbelievable sometimes.

But tonight. Well, I don't know any words to describe it. It was simply a terrific mass hysteria. For two hours 10 or 15 thousand people, mostly Sudeten Germans who crossed over into the Reich – Dresden is near the border, remember – yelled themselves hoarse. The yelling in a big stadium at homecoming when your side makes the winning touchdown would be nothing compared to what we heard tonight.

There seemed to be two yells, and they were not unlike some of our college yells at home.

One was:

Adolf Hitler, mach uns frei
Von der Tschechoslowakei.

Translated it would be: Adolf Hitler, free us from Czechoslovakia. But in German it rhymes and has a popular swing.

The other was the more familiar one:

One Reich, One Folk, One Führer.

And they yelled and yelled it, until you would have thought that their voices would have given in, or the roof of the building fallen through.

16

The principal speaker at this meeting in Dresden tonight was Herr Sebekovsky, the young Sudeten deputy. His voice, as it came roaring through the radio, choked with emotion. It was hard for me to think that it was this same young man, Herr Sebekovsky, with whom I talked quietly not two weeks ago in the Sudeten headquarters in Prague. In Prague, the afternoon we talked, he struck me as a quiet, young, business-like type. Then he talked and argued earnestly about the Carlsbad demands for autonomy within Czechoslovakia.

That was two weeks ago! It seems like an eternity.

Herr Sebekovsky addressed most of his words to his fellow Sudetens across the frontier, many of whom, no doubt, were listening to him on their radios.

"Sudeten brothers at home," he roared. "Keep your courage! The hour of your liberation nears!" And then there was a pandemonium of yelling in the hall for several minutes before he could say: "Keep your courage. And we will come to you. And this time, not without arms."

Knowing from my personal experiences in Sudetenland how many Sudetens felt, how they came out last week when we passed on the road and asked us nervously: "When are they coming? Are they coming? And when?" I imagine his words and his promise cheered quite a few people.

So much for the Sudetens.

Here in Berlin the press is full of little other news. I've got some of today's papers with me here and I'd like to give you an idea of what is in them.

Here's the *Angriff*: a typical headline about alleged conditions in Czechoslovakia. It says: WOMEN AND CHILDREN MOWED DOWN BY ARMORED CARS. SUDETENS COMPLAIN. Another headline in the same paper: CZECHOSLOVAKIA WRITTEN OFF. RESULT OF THE LONDON CABINET MEETING.

The *Deutsche Allgemeine Zeitung* has a front page headline, or will have in its edition tomorrow morning – I just got a copy – UNDER THE BLOOD REGIME. NEW CZECH MURDERS OF GERMANS. And the editor of the paper has a two column editorial entitled: DESPERADOES. I take it he refers to the Czechs.

The *Börsen Zeitung's* front page leads off with the headline: POISON GAS ATTACK ON AUSSIG? And the story alleges a Czech plan to use poison gas on the German inhabitants of the town of Aussig. Special agents of Moscow are blamed.

The *Hamburger Fremdenblatt*, one of the leading provincial papers has this headline: EXTORTION. PLUNDERING. SHOOTING. THE CZECH TERROR IN GERMAN SUDETENLAND GROWS WORSE FROM DAY TO DAY.

And the *Nachtausgabe*, a widely-read evening paper carries this frontpage headline: DANGEROUS CHAOS IN PRAGUE. MOSCOW HOPES FOR CATASTROPHE IN SUDETENLAND.

And practically all the papers play up the story about the alleged gas attack plans for Aussig.

Now I'm not here tonight to tell you how I personally see the situation in Czechoslovakia. But I think perhaps you will be interested in seeing how the picture is presented in the newspapers here in Berlin.

The day after tomorrow there is to be the meeting at Godesberg between Prime Minister Chamberlain and Chancellor Hitler. That little town is a hive of activity tonight.

A friend of mine – one of the advance guard of the army of foreign correspondents who will descend on the little town tomorrow – was down there today and he has just phoned an idea of what it looks like.

The whole town, he reported, was being gaily decorated with pine-tree branches and bunting and thousands of flags. Not only the Swastika flag. The Union Jack too. Thousands of Union Jacks.

The good people of the little town officially of course are not supposed to know exactly who the decorations are for – the meeting hasn't been publicly announced yet. But of course they have a pretty good idea.

The little Hotel Dreesen where Chancellor Hitler went to stay way back in 1926 after his release from prison, and whose proprietor became his friend, was also getting a dressing-up today.

The hotel lounge was refurbished this afternoon and decorated with bowls of flowers and German and British flags.

Chancellor Hitler will occupy the little suite which is reserved for him the year around. And probably the meetings will be held there.

Mr. Chamberlain probably will stay in a hotel in nearby Petersberg, one of the seven famous Rhine mountains.

One thing is certain: Mr. Chamberlain will certainly get a warm welcome.

In fact I get the impression in Berlin today that Mr. Chamberlain is a pretty popular figure around here.

Cologne September 21, 1938 23.35

Hello America! This is Cologne, Germany, calling.

I want to tell you tonight about the beautiful, peaceful, sleepy little Rhineland town of Godesberg where Chancellor Hitler and Mr. Chamberlain are to have their historic meeting tomorrow. Chancellor Hitler is due to arrive by special train at 10 in the morning and Mr. Chamberlain by air from London shortly after noon.

I left Godesberg a half hour ago to drive over here to Cologne.

Driving down the Rhine today you get a curious sensation. It's the sight of the British Union Jack floating over the Rhine. Side-by-side with the Swastika. It appears to be a very popular combination in this part of the world tonight.

Godesberg itself, a town of some 24,000 tranquil souls, seemed to be rubbing its eyes today.

It has seen Chancellor Hitler before, to be sure, both before he became this country's greatest figure, and afterward. For 12 years he has had a suite reserved for himself at the Hotel Dreesen.

But never before have the good inhabitants of Godesberg had the chance of seeing not only the ruler of the German Reich, but the head of the British Empire. And they're plenty excited about it.

This afternoon I strolled down the river to the Hotel Dreesen where Chancellor Hitler will stay. It's a building of nondescript architecture, like many another hotel of its kind which line the banks of the Rhine. Made of white brick and stucco. And on the river side is painted on it a huge sign which says: RHINE HOTEL DREESEN – SUMMER AND WINTER STOPPING PLACE.

Inside the hotel there was a great deal of bustle. Flowers and pine-tree branches were being brought in. Union Jacks and Swastikas strung up.

From the Chancellor's rooms – from the room in which he and Mr. Chamberlain will meet tomorrow – there is a magnificent view across the Rhine to the famous Siebenbergen – the seven mountains which rise steeply from the opposite bank of the river. On the top of one of them you could see the ruins of the famous castle of Drachenfels – or, the Lair of the Dragons – a historic landmark.

But the view from Chancellor Hitler's hotel was nothing compared to the view we got from Mr. Chamberlain's hotel. The British Prime Minister is to stay across the river, on the Petersberg, one of the seven mountains, rising a thousand feet about the water.

I took lunch there today.

Now Godesberg is not an important enough town for a bridge and so we had to ferry over. Incidentally, driving down to the ferry, I noticed many horse-and-buggies. Godesberg is that kind of a town. Once across the river, we sped past the horse-and-buggies, around several hair-pin bends, and in ten minutes were on top of the mountain and being ushered into the Petersberg hotel where Mr. Chamberlain will stay.

The view was superb. The Rhine flowed like a narrow ribbon between the mountains. Ruined old medieval castles stood perched on the mountain tops like worn jewels. The air was clear and we could see 30 miles up the river to the range of the Eifel mountains. It was the landscape that inspired Beethoven, who was born at Bonn, five miles down the river; and Goethe.

And Mr. Chamberlain's rooms are so placed as to give him the best possible view of this noble landscape.

I saw them today – the three rooms. The assistant manager of the hotel took me all through them.

In Mr. Chamberlain's sitting room, he pointed out a large Louis Quinze table. A stream-lined telephone with an automatic dial stood incongruously on one corner of it. Back of the table on the wall was a large painting, one of those Victorian, or perhaps pre-Victorian works that I suppose modern critics would call amusing and slightly sentimental. Someone said the title of it was: "The Torn Letter". That was the idea, anyway.

The room was full of bowls of immense yellow and pink chrysanthemums. A door led from the sitting room to an immense veranda, a hundred feet wide, from which Mr. Chamberlain can get the wonderful view which I just described.

The other rooms, a breakfast room and the bedroom were just nice, pleasant hotel rooms.

And so back to Godesberg. Godesberg, by the way, is a watering place, a cure-place. People come here for cures from the springs here. What kind of cures, you may ask? This evening one of the town fathers gave me some literature. I'll just read from that: "The Godesberg baths," it says, "are generally acknowledged to be of the greatest value in cases of heart disease, and in nervous cases where a tonic effect is desired."

Godesberg September 22 1938 18:15

Hello America! This is Godesberg, Germany, calling.

We're speaking to you from the Hotel Dreesen in Godesberg. In a room just above us here the Chancellor of the German Empire and the head of the British Empire have been holding their historic conference most of the afternoon.

I say historic, and probably it is, though events are moving so fast that some people here are beginning to think that the meeting between the two statesmen will be little more than a formality – that is, to fix up the details.

Because the word coming in here today is that the Sudetens, backed by the Reich, have already moved into Czechoslovakia. And that the Swastika flag tonight flies from those two Sudeten strongholds in Czechoslovakia, Aasch and Eger.

It does look from here as if the avalanche cannot be stopped.

Now as to the meeting upstairs in the Dreesen Hotel here.

Chancellor Hitler arrived this morning at 10 o'clock by special train.

Mr. Chamberlain, flying from London, landed at Cologne at thirty-six minutes past noon. Most of us were at the airport to meet him, but, as was expected, he had nothing to say. I thought he had a very serious look on his face, and little time was lost in formalities. Mr. Chamberlain was naturally preoccupied with the business at hand, so much so that he forgot his umbrella in the plane, and it had to be retrieved. Incidentally it was a beautiful day, with the sun out and very warm.

A guard of honor from Hitler's own personal bodyguard – crack S.S. troops in black uniforms and steel helmets – presented arms to Mr. Chamberlain and he acknowledged it by raising his arm.

Mr. Chamberlain did not meet Chancellor Hitler at once. He drove directly to his hotel on top of the Petersberg and after admiring the view had lunch with the British ambassador, Sir Nevile Henderson. At the hotel he remarked to friends: "I had a good flight. Weather was fine. We flew low and I could enjoy the landscape."

A little before 4 p.m., our time, Mr. Chamberlain climbed into one of Chancellor Hitler's Mercedes, drove down to the Rhine, and crossed on the ferry which we all use here to get across the river. The German Foreign Minister, Herr Ribbentrop, accompanied him.

At the Hotel Dreesen here, Herr Hitler was out on the terrace to meet his guest. They shook hands warmly and the Chancellor then conducted Mr. Chamberlain upstairs to the little conference room. After five minutes of formalities everyone withdrew, both the German and English advisers, and Mr. Chamberlain and Herr Hitler were left absolutely alone to talk and decide whatever fate they choose to impose upon Europe.

The only other person present was Professor Schmidt, Herr Hitler's interpreter.

It is too early yet to say with any authority what was said or decided.

Now, Mr. Chamberlain, it appears, came with some plans of his own to propose. They were said to be three.

1. An international commission for Sudetenland to arrange for the withdrawal of the Czechs and the transfer of the two populations.

2. An appeal by the four Western Powers for a period of peace and tranquility during which the present situation in Europe could be cleared up.

3. An international guaranty for what remains of Czechoslovakia.

That gives you an idea of what's in the air, but we'll have to wait a couple of day to see what comes of it.

And now for the news from the other side of Germany. According to reports here, the Czech troops and police withdrew today from the Eger sector, and it was immediately occupied by the Sudeten Legion, which crossed the Czech frontier from Germany where it had been arming all week.

Coming down to the hotel a few minutes ago I bought a copy of the evening edition of the *Kölnische Zeitung*. I want to read you the first story phoned by the correspondent of that paper from what until yesterday was Czechoslovakia but since today has become a part of the ever-swelling Reich. He dates his story from Graslitz, near Eger.

"This is the first telephone conversation to Cologne made from the Eger district since the Germans took over law and order," he phoned. "We German journalists crossed the former Czech border at 8.20 this morning, though with some difficulty.

"At 6.20 this morning it became known on our side that the Czechs were withdrawing. A terrific feeling of joy came over the people in the Klingen Valley, both Reich Germans and the Sudeten German refugees. With cries of 'The frontier is free! Sudeten Germany is free!' crowds stormed through the streets of Klingenthal." (Klingenthal is the town on the German side of the border.)

"We journalists," he goes on, "drove slowly down the road towards Graslitz, with the Swastika flag flying from our radiator. The streets through which we drove were crowded with people, shouting continually Heil! Heil! Heil! We could drive through the mass of people only very slowly. After a quarter of an hour we finally reached the market place, where a delirious crowd stopped any further progress of our car. We had to climb out of the car, and just then we saw the first Swastika flag being hoisted over the Czech district offices. I'm telephoning this from the local telephone central."

And then he describes how the last Czechs pulled out at 8.20 this morning, tanks forming the rear-guard.

And here's a proclamation to the population of Eger, which just comes in from the official German news agency, *DNB*.

"To the German people of the Eger district: 'Our homeland is free, and we join the Reich. In this great hour we ask all comrades to maintain absolute quiet and Order. Our police service, in agreement with the Czech state, takes over the organization of the front-fighters. The orders of the front-fighters are to be absolutely followed. To guarantee the handing over of our homeland without trouble, the entire population is asked for the time being to remain in-doors. German people of Eger, who through so many hard years have maintained themselves through strict discipline, in these last hours before the complete liberation, continue to maintain law and order.'"

From that official communiqué it appears as if the whole thing was done in agreement with the Czech authorities. And it was done peacefully.

Another *DNB* report from Eger also speaks of negotiations for the withdrawal having been worked out with the Czech police and military.

But there was one group of Czech soldiers which apparently did not withdraw immediately from Eger. The *DNB* reports that the *cemetery* there was still being guarded by Czech troops.

The *DNB* also emphasizes that the whole occupation today was carried out peacefully and orderly.

Well, events do move quickly. Just a week ago today I stood in the streets of Eger gazing at the front of the Hotel Victoria which had been partially demolished by machine-gun bullets and hand-grenades. Czech police and troops and armored cars and tanks were everywhere.

Just as week ago, that was.

Godesberg September 22/23, 1938 01:25

Hello America. This is Godesberg, Germany, calling

For the second time today, I'm talking to you from the Hotel Dreesen in Godesberg where for more than three hours this afternoon Chancellor Hitler and Prime Minister Chamberlain were in conference together.

What was decided or even what was discussed in the little room just above us here has not been made known.

All we know is that the talks did not come to an end after the first meeting, as they did at Berchtesgaden last week. An official communiqué said they would be continued tomorrow.

And then we have the appeal of the British Prime Minister issued from his mountain hotel above the Rhine tonight, pleading that there be no incidents in Sudetenland.

Shortly after Mr. Chamberlain left Chancellor Hitler's hotel at 7:15 this evening, his private secretary convoked the correspondents to his hotel on the summit of the Petersberg. The ferry wasn't working, we drove five miles down the river to Bonn to find a bridge, and arrived all breathless on the mountain top a half hour later. I'll read to you the statement from Prime Minister Chamberlain which we were given:

"The Prime Minister had a conversation with the German Führer which, beginning at 4 o'clock, was continued until shortly after 7 p.m. It is intended to resume the conversations tomorrow morning.

"In the meantime, the first essential, in the opinion of the Prime Minister, is that there should be a determination on the part of all parties and on the part of all concerned to ensure that the local conditions in Czechoslovakia are such as not in any way to interfere with the progress of the conversations. The Prime Minister appeals most earnestly therefore to everybody to assist in maintaining a state of orderliness and to refrain from action of any kind that would be likely to lead to incidents."

That was Mr. Chamberlain's appeal.

The evening newspapers available here divide their front-page headlines and space tonight almost equally between Mr. Chamberlain's meeting with the German Chancellor and the reoccupation of the Eger district by the Sudeten Germans which, according to the papers, began this morning.

The German press says that this occupation took place in an orderly manner and according to agreement with the Czech military and police.

"Wonderful Discipline – Indescribable Joy" – was the headline about it in the Cologne evening paper tonight.

And you can imagine that there was considerable rejoicing among the populace here when the news came that the Nazi Swastika flag was being hoisted everywhere in this district which only yesterday belonged to Czechoslovakia.

I was at Eger just a week ago today, and of course not a Swastika was to be seen. Events indeed are moving rapidly.

But today, say the German papers, the Nazi flag went up in quick succession on the city-hall, the town's church, numerous public buildings and then the private dwellings.

Well, it's 1:30 in the morning here now. I see the lights in Mr. Chamberlain's hotel up on the mountain across the Rhine are mostly out. The good folk in this town of Godesberg have all gone to bed.

Berlin September 24, 1938 24.05

Hello America! This is Berlin calling.

At least tonight, we seem to know a little more where we stand.

We still have six days of peace ahead of us. And just exactly one week from tonight we shall know whether it is to be peace or war.

To the extent that we know that much, the talks between Mr. Chamberlain and Herr Hitler which ended at 1.30 this morning at Godesberg have cleared the air. There was some confusion amongst us all at Godesberg early this morning as to what the British Prime Minister and the German Chancellor actually had accomplished.

But tonight, as seen from Berlin, it seems clear that the position is this: Herr Hitler has demanded that Czechoslovakia not later than next Saturday agree to the handing over of the Sudeten territory to Germany. Mr. Chamberlain has agreed to convey this demand to the Czechoslovak government. And by the very fact that he – with all the authority of a man who is the political leader of the British Empire – has taken upon himself the job of communicating Herr Hitler's demands to the Prague government is accepted here – and I believe elsewhere too – as meaning that he, Mr. Chamberlain, backs them up.

That is why few persons in Berlin tonight believe that Czechoslovakia will turn them down. That is why the German press tonight is coupling the names of Adolf Hitler and Neville Chamberlain as the real rescuers of European peace. That's why the German people I talked with in the streets of Cologne at dawn this morning waiting for my plane, and in Berlin this evening, still seemed to believe that there would be peace after all. And that Germany would acquire three and a half million Sudeten Germans and their beautiful and rich territory without bloodshed.

As a matter of fact, what do you think the new slogan is in Berlin tonight? It's in all the evening newspapers. It's this: "With Hitler and Chamberlain for Peace."

Mr. Chamberlain, without doubt, has become a very popular figure here in Germany. The *Diplomatic Correspondence,* organ of the German Foreign Office, writes tonight, "The German nation thanks Mr. Chamberlain for the efforts which he has made to establish a basis for shunting the threatening conflict towards a peaceful separation of Czechs and Sudetens. The Prime Minister, within a short week, has accomplished a valuable work in the service of peace. He realizes that the German demands still keep within the limits of the principles of self-determination which have been recognized in all responsible quarters."

And *Der Angriff,* most outspoken of the Nazi evening papers in Berlin, says that the warm reception which Mr. Chamberlain was given in Cologne this morning before boarding his airplane for London was only "a further proof of how this clever and far-sighted statesman has conquered the best sympathies of the German people."

And the same paper goes on to say how Mr. Chamberlain and Chancellor Hitler, quote, "have been working night and day for peace."

For the German press, the Czech President Beneš, on the other hand, has been working night and day for just the opposite, for war. And all the newspapers tonight which, as I said, publish the new slogan "With Hitler and Chamberlain for Peace," publish another one which they attribute to Czechoslovakia, and which runs like this: "With Beneš and Stalin for War."

Let's look at the headlines of tonight's and tomorrow morning's Berlin newspapers.

The front-page headlines of *Nachtausgabe* say: PRAGUE'S MOBILIZATION – THE ROAD TO WAR. ADOLF HITLER'S PLAN – A PROPOSAL FOR PEACE.

The headlines in the *Angriff* put it this way: PRAGUE'S RULERS SABOTAGE CHAMBERLAIN. GERMANY, ENGLAND AND FRANCE WANT TO SAVE EUROPEAN PEACE.

The *Börsen Zeitung* puts it even more simply: CHAMBERLAIN AND ADOLF HITLER FOR PEACE. ONLY PRAGUE WANTS WAR.

Herr Hitler, to get back to the news, returned to Berlin by air this afternoon and held consultations with his chief followers, including Field Marshal Göring, who, it was announced today, had completely recovered from his recent illness.

Here in Germany, we've been completely cut off from Czechoslovakia. No trains or airplanes came through today at all. And the telephone and telegraph service has been stopped. It was officially denied here tonight that Germany, through which most of the telephone and telegraph lines from Czechoslovakia reach the outside world, had cut them. Officials here said that the Czechoslovak Ministry of Posts today informed the international postal office at Berne that in accordance with Article 27 of the Berne Convention, all private telephone and telegraph communication from or to Czechoslovakia was being stopped.

Berlin September 25, 1938 23:40

Hello America. This is Berlin calling.

The news from Berlin tonight is that Chancellor Hitler is going to make what has been described here as a historic speech tomorrow evening at 8 o'clock, our time – 2 p.m. New York time.

Preparations were being rushed through tonight to enable every single one of the 75,000,000 Germans in this country to hear by radio the words of the Führer. It will also go out on short wave to many foreign countries. There will be few indeed, in Europe, or in the rest of the world who will not be able to hear the speech if they wish to. You can rather imagine that among the listeners will certainly be Mr. Chamberlain in London and M. Daladier in Paris.

In fact Chancellor Hitler's audience probably will be even greater than the one he had just two weeks ago tomorrow night when he made his famous speech at the closing session of the Nuremberg Party Congress. It was following that talk, you will remember, that events in Czechoslovakia and in Europe started marching with such bewildering speed.

The news that in this tense hour for Europe Hitler had decided to make a public speech burst suddenly at 5 o'clock this afternoon in Berlin.

I happened to be strolling up the Wilhelmstrasse a little before five on my way back from the American Embassy where I'd had a talk with our counsellor of embassy. Usually on a Sunday afternoon, the Wilhelmstrasse, on which, as you know, are located most of the government ministries, including Herr Hitler's Chancellery and the Foreign Office, – usually the Wilhelmstrasse is a very dead and quiet street on a nice Sunday afternoon such as we had today.

All the government offices are usually closed.

But this afternoon I thought I detected considerable activity – quite a bit of coming and going, as it were. I thought I saw the British ambassador, Sir Nevile Henderson, leaving the Foreign Office. And I knew that he usually did not call there on Sunday.

At about 8 o'clock tonight, early editions of tomorrow morning's papers were on the street and selling briskly. I bought one and this is the flaming headline I saw: The Führer to Speak Monday at the Sport Palace. Community Loudspeakers to Carry it to Every Corner of the Land.

And then down one half of Page One in great black type was the following Proclamation to the People issued by Dr. Goebbels. It's interesting to note that he issued it not as Minister of Propaganda and Public Enlightenment, but as "Reichs Propaganda Chief of the National Socialist Movement."

Above the proclamation in half-inch high type is a heading: HISTORIC MASS MEETING.

And this is it. I quote:

"On Monday, the 26 September, at 8 o'clock in the Sport Palace in Berlin there will be a great Popular Mass Meeting. The Führer will speak.

"This mass meeting will be broadcast by all German radio stations. Those who do not possess a radio apparatus will listen to it through community loudspeakers in every town and village in Germany. All party leaders in each district must begin immediately to prepare for the reception of the community broadcasts. There must not be a single person in Germany who shall not be a witness, by means of the radio, of this historic mass meeting."

Later on tonight the party leadership in Berlin added the following to the proclamation, addressed to the population of the capital:

"Entry to the Sport Palace mass meeting is free. The mass meeting will be broadcast by loudspeakers along the streets leading from the Führer's Chancellery to the Sport Palace. The Sport Palace will be opened to the public at 5 p.m.

"People of Berlin! Come out to the great People's Mass Meeting! If there is no place for you in the Sport Palace, then make for the Führer along his route a gigantic human wall and prepare for him a reception full of the feeling which moves us in these historic hours."

The Sport Palace, you may know, is the Madison Square Garden of Berlin. It seats about 15,000 people. In the days of the Republic, as since, it has been the scene not only of sporting events, but of great popular political meetings. Herr Hitler himself used to speak there before he rose to power, and I well remember that my first glimpse of him and indeed of his National Socialist movement was at a Nazi mass meeting at the Sport Palace six or seven years ago.

It seems curious to realize, incidentally, that at that time Berlin, which had a socialist and communist majority, did not take him very seriously. Outside of one newspaper, then edited by Dr. Goebbels, all the Berlin newspapers panned him the next day.

Well, that was all six or seven years ago.

Now, why did Chancellor Hitler suddenly decide to make a speech tomorrow? The newspapers here do not give an explanation, but here is one I heard in the Wilhelmstrasse tonight.

The Chancellor, it was said there, has decided to speak in order to answer a statement given out by the Prague radio station at 2.20 o'clock this afternoon. I did not hear that broadcast, but in Berlin it is charged that the Prague radio station accused Herr Hitler and Mr. Chamberlain of going further than the original terms of the Anglo-French agreement which was forced on Czechoslovakia last week.

Herr Hitler, I was told, will answer that accusation in his speech tomorrow night.

Now that brings us back to the famous German memorandum handed over to Mr. Chamberlain at Godesberg night before last.

According to German sources of information here, that memorandum merely follows the principles of the Anglo-French proposals for the partition of Czechoslovakia. On top of that, it is believed to demand the evacuation of the Sudeten territory by the Czechs within a certain time limit and the occupation by German forces. A study of Herr Hitler's own newspaper this morning, the *Völkischer Beobachter*, brings this out very clearly.

The chief foreign political expert of the *Völkischer Beobachter*, Dr. Theodor Seibert, also emphasizes that in his paper today. He calls the memorandum the "final peace proposals of the Führer." He says, incidentally, that Mr. Chamberlain accepted the job of handing over the memorandum only *with a heavy heart*, and adds, quote, "We have a very full understanding for Mr. Chamberlain." Dr. Seibert goes on to say: "Prague's position could be understood if the question of the so-called integrity of the Versailles Czechoslovakia really was being questioned. But as a matter of fact, not only did most of the public opinion in the Western Democratic countries already accept the proposition that the amputation of Czechoslovakia was unavoidable, but Prague itself, Beneš himself, accepted this fundamental before all the world. We understand that the new Sirovy government also notified London that it would stand by this acceptance."

That's the German version of the memorandum.

Now I want to say just a word about how the people look in Berlin in this critical hour.

A friend called me up from New York yesterday and wanted to know

28

if there was any war feeling, any of this "On to Prague!" fever among the population of Berlin.

The answer is that there is *none*. In the old days on the eve of war, the crowd used to demonstrate angrily before the embassies of the enemy countries. I made a point of it today to go past the Czech Legation. Not a soul outside, not even a policeman.

There is no war fever among the people in Berlin at all. Today, for instance, what did they do?

Well, they did what they do every Sunday when it is warm and sunny like it was today. They left the city and flocked out to those lovely lakes and splendid woods which dot Berlin and which make it one of the most pleasant cities in Europe in which to live. Thousands went to the Wannsee for what was probably the last swim of the season. The subways and elevated lines which take you out to the lakes and woods were jammed. You could hardly find standing room.

This morning I strolled through the Tiergarten, Berlin's Central Park, in the very heart of town. The good citizens were sunning themselves on the park benches, or playing with their children on the grass.

You had to rub your eyes to think that anything at all was the matter with this old world, with this old Europe.

I return you now to the CBS studios in New York.

Berlin September 26, 1938 01.45

Hello America! This is Berlin calling.

Well, at least on this fateful evening for Europe, we know where we stand.

Most of you, I take it, heard Chancellor Adolf Hitler's speech five hours ago at the Berlin Sport Palace.

If you did, you heard him say in a tone, and in words which left no doubt whatever, that he will not budge an inch from his position and that President Beneš must hand over to him Sudetenland by Saturday night, or take the consequences.

Those consequences – in this critical hour you almost hesitate to use the word – are war.

It's true Herr Hitler did not use the word himself. At least amidst the fanatical yelling and cheering in the Sport Palace I did not hear it, and I sat but fifty or sixty feet from him.

But no one in that vast hall – or none of the millions upon millions of Germans who gathered tonight in every town and village of Germany to hear the speech broadcast through community loudspeakers, or who sat quietly in their homes listening – had any doubts, so far as one can find out.

This is what Herr Hitler said, as I jotted his words down as they were being spoken: "On the Sudeten problem, my patience is at an end. And on October 1, Herr Beneš will hand us over this territory."

Those are the Chancellor's words, and they brought the house down with a burst of yelling and cheering the like of which I have never before heard at a Nazi meeting.

And if President Beneš does not hand over the Sudetenland on Saturday? Herr Hitler had a very categorical answer to that too. In no unfirm voice and with the crowd again cheering wildly before he had hardly finished the phrase, he said:

"Beneš has now in his hand, war or peace.

"He can grant the Sudeten Germans their freedom, or we will take it for them."

At this point, the 15,000 people leaped to their feet in a frenzy, raising their right hands in salute and yelling at the top of their voices in approval. It was a full minute before Herr Hitler could go on.

"The world must know," he went on, "that in my whole life I have never been a coward. I now go at the head of my people as its first soldier. No democratic phrases will suffice at this time. In this fateful hour, the whole German people are united behind me.

"We are determined. Herr Beneš can choose."

Those were Chancellor Hitler's very last words, and those of you who were listening to the broadcast must have heard the frantic cheering that greeted them.

Then the crowd started to yell in unison – much as our own college boys do at home – "The Führer commands, we follow." Over and over again they kept shouting it until I thought they'd take the roof off.

In good plain American, you can summarize it this way: Herr Hitler put it up to the Czechs to accept his demands by Saturday, or fight. And there we are.

There was a remarkable scene at the end. Herr Hitler sat down, and when the cheering had subsided, Dr. Goebbels arose and addressing the Führer said, "The German nation stands behind you in blind obedience, willing to follow where you lead, and in the spirit of German honor." Then he added:

"And never will 1918 come again!"

At this point not only the house rose to its feet to cheer, but all the cabinet members on the platform stood up, and Herr Hitler stood up. Herr Hitler stood up – he was facing in my direction, and I'll never forget the emotion on his face as Dr. Goebbels uttered those words that 1918 would never come again. Herr Hitler raised his right hand high up and brought it down in a gesture of approval and thankfulness, as if Dr. Goebbels had hit upon the right word to sum up the feelings in all of them. No 1918 ever again. No defeat like in '18.

It was a moment – it lasted perhaps ten seconds in all – that will remain in my mind the rest of my life, regardless of what is to come in the next days.

Now, don't think that after that unforgettable speech and the unforgettable scenes of enthusiasm which that speech evoked in the fifteen thousand people in the Sport Palace – don't think that there is a lot of war fever in the streets of Berlin tonight. When I drove up here a few minutes ago to the broadcasting house two miles through the center of Berlin, there was hardly a soul in the street. It was 1.30 in the morning, and everyone had gone to bed.

After the speech, I followed the crowd out and walked with it up the Potsdamerstrasse to the Potsdamerplatz. I was very puzzled. Because I was listening to what the people were saying. And they were not talking about war at all, but about how to get home, and whether there was time for a beer in their favorite beerhouse, or a coffee at the favorite café. No yelling; no slogans; no shouting, "On to Prague!" They were a good-natured bunch of people and you could see that they neither wanted war, nor expected it.

Berlin September 27, 1938 18:00

Hello America. This is Berlin calling.

Chancellor Adolf Hitler has replied to President Roosevelt.

The reply was sent off by cable to Washington this morning and is said here to be the longest message of its kind ever dispatched by the German Führer to the head of another state.

It gives an exhaustive analysis of the German position, and reviews the grievances of the Sudeten Germans since the war.

But the important thing for us is that Chancellor Hitler frankly informs President Roosevelt that he, that Germany, flatly rejects all responsibility if the present situation should come to a war. The responsibility, Herr Hitler maintains, is now with Prague.

Moreover, Herr Hitler tells Mr. Roosevelt in very plain words that a further postponement of the solution of the Sudeten question is impossible. "The possibilities," he informs our president, to quote him, "of arriving at a just solution by agreement are therefore exhausted by the German memorandum."

As you know that memorandum demands that the Czechs clear out of the Sudetenland by Saturday – just four days from now.

"It does not lie in the hands of the German government," Herr Hitler concludes his long message to President Roosevelt, "but in the hands of the Czechoslovakian government to decide whether it wants war or peace."

In other words, the German Chancellor has told President Roosevelt what he told the German people in his broadcast last night: that Prague must accept his demands peacefully, or submit to war.

And in this message to our President, as indeed in his speech at the Sport Palace last night, Herr Hitler makes it clear that he has made up his mind, and that he will not budge an inch from his position.

If Prague accepts the German demands: Good. Peace.

If Prague does not accept: Good. War.

You couldn't ask for it any plainer, if I may put it that way, in this critical hour for Europe.

Hitler received Sir Horace Wilson this morning and handed to him his reply to Mr. Chamberlain's letter. What Herr Hitler's reply is has not yet been officially made known. But in the Wilhelmstrasse this afternoon there was still some optimism and it was said that Herr Hitler's reply gives "new hope for a peaceful solution."

The feeling here this afternoon was that if Mr. Chamberlain, as is reported, was willing to guarantee that the Sudetenland would be given over to Germany without undue delay, then the German Chancellor would accept this, and there would be no resort to force on Saturday, even if the Czechs are not out by that time.

But at the same time it was emphasized that something definite must be done by October 1.

Munich September 29, 1938 18:00

Hello America. Hello CBS. This is Munich, Germany, calling. William L. Shirer calling the Columbia Network from Munich.

The Big Four of Europe – Herr Hitler, Signor Mussolini, M. Daladier and Mr. Chamberlain, have lost no time in getting down to the very serious business of trying to avert a world war over the Sudeten crisis.

Just a few minutes after Mr. Chamberlain landed at Munich airport at

11.55 today, and he was the last of the four to arrive, these four statesmen, who hold the destiny of Europe in their hands, got together in the Führer's headquarters here in Munich and began their discussions. There was so much speed about it that Mr. Chamberlain didn't even have time to go to his hotel. He drove right from the airport to the Führer's headquarters.

The first meeting was quite informal. It began at 12.30, our time. And the first feeling out of one another took place while the four statesmen nibbled at a buffet lunch, offered by Herr Hitler. It was what you might call a stand-up buffet lunch. The four men – no they weren't alone, Foreign Ministers Ciano of Italy, and von Ribbentrop of Germany, Sir Nevile Henderson the British ambassador, and M. Francois Poncet, the French ambassador were there too. As was also Field Marshal Göring, whose role in these days must not be overlooked by any means.

They all stood around in a small reception room, eating a light lunch, and getting acquainted.

For instance, Mr. Chamberlain had never personally met the Duce before. He had written him personal letters, but had never met him face to face. They started off with a friendly little chat. M. Daladier had never personally met either of the leaders of the two totalitarian states. And he proceeded to get acquainted with them. Actually, I'm told that during a considerable time, M. Daladier and Hitler stood in one corner and had a very long heart-to-heart talk. Herr Hitler has a warm spot in his heart for anyone who, like himself, fought the last war in the trenches as a common soldier. M. Daladier had done just that, in the front lines in France. It may have been that the two fought literally opposite each other some time between 1914 and 1918. At any rate, they stood together today and had a long friendly chat.

After this stand-up buffet was finished, the four statesmen gathered around a table and discussed briefly how their work would proceed. The talks were necessarily slow because of language difficulties – everything had to be translated in French, German and English.

It's generally believed that they decided to devote the day exclusively to trying to find a solution of the Sudeten problem.

Whether or not these four men on whom so much depends will be able to do any more than work out some agreement by which a world war can be averted at this eleventh hour over Sudetenland we do not yet know. And we won't know until later on this evening.

[*The rest of Shirer's broadcasts covering events at Munich have been lost.*]

33

With the German Army of Occupation in Czechoslovakia October 2, 1938

Just as Hitler promised and Mussolini, Chamberlain and French Premier Daladier agreed, the German army marched into Czechoslovakia at two o'clock yesterday afternoon.

I went with it.

It was a very peaceful occupation. Not a shot was fired. Only once did we run into the slightest danger – of which more later. The whole thing went off like a parade, even to the military bands and regimental flags and Sudeten girls tossing bouquets of flowers at the troops and throwing kisses at them.

And yet this was the German army which forty-eight hours ago was girded for war. Today it functioned with that clock-like precision which has given the Reichswehr its reputation. And it was ready for all eventualities. Only none of them occurred.

It's not true that Germans marched in a minute after midnight Friday night and with tremendous force.

I stood on the Czech-German frontier at Sarau, thirty-five miles east of Passau, general headquarters of the army occupying district number one on the south-west tip of Czechoslovakia, and from where we set out at noon. At exactly 2 p.m., by synchronized watches, the march began. And though the roads from Passau to the frontier were lined with troops, artillery and supply trains, only a handful took part in the occupation today.

It was truly a symbolic occupation. The Czech forces had withdrawn during the night, taking their arms and military supplies with them, but nothing else, and observing the conditions of withdrawal perfectly. There was no contact in my sector on the extreme right wing of the German army throughout the day. Even with field glasses we saw no Czech troops.

All the way up from Passau yesterday, driving with a German army staff captain who told me he had been captured by American troops in the Argonne shortly before the World War ended, we passed long lines of motor vehicles chugging towards the "front". There was artillery, mostly 105s, which of course was not used, and which had not even crossed the frontier tonight, and batteries of anti-aircraft guns nicely camouflaged. These also were not used, as there was not a single plane in the air today on either side.

Field kitchens were smoking by the roadside, serving up food to the hungry troops. At one place we passed a motor-train of fifteen pontoon bridges.

"In case the Czechs blow up the bridge over the Moldau," my guide explained.

A couple of hours later, though we were not allowed to advance further than the German outpost 1,500 meters from the river, we could see that the bridge over the Moldau had not been blown up after the Czech troops withdrew over it.

A grey mist hung over the beautiful mountains of the Bohemian Forest as we stood waiting for the zero hour at 2 p.m. The German soldiers had full wartime equipment – steel helmets, heavy packs, gas-masks. And they looked ready for anything. There were a few tanks and armored cars, and machine-guns were all ready for action. I also noticed anti-tank guns about.

As the commanding officer, a colonel, later told us, the Germans were taking no chances. That's one of the reasons they didn't go in last night, when a few well-placed guerrilla irregulars, equipped with machine-guns, might have caused some unpleasantness.

Even yesterday afternoon the commanding officer kept a sharp lookout for road mines. In the end he discovered one, and it came near to blowing our car and its passengers to bits.

At 2 p.m., on a simple command of the commanding officer, the Germans moved slowly forward up the main road, scouts with machine-guns and automatic rifles covering the flanks in the woods. Tanks and armored cars went up side by side with anti-tank guns. The German army moved forward ahead of us, machine-like, but carefully.

In five minutes we reached the Czech custom house. It was deserted, but outside delirious Sudeteners had already started to erect a triumphal arch of telephone poles, decorated with pine branches, and over which they had already scrawled a sign: "Sudetenland Welcomes its Liberators."

And then from across the fields between the woods the peasants started to emerge, jumping up into the air, raising their hands in the Nazi salute and screaming at the top of their voices "Heil Hitler!"

At this moment the correct military advance of that part of the German army which I was watching became very incorrect. They broke all the rules of strategy. Somebody sent back to the rear for the band. It came up on the double, and the rest of the advance was made up the main road behind a full military band tootling old German marches, the regimental flags following. On the flanks the scouts still crept along the edge of the woods, and the armored cars scooted about, but the main force marched up the road, now lined with a happy, shouting population.

The womenfolk, attired in their best Sunday peasant costumes of richly-colored embroidery, tossed flowers at the troops. A bushel of flowers must have fallen into my own lap, though I brought up the rear.

The menfolk, in their mountain costumes, had put on white collars and their best Sunday go-to-meeting hats. They also cheered and heiled.

In the meantime, engineers had inspected the tank obstructions near the customs house. They looked pretty formidable to me. They consisted of several rows of heavy iron rails, buried in concrete placements.

But a German captain of engineers came running up, laughing.

"They're childish," he insisted. "Look at them. They wouldn't hold you up five minutes. Childish and laughable, I tell you."

"But why?" I asked him. And he explained that they had only been thrown across the road to the edge of the forest, but that one single artillery blast would have uprooted enough trees at the side of the tank barrier to open a road for all the tanks in the world.

I'm no soldier. I know nothing about it. I'm only telling you what he said.

We marched on about three-and-a-half kilometers altogether, and then the colonel called a halt. That was all for the day, and it was over almost before it began. Before us lay the Moldau River, and beyond the withdrawing, invisible Czech army.

A young captain came up to explain, almost apologize for, the carefulness of the German troops, as he put it. He himself had come up to the frontier just before dark last night to reconnoitre and had spied, he said, five Czech machine-gun nests, manned by a total of about twenty Czech troops. He had sketched their positions, but just as they were leaving, about 8.30 p.m., the Czechs dismantled their machine-guns and withdrew. At least that's the way it looked, but as he said, they took no chances and had those machine-gun posts covered in the advance today. As it happened, they were found entirely deserted.

The biggest village in the district was a little place called Unter Moldau, a hamlet of 400 souls, that lay outside our lines, down by the river which was in no-man's land. About three, the whole village flocked up the road to greet the troops with a wild ovation.

At their head was the burgomaster. I collared him when he had finished saluting and heiling and welcoming the troops, and we had a little talk by the side of my car. He was a typical hardy mountaineer with the most beautiful flying walrus mustache I've ever seen, and a grizzly, deeply-lined face. And he was all dressed up. He introduced himself as Josef Schwarzbauer, which means "Black Peasant".

He seemed most peeved at the fact that the Czech police had confiscated all the radios in the town and he and his flock couldn't hear Hitler's Monday speech or get any news of what was going on in the world.

He said they didn't even know of the Munich Agreement until Sudeten Legionaries crossed over after dark last night and told him the news. About 9 p.m., he said, the Czech military and police convoked him and politely turned over all power to him, but he was more worried about

36

getting the radios back to their owners than anything else. When this was done, and the Czechs pulled out, the village gave itself over to a right good celebration, he said.

About 500 peasants are spending the night within the German lines, as some of their villages were still occupied by the Czechs. It made a nice little job for the army command to feed them.

Later in the afternoon we drove over to the extreme right wing, and it was here that we got our only real thrill of the day. A soldier was guarding a small bridge and motioned to us to stop, but the driver didn't see him at first and only stopped when the soldier flung his body in front of the car. I thought he looked a bit nervous, the soldier. We jumped out of the car to find that we had driven within about five feet of a fully-loaded mine. It was being guarded until the engineer corps could get there to take it apart without danger of explosion.

The German officers with me thought it was a good joke. "They never would have found the pieces of us or this car," they laughed.

A little further on up the road, some engineers were cutting through a barrier of logs across the road. They cut through them with a wonderful contraption, a gasoline-powered handsaw operated by two men that cut through a huge log like a knife through butter. They removed the whole obstacle in about an hour.

I was surprised at the atmosphere in this new German army on the march. There was very little heel-clicking or stiff, overzealous discipline. Rather, a surprising comradery between officers and men, and between senior and junior officers.

Altogether, it was very much like a holiday parade, the whole occupation.

And it came so near to being something much more grim.

Telephoned to Murrow March 17, 1939, 23.30

[Shirer had just returned to Geneva from Rome, where he covered the election of Pope Pius XII, when news came that the German army had occupied Bohemia and Moravia and that Hitler had announced their annexation to the Reich. Unable to get to Prague himself, Shirer called this report in to Ed Murrow in London.]

I have just been on the telephone to some of the American correspondents in Prague. It is not wise for them to say much on the phone in a city under strict German military dictatorship, but they were able to indicate enough. The terrible tragedy, they said, continued.

One of the correspondents reported that the cleaning-up operations of the Gestapo went on today at even an accelerated tempo. No one knows, he said, what the fate of those arrested by Himmler's gang of 800 secret police is. There is no way of finding out. But the trucks of the dreaded Black Guards, he said, thundered through Prague all day today, rounding up those whom Hitler considers undesirable.

By the weekend, my informant reported, most of the thousands of German political refugees who had taken refuge in Czechoslovakia and who were caught like rats in traps, are expected to be rounded up. People in Prague, he said, are shuddering as to their outcome. Besides the émigrés, Jews and Czechs were also being arrested wholesale. Apparently any Czech who had anything to do with Beneš is earmarked for arrest. Also hundreds of Social-Democrats and communist Czech leaders.

The booing and hissing with which the Prague populace greeted the first German troops on Wednesday has now given way, one of the American correspondents said, to a stoic, bitter resignation. The people in the street, he said, went their way today silently, but with almost indescribable bitterness written on their faces. The Czech people, he emphasized, show not the slightest sign of accepting their fate subserviently or of kowtowing to their military conquerors. When German troops passed in the street today, he noted how the Czechs turned away their faces and went grimly – some still with tears – on their way.

Most of them, he told me, can hardly realize yet that it has happened, and none *how* it could happen. But the Czechs are a people with a dour, stubborn hope and most of them seemed to think, he explained, that their present subjection cannot last long.

One of the correspondents in Prague tonight hinted that worse things are in store yet, but I could not catch his allegorical language and I couldn't make out what he wanted to say.

As for Geneva, what is left of the League is of course in the deepest despair imaginable. The atmosphere around the secretariat has been very blue anyway because of the dismissal for reasons of economy now going on of a large number of officials and employees. The rest – those who still keep a job of some kind – are since Wednesday thinking about another job anyway.

As for Switzerland, it has taken events this week calmly, though the press has with considerable bravery, considering the German pressure on this country, attacked Germany savagely. Today one of the members of the Swiss Federal Council was quoted as saying the Swiss would fight if attacked. Every Swiss I've talked to takes it for granted. But they're wondering, if they're not exactly next on the list of Germany's intended victims, how far down the list they are. Not very far, they think. One important thing is that Nazism has made no headway at all among the German Swiss, who form a majority of the population of this country. The German Swiss are even more violently anti-Nazi than the French Swiss.

Traveling through Switzerland, as I have recently, one notices many more soldiers than usual. Well, it's understandable, isn't it?

Berlin April 20, 1939. 16.00 GMT

Hello America! This is Berlin calling.

Adolf Hitler, Chancellor and Leader of the Third Reich, is fifty years old today. And here in Berlin he has surely had a birthday celebration such as no other ruler of our time has ever had.

I don't know whether he had a birthday cake with fifty candles or not. That would be quite an ordinary thing to have.

But I do know that I've never seen so many flags, standards, golden eagles and floodlit pylons in my life. Nor so many glittering uniforms, or soldiers, or guns. Nor so many people at a birthday party. There must have been – last night, when in a blaze of floodlights, Herr Hitler opened his new monumental avenue through the heart of Berlin – there must have been nearly two million people in the streets. And this morning at least as many people lined the great East-West boulevard for the great military review which has just ended.

That parade – from which I've just rushed away to come here to the studio – was, of course, the culminating event of the two-day birthday celebrations.

And it was – if I may so put it – *some* parade!

It just happens that I've seen all the big military reviews here since Herr Hitler came to power. And I've seen some pretty big ones in France and Italy.

But today's parade of the cream of the new German army must certainly have been the greatest display of military power that modern Europe has ever seen. Not even the old imperial Germany – I'm told – ever saw anything like it.

The Berlin crowds – usually a jovial lot who like a good, colorful show – struck me as being in a pure holiday mood. They liked what they saw all right, but there was nothing grim about them. The Führer's birthday was a national holiday, with the result that all the youngsters of the city were in the front row – that is, behind the S.S. and S.A. guards who lined the streets – with the elders, usually the whole family – father, mother, uncle, aunt – grouped behind. These people didn't strike you as thinking much about war, even though they were looking at the men and the machines which will fight it, if it should come. The hot-dog stands and the beer stands did a tremendous business during the whole time. It was that kind of a crowd.

Among the street decorations along the line of march, were great banners, thirty feet long, hanging from specially erected posts. They were the banners of the German "Gau" or districts in which the Reich is now divided up. You couldn't help noticing at least three banners with the inscription "Danzig" on them. And indeed the last thing Herr Hitler did before he left to review his troops, was to receive a delegation from Danzig which had come to name him an honorary citizen of the Free City of Danzig.

I might add that earlier in the day Herr Hitler received formal birthday congratulations from Dr. Hacha, President of the Protectorate of Bohemia and Moravia, as well as from the Protector himself, Reichsminister von Neurath. Dr. Tiso, the Prime Minister of Slovakia, which is also under German protection, as you know, also called in person to offer his congratulations to the Führer.

From 11:25 this morning until 3:25 this afternoon I stood in the press stand by the side of the place Herr Hitler and his generals, his cabinet and his guests of honor, took the salute. All that time, for four hours, we saw these steel-helmeted troops, moving with the precision of a mighty machine, goose-step by.

They didn't all goose-step, of course, because a large part of an army nowadays moves on wheels. And overhead, at the beginning, we saw a sample – a pretty good-sized sample, I thought – of that deadly new weapon, the air force.

Herr Hitler, who as far as I could see showed no sign of strain, was clad, as usual, in his brown Nazi party uniform, with his Iron Cross hanging from his breast. He took the salute standing on a platform under a canopy in front of the Technical High School. For those four hours he saluted literally every platoon, every tank, every truck.

Under the awning of this canopy, was a large red-plush, golden-gilded chair. Slightly back of this were other chairs. The first chair, which looked quite imperial, was for Herr Hitler, those behind for his aides and generals.

Actually, when the German Chancellor drove up in his big Mercedes to the reviewing stand at 10.20 this morning, he gave the three seats to his right and left, not to the three heads of the defense forces, but to three others. They were Baron von Neurath, his protector for Bohemia and Moravia, and Dr. Hacha, the president of these provinces, a small, forlorn-looking figure next to the towering Neurath in a glittering uniform. Dr. Hacha was the only one on the platform not in uniform. He bobbed up and down, removing his silk hat as he did so, each time a Reich flag passed, which was every two or three minutes. The third man was Dr. Tiso, premier of Slovakia. Back of these three sat the heads of the defense forces, Field Marshal Göring in a resplendent uniform, General Keitel, chief of the army, and Grand Admiral von Raeder, chief of the navy.

As for the review itself – I don't think Europeans or Americans have ever seen anything quite so big, and impressive. It was one more demonstration to Germans and to the world that this country has a mighty armed force.

All the streets of the capital are a sea of flags and bunting, and meandering about last night I noticed that in almost every shop window the display goods had been removed and replaced by either a picture or a bust of the Führer around which spring flowers and evergreen branches were placed.

I find the newspapers and weekly magazines here – all of which devoted special numbers to the birthday anniversary – interesting, even instructive. None of them fail to recount what, after all, Hitler has done for Germany, and his long list of successes are enumerated and recalled in some detail: the proclamation of conscription, which paved the way for the great army which we saw today; the march into the Rhineland; the Anschluss with Austria; the liberation – as they put it here – of the Sudetenland; the occupation of Czechoslovakia; and last – it was very recent – the return of Memel.

There are suitable pictures to illustrate these triumphs and you get the impression from the people in the street that they feel pretty good about these things, and certainly proud of them. They seem to feel that they have got somewhere and are going places, as a nation.

London April 23, 1939 10.10 GMT

It is not my job to hop about Europe in these critical days, and then take up your time by reporting to you my own personal opinions or prejudices about this country or that, and which is right or wrong, and what I think we Americans ought to do about it.

Surely our job as American broadcasters is to report to you as objectively as we can the facts and the trends and the atmosphere we find in these nations of Europe. And having done that, let you draw your own conclusions. We are simply reporters.

For obvious reasons, I spend a great deal of time in Germany these days. I was there Thursday, to see that unforgettable four-hour birthday parade of Germany's military might. I was there three weeks ago to hear Herr Hitler throw down his challenge at Wilhelmshaven to the powers which he claims are trying to encircle the Reich. I was at Godesberg and Munich. And I was permanently stationed in Berlin from 1934 to 1937.

Perhaps that gives me some excuse for a few minutes now, to point out to you – not how much we may feel that Germany is in the wrong, but actually how the German people see the present situation, and why, and what they intend to do about it – or rather, what their leader intends to do about it, and how far the German people will back him up.

Now you and I will make our reservations on practically all of these points. I'm only saying, that that's what the German people think.

Now naturally these views of the situation which the German people do hold have been largely hammered into them by a controlled press and radio, and it goes without saying that they rarely have a chance to get the news as it is presented elsewhere. But that does not alter the fact that those views are held – and stubbornly held, too.

From talks with many simple citizens – the majority not Nazis – and after checking up my information with many of the American correspondents in Berlin, it seems to me that the majority of the German people today believe:

First, that Great Britain, backed by Daladier, Stalin and Roosevelt, is forging an encirclement of Germany designed to crush the Reich.

Secondly, that Hitler is right if, profiting by the lessons of 1914, he desires to break that encirclement before it is successfully completed.

Thirdly, that eastern and south-eastern Europe is a natural part of Germany's *Lebensraum* – or space necessary for its existence – and that neither Britain nor anyone else, including America, has any right to interfere with Germany's action there.

Fourthly, that Hitler, whether they like him or not, will get what he wants in eastern Europe, and get it – as he got Czechoslovakia at Munich – without a war.

Fifthly, that there will therefore be no war, and that they – the German people at any rate – do not want war. And that war can only come if the "encirclement powers", jealous of Germany's success, attack the Reich, in which case they will gladly fight, and this time, they say, Germany will win.

And sixthly, the mass of the German people, whatever they thought of Hitler before, or even though they still do not like many aspects of the régime, do feel that he has outsmarted the "foreign tyrants", as they call them, who were trying to keep Germany down, and that he has restored it to its proper place in the world. And that without a single shot being fired, nor the life of one German soldier sacrificed.

Remember, these are the people who went through the blockade. That blockade spelled semi-starvation. They remember that.

Now what actually is Germany's goal towards which it is racing with such speed? Because there is a time-factor involved. Neither Germans nor foreigners in Berlin believe for one second that Hitler will stop now – halfway on his road.

The goal is the domination of eastern Europe down to the Black Sea, or as the Germans put it, the Reich's *Lebensraum*, or living-space. I got the impression in Berlin last week that this does not necessarily mean that Hitler intends to annex the countries in his way, as he did Czechoslovakia. He might very well be content to leave them their independence, provided they maintain governments friendly to him and give him what he wants economically. But what Germany envisages economically in this territory we know from the German Finance Minister, Herr Funk, who described it as a "compound economy from the North Sea to the Black Sea".

That's Germany's goal, and if it reaches it, it will not only be the most powerful country in Europe, but it will be invulnerable to the blockade which lost it the last war. The raw materials and the food so necessary for its existence will then be available in its own back-yard.

Why the speed to reach that goal?

Because Germany must hurry to complete its tasks while it can still bear the tremendous economic, financial and psychological strains. The Nazi economic machine is now at its peak. So is the military machine.

But there are limits – limits to the financing of essential raw-materials and food from foreign-exchange reserves, to the maintenance of long working hours on unincreased wages, while the cost of living rises. And probably there is a limit – though no one knows what it is – to borrowing. The published Reich debt increased last year by four billion dollars, according to the official rate of exchange, and it is increasing this year at the rate of nearly 400 million dollars a month.

In the meantime, the food situation does not get any better, and in Berlin they tell you that the iron fences of Germany are being melted down for more important functions.

And now from London comes the dreaded specter of what the Germans believe is encirclement and which threatens to deprive them of their goal.

That explains the haste.

Peace? Yes, but in Berlin last week I heard a new expression. People there spoke of a *German Peace*. And it was explained that it meant a peace ensured by the German army. The paper of Hitler, the *Völkischer Beobachter*, on Friday after the military parade, put it this way: "This army is for us the shield and the security for Peace, which admittedly is a German Peace, and which will ensure for a powerful people its necessary rights. The world," it concludes, "must realize this and draw some

43

practical conclusions from the fact that the German army has now been brought to completion."

Geneva May 7, 1939 22.06 CET [Central European Time]

This is the first weekend I've been able to spend in my temporary home in Geneva since the German army walked into Prague nearly two months ago. Maybe it's a good time to look at things in a way that is only possible from this peace-loving – but also liberty-loving – land of Switzerland where the people you talk with still seem to be in their right minds.

Now, before I get to the latest crisis news, a word about another matter, not unconnected with the crisis to be sure, which is splitting European heads just now. A front-page editorial in my morning newspaper, the *Journal de Genève*, today begins with this sentence : "Will the United States intervene in case of a European war?"

It's a question I've been asked dozens of times in Rome, Paris, London, Berlin and Warsaw in the last few weeks. You at home, of course, know the answer better than I do. But perhaps it may interest you to know the feeling of Europe on that matter.

Subject to correction by my colleagues Ed Murrow and Tom Grandin in London and Paris, I got the definite impression in those two capitals that Britain and France count quite definitely on American industrial aid in wartime from the outset. And they don't think we will be really very long in actually entering the war on their side.

The German attitude is very interesting. The Germans don't think we'll come in again. But if we do, they appear to think – as they did in 1916 – that it won't make very much difference. That may strike most Americans as strange, in view of recent history, but there it is. Why it is, I don't know.

I got perhaps a hint at the answer in Berlin last week. An acquaintance of mine told me that America could never ferry over two million soldiers the next time.

"But that's what you said in 1917," I countered.

Well, he had an answer. You can sum it up in two words: Airplanes. Submarines. He thought the new high-speed bombers and the increased efficiency of submarines could easily prevent troops from landing in either France or England, or even Ireland for that matter. I'm no military expert and I don't know. Perhaps Washington does.

The big news of course in Europe tonight is the agreement reached in Milan today by Herr von Ribbentrop and Italian Foreign Minister Count Ciano for a military pact between the Axis powers. My friends in Berlin and Rome told me on the telephone a few minutes ago that this was being hailed in the two capitals tonight as a tremendous blow to the alleged encirclement policy of France and Britain. About an hour ago I heard the Berlin news broadcast hail it as a great boon to European peace.

According to my informants in Rome, the plan is to draw into this Italo-German military alliance both Spain and Hungary and perhaps later Yugoslavia. Italy and Germany, according to the same source, will also try to get Japan to join.

With Russia, since the retirement of Litvinov, becoming an increasingly doubtful factor in the so-called Democratic Peace Front, Rome and Berlin, along with their satellite nations, would certainly seem to be in not a bad military position.

Another thing came out of those Milan conversations, according to my information from Rome tonight. Italy, I'm told, agreed to back Germany's demands on Poland. Not only that, but to back them by using its influence in Warsaw, which is not wholly inconsiderable, to get them accepted. The idea seems to be that in return for Danzig becoming a part of the Reich and Germany getting its motor-road across the Corridor, Italy herself would take part in a guarantee of Polish economic rights in Danzig.

Whether the Poles would accept this is of course another matter.

And perhaps most important of all, many foreign correspondents at Rome tonight seemed to feel that today's Milan meeting was historic not so much because of the military pact but because, in their opinion, it definitely and finally sealed for a very long time Italy's alignment in Europe. If there were doubts yesterday, they say, there can be none tonight.

[While still in Geneva, Shirer took advantage of the absence of Nazi censorship of the mails to write to Paul White, CBS's Director of Public Affairs in New York.]

May 8, 1939

Dear Paul:

You may be interested to know how the Nazi government is now checking up on the American networks. According to an informant of mine in the RRG [Reichs Rundfunk Gesellschaft], the German government at first ordered RRG to refuse facilities to both CBS and NBC for Hitler's Reichstag reply to Roosevelt. At the same time it specifically ordered that Mutual was to have exclusive facilities. Only after our refusal to take orders from Germany as to who and what we put on our network, plus the fact that the RRG itself pointed out to its own government the dangers of shutting out the two big American networks, did Berlin give up its original plan to give the speech exclusively to Mutual. In fairness to

Mutual, I don't think it knows anything about this. But you can see how important it was that neither Murrow nor I nor you in New York gave in an inch to Nazi demands about our commentators. Actually, by taking this attitude from the first, we helped RRG tame its own government on this point.

In Berlin the other day I nosed around a bit to see if I could find out the reason for the Nazi government's attempt to muzzle us at this particular time. I found out this: that the Wilhelmstrasse [the German Foreign Office] had received very elaborate reports from all over the United States on how American radio stations handled Germany in their news and commentary. Several German agents worked on the job. Their conclusion was that both CBS and NBC were very "anti-German", "distorting" German news and "attacking" the Fatherland. Their recommendation was that these two networks be denied facilities on the next big story from Germany, with Mutual getting all the facilities it wanted. With typical German mentality they thought that such a "disciplining" would make us good boys thereafter!

I thought maybe you in New York would like to know that you were being spied upon, but naturally please treat this as confidential.

Paris June 1939. Joint broadcast with Ed Murrow and Thomas Grandin of the Paris CBS staff.

GRANDIN: This is Thomas Grandin. Today Bill Shirer and Ed Murrow are passing through Paris, and, for the next few minutes, the three of us are going to continue a conversation we've just been having in a café. Now, Ed, certain people here in Paris claim the British are convinced that war is inevitable. It's said the British don't believe that Germany and Italy merely want Suez or Gibraltar or Danzig, but *everything*. The British, I've been told, are working with great determination in an effort to save peace, but they're really at the stage, it's claimed, of working to assure a victory in the next war. How about it?

MURROW: Nothing is inevitable to the British. I came over on the Dover-Calais boat yesterday, and it was loaded to the gunwales with Englishmen and their cars, off for a holiday on the Continent. Most of them were talking about a peaceful summer, and quoting their favorite astrologer in support of that belief. By the fall, Britain will have three quarters of a million men under arms. There's a boom in the making. Unemployment figures are going down every month, but it's all based on re-armament. As to the inevitability of war, didn't you read this week's statements by Mr. Chamberlain and Lord Halifax [the British Foreign Secretary]? They

46

said, in effect, that any and all of Germany's claims might be settled around a conference table.

SHIRER: That sounded like appeasement to me.

MURROW: It sounded like appeasement to a lot of people in London too. But appeasement is a more attractive proposition, when you live in the best bombing target in Europe. What's your alternative, Shirer, to appeasement?

SHIRER: Well, you tried appeasement in September, and would you say that it was a success?

MURROW: Most people in London seem to feel that it left something to be desired.

SHIRER: Then what makes you think it will work now?

MURROW: I don't think it will.

SHIRER: That's what most of the people on the Continent think too.

MURROW: What's the feeling in Paris, Grandin?

GRANDIN: There are partisans of appeasement here in France. Some of the extreme conservatives, and also, oddly enough, a certain section of the socialist party too. But, on the whole, Paris doesn't seem to welcome this latest British move.

MURROW: I'm not saying that appeasement is the keynote of British foreign policy. But I do say that the appeasers are still there. That they would like to avoid a hard and fast commitment to Russia, and their case is stronger than you might think. After all, they can always say, "This is better than war." And in spite of Britain's growing strength, war isn't exactly popular on the other side of the Channel.

SHIRER: Well, so far as that goes, don't get the idea that war is popular in Italy or Germany. So far as the people themselves are concerned, they don't want it any more than the English or French.

GRANDIN: I agree – it's certainly true of the French. They're good fighters but hate to fight.

MURROW: Maybe this latest move by the Vatican will provide the solution.

SHIRER: There's no doubt that the Vatican is working very hard for peace. Of course, it's very difficult to get concrete information as to exactly what the Pope proposes as a basis for peace. Though he's denied it, some people persist in thinking that the Pope is trying to negotiate a peace

47

before Britain, irrevocably, ties up with Russia in the non-aggression front. They say that this delay of London in pushing the negotiations with Moscow to completion, and also the nature of the overtures made last week to Germany by Mr. Chamberlain and Lord Halifax, are not unconnected with the Vatican's peace moves.

GRANDIN: On the other hand, certain people here in Paris feel that the statement was intended for use as counter-propaganda against the German people's growing belief that they are being aggressively encircled. Now, Bill, would you say that the German people really believe that?

SHIRER: They certainly do.

GRANDIN: Some French observers say Chamberlain and Daladier are giving Hitler a last chance to negotiate.

MURROW: Do you think he will accept the invitation?

SHIRER: No.

GRANDIN: Why not?

SHIRER: His methods are changeable, but his purpose is inflexible. He has a goal. A program. And they're only half fulfilled.

MURROW: But the program doesn't seem to be working out too well. What about the recent troubles in Czechoslovakia?

SHIRER: Yesterday, the foreign correspondents in Prague received an order from the German authorities not to publish anything on the shooting at Kladno and Nachob, except the official commentaries. But despite the censorship, we know that there have been many outbreaks in Bohemia and Moravia during the last few days. Some people now believe that perhaps these incidents have not been as spontaneous as we first thought. As a matter of fact, there's a consistent rumor now going around the capitals of Europe that Hitler, using these outbreaks as an excuse, intends, within the next few days, to liquidate the so-called "Protectorate", and annex Bohemia and Moravia outright, as provinces of the Reich.

GRANDIN: Well what would be the real significance of a move like that, if it's taken?

SHIRER: It may be a precautionary measure, in view of possible developments toward the end of the summer.

MURROW: What do you mean by that?

SHIRER: Well, after the harvest in August, it seems to most people that you're going to have to solve some questions, either by appeasement, or by something more serious. Isn't that also the feeling in France, Grandin?

GRANDIN: Yes, it is. It's thought there will be trouble in August. And France isn't slowing down on defense measures. More than a million men, I suppose, are still mobilized. M. Daladier recently published certain measures with respect to these men. The only leaves being granted are for forty-eight hours, except in the case of farmers. The contingents now serving will be kept under arms until September and October. There has also been a project before the Chamber of Deputies here, by which all elections of congressmen will be postponed, so as to prevent any sort of political weakness inside France. It seems that M. Daladier will probably be able to put this project into effect by decree. There is an amazing spirit of confidence here in France, among the people. Financially, the country is much better off.

MURROW: That may be true, and I suppose the same thing could be said of England. But basically, both Britain and France seem to be getting into the same position as Germany, where the economy of the country is based upon re-armament, where the largest customer for most industries is the government, and where normal business, other than that dictated by defense, is at a standstill. The experts in London have been saying for years that Germany couldn't stand the strain of a transfer from wartime to peacetime economy. If things go on as they are now, Britain will be in a similar position. Of course, no one expects that any country is going to be faced with the happy prospect of producing houses and civilian essentials, instead of guns, planes and ships, in the immediate future. So things are likely to go on as they are, for some weeks or months, anyway. In the meantime, everyone is waiting to see whether Britain and Russia are really going to get together.

SHIRER: Well, Ed, are they?

MURROW: I'm no prophet, but a lot of people in London are getting worried. The government seems to be delaying matters, they're sending Mr. Strang [a British diplomat] to Moscow, who certainly isn't empowered to conclude a final arrangement. Then, too, the British Government's appeal to Germany to negotiate isn't likely to help matters along any. The Russians seem to feel that the Axis can't be reasoned with, and that a display of overwhelming force is the only thing likely to prevent further aggression. British hopes, in connection with the Russian agreement, have been postponed many times. And I wouldn't be surprised to see them disappointed again. The Russian demands are high, and the British are likely to accept them only when they become convinced that no other formula, such as the mediation of the Vatican, for instance, will solve existing problems.

49

SHIRER: Do the British feel that their so-called Anti-aggression Front can hold up without the Russians?

MURROW: The whole Anti-aggression Front has been created piecemeal. The guarantee to Poland is a liability, until such time as the Russians come in. How do the French feel about it, Grandin?

GRANDIN: The French signed an alliance with Russia back in 1935. There are a number of people who object to this pact, on the ground that Communists can get a hold on French internal politics in this fashion. But the majority opinion here is certainly in favor of closer co-operation with Russia. They mention Richelieu's statement that foreign alliances and internal politics have nothing to do with each other. There's no doubt that most Frenchmen think the full Triple Alliance – France, England, Russia – absolutely essential, if possible German aggression is to be prevented.

MURROW: Of course the Germans haven't been exactly idle during these last few weeks.

SHIRER: No, you can't say they have. For instance, they did some very useful work with Prince Paul of Yugoslavia during his recent visit to Berlin. As a result, I don't think that you will find Yugoslavia in the Anti-aggression Front. On top of that, they signed a so-called non-aggression pact with Denmark, thus breaking up a certain unity in Scandinavian policy, and they also made non-aggression pacts with Estonia and Latvia. If I may change the subject, for a moment, Ed, was there any reaction in England to the tremendous reception which the King and Queen got in America?

MURROW: Most of my English friends seem to think that the reception was almost too good to be true. According to the press, New York went crazy. Not much mention was made of the fact that certain American senators and congressmen refused to attend the official reception in Washington. It's generally believed that an invitation was extended to President Roosevelt to visit London. There's no question that he would get a tremendous reception. At the same time, most people seem not to expect to see the American President drive down Whitehall. But I see that our time is almost up, and since he's sailing for New York next week, I think we ought to let Bill Shirer say . . .

SHIRER: We return you now to America.

July 1939

[Shirer sailed to New York on June 17 on the maiden voyage of the Mauretania. While in the U.S. he gave a number of talks. This is from the one he gave on July 14, 1939.]

When I left Europe on June 17th it did look as if there would be peace until fall. There were at least three reasons.

First – and this is the most important – because all the nations want to gather in their harvests – especially the Axis powers which are short of food, and shorter on the foreign exchange with which to buy it from outside. You can't start a war on an empty stomach.

Second. So far as is known, Hitler has not yet made up his mind exactly how or exactly when he is to try to get Danzig, and the other things he wants from Poland. Apparently, also, Mussolini's mind was not made up as to what he was to do – if anything – as the very much junior partner of the Axis.

Third. Both sides were still trying to assess first, the other's strength, secondly their own. This was especially true of Berlin and Rome. The entry of Turkey into the Anti-aggression Front was a bad blow for both of them – almost the first big blow, I'm tempted to say, that they've had since they started moving. That made them sit back and think. Russia's finally making up its mind made them sit back and ponder even more. For if the Triple Entente, which defeated the Central Powers once, was really being reborn – and this time with the addition of Turkey and Poland – then here was something which could not be wafted away by mere fiery speeches or noisy sword-rattling. Hitler and Mussolini are no fools. They calculate very coolly and thoroughly. And though it may be different in the end, so far you have to admit that they have never taken undue chances. Abyssinia, Albania, Austria, Czechoslovakia, Memel, Spain were pushovers. It may well be – though I know people who are still skeptical – that the days of the easy conquests are over. But if that day is over, then you can understand that one reason for the lull in Europe at the moment is that the dictators are taking time out to think it over.

The possibility of a Russo-German tie-up. I saw this described in an American magazine the other day as "Europe's Secret Nightmare", and I have no doubt that many people were convinced by the author's ingenious arguments: Because the two countries complement each other so perfectly economically; because they are both dictatorships; because they both are on the road to state-socialism (though on this point I would make some reservations); because they both stand to gain by the rout of the British Empire. And because such a partnership could dominate Europe, if not the world. These are some of the reasons advanced.

But there is one reason which would seem to rule out the possibility of an alignment between German and Soviet Russia. It's this: Hitler's goal is the occupation and annexation of a vast part of Russia. How are you going to play ball with a man who covets your house and intends to settle in it if he can, even if he has to hit you over the head with his bat? And moreover *says* so.

Because he does in *Mein Kampf,* that Nazi bible which we all have to go to to divine what the Führer may have in his mind next. Hitler in *Mein Kampf* says very plainly that Germany will only be a great nation when it acquires a much larger territory in Europe. From where is that territory to come? Hitler very obligingly gives us the answer. It is: *From Russia.*

A second reason is that if Hitler were to make a deal with Russia, the Japanese alliance, or whatever you call their present understanding, falls through automatically. Now the strange tie-up between Japan and Germany is not so strange as it seems, if we look into it for a moment. It's valuable to Germany first as a part of a general threat to Britain and France – and to a lesser extent, the U.S. – in the East. Secondly, if and when Russia is to be conquered, it confronts Russia with a war on two greatly distant fronts, thus making Germany's job of conquering European Russia much easier. This second point is also the reason for Tokyo's friendship with Berlin – that is, if Japan is to get the Russian maritime provinces as well as Mongolia and a big slice of Siberia, Germany's military effort on the Western Front is absolutely necessary. Unless Japan ruins itself as a Great Power in China, and thus can no longer threaten the three Democracies in the Far East, there is little evidence that Hitler will ditch Tokyo. Along the path that he has apparently chosen, it is too valuable an ally.

[Shirer returned to Europe on the Queen Mary and after stop-offs in London and Paris, and also in Geneva where his wife and infant daughter took up residence, he returned to Germany on August 9. While in Berlin he lived at the Hotel Adlon and visited Geneva every few weeks.]

Gdynia, Poland August 13, 1939 18.45 Central European Time

[Although the Treaty of Versailles of 1919 had included Danzig (Gdansk) in the so-called "Corridor" that gave the newly revived Poland access to the Baltic, it was allowed the semi-autonomous status of a "Free City" and its population remained largely German.]

Hello America! This is Gdynia, Poland.

Gdynia, as you know, is Poland's great port on the Baltic. Fifteen years ago it was a sleepy fishing village of 400 souls. Today, it's the largest port on the Baltic, with a population of 150,000 and the most modern docks in Europe.

Twelve miles down the sandy shore is Danzig. I've just come over from there, because this was the first place where I could find a microphone. I started by taxi, but the driver got cold feet about crossing over into Poland so I came on by train.

And I'd like to talk a little about Danzig – this powder-keg of Europe where we've all been hearing the war would start.

Well, maybe it will. But you'd hardly think so if you were there, as I've been the last few days, ambling through its peaceful medieval streets, flanked by the steep-gabled old patrician houses that look exactly the same today as they did centuries ago when Danzig was one of the great Hanseatic cities.

I don't say there isn't any tension in Danzig. But I do feel that it is less – much less – than I've found in recent weeks in Berlin, London or Paris.

Actually, as you mingle with the people in the streets or sip a beer with them in one of their pleasant beer gardens, or saunter out to the beach with them – and today practically the whole town invaded the seashore to get away from the heat – it really is difficult to imagine that the whole of Europe is threatening to go to war over them – over these half million citizens of the Free City of Danzig with their 760 square miles of sandy land along the Baltic.

Of course, that isn't the whole story. It isn't as simple as that. In a large sense, Danzig is not really the issue. It is only a symbol – for both sides. The issue of course, for the Poles, is the future of Poland as an independent nation with a secure outlet to the sea. For the Germans it's the future of East Prussia cut off from the motherland, the future of the whole German stake in the East. And for most of the rest of Europe the issue is that of German dominance on the continent.

I'm not sure after a few days in Danzig that the Danzigers realize the immensity of the issue. They see it in more simple terms. They're German, and they say: why can't we join Germany if we want to?

And they think they will join Germany – soon. And without a war. There you have the answer as to why there is not so much tension in Danzig as you would expect. The Danzigers won't discuss with you *whether* they're going back to the Reich. But only *when*. They have an almost touching faith in Hitler being able to swing it when the proper time comes.

Now, the one outstanding impression that we who've been in Danzig this past week received is that Hitler is not going to push matters as rapidly as most people thought. It looks as if nothing sensational will happen here before his speech at Tannenberg on August 27th, or even before the Party Congress at Nuremberg the first week in September.

There are two reasons for saying this.

First, the Nazi leader here, Gauleiter Albert Forster, returned on Wednesday from Berchtesgaden where he had seen Hitler. Many nervous people thought he was returning to throw down the gauntlet to the Poles. He did nothing of the kind. His speech the next day was comparatively mild, and contained nothing new. Also, on the same day – Thursday – one of Forster's chief lieutenants, who had been with him to Berchtesgaden, told the foreign correspondents that the Nazis had no intention now of precipitating events and he gave the very definite impression that Hitler had decided to play for time.

Why? Perhaps it's this: The second reason.

Last weekend the Poles very firmly called a halt to what they conceived to be the constant nibbling away of their position in Danzig. And they succeeded. Danzig – no doubt on orders from outside – gave way.

You remember the incident.

A week ago Friday, the Polish customs officials in Danzig – or at least those on the East Prussian frontier where most of the German arms are coming in – were informed by Danzig customs officials that they must cease doing their job. Now this, if carried out, was a very important step. It not only meant that in the future arms would flow over from East Prussia without hindrance. It also meant that the Poles were losing one of their most important grips on Danzig, that is, control of the customs. And since German tactics in Danzig obviously are to nibble away one by one successive Polish rights until in the end there'll be nothing for anybody to fight for – certainly nothing that Europe will go to war for – the question was : Will the Poles call a stop, and if so, just where?

The answer came in the late hours of that Friday night. Poland sent the Danzig Senate an ultimatum. Either the order against Polish Customs inspectors would be withdrawn or Poland would take certain measures. The Polish Commissioner-General in Danzig, Mr. Chodacki, demanded a reply by 6 p.m. Saturday. It was a real ultimatum, with a time-limit.

Now, here was a golden opportunity for a showdown. Danzig – if Germany really wanted a showdown – could ignore or turn down the Polish ultimatum. Then the Poles would either have to make good their threat or suffer a setback that might well have proved fatal. And if the Poles stuck to their guns, then the Germans would have to do likewise – and I hardly need to say what that might have brought about.

What happened? In the end, the Germans – or, if you prefer, Danzig – gave way. Herr Greiser, the president of the Senate, telephoned the Poles that he knew nothing of the order discharging their customs men and that, in any case, it would not take place. The next day Gauleiter Forster, the Nazi boss of Danzig, flew to Berchtesgaden to consult with Hitler. And the Polish customs officials stuck to their posts.

Now to observers in Danzig this incident meant just this: That Chancellor Hitler was not ready, or did not want to move yet. That he still is biding his time, waiting for a more favorable moment. And also that there are limits in Danzig beyond which you cannot push the Poles.

Some people think those limits have already been pushed pretty far. For instance, the Poles have done little or nothing to prevent the militarization of Danzig. It is difficult to give you a precise idea of how far that militarization has proceeded, but, as Forster said in his speech Thursday, Danzig has certainly taken measures in the last few weeks to defend itself.

Actually you see very little. Every morning in my hotel in Danzig I would bump into two or three German army officers who were staying there. The barracks are crammed and they are feverishly building a new one outside the city. In the streets you see about as many army cars and trucks as you would in any German garrison town. I noticed they all had Danzig license plates, but there's no doubt where they came from. There is a considerable hinterland outside the city – 750 square miles of it – and most of the roads leading in from Poland are blocked with tank-traps or log barriers. They reminded me of Sudetenland just a year ago.

The two strategic hills of Bischofsberg and Hagelberg have been fortified. And, according to neutral sources, a considerable amount of arms have been run in under cover of night, either through the port of Danzig or across the Nogat River from East Prussia, which borders the Free City on the east.

These arms consist mostly of machine-guns, anti-tank and anti-aircraft guns and light artillery. Apparently they have not been able to bring in any heavy artillery.

The report that there are at least 40,000 men under arms in Danzig is, I think, exaggerated. The best estimates put the number at 15,000, about half of them brought in from the Reich.

Incidentally, most of the arms brought in are said to be of Czech manufacture.

A curious thing about Danzig. To a visitor like myself it seems to be already about as Nazified a city as you can find. All the Nazi uniforms you see in Germany you also see in the streets here. The Senate which, according to the Constitution, governs is completely Nazi. But the real power is in the hands of the party leader, Gauleiter Forster, who was appointed by Hitler, takes his orders from him, and is responsible only to him. Thus, through Forster, Danzig, in so far as it is independent of Poland, already is ruled from Berlin or Berchtesgaden.

A word about this man Forster, who holds such a key post in Europe

55

today. In the first place, he's not even a Danziger. He's a Bavarian, comes from the ancient town of Fürth . He was sent up here five years ago by Hitler to take charge. In a way he's typical of the men whom the Führer picks for the difficult jobs. He was just thirty-two when he got the post; he's thirty-seven now. Youthful, energetic, fanatical when it comes to Nazism, a good public speaker. Some say he's impatient and would like to push the Danzig affair much quicker than it's being pushed. But of course he's completely loyal to Hitler and I'm told the Führer has complete confidence in him.

Well, there you have the picture as it looks on the spot. On this 13th day of August, all is quiet in Danzig. Even though the danger of war hangs over their heads, the people of Danzig were also thinking of other things today. Of the coolness of their beaches along the sea, of the fact that the European Astronomy Society in convention there yesterday decided to name a newly-discovered star after Danzig. And last, but not least, of how their football team, which Herr Forster packed off by airplane yesterday to play his home-town team of Fürth in Germany, will make out. There was more space about that football game in the Danzig press today than about anything else.

Berlin August 22, 1939 23.30

Hello America! This is Berlin.

Nazi Germany and Bolshevik Russia getting together! Well, even in Berlin where as a foreign correspondent I've seen many surprises since Adolf Hitler came to power in 1933 – even here in Berlin people are still rubbing their eyes.

Not that they don't like it. You may be surprised, but the fact is that they do like it. Judging from the reaction of the people in the street it is a very popular move. Only for all of them, it has come a little sudden. Like everyone else all over the world, they had no warning.

I rode around Berlin today on buses, street-cars, the elevated and subway. Everyone had their head buried in a newspaper. And in their faces you could see they considered that what they read was Good News.

But consider what they read. I mean, you all know that before yesterday Bolshevik Russia was not exactly the idol of the Nazi press. But look today. I have the *Angriff,* always the most fiery of the Nazi afternoon papers, here. It rejoices that the old traditional friendship between the Russian and German peoples has at last been revived. Here are its words: "The world stands before a towering fact: two peoples have placed themselves on the basis of a common foreign policy which during a long and traditional friendship produced a policy of common understanding. It is certain that the renewal of these ties has many good possibilities both in the economic and political fields."

The *Angriff* admits, as do the headlines in all Berlin papers today, that Herr Hitler's decision to conclude a pact with Russia marks a turning point in Germany's course. The German people, it concludes, will applaud this change. I quote: "The decision of the Führer is so popular because the simplest man among the German people sees that it means the rebirth of the historical German-Russian policy, which for so long in history proved its importance."

All the other newspapers carry similar comment. Karl Silex, the well-known editor of the *Deutsche Allgemeine Zeitung*, calls the new German-Russian tie-up a "natural partnership".

Now why has this sudden Nazi embracing of the once-hated Bolshevik proved so popular among the people throughout Germany? The answer is simple. And it's important to see it very clearly. It means for every man, woman, and child in Germany say above the age of twelve, that the dreaded nightmare of encirclement has apparently been destroyed.

Yesterday the German people had this terrible nightmare. Britain and France on the West. Not so much Poland, but sprawling, powerful Soviet Russia on the East. The same set-up as 1914. Now, overnight, this dreaded thing that they all feared seems to have collapsed. There will be no long front against Russia to hold this time.

This is the sort of reasoning that I've heard from a score of Germans today, Nazi and non-Nazi. And the same thread runs through all the front page editorials.

No wonder then that a few minutes ago I picked up one of the early editions of tomorrow morning's newspapers and read – I must admit, still a little astonished – a glowing dispatch from Moscow in which those two arch-Bolshevik newspapers, *Pravda* and *Isvestia,* were quoted approvingly.

Now don't think that the Russian thing was the only story in the German newspapers today. There were two others. First – and I must admit that the Germans seemed to find it pleasant reading – was a long account of the shock which the other capitals of the world received when they got the news last night. A typical headline ran: CONSTERNATION THROUGHOUT THE WORLD

The second story, more important, reminded us all that back of everything – or above it, if you like – remained the question of Poland, the question of Danzig. Some of the headlines tonight read: POLES THREATEN DANZIG WITH HUNGER BLOCKADE. Another: DANZIG NEEDS ITS HINTERLAND. I need hardly point out that the "hinterland" of Danzig is Poland as it now is. Another headline: POLAND CONCENTRATING TROOPS.

Now most people here in Berlin tonight feel that things are moving fast. I'm told that unless there is a hitch, it's expected that Herr von Ribbentrop and Mr. Molotov [the Soviet Foreign Minister] will finish their work in a day or two. Imagine that! A day or two! That takes us to say, Thursday, if matters go according to schedule.

After that, as one official in the Wilhelmstrasse put it to me tonight, the question of Danzig and some other matters with Poland become ripe. Germany, he left no doubt, expects a settlement. My official did not see why it should not be a peaceful one if, as he said, the Poles were "reasonable".

So it may well be that towards the end of the week the uncertainty and the tension which has hung so long over Europe may be solved – one way or another.

In the meantime, Germany is anxious to know what Great Britain will do. I've heard that question on many lips in the Wilhelmstrasse tonight.

The official British statement was picked up on the radio here a couple of hours ago. But the first reaction here is that it does not entirely clear up matters.

And to end with some news which at 9.45 has just come in: Herr von Ribbentrop and his staff left tonight in two big Condor airplanes for Moscow. They'll stop overnight in Königsberg and arrive in the Russian capital in time to begin talks at noon tomorrow.

One other item: most of the British and French correspondents left Berlin tonight to rejoin their respective countries.

Berlin August 24–25, 1939 03.30

Hello, America. This is Berlin.

It's 3.30 in the morning here, and still, so far as we know, there has been no irrevocable step, no plunge into war.

The city of Berlin is quiet. As a matter of fact, so far as the appearance of the streets and the people going about is concerned, this has been a perfectly normal evening. No crowds, no noise, no shouting.

But what may prove to have been a very decisive conference has been going on most of the evening at Herr Hitler's Chancellery in the Wilhelmstrasse here in Berlin.

The German Chancellor himself suddenly arrived here at 6.00 this evening, followed by Herr von Ribbentrop who flew in from Moscow at 6.45. They were immediately closeted together in the Chancellery. The German Foreign Minister gave a full report of his talks with Mr. Stalin and Mr. Molotov, and events in London, Paris, Warsaw, and elsewhere were undoubtedly considered.

Later they were joined by Field Marshal Göring and the heads of the defense forces. What they decided we do not know yet. No communiqué has been issued, no information given out. The meeting broke up sometime after midnight.

Now, don't picture Berlin as full of a war-fevered populace, shouting for battle, and yelling, "On to Warsaw!" Things have changed since 1914.

There have been no crowds in the Wilhelmstrasse or any place else in Berlin tonight.

Karl von Wiegand, the veteran American foreign correspondent who flew in here today from Paris, was noting that. Karl was here in August, 1914, and he was telling me tonight about the feverish excitement of the people in the streets, of how they shouted and sang and threw flowers at the marching troops. That was in 1914. There was none of that here today. I must admit I didn't even see any marching troops.

Now tomorrow morning, or rather this morning, for it's Friday here already, the last editions of the morning papers take a graver view than did the afternoon papers. Poland is described as ready to strike.

I'd like to read you some of the headlines in the newspapers which the German people will read later this morning when they wake up.

The bannerline in the *Morgenpost* reads: POLAND HAS MOBILIZED – ON EVE OF POLISH COUP AGAINST DANZIG and then the next line: THE WARSAW GOVERNMENT NO LONGER MASTER OF THE DECISIONS OF THE ARMY.

The general idea expressed in the flaming headlines of all the German newspapers is that Poland has surrounded Danzig with a whole division of troops and may go in any moment. A further idea in the headlines and in the dispatches printed in the Berlin newspapers this morning is that Poland is threatening Germany with offensive measures.

The chief front-page headline in the *Deutsche Allgemeine Zeitung*, for instance, says: OFFENSIVE PREPARATIONS BY POLAND.

And all papers print in large black type a DNB [the official German news agency] report from Danzig which gives details of this Polish division that is reported to have surrounded Danzig, that is – on the west and south, because the eastern border of Danzig is common to East Prussia. According to this German report, the division comprises three infantry regiments, a regiment of artillery, and all the other units necessary for a division at war strength.

Incidentally, there are some very interesting photographs on the front page of the Berlin newspapers this morning. The official Nazi paper, the *Völkischer Beobachter*, carries a flaming headline, POLISH ARMY READY TO STRIKE – THREATENED OCCUPATION OF DANZIG – WAR PREPARATIONS ON THE ENTIRE GERMAN-POLISH BORDER. This paper, organ of the Nazi party, carries two large photographs of Mr. Stalin and

59

Herr von Ribbentrop chatting amicably together during the signing of the Russian-German pact yesterday. Mr. Stalin wears a light colored blouse, and he and Herr von Ribbentrop seem to be in the best of moods. Most Berlin papers will carry these photographs this morning.

Official reaction to Mr. Chamberlain's statement in the Commons today is negative. The Germans still stick to their standpoint that the present difficulties concern them and Poland alone, and are no business of the British. I say that's the German standpoint.

So it is not surprising that the morning papers today, Friday, will carry very little about the London statement or the speeches in the House. What is going on in England is being played down.

One headline I saw about Lord Halifax's speech described it as demonstrating ENGLISH HEARTLESSNESS AND SHAMEFULNESS.

All in all you can say that the Germans show no signs of giving way to British entreaties not to continue whatever course they've decided upon.

And so if this has been a crucial evening, the great decisions, which we still are ignorant of, will probably make themselves known very clearly tomorrow.

Berlin August 26–27, 1939 24.30

Hello, America. Hello, CBS. This is Berlin.

I don't know whether we're going to have war or not. I don't know what the situation is in the other capitals of Europe tonight. We don't have much news from them here.

But I can tell you that in Berlin tonight – thirty minutes after midnight – the feeling is that we are either in for war or a peace based on the fulfillment of Germany's demands against Poland.

And that shortly after noon tomorrow – our time – early Sunday morning by your time – after Sir Nevile Henderson, the British Ambassador, has flown back to London and had time to confer with Herr Hitler – we shall probably know pretty definitely whether it's to be peace or war.

Now, it may surprise you to know – frankly it surprised me – that in the Wilhelmstrasse tonight there is a great deal of optimism about prospects for peace.

Not that preparations for war are not speeding ahead. We've seen evidence of that all day today. You just had to visit any Berlin station tonight to see the reservists packing off to see that.

But in the government offices along the Wilhelmstrasse the feeling of optimism continues. Now why, do you suppose?

Well, for the reason, I think, that events have not yet got past the diplomatic stage yet. There are certain proposals in the air. We have no definite official information as to what they are exactly. But it is no longer a secret here – at least that's what we're told – that British Ambassador Henderson carried back to London today a certain solution suggested by Herr Hitler. And the fact that Sir Nevile spent so much time with Mr. Chamberlain, and that he also took part in lengthy cabinet discussions in London this afternoon – this is interpreted in Berlin tonight as meaning that the British government is at least considering whatever Herr Hitler had to offer – in other words, that a diplomatic solution is still possible.

From the tone of tomorrow morning's press, copies of which I've just seen, Germany demands not only Danzig and the Corridor, but everything that she lost to Poland in 1918. Now about an hour ago I was given to understand by a very high source that the actual German demands, as outlined to Ambassador Henderson, do not go so far. There is talk, I mean, of a return of Danzig and the Corridor to the Reich, with Poland maintaining Gdynia as an outlet to the sea, with a road to it from the interior of Poland.

We must now wait until the crucial meeting between Herr Hitler and Sir Nevile Henderson in the Chancellery here tomorrow. The British Ambassador is expected back around noon, and will be whisked right to Herr Hitler's study.

On the outcome of that meeting hangs the fate of Europe, and perhaps more than that.

In the meantime, preparation for war goes on. The roofs of this city are cluttered with anti-aircraft guns. I can see one from the window of my room in a local hotel, and no doubt if I peeked out of the window of this radio studio from which I'm talking I could spot another.

And in the principal railroad stations in Berlin tonight, the platforms were jammed with reservists who had just been called to the colors and were saying good-bye to their women folk.

In the stations too you saw another reminder of the situation – announcements that starting tomorrow, Sunday, the regular train schedules were off. Everyone knew what that meant.

I also noticed many foreigners, including some Americans, getting off on trains west-bound. Sleepers were sold out, but they seemed quite willing to sit up all night.

And I'm just informed by *DNB* that beginning Monday certain foodstuffs, soap, coal, textiles and shoes will be rationed. Cards for rationing will be distributed within twenty-four hours by the burgomaster of every city. It was announced that bread, cocoa, eggs, and flour will be exempted, there being plenty on hand.

Perhaps the most serious announcement of all for Germans was the one issued late last night that the annual Nazi Party Congress at Nuremberg had been called off – an unprecedented step. Whether it is held later, it was added, would "depend upon circumstances".

⋙

Berlin August 28, 1939. 19.52

Hello, America. Hello, CBS. This is Berlin.

The sands are running fast. Tonight here in Berlin we should have a decision whether it's to be peace or war.

It's just eight minutes to eight, Berlin time, and Sir Nevile Henderson, the British Ambassador, is due to arrive any minute now from London.

A big Mercedes car is waiting for him out at the Tempelhof airdrome and will rush him to Herr Hitler's Chancellery in the Wilhelmstrasse as soon as he arrives.

The outcome of this historic meeting is in the lap of the gods.

Although word has sifted through this afternoon that the British government cannot accept the demands which Herr Hitler made public last night – namely, a return of Danzig and the Corridor to Germany – the Wilhelmstrasse when I left it a few minutes ago was maintaining silence, preferring to wait until it knew what Ambassador Henderson brought back.

The feeling in German government circles on the eve of this crucial meeting is still firm. And the entire press this evening maintains that Germany cannot and will not compromise; that the Reich will not budge an inch from its demands on Poland for the return of Danzig and the Corridor.

It is not entirely ruled out, of course, that the British answer, which, it's believed, contains certain counter-proposals, may necessitate a reply.

But the tension has become so terrific, that it does not seem possible to anyone that it can long continue, probably not past tonight, without events taking a turn one way or another, or as the Germans say: "*So oder So.*"

In the meantime, Germany seemed already on a complete war footing today. Housewives stood in lines beginning early this morning to get their ration cards. It was the first time since the World War that these cards had made their appearance and the people, who had hardly believed a couple of days ago that war was possible, certainly looked grimmer as they stood patiently waiting for their cards.

With true German efficiency the rationing system swung into operation very smoothly. At any store today if you wanted certain foodstuffs, or soap, or shoes, you had to show your card; otherwise you were politely turned down.

The newspapers and the radio have assured the population several times today that there is food and clothing and soap and shoes and fuel enough for every German; that the rationing was only resorted to in the interests of fairness to all.

By everyone taking the new measures with good grace, the people are told they are helping to defend the freedom of Germany. Most papers praise the German woman for the calmness with which she has taken not only the rationing of foodstuff and materials, but also the spirit with which she has seen her menfolk – husbands, sons or fathers – off to the army in the last few days.

The military took an ever-increasing part in the picture in Berlin as the day advanced. Cars with high army officers sped up and down the Wilhelmstrasse, or down the Tiergartenstrasse to the War Ministry in the Bendlerstrasse. Many cars and motorcycles were requisitioned. I saw several civilian motorcyclists who had been called up with their vehicles. They received an army armband and could be seen speeding through the streets carrying messages.

Despite the needs of the armed forces, the gasoline situation improved today. I was able to buy two gallons a few minutes ago, which enabled me to get here in time for this broadcast. Men from the air service supervised the tanking up.

Squadrons of big bombers have also been roaring low over the city in formation.

In other words, though the talking stage has not yet been completely abandoned, the grim preparations for the worst go on. I understand no trains from Germany crossed any borders today, but those foreigners trying to get out were able to proceed as far as the frontier, and then either walk or get some kind of transportation to the other side of the border.

Note that Germany has already assured Belgium, the Netherlands, Luxembourg and Switzerland that it will respect their neutrality in case of war. But tonight we heard that Holland had decided to mobilize.

Well, all depends now on the talks which will be beginning here in a few minutes between Herr Hitler and the British Ambassador. We'll be on the air later tonight to tell you what we can about them.

Berlin August 28–29, 1939

The British Ambassador arrived at 8:30 p.m. Berlin time at the Tempelhof airfield. Considering the strain he's been through the last few days he looked fit enough. He was met at the airport by two secretaries of the British Embassy and a German official from the Foreign Office.

Sir Nevile got into his own car, now familiar to people in Berlin by its license number "6", and drove straight to the British Embassy, which is in a yellow building near the top of the Wilhelmstrasse where it runs into the Unter den Linden.

As he drove up the Wilhelmstrasse he passed the Chancellery within which Herr Hitler was busy conferring with Field Marshal Göring, Dr. Goebbels, General von Brauchitsch, General Keitel, and other high military, air force and naval leaders. All the cars of these visitors were lined up in front of the Chancellery, which actually is but a stone's throw from the British Embassy.

Ambassador Henderson remained in the British Embassy for nearly two hours. At 10.25 he stepped out of the Embassy, got into his car and drove down the street a distance, say, of 200 yards, and turned into the new Chancellery. I happened to be one of the small crowd outside trying to get a peep at the outer trappings of this historic meeting. We got a glimpse of the spectacular-looking Courtyard of the Ambassadors, as it's called. It was floodlit and reminded you of some Grecian courtyard you've seen in a drawing someplace. At the far end, before the great stairway leading to Herr Hitler's room, two black-uniformed guards in steel helmets and fixed bayonets stood motionless at the salute as the British Ambassador strode slowly up the steps, Mr. Chamberlain's all-important message in his pocket.

I should have estimated the crowd standing in the Wilhelmplatz outside the Chancellery at about 500, all told. They stood there silently, patiently, waiting to see Ambassador Henderson emerge, waiting, of course, as were we all, for the decision – whether there was to be peace or war.

Over in the Kaiserhof Hotel, where Hitler used to stop in the days before he came to power, the newspapermen – German and American mostly, one or two Dutch, a Swede and a Swiss – waited. The phone would ring from Amsterdam for the Dutchman. He would come back and say, "Well, Holland has mobilized. Our Queen has made a broadcast."

Again the phone would ring. This time for the Swiss. He'd come back after talking with his office in Basle. The Swiss had done it too: mobilized.

In the meantime, as the night wore on, troops thundered through the streets, eastward-bound towards Poland. They weren't the crack units with the magnificent equipment which I had seen parade before the Führer on the occasion of his birthday on April 20th.

Most of these troops were being transported on the most strange-looking vehicles you could imagine. Moving vans, grocery trucks, florists' delivery wagons, and so on.

When I left the Broadcasting House after my last broadcast at 8 p.m., I followed one of these motorized units that had been hastily assembled from requisitioned cars and trucks.

It roared right through the middle of town down the new East-West Axis towards the east. There was some artillery and every few cars an anti-aircraft machine-gun mounted on a delivery truck. Few people were there to see the troops. The streets were half-deserted and half-dark.

Berlin August 29, 1939 0200

Hello, America. Hello, CBS. This is Berlin.

Well, the crucial meeting between Herr Hitler and the British Ambassador in Berlin, Sir Nevile Henderson, has taken place.

And the least you can say in Berlin at two o'clock this morning, two and a half hours after their talk of an hour and a quarter broke up – the least you can say is that certainly the armies are not going to start marching tonight.

If they were, all the street lights wouldn't be shining so brightly as they are.

But we have a little more to go on than just that Berlin doesn't look like it is expecting war tonight.

From all that we can learn in the Wilhelmstrasse, the Germans are by no means pessimistic about the situation after receiving Mr. Chamberlain's communication and the verbal supplement which Sir Nevile Henderson added to it when he conferred with the Führer tonight.

Unless our first information is entirely wrong, the door seems to have been left open by both sides for further negotiation. They're going to talk further before going to war.

From the meager information we have on the contents of the British communication – and no word has been given out about it officially – it's said here that Great Britain opens up certain possibilities for a very far-reaching and general settlement in Europe.

At any rate, it is important that whatever the British offered, it was not rejected. And it may be even more important that the first reaction along the Wilhelmstrasse after the talk had ended was one of optimism. That seems to indicate that the chances for peace are still not bad, but of course we don't know yet what kind of peace, if it is to be peace.

The talk between Herr Hitler and the British Ambassador, which was held incidentally in the presence of the German Foreign Minister, Herr von Ribbentrop, got underway at 10.30 and ended at 11.40 p.m. Berlin time.

Sir Nevile then drove up the street to the British Embassy and Herr Hitler immediately went into conference with his Foreign Minister and Field Marshal Göring, who was present in the Chancellery during the

65

talks with the Ambassador, but apparently did not take part in them.

Only the briefest of communiqués was issued by the official news agency after the talk. It said simply that, "The Führer tonight at 10.30 o'clock received in the presence of Foreign Minister von Ribbentrop, the British Ambassador, Sir Nevile Henderson, who brought a communication from the British Cabinet." Later it was learned that the Ambassador supplemented the communication verbally.

Judging by the fact that Sir Nevile waited two hours at the British Embassy after his arrival from London tonight – he arrived at 8.30 p.m. – before seeing the Führer, it is likely that he sent over the London communication for Herr Hitler to study as soon as he arrived. This gave the German Chancellor a chance to see what London was offering before discussing the consequences of the note personally with the Ambassador. That the two men could talk for more than an hour was accepted by many observers as an indication that conciliation was in the air.

In fact we were given to understand that Herr Hitler answered immediately certain points in the British communication, and that these will be taken back to London tomorrow by a Mr. David Boyle, who accompanied Sir Nevile to Berlin tonight, and communicated to Mr. Chamberlain before Parliament meets.

Berlin August 30, 1939 23.45

Hello. The football – so to speak – of this diplomatic struggle which is the prelude to war or peace in Europe was kicked back to Berlin tonight. With what result we don't yet know.

If, as we hear here, the British government is remaining firm, so, for that matter, is the German government.

At any rate, we don't know yet what the reaction is to the British communication of this evening, or what is going to be done with it.

But it may well be that tonight will be the decisive one we've all been waiting for. Nobody knows for sure that it will be, but there is a feeling in the air that it may.

It's significant that the *DNB*, the German official agency, has announced it will be issuing news all night tonight. This is the first time since the crisis began that the *DNB* has remained open all night.

The early morning-edition of tomorrow morning's papers play up the general mobilization in Poland, which the press here says was ordered at 2.30 this afternoon. One paper tells its readers how this order spread panic across the frontier.

First press reaction to the Polish mobilization here in Berlin is to assume that, by mobilizing, Poland has placed the blame for eventualities on itself. "The Responsibility Is Now Established", says the *Lokal Anzeiger*.

Now all depends on Hitler's reaction to London's proposal. When I left the Wilhelmstrasse half an hour ago we didn't know yet even whether or not the London message had arrived. But you can take it that Herr Hitler, Herr von Ribbentrop and Field Marshal Göring will go over it tonight. Everything depends upon what they decide.

Berlin August 31, 1939 02.40

[This broadcast was made 2¾ hours after the previous broadcast.]

Hello America. This is Berlin.

The first thing to say from Berlin tonight is that there seems no likelihood of there being any definite decision about what is in store for us, tonight.

Most everybody here, except newspapermen and broadcasters, has gone to bed, it being nearly 3 a.m., Berlin time. That goes for the officials in the Wilhelmstrasse too.

Earlier in the evening there were some here who believed that possibly the showdown might come late tonight. The official German news agency got orders to keep going all night. But as the evening wore on and the latest of the British notes did not arrive, tension relaxed.

Actually, as you probably have heard in the news bulletins, the British note was delivered here about midnight. Since it supposedly had been dispatched from London at about 5 p.m., our time, it took somewhat longer than the other notes. Whether that's a good or bad sign, I don't know. At any rate, instead of the more spectacular spectacle which we had Monday night of the British Ambassador rushing back here by airplane, and hurrying to see the Führer, today's note came through the regular diplomatic channel and was delivered at midnight not directly to Herr Hitler in his Chancellery, but, as are more ordinary communications, to the German Foreign Minister at the Foreign Office.

The pessimists here immediately concluded from this procedure that the English note was negative – the optimists just the opposite.

As in the case of all these written communications passing back and forth between London and Berlin, tonight's note from London was supplemented by a talk between the German Foreign Minister and Sir Nevile Henderson. Their talk lasted about forty minutes – rather longer than expected. When it was finished, Sir Nevile walked up the

Wilhelmstrasse to the British Embassy and Herr von Ribbentrop took the British note to Herr Hitler.

In the meantime, there has been great activity all day in the Chancellery, and about midnight the announcement was made that Hitler had appointed what amounts to a War Cabinet. It is to be headed by Field Marshal Göring and will consist of five other cabinet ministers – Herr Hess, the Führer's Deputy; Herr Frick, the Minister of Interior; Herr Funk, the Minister of Economics; Herr Lammers, the Chief of the Chancellery; and General Keitel, Chief of the High Command of the Armed Forces.

The war cabinet, which will be called the Ministerial Council for the Defense of the Reich, was given sweeping powers by Herr Hitler. Whatever it decrees becomes law, unless Herr Hitler himself decides otherwise.

Creation of a war cabinet seems to have been Germany's first reaction today to the general situation, though it was no doubt decided upon before the contents of the British note were known, but after reports of the general Polish mobilization had been received.

So there we stand. Germany no more than any other nation gives no sign of receding. But people here agreed that the exchanging of notes cannot go on indefinitely and that the show-down is fast approaching.

Tomorrow, after Herr Hitler has had time to study this last British note, may be a very important day.

Now before signing off I'd just like to inform those who are listening to me that in case important news breaks tonight we plan to go on the air on a moment's notice from Berlin and we'll be using the same transmitter that we're on now from Berlin to New York, that is, station DJB, until 22.50 – Berlin time – and after that another station.

Berlin September 1, 1939 08.15

Herr Hitler has at last decided to resort to force against Poland. The decision came in the early morning hours of today, Friday.

In a proclamation to the army dated this morning Herr Hitler says:

Poland has refused my offer for a friendly settlement of our relations as neighbors. Instead she has taken up arms.

The Germans in Poland have been victims of bloody terror, hunted from house to house. A series of frontier violations that a Great Power cannot accept, proves that Poland is not willing to respect the

Reich frontiers. To put an end to this foolhardy situation, I am left with no other means than from now on opposing force to force.

The German army will lead the struggle for the honor and vital rights of resurrected Germany with hard determination.

I expect that every soldier, filled with the great traditions of the eternal German soldiery, will fulfill his duty to the last.

In every situation know that you are the representative of National Socialist Greater Germany.

A. Hitler

Now this was made known about five a.m. here, and extra editions immediately went on to the streets. But the people probably don't realize it yet. I noticed them this morning going to work as usual. Work on a building across from my hotel started as usual this morning.

It's a gray day here with overhanging clouds. So far absolutely nothing unusual about the picture in Berlin except that the radio is going full blast alternating with martial music and announcements. Some of those announcements are:

That military operations in the Bay of Danzig and all over Poland must be reckoned with.

That all schools are ordered closed.

That all foreign nationals in Poland remain there at their own risk.

That all but military aviation is prohibited over the Reich territories.

So far, no news of hostilities.

Berlin September 1, 01.15

Hello. This is William L. Shirer in Berlin.

It's just quarter after one in the morning Berlin time, and we're halfway through our first blackout. The city is completely darkened, and has been since seven o'clock.

It's a little bit strange at first, and takes some getting used to. You grope around the pitch-black streets and pretty soon your eyes get used to it, and you can make out the whitewashed curbstones – and there's a blue light here and there to guide you – and somehow you get along.

Every window in Berlin tonight is curtained with heavy black paper. Behind the darkened windows the people sit in their homes and listen to the radio, which plays martial band music, or a stirring symphony from Beethoven or Brahms, and every once in a while you get a news announcement or a repetition of an announcement that you may have

69

heard earlier. We have heard several times the broadcast of the official evening communiqué of the High Command of the German army which informed the people tonight that the armed forces had achieved by the end of the day all their military objectives in Poland – that is, for the day.

We are still in the dark as to what England and France are doing, though the newspaper correspondents who get news from Paris and London cabled back from New York kept a watch in the darkened Wilhelmstrasse tonight to see the result of the démarche which the French and British ambassadors made there this evening. There seemed little prospect that what they were demanding would be agreed to on this side.

One curious thing about Berlin tonight. The cafés, restaurants and beerhalls are full. I went out a couple of hours ago to get a bite to eat. My restaurant looked so dark outside I thought it had shut down. But once I got through the double set of curtained doors, I found the restaurant very light and full of people. I had no trouble in getting a good meal, a glass of Pilsner beer and a cup of coffee. It was a vegetarian day, but I got plenty of vegetables and eggs.

We had our first air-raid alarm early in the evening and it happened just before I was to broadcast so that I had to write my notes in an air-raid cellar. Actually, no enemy planes came over, nor have any up until now, though a couple of hours ago the moon came out and some of us thought there might be something doing. But nothing happened.

The isolation that you feel from the outside world on a night like this is increased by a new decree issued tonight prohibiting the listening in to foreign broadcasts. From now on you can't listen to them.

As to actual happenings here today, you know them by this time: The Reichstag session this morning, Herr Hitler appearing in a field-gray soldier's uniform which he said he would not doff until victory had been won; his thanks to Italy for diplomatic support but his acceptance that Germany would now fight alone; the proclamations to the armed forces, especially that of General von Brauchitsch which ended with the words "Forward with God for Germany!" And the news of the return of Danzig to the Reich.

Now how, do you think, is this war being presented to the German people by the press tonight? In the first place the military operations are exclusively termed "a counter-attack" against Poland. Poland is held entirely to blame for what she is receiving, and England is held responsible for not making Poland accept what all the papers, and what indeed Herr Hitler described today in the Reichstag as "Germany's very generous offer to Warsaw".

A word about Americans here. Our Embassy today gave Americans a last chance to get out by a special train which will take them to the Danish border tomorrow morning. At Flensburg, where the train stops on the

German side of the frontier, the passengers will be taken across the border in busses. All the wives and children of Embassy and Consulate staff members will be evacuated on that train tomorrow. The Embassy tonight distributed gas-masks to its staff.

So there we are. And as long as radio keeps going, I hope to be on the air again tomorrow to tell you what I see from Berlin.

Berlin September 2, 1939 16.15

Hello. This is William L. Shirer in Berlin.

Germany entered the second day of hostilities today, with the papers confidently reporting that German troops were advancing everywhere against Poland.

People seemed to be a little more cheery today after the first night of a blackout, which takes some getting used to for everybody concerned. After, say, about 1 a.m. this morning, when it became fairly evident that if the Poles were going to send over any planes they would have come by that time, most people went to sleep. Taxis, creeping along with little slits of light to identify them, did a big business all through the night.

Outwardly, the town, I thought, had a fairly normal aspect today. Shops were open, though of course your purchases were subject to your having a ration card for those things which are being rationed. Work on new buildings went on as usual. There were not nearly so many cars as usual on the streets, and a special appeal was made to the population not to use their automobiles except for very necessary things, and only when other transportation was impossible.

It's announced that all schools will be closed until further notice.

The decree last night against listening to foreign broadcasts was welcomed today by the press as something self-evident in view of the lies which would be broadcast towards Germany by the foreign broadcasters.

The German High Command today reports that the German advance into Poland was going along according to schedule:

"German troops are advancing steadily everywhere despite heavy resistance and blown-up roads. German forces captured Teschen, advanced up to Pless Nikolai, occupied Wieroszow, east of Kempen and also Klobuch Schildberg. In the Corridor the German forces reached the important railway line between Bromberg and Gdynia near Culm."

The special railroad coaches which were expected to evacuate American women and children from Berlin and take them by rail to the Danish frontier did not leave this morning. Because some could not reach the German capital from the provinces in time to make the train and because those already here wanted another day in which to pack what belongings they can take out, and make arrangements for the rest, the American authorities here changed their plans. The Americans will now be evacuated in special cars to be attached to a regular train leaving the Lehrter station for Warnemünde on the Baltic Sea tomorrow morning at 8.45. From Warnemünde the Americans will be transported in a Danish boat directly to Copenhagen.

With the departure of this train tomorrow, only those Americans will be left here who belong to the Embassy and Consulate staffs, and a handful of newspapermen and radio reporters.

It's expected that the American Embassy will take over the interests of the embassies of both France and Britain. All plans for this were completed this morning.

When I visited our Embassy this morning, workmen were busy tacking up black paper over the windows. The blackout caught the Embassy a little by surprise last night, and though the chargé d'affaires and many of the secretaries worked through most of the night, they had to congregate in two or three rooms, as the others were not equipped for a blackout.

The press announces that the town will be blacked out every evening from now on.

I'll now give you a picture of the German press as it looks on the second day of hostilities. The official Nazi paper, the *Völkischer Beobachter*, had a two-line banner across the front page in red ink and it says: THE FÜHRER PROCLAIMS THE FIGHT FOR GERMANY'S RIGHTS AND SECURITY. Most of the other morning papers have similar headlines.

The *Angriff* plays up a story that the German air force made a demonstration flight over Warsaw, and describes the panic of the Polish population at the sight of the mighty German air armada. No mention of any bombs being dropped is made. It is called merely a demonstration flight.

We're also getting the first photographs of action in the papers this afternoon. On the front page of the *Börsen Zeitung*, I notice a photograph of a burning building. The caption on it says that it's the home of a German in Poland. Another picture shows an armored-car group advancing up a road. There are also photos of airmen loading bombs into the bomb-racks of German airplanes.

It is again officially stated here this afternoon that Germany is confining its aerial bombardments in Poland to purely military objectives. And the *DNB* issued for publication this afternoon Herr Hitler's reply to President Roosevelt's appeal not to bombard open cities or the civilian population.

Berlin is still in the dark about what the British and French will do. Up until a couple of hours ago the ambassadors of the two countries had not asked for their passports. But they were all packed up ready to go.

Comments with some indirect quotations from Chamberlain's speech yesterday are published. The best German reaction to that speech I have seen I can give by quoting the full headline over an editorial in the *Nachtausgabe* tonight. It says: OUR SOLDIERS MARCH FOR GERMANY'S HONOR AND SECURITY – CHAMBERLAIN IN THE CHAINS OF THE WARMONGERS – ENGLAND HAS INVITED UPON ITSELF A FRIGHTFUL GUILT – THE BRITISH PRIME MINISTER DISTORTS THE FACTS.

News of the general mobilization in France and England is published, but that is all.

CBS Berlin Sunday September 3 , 1939 18.30

The extras are out on the streets here in Berlin now. The newsboys are giving them away, and those in the streets are grabbing them up. I have the first one here – it's the *Deutsche Allgemeine Zeitung*. And here's its headline:

BRITISH ULTIMATUM TURNED DOWN

ENGLAND DECLARES A STATE OF WAR WITH GERMANY

BRITISH NOTE DEMANDS WITHDRAWAL OF OUR TROOPS IN THE EAST

THE FÜHRER LEAVING TODAY FOR THE FRONT

And then in big black type are published all the official statements which we've been receiving over the radio since noon when it became known that England considered itself at war with Germany.

The headline over the official account is GERMAN MEMORANDUM PROVES ENGLAND'S GUILT.

And then are published Herr Hitler's various proclamations, first to the East Army, then to the West Army, then to the German People, then to the Party.

I won't read them over because you've undoubtedly had them from the news agencies already. But the note that runs through them all is that England alone is guilty for what has come to pass today. As the German memorandum handed to Ambassador Sir Nevile Henderson puts it: "The British government carries the responsibility for all the unhappiness and suffering which now will come over all the peoples." And a little further on in the memorandum these lines: "The German people and its government have no wish, as does Great Britain, to dominate the world."

One must also point out the important proclamation to the Party by the Führer which begins with this sentence: "Our Jewish-democratic world-enemies have brought it about that the British people are now in a state of war against Germany."

You notice also in Herr Hitler's proclamation to the East Army the friendly references to Russia and the mention that Germany and Russia are the two strongest nations in Europe.

Now, so far, no mention is made over the radio or in these newspaper extras about France. France has not yet been mentioned. Also, no mention is made of what Italy will do.

Now, what happened here this morning – and it's been one of those lovely warm September Sundays that Berlin always has at this time of year – what happened can be told in a few words.

At nine this morning the British Ambassador called on the German Foreign Minister and handed him a note from the British government giving Germany until 11 o'clock to accept the British demand that Germany withdraw her troops from Poland.

Everyone waited anxiously, and when Sir Nevile returned a little after 11 to the Wilhelmstrasse he was handed the German reply in the form of a memorandum. It was negative, and you all know what followed in London.

I was standing in the Wilhelmstrasse about noon when the loud-speakers there suddenly announced the news that England had declared a state of war with Germany. There were I should say about 250 people standing there in the sun. They listened attentively to the announcement. When it was finished there was not a murmur. They just stood there like they were before.

The German radio was on the air for some time, the announcer reading the official communiqué and the various declarations. But it was four hours before the extras were on the streets with the news.

In the meantime fifteen or twenty members of the British Embassy gathered in the garden of the Hotel Adlon. You would never have known from their talk or behavior that anything much had happened.

There have been absolutely no demonstrations of any kind in front of the British or French Embassies. When I passed them about two hours ago one policeman stood in front of each, and they had nothing to do. People passed the Embassies but hardly paused to look up.

The members of the diplomatic staffs of the British and French Embassies will be taken to the Belgian frontier tomorrow morning in a special Pullman train. I noticed when the German authorities were conferring with both the British and French about transportation arrangements, they were all exceedingly polite and correct to one another in every way.

Special coaches carrying American women and children left Berlin this morning. When I dropped into our Embassy a short time ago, our officials were worried because no news of the train had been received. But just as I was leaving – about two hours ago – a telephone call came in that the train had reached Warnemünde all right, and the Americans transferred to a Danish ferry-boat there. They should be in Copenhagen this evening.

There are about fifty Americans left here, and perhaps of these a dozen are women. Some of the wives refused to leave their husbands today.

This afternoon the American Embassy formally took over the interests of France and Britain here.

Berlin September 3, 1939 19.45

Hello.

The world war is on. The newsboys have ceased shouting it. The radio, too, because now the radio is playing a stirring piece from the Fourth Symphony of Beethoven. Sometimes the music stops and the proclamations which the German Führer issued at noon today are re-read – his proclamations to the East Army, to the Army of the West, to the German people and last of all, to his own party, the National Socialist German Workers' Party, to give it its full name. Then the music goes on and people huddle close to their sets for the next piece of news that this tragic day of September 3, 1939, may bring.

There is no excitement here in Berlin. There was, we are told, in 1914, and it was tremendous. No, there is no excitement here today, no hurrahs, no wild cheering, no throwing of flowers – no war fever, no war hysteria.

But make no mistake, it is a far grimmer German people that we see here tonight than we saw last night or the day before. Until today, the people of this city had gone about their business pretty much as always. There were food cards and soap cards and all that, and you couldn't get any gasoline, and at night there was a complete blackout, but the military operations on the East seemed a bit far away – two moonlight nights and not a single Polish plane arriving over Berlin to bring destruction – and besides, the papers said that the German troops were advancing victoriously all along the line, that the Polish air force had been destroyed. Last night Germans talked of the Polish thing lasting but a few weeks, or months at the most.

Few here believed that Britain and France would move. They had been accommodating before. Munich was only a year ago. The Polish business was Germany's concern, not that of the Western Democracies. It would be over soon. And yesterday, when it seemed that London and Paris were hesitating – they had already hesitated for two days – there was considerable optimism among those I talked to.

But today it's different. A world war is different. The people here are also different. They're grim.

It's just become dark here and Berlin begins its third blacked-out night. So far, no air-raid alarms, but as I said, the evening is still young. No one knows what will happen. But everyone who has one keeps his gas-mask nearby. Few Americans, outside the Embassy and Consulate staffs, have a mask.

And here are some of the little things I've noticed today in Berlin.

For instance, we get our first idea of how radio broadcasting functions under the conditions of today. Yesterday, all German radio stations played martial band music, or selections from Beethoven and Brahms throughout the day, breaking into the music from time to time with news announcements. Some of these announcements, such as advice to the population about air defense, or the official communiqués of the High Command of the German army were repeated several times, so that no one would miss them. But since you can't broadcast news bulletins all day long, the result was, in the minds of the competent authorities, that the martial music became monotonous.

So today the music was to some extent cut down, and the radio merely remained silent until there was news to broadcast. People in their homes and offices kept their radios on in order to hear the latest news or instructions, but were able to get on with their work during the silent periods. Yesterday it was difficult to work with the music blaring away, but today that aspect was largely eradicated. You might say that that is the first lesson the broadcasters have received from war-like conditions.

Here's another item that interested me. The papers tonight explain to their readers why it is advisable during air-raid alarms to keep their windows not shut, but *open*. The instructions are to open wide all your windows before you hurry to the cellar. It's explained that in case of an explosion, the glass in the windows is much more liable to fly in bits in all directions, and thus cause considerable damage, when the windows are left closed. It's also pointed out to those who might think that by leaving the windows open you, so to speak, invite the gas – if there is gas – to come into your house – it's explained that gas is heavier than air, and therefore will not enter your house.

Berlin September 4, 1939 19.45

Hello. This is William L. Shirer in Berlin.

The foreign correspondents were summoned to the Wilhelmstrasse shortly after noon today and given a denial that any German submarine had sunk the British ship, *Athenia*, with 240 Americans aboard. *[The Athenia was sunk 200 miles north-west of Ireland at 2 p.m. on September 3, with 112 deaths.]*

The story was dubbed propaganda designed to influence the American people.

In German quarters it was suggested that the vessel may have hit a mine, or maybe a boiler blew up, but that it was not the work of a German submarine.

The Wilhelmstrasse insisted that all German vessels of war had been given strict orders to observe all the rules of the sea. This would mean – it was explained in Berlin – that German warships would only force enemy passenger or freight ships into German or neutral ports, but never sink them, unless the German boats were fired on first.

In this connection I would like to point out to you that I am not here to try to report what is going on outside this country. My assignment is to tell you what news and impressions I can pick up here in Berlin. And what I've just told you is exactly what we've been told here today in official German circles.

In the meantime, according to the official communiqué given out today by the German High Command, the armies of the Third Reich continue to smash through Poland. Victories are reported on each and every front. But I notice for the first time in an official communiqué that "sharp fighting" is reported. Obviously, this campaign against Poland is turning out to be no walk-over. Heavy fighting is going on. The German communiqué speaks of a Polish cavalry attack on German territory in East Prussia, but says it was repulsed. The paper *Nachtausgabe* headlines this with a big exclamation point and says: CAVALRY ATTACKS TANKS! The communiqué also tells that fighting is still going on before the fortified town of Graudenz, which as you can see from your maps, is but a few miles from the German border of East Prussia.

Great activity of the German air force in Poland is also reported today. The Germans state they've destroyed several important Polish railroad lines, notably Kutno-Warsaw, Krakow-Lemberg, Kielce-Warsaw, Thorn-Eylau. The Polish railroad station of Hohenfalza, says the German army communiqué, lies in ruins, after an aerial bombardment.

And the Corridor has been so well cut, that this morning for the first time, says the communiqué, German troops reached East Prussia overland.

On the sea, the only mention of any action is against the tiny Polish navy. The Germans say they sank two Polish submarines, and that an air attack sank the Polish destroyer, *Wicher*.

The staffs of the British and French Embassies got away this morning in two special trains. It's one of those weird things about war that while the killing goes on, all the diplomatic niceties are strictly observed.

Each of the two ambassadors, for instance, was given a Salon car and the rest of the staff had Pullmans. They were accompanied to the Dutch frontier by officials from the German Foreign Office and German army.

Herr Hitler, who left Berlin by special train last night, spent the day somewhere on the Eastern Front.

As to Berlin, we've had another Indian summer day, and that strange phenomenon of the German capital appearing so normal that except for the papers and the radio and the few motorcars on the street, you'd hardly know that a world war was on.

The bricklayers continued to work all day on a new building across from my hotel. And when I came down to the lobby of the hotel for a few minutes this afternoon, the orchestra was playing sweet tunes at tea time, just as it has every afternoon for years. It gave me a strange feeling. I'd just as soon skip the sweet music now, if you know what I mean.

Berlin September 5–6, 1939 04.30

This is Berlin. William L. Shirer.

Another blacked-out night half over, and no bombs or even leaflets over Berlin.

The thing that is puzzling a lot of people here is the Western Front, which apparently isn't a front – yet.

We are told again in the Wilhelmstrasse tonight that up until this evening not a shot had been heard in the West. And the Germans added that so far as they were concerned there wouldn't be any shots unless the other fellow fired first.

I might also point out that no mention is made in the German press of France being an enemy – all the bitterness of the German editorial writers is concentrated on the English, who are accused of being responsible for the whole war. If France and Germany are at war, the average German tells you, it's a strange kind of war. And he wouldn't mind keeping it that way.

The only English activity reported so far today is a report that late this afternoon four English observation planes flew over Hamburg, and the Germans say they brought down two of them.

But if no shots are being fired on the Western Front, plenty are being fired on the Eastern Front. The communiqué of the High Command today speaks of heavy fighting, and Berlin does not consider that it is having a walkover in Poland. Aside from the break through the Corridor two days ago, the biggest German victories since the fighting started were reported today. They were the capture of Kattowitz, the most important industrial town of Polish Silesia, and of Graudenz, a well-fortified Polish town near the south-east tip of East Prussia. Now it's obvious that the favorite German strategy of pincer movements is developing fast.

Undoubtedly the biggest battle of the war has been over Graudenz, where the Poles are said by the Germans to have fought very stubbornly. But with the Germans driving eastward south of Graudenz, and south from East Prussia east of the town, it was in danger of being cut off. The same with Kattowitz, which lies close to the German border. Two German forces, whose main goal is Krakow, have penetrated eastward into Poland both north and south of Kattowitz, and clearly it could not have been held unless the Polish forces were willing to be cut off and fight a suicidal siege.

It's also evident from what we learn from the only American correspondent who's been to the front that not only the Polish army is fighting, but that Polish civilians – men, women and even boys – are fighting desperately from house to house.

The bulk of the German population, which of course is not at the front, got a glimpse at least of the *sound* of war when the German broadcasting company broadcast from the front-line. It sounded plenty realistic, with a terrific roar of artillery, machine-guns and very often the roar of airplanes – I imagine they were German – very audible.

Now as to the sinking of the *Athenia*, which, as you know, the German government strenuously denies having had anything to do with, there is considerable editorial comment in the Berlin press today. All the papers state that it is just another attempt to influence American opinion to come in on the side of England. To cite a typical editorial, the foreign editor of the *Völkischer Beobachter*, the official Nazi newspaper, suggests today, "If the *Athenia* was really torpedoed, then it could only have been by an English U-boat. Probably," this editor goes on, "the *Athenia* was not even torpedoed. Most probable is that it was a boiler explosion. It's also possible that Mr. Churchill *[then First Lord of the Admiralty]* touched off a small bomb in the ship in order to be able to give the world an alarming report." That's how the editor of the *Völkischer Beobachter* sees it.

Now the morning papers are just in, and their headlines are different from those this afternoon which spoke of victories in Poland. Tomorrow morning's *Lokal Anzeiger* headlines as follows: TERRIBLE BESTIALITY OF THE POLES – GERMAN FLYERS SHOT – RED CROSS COLUMN MOWED

DOWN – RED CROSS NURSES MURDERED. The first headline refers to a report published in the press here that the Poles executed thirty-one German flyers who had made parachute landings.

Another headline tells of how many English planes were shot down. The latest figures on that now are that in the raids on Cuxhaven and Wilhelmshaven ten out of some twenty or twenty-five English bombers were shot down.

Berlin September 8, 1939 23.30

This is Berlin.

As you know by this time, the German High Command announced this evening that German troops have entered Warsaw. Armored and motorized troops, we are told, reached the Polish capital at 5.15 this afternoon, Central European Time.

Judging by the communiqués, they had been pushing forward from the south-west at the rate of twenty-five miles a day. Yesterday afternoon they were stopped for a short time on the road to the capital, but before noon, according to a communiqué published this evening, they were about fifteen miles outside Warsaw. They must have pushed ahead very fast to have reached the city by 5.15 p.m.

Exactly what has happened to the Polish Army one doesn't yet know. It would appear, on the basis of information here, that a large Polish force which had been holding the Posen sector, way to the east of Warsaw, may be trapped. Someone remarked to me awhile ago that the Germans may have pulled another Tannenberg *[the decisive German victory over the Russians in 1914]*, but it's better to wait for further news before judging as to that.

The news of the taking of Warsaw was first given to the German public over the radio at 7.15 this evening. Immediately afterward, a band played *Deutschland über Alles* and the *Horst Wessel* song.

But don't think there was any wild rejoicing on the streets of Berlin tonight. There wasn't. With these complete blackouts, it would be pretty hard to celebrate anything. After the news, I groped my way down the Wilhelmstrasse, which was as black as ink, bumping into silent pedestrians but reaching my subway station without any serious bruises. Because my subway runs above ground for a few blocks up-town, the cars were almost completely darkened, and I huddled in my place, along with a few hundred others, everyone silent in the darkened train. There won't be any Extras out, because you can't sell papers when you can't see the customers in the street. This war is certainly different.

80

Now as to the West Front, I can only repeat what I've been saying every night – we have no news of any action there. We ask the Wilhelmstrasse twice daily, and tonight we got the same answer, except that English reports that there had been some action there were denied. In this case, your guess may be better than mine.

Tomorrow it's announced that Field Marshal Göring will make a nationwide broadcast at 1 p.m., our time. I'm told he'll speak from a munitions factory.

The papers play up in Berlin tonight the decrees invoking death penalties. There are a number of things involving defensive matters – broad term – for which people in this country may be executed. The first person to be executed is reported today. He was one Johann Heinen of Dessau, and he was shot yesterday for refusing to take part in necessary defense work.

No air-raids here so far tonight.

Berlin September 11, 1939 23.30

This is Berlin.

The headline that struck me tonight was in a Berlin newspaper called *Deutsche Allgemeine Zeitung.* It was a bannerline clear across the front page and it said: THE POLES BOMBARD WARSAW. I thought it was a misprint until I read the story under it, which turned out to be the official communiqué of the High Command. The paragraph that made the headline read as follows: "Polish artillery of every caliber opened fire from the eastern part of Warsaw against our troops in the western part of the city."

According to information here, some very heavy street fighting, which the German News Agency tonight describes as "senseless and insane", is going on there. This report, besides telling of the Polish artillery fire, admits that the Germans are dropping bombs on the city, but of course – it adds – on fortified points and other military objectives. The German report also tells of terrible fires sweeping the city, with the fire brigades helpless because barricades block the streets.

At any rate, Warsaw still seems to be holding out.

I have just received – and I pass it on to you without comment – an official denial from the German Admiralty of a French report that the German submarines U-26 and U-27, which recently visited Iceland, were involved in the sinking of the *Athenia*. The German Admiralty says that the U-27 arrived back in Wilhelmshaven on July 29th, the U-26 returned to Kiel on July 30th, and that both vessels were at their home ports when hostilities broke out.

Well now, this country continued today to put its population on a wartime basis. Such food products as grain, dough products, meat, milk and other dairy products, sugar, marmalade and spices were placed on the ration list. It was announced that such things as table-cloths, dress clothes and carpets would not be manufactured during the war, only life-necessities in the way of clothes would be made. And beginning September 20th only motorcars serving the public interest will be allowed to circulate. They must all carry a special sign, or they won't circulate. The mechanized German armies, of course, burn an awful lot of fuel. This country imports most of its oil. Therefore the civilians must stop using it.

We don't hear much from Bohemia and Moravia these days – an occasional quotation from a Czech paper in Prague praising Germany's action against Poland, an item that German police have taken over police functions in the Protectorate. But today the Protectorate government warned Czechs that fighting in a foreign army was equivalent to high treason and would be punished as such, also that Czechs in an enemy army captured by Germans knew the consequences. I took that to mean that any Czechs serving with, say, the French army who are captured by the Germans would be shot as traitors.

Now some may be wondering about those four million Jews in Poland. I haven't seen anything in the press about what is to happen to them, but the *DNB* agency mentions the matter for the first time in a report tonight. It says: "We promise the Germans that never again will Polish Jews come to Germany. The solution of the Jewish problem in Poland will contribute to ordered relations between Germans and Poles."

Berlin September 14, 1939 23.30

This is Berlin.

Funny thing about these blackouts. There's an iron lamp-post about a hundred yards from my hotel. Two nights running now I've stumbled into it. Night before last, my knee hit it, and I limped out here to the studio. Last night my head struck it, and I'm afraid my broadcast was a little foggy.

Tonight I determined to miss that lamp-post at all costs, even at the cost of signaling enemy flyers – if any. I flashed my flashlight on it, twenty yards away, and felt rather proud of myself for routing my enemy so easily when the Polizei suddenly jumped out of the darkness and asked me what the idea was. My English accent in German didn't make me any less suspect. And, as a matter of fact, I forgot what German I knew. It looked for a moment as though I might spend this evening in jail, but finally I explained to them about that deadly lamp-post, and they let me go, and here I am.

As for news, the papers in Berlin play up the surrender of Gdynia, the capture of 60,000 Polish prisoners at Radum, south of Warsaw, and a story that Warsaw has now been completely surrounded. Gdynia – I can hardly believe that I was broadcasting from there only a month ago – surrendered because the civil population had gone without food for two days.

For the first time the High Command speaks of the French employing stronger forces on the Western Front than heretofore, but states that they were repulsed between Saarbrücken and Hornbach, and that anyway they've not yet got to the Siegfried Line.

The German papers also feature Moscow dispatches about Polish planes violating the Soviet frontier. Many people I've talked with here think Russia may attack Poland.

And then the *DNB* correspondent with the Führer tells us today of how Polish Jews are being put to work on the roads. The party stops near Lodz to watch them for a minute. "Hundreds of Jews – some of them clothed in caftans and with a greasy dirty East-Jewish headpiece on their heads – were at work on the road making it passable. German auxiliary police superintended their work – the first productive work these Eastern Jews ever did in their lives."

Berlin September 15, 1939 23. 51

Good evening.

It was just two weeks ago this Friday morning that the Germans began what they call their great counter-attack against Poland. In fourteen days the mechanized German military machine has rolled back the Polish army some 200 miles, captured 100,000 prisoners, including entire divisions with their staffs and guns, surrounded the capital and – so it is believed here – practically liquidated Poland in a military sense.

Today one German army stands before the citadel of Brest-Litovsk, where Germany dictated a harsh treaty to Bolshevik Russia in 1918. Another German army is rapidly cutting off Poland from Romania, thus not only making impossible a Polish retreat into that country, but also bringing Germany to the border of Romania and its precious oil-fields and its large wheat stocks. A special minister of King Carol's court sits in Berlin today, assuring Germany of his country's neutrality and of its desire to trade its oil and grain against whatever Germany can swap in return.

To be sure, a gallant Polish army, completely surrounded at Kutno, seventy-five miles west of Warsaw, continues to hold out. But for how long? Warsaw too holds out. But for how long? The war in Poland – to Berlin at least – seems almost over. Already one hears of German divisions being recalled for duty in the West.

It's been a terrific blow. A month ago, in Warsaw, I canvassed a number of foreign military attachés. They assured me it would take the Germans six months to reach Warsaw, even if Britain and France stayed out. The foreign military attachés here in Berlin disagreed. One of them insisted – and none of us believed him – that the Germans would liquidate the Poles in a fortnight. Probably he knew something of the effectiveness of the German nutcracker tactics, of the deadliness of their armored divisions that have shot through Poland these past days like great steel fangs, piercing the country until organized military resistance on a line was made impossible.

What now, then? The German armies tonight are more than 100 miles east of the old 1914 German-Russian border. The country they are advancing into now is peopled largely by Russians or Ukrainians. I don't know what the plan is, but I've heard many here today hazard the guess that Russia will now step in and occupy the parts inhabited by Russians.

More than that, there is much talk of peace here. Items in the papers about the Italian Ambassador in Berlin having talks in Rome, about the French Ambassador in Rome having talks in Paris, and so forth. And talk that in the end Mussolini will step in with a peace proposal which perhaps the French, perhaps even the British, might accept, and which Germany, Italy, and Russia certainly would accept. So far it's only talk, but I pass it on to you for what it's worth.

As for other news, American neutrality is more and more getting the headlines here. Senator Borah [of Idaho, a leading isolationist] is on the Berlin front pages. The Börsen Zeitung headlines: SENATOR BORAH WARNS AGAINST THE WAR AGITATORS IN USA.

Another headline in the Nachtausgabe tells us: AMERICAN PRESS REACTION TO BRITISH HYPOCRISY – SHAMEFUL LIES AN INSULT TO INTELLIGENCE OF AMERICANS. In this case "American press reaction" turns out to be an editorial in an American paper called the Gaelic American.

Berlin September 16, 1939 23.40

Good evening.

Every German I've met today commented favorably on Colonel

Lindbergh's broadcast. The story gets a good play in the Berlin newspapers, though there is no editorial comment. The headlines appear to show sympathy for Colonel Lindbergh's viewpoint. The *Börsen Zeitung* headlines: WHERE AMERICA'S FRONTIERS LIE – COLONEL LINDBERGH WARNS AGAINST THE AGITATION OF THE WESTERN POWERS. Other headlines are similar. The *DNB* dispatch, dated New York, points out: "Lindbergh clearly enough alluded to the anti-German agitation in America when he warned against malicious propaganda. The speech of Lindbergh created a strong impression throughout America."

I hardly need to point out to you that Germany naturally hopes that America will not aid its enemies nor come into the war on their side.

Here's an item about hoarding. An American woman I know bought a tin of sardines today. The grocer insisted on opening the can in the shop. Reason: you can't hoard tinned food if your grocer opens it before he hands it to you.

As to war news, the Germans announce the capture of Bialystok, on the main line from Warsaw to Moscow, and Przemysl, in south-eastern Poland. Obviously, the Germans are trying to cut off what is left of the Polish army from retreating into Romania or the Baltic states. Warsaw still holds out, though the Germans are in the eastern suburb of Praga across the Vistula. The Polish divisions completely surrounded at Kutno are still fighting gamely. The war communiqué today speaks of the Germans throwing in fresh forces against them.

But for the Germans, the Polish war is as good as over. The people here think now that peace may come. That Britain and France, by their skirmishing on the West Front, have formally kept their word with Poland, and are now ready to talk Peace. "What's there to fight for now?" they ask.

Here's another question you may have been asking. Do the German people – with their controlled press and radio – know that the British and French maintain that they are fighting not against the German people, but only against Nazism? The answer is: they do know it. The newspapers have published it several times. Take today's *Frankfurter Zeitung* which in a Rome dispatch states Franco-British war aims as: "A war for three years or longer – destruction of the Nazi régime, with all the consequences which that would bring." The same dispatch also mentions the war aims of the Allies as including the liberation of Austria, Slovakia, Bohemia and Moravia, as well as Poland.

No, these things are in the papers for Germans to read if they want to.

We asked the Wilhelmstrasse today about outside reports of wholesale arrests of Catholics in the Protectorate. Answer of the Wilhelmstrasse: A few arrests have been made in Bohemia and Moravia of Jewish elements or followers of Beneš. A few priests were among those arrested, not

85

because they were Catholic priests but because they were politically dangerous.

The first German war-correspondent was killed yesterday. A piece of shrapnel got him just as he had finished a dispatch for his paper, the *Angriff,* which publishes it tonight.

And here's a headline in the *12-Uhr Blatt* that interested me: CRIMINAL METHOD OF THE USA AMBASSADOR IN POLAND TO CREATE WAR FEVER. This Berlin paper objects to Ambassador Biddle's telegrams to Washington about the bombing of open towns. The paper denies the Germans did any such thing.

I've just been informed that Prince Oscar, grandson of the Kaiser, has been killed in action on the Polish Front. He was twenty-four, and a lieutenant.

An inspired statement from the Wilhelmstrasse tonight warned neutral countries – especially those of the Oslo Group – against letting Britain dictate to them as to what they can import and export. Germany, it was said, cannot accept a conduct of the neutrals incompatible with strict neutrality, even if Britain tries to force such conduct upon them.

Berlin September 17, 1939 14.00

Good morning. This is Berlin.

The news this morning sort of gallops so far ahead of your imagination that you can't keep up with it. You can hardly comprehend it. Or at least I can't.

There are the two stories.

The first is that the German High Command has given Warsaw an ultimatum that if it doesn't surrender within twelve hours it will be bombed and bombarded.

The second story is that at six o'clock this morning, Moscow time, Red Army troops began an invasion of Poland along the entire Russian-Polish frontier.

Now, what else can you say except to state the naked facts, which speak for themselves?

Warsaw in peacetime had well over a million people living within the city limits. I don't know how many are there now, but probably a half million, of whom perhaps not less than half are women and children. Are they all to die now, to be smashed to smithereens by bombs and shells, because they won't surrender? Apparently they are. In just an hour and ten minutes from now, if they don't give up the fight. That's made plain in the German communiqué this morning.

86

So far we've had no news from Warsaw as to whether it's surrendered, whether the women and children were evacuated this morning – the Germans gave twenty-four hours to evacuate hundreds of thousands – or what has happened. But the Germans stick to their word. If no surrender, Warsaw will be treated as an area of military operations. That means that one of Europe's largest cities will be blown up by the German army, and a good share of the human beings living there with it. Certainly history knows no parallel.

And another thing. The Germans say it is the Poles in Warsaw who are violating international law by making their civilians help defend the capital. But as I say, I just can't follow the things that are happening in this war.

On the same pages this morning that headline Germany's ultimatum to Warsaw, is a German answer to France repeating that Herr Hitler is determined not to wage war against women and children, but accusing the English blockade of doing this and threatening the most horrible consequences in revenge.

The other piece of news that defies imagination – or at least mine – is the announcement here that at six this morning, Russian troops marched into Poland. Russia, of course, had a non-aggression treaty with Poland. Moscow now says that no longer holds good because no Polish government exists, though the Russian note was handed, please note, to the Polish Ambassador in Moscow just as though it still recognized the Polish government. Moscow, we are told, still maintains that it is observing strict neutrality in gobbling up the Russian and Ukrainian parts of Poland. It claims it is going into Poland to restore law and order. What ages ago it seems now – but it really wasn't ages ago – that I sat in Geneva or in other capitals and heard the Russian statesmen talk about common fronts against the aggressor, and so on. And now Soviet Russia stabs Poland in the back, and the Red Army joins the Nazi army in over-running Poland. All this, of course, is heartily welcomed in Berlin this morning.

Berlin September 20, 1939 23.45

There's still a lot of talk about peace in the newspapers today. The German press plays up two points. First, that Germany, by annihilating the Polish army, has achieved its war aims. Second, that Germany has no war aims against Britain and France and hence has no desire for a bloody war against the Western Powers.

Now the German press never differs with the German government, so you can draw your own conclusions.

"Why should England and France waste the blood of their nations against our West Wall?" asks the *Frankfurter Zeitung*. "Since the Polish state has ceased to exist," it argues, "the treaties of alliance with it have no more sense." All the other German editorial writers argue similarly tonight.

Last week I mentioned that German military circles hinted that the battle due west of Warsaw looked like another Tannenberg. Today a general-staff officer confirmed this to us. The battle will probably go down in history as the Battle of Kutno, after the town of that name. The High Command, usually very sparse with its adjectives, today describes it as one of the most destructive battles of all time. Not only does the number of prisoners taken put Tannenberg into the shade, but the High Command for the first time mentions "extraordinarily heavy and bloody losses of the enemy". We questioned the General-Staff officer about that today. He pointed out that the Russians at Tannenberg lost 92,000 prisoners, and 28,000 dead. Yesterday at Kutno the Germans took 105,000 prisoners alone; the day before 60,000. And he hinted that the Polish losses in killed and wounded might also be much heavier than the Russian losses at Tannenberg.

After three days at the front – during which we finally saw an actual battle – I can see why the Polish losses have been so terrific. The Poles had no defense against the devastating attacks of the German bombers and German tanks. It gave you a queer feeling to see a German plane swoop down to within 150 feet of the Polish lines and bomb and machine-gun them as if in target practice. The Poles had no weapons to defend themselves against such things. Against tanks the Poles used cavalry, and the result was terrible – for the cavalry.

Here are some items before I close. It's announced here that a number of German army officers have left for Moscow. Apparently their job is to agree with the Russians as to the line on which their two armies in Eastern Poland shall stop.

Official quarters take issue with Ambassador Biddle for allegedly sending news reports about bombing of open towns in Poland. They charge it's a maneuver to influence Congress today and claim that anyway the Ambassador is violating Romanian neutrality by sending such reports from there.

In the Saar village of Ottweiler yesterday the Germans buried with full military honors Lieutenant Louis Paul Dechanel of the French army. His father had been a president of France. The Germans say he died a hero's death leading a detachment against the West Wall. At his burial a German band played the *Marseillaise*.

General von Brauchitsch, commander in chief of the German army, has gone to the West Front.

Berlin September 21, 1939 01.00

Good morning.

Germany today, like a good share of the rest of the world, turns its eyes on Washington. Of course, the country is still flushed with its overwhelming victory over Poland. But last night General von Brauchitsch, the commander in chief of the army, in an Order of the Day to his troops, officially announced that the operations against Poland were concluded.

For Germany, the war – or as they called it here, the counter-attack – against Poland is ended. In eighteen days this terrific fighting machine which is the German army has destroyed Poland, annihilated its armies, chased its government from Polish soil.

Well, now that this part of the war is over, people are wondering what next. And that's where America comes in. And that's why Berlin is paying a good deal of attention to what transpires in Washington today.

I gather from the press comment this morning that Germany would certainly not be surprised if Congress passed the "Cash and Carry" Bill, *[modifying the Neutrality Act to allow the Allies to buy American weapons]* though the Germans naturally hope that it won't. But it is interesting to note that the role of America in the present international mess is being considered here in Germany for the first time. Until now, we were out of the picture completely.

Today, for instance, the *Börsen Zeitung* carries a long editorial headed: AMERICA AT THE CROSSROADS. The paper complains that the American press, which incidentally it says is nearly 100 percent Jewish-controlled, has not been fair to Germany. It accuses our press of having printed lies about alleged German atrocities in Poland which were fed to it by the British propaganda service. "Without doubt," it tells its readers here in Berlin this morning, "the majority of the members of Congress and also the President are in sympathy with the Democracies." But the *Börsen Zeitung* sees some hope in what it calls the "Front of Reason" in America. In that front it puts Senators Borah and Clark, Colonel Lindbergh and Father Coughlin *[the anti-semitic "radio priest"]*. Well, tonight, when I talk to you again, it'll be interesting to report on what the German reaction is, after Berlin has heard what the President has to say.

Berlin September 22, 1939 01.00

Good morning.

My eyesight isn't any too good, but I'm not blind. And I've been going

89

over every word in the morning papers here in Berlin, and I can't find any mention of President Roosevelt's special message to Congress, except in one paper.

The *Deutsche Allgemeine Zeitung*, in a front-page review of world events – a daily column dated Berlin – devotes part of one sentence to mentioning that the President asked Congress to change the Neutrality Law by lifting the arms embargo.

Not a line in any other Berlin newspaper that I can find.

Now in the Wilhelmstrasse last night, American correspondents were told this: that President Roosevelt's speech was no surprise in Berlin. But that it would be premature for Germany to draw any conclusions until Congress had had its word. But these official quarters made no attempt to hide from us that in their opinion the repeal of the arms embargo might in the end endanger the relations between the United States and Germany, and that if American arms and munitions were to stream towards England and France, the likelihood of incidents was certainly increased. Also that friction between the two countries would be bound to increase. Finally, the Germans pointed out that the repeal of the embargo benefits England and France exclusively, and therefore is one-sided and not neutral. Other points in the President's address were heartily approved here, such as keeping American ships and citizens out of the war zone, and the banning of war credits.

So much for official reaction. I understand the text of President Roosevelt's message was wired to Herr Hitler at the front last night, and we are not likely to know his reaction for at least some days.

The Berlin papers themselves play up today stories about the Polish campaign, about the last Polish resistance being broken in East Poland and about the heroic deeds of certain units of the German army.

The most interesting story, however, is the German reaction to the assassination of the Romanian Prime Minister in Bucharest yesterday. With one accord, the German press sees the long hand of England and the British Secret Service as responsible. THE GUILT POINTS TOWARDS ENGLAND is the head over a front-page editorial in the *Völkischer Beobachter*. And the same paper dates a story from Bucharest under this headline: A CRIME OF THE BRITISH SECRET SERVICE. The dispatch argues that Britain tried to break Romania's neutrality but failed because Premier Calinescu stood firm. Therefore – and here I quote – "England did what it has always done, it took to murder. The man in the street of Bucharest concluded that only England and France had an interest in murdering the premier." As to the fact that the murderers belonged to the Fascist Iron Guard, the dispatch argues that they were either crazy, or were purchased to do the murder as provocateurs.

Berlin September 24, 1939 01.14

Last Tuesday, the 19th of September, I saw one of the last battles of the Polish war, the fight around Gdynia, the great Polish port on the Baltic. That night I went over to Danzig to broadcast an impression of it, but my talk didn't get through.

Tonight I'll say just a word about it, because it was the only battle that any of us correspondents saw in Poland. And it gave us a first-hand idea of just how the German army could conquer Poland in three weeks.

I myself had been in Gdynia only a month before, and had broadcast from there. On Tuesday I found myself on a hill in the midst of the city, which had been occupied two days before. The hill was an observation post. Officers stood about, peering through field glasses.

Two miles to the north of us – across the city – on a ridge that stretched for seven miles inland from the sea, the killing was going on. You could hear the deep roar of the German artillery – the Poles had none – and the rat-tat-tat of the machine-guns on both sides. Over our heads came the huge shells of the battleship *Schleswig-Holstein*, anchored ten miles to our rear, in Danzig. Its twelve-inch guns were firing at the Polish positions twelve miles away. Fortunately, they did not fire short, or I wouldn't be here. The sound of those shells exploding, or of the bombs from the airplanes, was deafening. But I'll be frank. We heard an awful lot. But in modern warfare you don't *see* very much. We saw the shells and the bombs exploding, the cloud of smoke, the mass of flying dirt or debris. And the flames shooting up when a German shell hit the roof of a building from which Polish machine-gunners had been firing. But you couldn't identify the Polish and German lines. The infantry on both sides kept well under cover. Also the tanks. Only when the German infantry, led by tanks, advanced could we see how the battle was going. Even then it was difficult, because the infantry constantly took cover, and a camouflaged tank at two miles, when it's not moving, looks like a bush.

At night-time, of course, you could see the flaming buildings and see the sky lit up when the big guns went off. We had watched the battle the night before from the pier of the summer resort of Zoppot, and it was an awesome sight. I could hardly believe that on a peaceful night five weeks before I had run into my friend, John Gunther, on that pier at Zoppot, and that we had sat there far into the night arguing as to whether the guns would go off or not in Europe.

As to the battle the next day, the Poles were in a hopeless position. German forces surrounded them on three sides, and the sea, from which German destroyers were peppering them, cut them off on the fourth. Yet they had fought gamely on this last ridge for several days, and they fought on that day until nightfall, when they surrendered. It shocked me that the

Poles had no artillery. If they had, of course, we wouldn't have been so near. During the morning they tried to use two anti-aircraft guns against advancing German infantry and tanks, but it was useless. In the meantime, the German artillery pounded away at the Polish positions, and when they had been battered down, the infantry went forward relentlessly – every half-hour, by my watch, a new charge. I tried to spot through my field-glasses the Polish infantry retreating, but couldn't pick them up. Apparently they were either killed at their posts, or surrendered. Watching there, you hoped that they had surrendered. Because to have retreated in the open under the withering German fire would have been almost suicide. I don't know how many Polish troops were there when the battle started, but at nightfall, when they surrendered, 15,000 came out alive.

As to aircraft, there's little to be said. You'd see the German bombers dive to within 150 feet of the Polish lines, drop their bombs or let fire with their machine-guns, and then soar up again as if they'd been target-practicing. You would have thought that a machine-gun or even a rifle would have brought them down. But all escaped. I got the impression that it was this constant bombing and machine-gunning from the air that broke the back of Polish resistance more than anything else. The Poles had no defense against it; no way of moving their troops without subjecting them to decimation from the air. It was one-sided warfare.

And all through the battle you got the impression of the German army moving with machine-like precision, like a steamroller, but a fast one. Not the slightest sign of strain or excitement among the German officers at our observation post. They reminded me of the coaches of a championship football team who sit calmly on the sidelines and watch the machine they've created do its stuff.

Below us in the streets of the town, women with their youngsters – Poles – stood around in little clusters, listening to the din of the guns and the rattle of the machine-guns. The bitterness, the anguish on the faces of those women, was indescribable. "Tragic and grotesque," a newspaperman muttered to me. Grotesque that we should be standing there watching the killing as though it were a football game – and we comfortably off in the grandstand. Watching that, and the bitter faces of the women in the streets below. Well, it was your job, but that gave you little comfort.

Berlin September 24, 1939

Good morning. This is Berlin.

This fourth Sabbath Day since the war started has been spent by the people of Berlin in church, and lining up for the new monthly food-cards which go into operation tomorrow. No meat, bread, milk, fats and such things will be obtainable in Germany after today except through foodcards, regardless of whether you eat at home or in a restaurant.

Now the papers this morning all play up on their front pages the amazing report of the German High Command explaining in some detail how the Polish war was won so easily and so quickly. And most of the papers carry long editorials glorifying the army and praising its wonderful achievements during the past few weeks – or, I should say, days.

Some almost unbelievable things come out of that report of the High Command. Things like this:

That the fate of Poland was really decided in eight days. By that time the German army had already obtained its main strategical object, that is, the trapping of the main part of the Polish forces within the great elbow of the Vistula River. The remaining ten days were merely taken up in wiping out that Polish army in one of the bloodiest – I mean for the Poles, not the Germans – battles in history.

Some other things: that 450,000 Polish troops were captured, 1200 guns taken and 800 airplanes either destroyed or captured, and that at the end of eighteen days not a single Polish division, not even a brigade, was left intact.

Well, the German papers are very proud of all that this morning. So far there have been no casualty figures published. The High Command said they're comparatively very small, and that they will be published shortly.

Some people here in Berlin are sure that now that the Polish war is over, we may see a German Peace Offensive, directed against the West, especially France. Mussolini, these people say, would play his part in it.

I've just come from the Wilhelmstrasse, where we correspondents had a conference with Dr. Goebbels. He devoted most of his time to Mr. H.R. Knickerbocker *[the American journalist]*, whom he called an international liar and counterfeiter. He objected to a story he attributed to Knickerbocker to the effect that the Nazi leaders had shipped out a lot of Nazi gold in case they were forced to quit the country after a German defeat. Dr. Goebbels revealed – and this is a new technique which interested me – that on Thursday he had had the German short-wave radio stations call Knickerbocker and challenge him to produce his proof about this Nazi gold being planted abroad. Dr. Goebbels said that he had offered Knickerbocker 10 percent in cash of any sum which the American correspondent could prove the Nazis had deposited abroad. "We gave him in our radio call until midnight last night," said Dr. Goebbels, "to answer. But no answer came."

Berlin September 25, 1939 24.46

Good evening. This is William L. Shirer in Berlin.

The Germans tonight claim another big victory of their air force over the British fleet.

According to an official announcement read over the German radio at 10 p.m. – about three hours ago – German bombers today made several successful attacks on units of the British fleet in the northern part of the British Isles. The Germans claim that their flyers scored direct hits on four British warships, and that all their planes returned safely to their bases.

Just where the attack occurred, we are not informed. It's merely stated that it took place 560 miles from the German coast.

The Germans were so pleased over the exploit that after the radio announcer had read the news at the beginning of the regular news bulletin, he stopped while a band broadcast a patriotic march and a choir roared the new popular anti-English song: "We're Marching Against England". Then the news bulletin was continued.

The announcement added that it was "absolutely established" from the observations of the German flyers that four British warships had been hit, and that they were direct hits. What kind of warships they were – whether they were big or small – is not disclosed.

The German communiqué offered another piece of interesting information. It said that the German flyers were subject to heavy anti-aircraft fire, but said not a word about any British chasers having taken to the air to fight. You assume from the German report that none did. And that raises the question – if the German version is correct – why not? I understand that the Germans themselves are puzzled by this. They say they've made several flights with heavy bombers to objectives five and six hundred miles from Germany, and that often no British pursuit plane has appeared at all.

Most neutral observers here feel that it is still too early to pass any judgment on that old controversy of airplanes against warships. But I have the feeling here that in German military circles the idea is growing that airplanes may prove the masters before this war is over. Of course, you could add that they'll have to, if Germany is to win.

The Germans are also making quite a bit today out of an item in the High Command's daily communiqué which told of a U-boat having destroyed a British "Q" ship. These vessels, disguised as merchant ships, were a nightmare to German submarine commanders in the last war. And German editorial writers tonight are almost beside themselves in commenting on this form of warfare, which they claim is against all the rules of the sea, and is nothing but attempted murder. Says the *Börsen Zeitung*: "The English know that in open battle they are not up to the

94

Germans either on the sea, in the air, on the land, or in politics. So they take to mean murder. All the harder will be the sentence which the German soldier will bring about."

You see the bitterness there, the anger?

The German High Command says, by the way, that the English "Q" ship, a vessel of 7,000 tons, was disguised as a Dutch boat.

As I've already reported, clothing-ware is being rationed here. I see that the authorities have now laid down strict rules as to the amount of cloth you can use in a suit. If I order a new suit my tailor must make it out of a piece of cloth exactly 3.1 meters long by 144 centimeters wide – about three yards by a yard and a half. I'm afraid that'll force me to resort to my boyhood short trousers again. For a young woman's suit, you're allowed a piece of cloth 2.45 meters long and 124 centimeters wide. Tall women are allowed a few centimeters more of precious cloth.

New rules are also laid down for the length of socks and stockings but I haven't time to go into that.

Berlin September 26, 1939 24.51

Good evening.

With the counter-attack against Poland ended, German interest today turned towards the West. For the first time since the war started the Berlin newspapers tonight play up the Western Front and the report that a German U-boat sank a British destroyer.

No word here in Berlin about any serious fighting in the West. The High Command still speaks merely of skirmishes. And the papers headline that eight French planes were shot down in air battles.

But there's still a lot of talk here about a German Peace Offensive in the West. Judging from what you read in the press, and hear in the Wilhelmstrasse, Germany seems to say: Why fight there in the West? Poland is finished. No amount of blood spilled on the Siegfried Line will make Poland what it was before. Besides, Poland is no longer a purely German affair. Soviet Russia has half of it now.

Seven members of the American Consulate staff at Warsaw arrived here tonight and put up at the Adlon. Considering the bombardment they went through, they were in excellent spirits.

They brought with them a tattered American flag which was flying on the Consulate when a German shell pierced the front part of the building and blew a big hole in it. Fortunately for them, they had taken refuge in the Embassy, which was not hit. Curious thing – despite the bombardment and the continual bombing, they said the water supply, electricity, even the telephone service were all functioning in Warsaw when they left. Another thing. The first they knew that the Germans were even near the city, they said, was when a German shell arrived. The suburb of Praga, they said, was in ruins, and Warsaw had also been badly damaged.

For the first time the German High Command communiqué speaks today of dive-bombers working on Warsaw – that is, it points out, on military objectives there.

Berlin September 27, 1939 24.45

This is Berlin.

This has been a day of good news for Herr Hitler.

Warsaw has capitulated after a heroic but hopeless stand. And in the first battle in history on the open sea between naval ships and airplanes, Germany claims a resounding victory for its air force that possibly may have consequences unforeseen when this war started three and a half weeks ago.

First about Warsaw. At 8.10 tonight the radio stations of Germany stopped whatever they were doing and broadcast the following communiqué from the High Command: "Warsaw has unconditionally capitulated. The formal giving over of the city to the German High Command will probably take place September 29th" – that would be the day after tomorrow. The communiqué added that the Polish troops in Warsaw numbered 100,000 men. As has been the case with other victories in this war, the radio then broadcast the two German national anthems.

As you know, the Germans declined to consider Warsaw as an open city after it refused to surrender, and a devastating attack that pierced the first two defense lines began yesterday. It appeared obvious to everyone that if this continued more than a million civilians within the city would perish. This morning therefore, "impressed by the German attack," as the High Command put it, the Polish commander offered to surrender. From the very beginning – as I've told you before – the German press had considered the defense of Warsaw as a criminal act on the part of the Poles.

So ends the Polish War, with Poland divided up as it was before 1914 between Germany and Russia. Whether a buffer Polish state – there are 20 million Poles, remember – is to be set up will apparently be settled by Herr von Ribbentrop and Stalin in Moscow in the next few days. The German Foreign Minister arrived there tonight. In the meantime, Herr Hitler has appointed General von Rundstedt as head of the military

96

administration of occupied Poland, with Reichsminister Dr. Frank, an ardent Nazi, under him in charge of civil administration.

A word about that other piece of good news for the Germans. History yesterday witnessed the first battle between a fleet and airplanes. The engagement took place in the North Sea. The Germans claim to have destroyed a British aircraft-carrier and damaged a battleship without losing a single plane themselves. If that is so, you may have there the answer to the question that has been fought over by the experts for the last ten years: can airplanes destroy a battle-fleet? The Germans are saying a decided "Yes" to that tonight.

We asked an officer of the High Command tonight why the Germans said the aircraft-carrier was "destroyed" and not "sunk". He said a 1,000-pound bomb had scored a direct hit and wrecked it, but that German planes had not stayed to watch whether it sank or not. He also said that two 500-pound bombs hit the British battleship, one forward, the other amidships.

It will be interesting to compare this German account with what the English say. That's a privilege you have, and I haven't.

Berlin September 28 , 1939 23.45

Hello, America. Hello, CBS. This is William Shirer in Berlin.

You've been reading a lot these days about the German submarine warfare. During the first month of the war, German U-boats have taken a considerable toll of merchant shipping already. They have sunk one of Britain's seven aircraft-carriers, and also, I believe, one British destroyer.

People over here talk about a "hunger war". That is, the British blockade is designed to starve out Germany. The German submarine warfare is to prevent foodstuffs, among other things, from reaching the British Isles, and thus to starve out Britain.

In our newspapers we've read a good number of accounts of ships being sunk by German submarines. How could a U-boat, you might ask, creep up to an aircraft-carrier, protected by destroyers, and sink it? Or what about that story the other day that a German submarine had sunk the British freighter *Royal Sceptre* without warning, without giving its crew time to take to the lifeboats, thus abandoning them to their fate? Or that report of Mr. Churchill's in Parliament this week that a German U-boat commander had sent a radio message to him, notifying him of the sinking of a ship, and that that commander had been captured?

It occurred to me that it might be interesting for you and me if I could go to one of those submarine commanders and see how these stories looked from his angle. I don't think a submarine commander has ever been interviewed in wartime before. I know that one has never been interviewed over the radio before.

Well, with me here at the microphone in Berlin is Lieutenant-Captain Herbert Schultze, commander of a German submarine. He tells me he has just returned from one of those voyages in the North Atlantic.

He's a young fellow, as are all these men engaged in what must certainly be the world's most dangerous job at the moment. I asked him a moment ago where he was during the World War. He said, "In grade school."

Well, Captain Schultze left his submarine in port today, and has come to Berlin and he says he's ready to answer any questions I want to put to him. He asks me to apologize for his English, but as you will see, that's not necessary.

Well, Captain, first, what kind of submarine do you command?

SCHULTZE: I am the commander of a medium-sized German U-boat.

SHIRER: Where were you working?

SCHULTZE: In the Atlantic.

SHIRER: What kind of success have you had? Did you meet any ships?

SCHULTZE: Unfortunately I did not meet any enemy warships, but I did have a part in some successes which perhaps you have heard about in the newspapers or on the radio.

SHIRER: Could you give me a few details about that?

SCHULTZE: I would like to tell you about the sinking of the British merchantship, *Royal Sceptre*. There have been many stories abroad. Here is what really happened. The *Royal Sceptre* was bound for England with a cargo of grain. One day I sighted her. I rose to the surface and fired a shot of warning across her bows. In the language of international law that meant: "Stop at once, you are to be searched by a warship."

The *Royal Sceptre*, however, did not stop. Instead she answered by turning tail. I signaled, "Make no use of your wireless," and then heard the wireless operator sending out an SOS message, saying he was being fired at by a submarine and giving his position. Seeing that he was disobeying my orders, and by reporting my position was guilty of a hostile act, I was regretfully forced to stop him from doing so. The only means I had was to open fire with my gun. We scored several hits on the *Royal Sceptre*. These caused her to stop. Her crew took to the boats.

The radio operator, however, stayed aboard and continued to report his position. He was, by the way, an exceptionally fine and brave fellow.

I say that here because I shall scarcely have an opportunity to shake hands with him personally. The lifeboats made no attempt to come nearer, so I had to go up to them to ask whether I had wounded anyone and if they had plenty of provisions.

"Supplies sufficient, nobody wounded," was the answer. I then had the wireless operator fetched from aboard.

SHIRER: When did you sink the ship?

SCHULTZE: I sank the *Royal Sceptre* only after I saw the smoke of a ship on the horizon. I called out to the men in the boats to wait until I could send help. They waved a happy and friendly farewell and yelled, "Hurrah!"

SHIRER: Just a minute, Captain. I heard a report that the English crew was left to shift for itself and was believed drowned.

SCHULTZE: That is not true. I tell you what happened. In the meantime we had picked up a radio message from the American ship *Washington* saying that it was eighty miles away and would be on the spot at midnight. To make quite sure, however, I set my course for that smoke trail. It turned out to be the British steamer, *Browning*. I set my flag-signal "intend to communicate with you." I wanted to tell the *Browning* to take the crew of the *Royal Sceptre* aboard. The *Browning* sights us and our signal. But to my surprise the crew manned the boats in a panic. Before I can even draw closer to give my peaceful message all the passengers and crew of the *Browning* have left the ship. I now had to make it clear to these people that they were to get aboard again in order to go and save the crew of the *Royal Sceptre*. The joy and relief of those in the boats surprised us. Did they believe us to be barbarians? Taking to the boats in a panic like that as soon as the German U-boat comes in sight? The captain of the *Browning* – as I have now heard to my great satisfaction – has obeyed my orders to save the crew of the *Royal Sceptre*. And also, incidentally, my order not to make use of his radio until he should reach port. He has now, I hear, landed the crew of the *Royal Sceptre* safely in the harbor of Bahia in Brazil.

SHIRER: Well, Captain Schultze, did you have any other experiences on this assignment?

SCHULTZE: Well, I sent Mr. Churchill a radio message.

SHIRER: Ah, you are the one! But I thought he had been captured.

SCHULTZE: Yes, that is what Mr. Churchill told the House of Commons a day or two ago. He even said that I was well treated. That, at least, is correct, although he has apparently got my position wrong.

SHIRER: What happened exactly?

SCHULTZE: When I sank the British ship *Firby* I sent the following radio message: "Transmit to Mr. Churchill: I have sunk the British steamer *Firby*. Position x degrees North, x degrees West. Save the crew, if you please."

SHIRER: Did you get a reply?

SCHULTZE: No, except through his speech in Parliament. And I was glad to hear that the British crew was saved.

SHIRER: Well, Captain Schultze, thank you very much.

SCHULTZE: Not at all.

SHIRER: I have just been speaking with Captain Herbert Schultze, commander of a German submarine, who came up here to Berlin tonight to tell me about what he has been doing. Incidentally, I was just told he's been awarded the Iron Cross for performing those things he's just described.

Shirer CBS Berlin October 1, 1939 15.10

Good Morning. This is Berlin.

Today is Germany's Thanksgiving Day. The Germans don't celebrate with turkey, as we do at home. But on this day they do give thanks, as do we on ours, for a bountiful harvest.

In other years, to celebrate Thanksgiving, there was a great mass-meeting of farmers on a mountain top near Goslar, in Western Germany. The Führer always came and delivered a speech.

Today this celebration was called off on account of the war. There was no mass-meeting, no speech from Herr Hitler. Instead Herr Hess, the deputy-leader, addressed the nation over the radio.

The German harvest this year has been a good one, he told the nation. Britain cannot starve us out. I was struck by the way he singled out Great Britain as the single enemy. Not a mention of France. His whole attack was concentrated on England.

Well, the German harvest, according to the September estimates, has been a good one this year. This moves a morning paper here in Berlin to comment editorially as follows: "God Almighty therefore is not only on the side of the strong battalions; he also helps the right side. He also helps us to destroy the effort of the English Jews and their comrades to win by a Hunger Blockade. The German farmer has assured us bread and milk

. . . God Almighty was with our soldiers; God Almighty was with our farmers. Let us all be with God Almighty." That was a quotation from the Berlin *Lokal Anzeiger*.

Now, with today there begins a very crucial week in Europe. Germany is mustering every political card in the deck to induce Britain and France to call it quits, now that Poland has been destroyed and divided up between Germany and Russia.

Count Ciano, the Italian Foreign Minister, arrives here at five – that is, in about two hours from now – and will be immediately received by Herr Hitler and Herr von Ribbentrop. Obviously, Italy is to be drawn into the Peace Offensive launched by Germany and Russia after they signed their new agreement Thursday.

It may seem a little strange to you to suddenly see Germany filled with so much peace talk. But there it is. The *Völkischer Beobachter*, official Nazi paper, has a front-page editorial this morning: "The People Want Peace." And it argues that not only the German people, but the French and English, and all the neutral people also want peace.

Now, as I understand it, Mr. Chamberlain will make a declaration in the Commons tomorrow about the German-Russian proposals. It is possible that Count Ciano, acting as peacemaker, might, after he has seen Herr Hitler here this evening, still have time to transmit more details of what kind of peace Hitler and Stalin are offering to the British Prime Minister before his speech tomorrow. At any rate, the Reichstag, which has been called for this week will meet soon after Mr. Chamberlain has had his say. If there is a chance for peace, I imagine Herr Hitler will make a grandiose Peace Speech. If the German hopes for peace are dashed, then the Reichstag will hear another kind of speech.

So, it will be a crucial week. The German view is that, as the heading of an editorial in the *Börsen Zeitung* puts it, "This is the last chance for peace." The paper argues that the new tie-up with Moscow makes it impossible for England to win the war or achieve its war-aims. And it plays up a theme I've seen often in the German press the past few days. The theme is this: If England wants to fight Germany over Poland, it must automatically fight Russia too. Well, that's the Nazi view.

Berlin October 3, 1939 24.47

Good Evening.

There is very little reaction to Mr. Chamberlain's speech here in Berlin so far. But from what I can learn the Germans were not particularly pleased with it. Saying that may mean more to you than to me, because I

101

don't know what Mr. Chamberlain said. You probably do. I can only guess.

At any rate, the Wilhelmstrasse told us tonight that such an important speech at this critical time would take some reading and going over before any conclusions were drawn.

You may be sure that those conclusions – whatever they are – will not be made public until the Reichstag meets towards the end of the week to hear Herr Hitler draw them himself. Because of the peculiar nature of modern war, the exact date of the Reichstag session is being kept secret. But I can tell you that it will start at noon, Berlin time, so at home you'd have to get up early to hear it, 6 a.m. in New York, 5 a.m. in Chicago, and so forth.

In the meantime the German press and radio continue their Peace Campaign. The *Nachtausgabe* tonight has a flaming banner-headline: AN APPEAL TO THE NEUTRALS – FIGHT FOR PEACE. And Germans here point to Rome, from which some people think the next peace move may come.

I heard another suggestion here in Berlin today. It was that President Roosevelt might be called in as peacemaker. When you stop to think of it, my informant said, he is in a key position for such a job, as head of the only great neutral power that has not either taken sides or is at war. That is, Russia seems now tied to Berlin. Italy is still in the Axis. Japan has a war on her hands *[Japan had been at war with China since 1931]*. That leaves the United States.

Incidentally, the Wilhelmstrasse told us today that Germany was glad that our Embargo Bill was not being rushed through and that a lengthy debate over it would take place. This showed, we were told, that no hasty decisions were being taken in Washington. About an hour ago I heard a German radio commentator praise Senator Borah's stand. That neutrality legislation of ours looms larger in German minds, as the day for the crucial vote approaches.

I'm puzzled about a radio broadcast I picked up from London last night. It spoke of British planes flying over Berlin. I'm just wondering why they didn't sound the air-raid alarm here, or if they did, why none of my friends nor I heard it.

Berlin October 4, 1939 24.47

Good Evening.

The church bells have been ringing today, and millions of Swastika flags have been flying from the houses of Germany to celebrate the occupation of Warsaw and the victorious end of the "counter-attack" against Poland.

And yet – strange thing – not a word about the church bells and the flags on the front pages of the three leading evening Berlin newspapers tonight.

The Polish war may be over, but there is another war still on, and German interest is really centered not on Warsaw, but on three things. Will the Peace Offensive succeed? How is the war at sea against England going? What will America do?

Take the last question first. To be perfectly frank, the United States did not appear to matter much one way or another when this war began. Now our little debate in Washington on the Embargo Bill has suddenly become front-page news in the German Press. The *Börsen-Zeitung* has a front-page editorial tonight entitled AMERICA WANTS PEACE.

The *Nachtausgabe* also has an editorial. It's headed: U.S.A.: JEWS HAVE THE GREATEST INTEREST IN WAR. And it argues that America is not nearly so anxious to join the war on the side of England as are – and here I quote– "Herr Roosevelt and his Jewish camarilla". The editorial then presents Senator Borah's case against the Embargo Bill.

But I get the impression here in Berlin that Germany entertains little hope that the Embargo Bill will be defeated in Congress.

The German press makes much of the announcement today that German warships have held up seventy-eight neutral steamers in the last four days, and brought some of them, which carried contraband, to German ports. In this connection official circles here deny that German submarines have orders to sink armed merchant ships on sight. They will be attacked only when they make use of their arms, say the Germans, who add that an armed merchant ship is not to be treated as a warship just because it carries a gun – only when it makes use of the gun.

And now we've just got word in that the Reichstag is to be called Friday at 12 noon, Berlin time, 6 a.m. New York time. So on Friday we'll probably know the kind of peace which Hitler is prepared to offer to Britain and France and to Europe. He himself will speak, as always when the Reichstag convenes.

Tomorrow, it's reported, Herr Hitler will fly to Warsaw, to make a triumphal entry into the Polish capital.

But interest here is centered on what kind of a peace he may propose on Friday when the Reichstag meets.

Berlin October 5, 1939 14.05

Good Morning. This is Berlin.

There's nothing so far in the Berlin newspaper about it, but I understand that Herr Hitler is in Warsaw today to watch his troops complete the occupation of the Polish capital.

He is due to return here tonight to complete the draft of his big speech before the German Reichstag at noon tomorrow.

What will Hitler say tomorrow? What kind of a peace will he offer to a Europe whose peoples certainly want peace – if it's a just peace? What will he do about Poland? Set up a buffer state around Warsaw? An independent state? A protectorate? Or no state at all?

These are some of the questions being asked in Berlin today in political and diplomatic quarters. But Hitler keeps his secrets well, and we here are just as much in the dark as to what he will definitely propose in the Reichstag tomorrow as is the outside world. The German papers say nothing. They devote themselves to other matters. The Wilhelmstrasse is mum. It has no wish to anticipate the word of the Führer.

The general feeling here in Berlin is that Hitler will offer fairly comprehensive peace terms, including the establishment of an independent Poland – not like the Poland of a month ago, to be sure, but a considerable chunk of territory surrounding Warsaw which would include, say, some 15 million of the 20 million Poles who lived in the former Polish state. I gather that the new Poland would have about the same status as Slovakia – that is, it would be nominally independent and actually more independent than the Protectorate of Bohemia and Moravia, which of course is not independent at all, and in size it would be somewhat larger than Slovakia. Economically, it would be dependent upon Germany. These same quarters think that the Führer will tell the West that now Germany *and* Russia are in possession of Poland, any Allied war aims to restore it completely are futile, and would necessitate a war not only against Germany but against Russia.

That's an angle which the Wilhelmstrasse has been emphasizing this week.

Of course there are some observers here who think that Germany's position is so strong that Hitler will not go out of his way to offer too generous peace terms to the West. There has always been a school of thought in Germany which believes that Germany could never assure itself of its proper place in the sun until England was brought to terms and at least convinced that it must stop meddling in continental matters.

I give you these two points of view for what they're worth. But by tomorrow at this time we should have a pretty good idea as to whether this war is to end or, as they say here, really to begin. Note that: "really begin". Because in Berlin's view it has certainly not begun yet on the Western Front, and even on the sea it's been rather mild. What may happen there, when thousands of airplanes go into action in the West and over the North Sea is something best left to your imagination. So far only a very few airplanes have been used by both sides.

One thing the Germans tell me their planes will not drop – if the others don't as the war goes on – and that is bombs full of gas or bacteria. But of course there are plenty of other things they can drop that spell destruction.

Berlin October 5, 1939 24.47

Good Evening.

I saw a German newsreel tonight. It was a private showing, and I don't know whether the film is being shown in public here, or whether you'll get a chance to see it over there. But I suppose you will.

There were two things that interested me.

First, the pictures of the bombardment of Warsaw. They were very realistic. The cameraman was working just behind the big guns. And you could see batteries of German heavy artillery pounding away at almost point-blank range at the city of Warsaw.

The city itself – well, you could hardly see it. You could see only the flames and the smoke – mostly the smoke. In all my life I've never seen such a huge cloud of black smoke. It seemed a half-mile high and it covered the whole expanse of the sprawling city. I have been in that city often, I was there just before the war broke out. But I had never realized how sprawling it was until I saw the smoke today that hung so heavily over it.

The big guns kept going off and the announcer kept explaining that the city of course was a fortress, hence the shelling. What has happened to the million people in the city – how many have survived, we don't yet know. Two American correspondents who were chosen to go there yesterday and report for us all did not get back tonight as planned. They won't be back until tomorrow. And tomorrow, I suppose, world interest will be centered on the Reichstag speech of the German Führer.

He himself flew to Warsaw today and held a triumphant review of his troops. Tonight, he flew back to Berlin to give the finishing touches to his speech before the Reichstag tomorrow.

The Reichstag begins at noon. I shall be there and will be on the air at 11 a.m., New York time, to report on it.

I mentioned a second thing in that newsreel that interested me. It was a series of shots showing Polish Jews with long beards and long black coats working on the road gangs in Poland.

Berlin October 6, 1939 17.02

This is Berlin.

Many of you heard Hitler's speech in the Reichstag this morning. All of you know by this time what he had to offer Europe in the way of peace. Berlin now awaits the reaction of Britain and France. In the meantime, a word about the Reichstag session itself.

Five weeks ago this morning on a cold, gray day, I attended another session. Hitler was announcing the march into Poland, the beginning of war. He was defiant, and so were the members of the Reichstag. A tense feeling hung over the meeting.

Today, sitting there in the Kroll Opera House where the Reichstag meets, I had an entirely different feeling. Outside it was sunny and warm. It is true that on my way I saw numerous batteries of anti-aircraft guns surrounding the building for many blocks. But outside that, no feeling that we were in the midst of war. The crowd along the streets was small, but good-natured.

Same atmosphere within the Reichstag. The deputies, standing at their places, all in uniform, waiting for the session to open seemed almost jovial. The members of the cabinet – up on the stage where the opera singers used to perform – stood about chatting easily – Ribbentrop with Admiral Raeder, Dr. Goebbels with von Neurath, etc.

Then Hitler came walking smartly down the aisle. He wore a double-breasted gray army coat, with black trousers. Back of him was Hess, his deputy, in a storm-trooper's shirt, then Herr Himmler, the police chief, in field gray.

Herr Hitler, as he spoke, was more calm, more confident, less emotional than I have seen him in a Reichstag speech for a long time. Sometimes he read so fast it was difficult to catch his words. The Reichstag members also did not jump up so often and yell and applaud as they usually do: only once, when he said he did not doubt for a second that Germany would win. They applauded his appeal to France for friendship.

For the first time that I can remember, Hitler omitted a peroration to his speech. His last sentence, his thanks to God for the German victory, and his appeal for peace, was spoken in a low, matter-of-fact voice. I have never heard him end a speech in that tone before.

Afterward, in the lobbies where the deputies stood around and talked, you would have thought that peace already had been achieved. That was the atmosphere. And by the time we left the Reichstag, the soldiers were driving away with their anti-aircraft guns.

Hitler said it was his last peace offer. So far as I can ascertain, there will be no diplomatic move from Berlin to back it up. The feeling in

106

the Wilhelmstrasse when I left to come up here was that Germany will now wait to see what response is forthcoming from London and Paris.

Berlin October 6, 1939 24.47

Good Evening.

Adolf Hitler has spoken. In a speech to the Reichstag that lasted an hour and a half and was broadcast around the world he made public the kind of a peace he was prepared to offer after his destruction of Poland.

Most Germans, I think, find it a good peace. At least that is the opinion of the foreign correspondents here and also of all the Germans I have had time to talk to today.

The Germans find it a good peace and they hope that London and Paris will accept it. In fact, if you said to a German here in Berlin tonight that well, maybe Britain and France won't accept it, he would stare at you in amazement. He would say, as more than one has said to me this evening, "But why not? The Führer said he had no claims against them. He only wants peace with them. And now is the time to get it."

At the press conference in the Wilhelmstrasse tonight, one skeptical newspaperman asked how the Western Powers would be assured that Herr Hitler had no further demands, since that had been said before. The answer was that only now are the real foundations for a lasting peace in the interests of all there.

The Wilhelmstrasse struck me today as placing great weight on the idea that the neutrals, especially their leaders – figures like the Pope, the King of the Belgians, the Queen of the Netherlands, President Roosevelt – would welcome the Hitler Peace Proposals and perhaps bring pressure on Paris and London to consider them.

The Wilhelmstrasse thought tonight that it would be at least a week before the official reaction from Britain and France is forthcoming. Apparently Germany has no intention of making the offer any more definite by presenting it to London and Paris by diplomatic channels. One official pointed out to us that, strictly speaking, the speech was not a peace offer (*Angebot*), but a statement of Germany's readiness for peace. It was a statement of Germany's long-term policy.

Berlin October 8, 1939 15.10

Good morning.

Germany waits – and I must say waits hopefully – for the answer of Paris and London to what the Nazis consider was a very generous peace offer from Herr Hitler.

It is now admitted in the German press that the newspaper reaction in the capitals of the Western Democracies has not been very encouraging. But the Wilhelmstrasse seems content to wait for more official reaction from London and Paris. Mr. Chamberlain's expected speech in the House on Wednesday is awaited with particular interest.

In the meantime, the German press and the German radio continue a barrage of articles and talks to convince the German people that England and France alone will be to blame if the war continues. And that, if it does go on, Germany will have clean hands, and will be only defending itself against Franco-British aggression.

I must admit that most of the Germans I talk to certainly believe that already. Hitler's Reichstag speech apparently convinced them.

In the meantime, too, you can feel the effort here to make life in Germany as normal as possible until this curious kind of war in the West is either stopped or made much more serious than it has been up to now. Berlin today has one of the heaviest sport programs of the year. The races at Hoppegarten will attract a big crowd this afternoon. Besides this the following events are scheduled in Berlin alone: one track-meet, a bicycle race – bike racing is as popular in Germany as is baseball at home – between Germany and Hungary, two hockey matches, two rugby-football games, one wrestling match, one amateur boxing show, one weight-lifting contest, two hundred hand-ball games, and one hundred soccer-football matches including league games. Soccer, of course, is the greatest sport in Germany.

And the entertainment industry is not lagging behind the people who promote sports. This morning papers carry a whole page of advertisements of the various opera houses, light-opera houses, theatres, musical comedy shows and concerts, not to mention the movies. One film house advertises that rare thing in Germany now, an American film, and its advertisement features the familiar picture of Clark Gable.

Reading the sport pages and the theatre pages of the morning papers today, you would hardly believe that a war was on. Why, even a new murder mystery – an unsolved murder of a lady slain in a circus ground here – threatened to push the war news off the news pages in Berlin.

Berlin October 9, 1939 01.15

Good evening. This is William L. Shirer in Berlin.

To show you just how scarce spot news in Berlin is tonight – I have here the early editions of the two Berlin Monday morning newspapers, *Der Montag* and the *Montag Post*, which I bought on the streets at 7 o'clock tonight.

And the leading front-page story in both papers is a dispatch from Madrid quoting the foreign political editor of a Spanish paper called *Arriba*. This Spanish editor has it figured out that the fate of the earth depends upon the acceptance or the turning down of Adolf Hitler's Peace Offer by Great Britain and France. And that therefore the fate of the world at this present juncture is England's responsibility alone.

Now that is exactly the German view. The Spanish editor couldn't have it more exactly if he were in Berlin and, I suppose, that's why it is the leading story in the Berlin papers tonight.

You have probably already heard the rumor that Field Marshal Göring may go to Rome next week to see the Duce and then – with Mussolini – try to bring in President Roosevelt as peacemaker. From more than one source today I have heard the name of Roosevelt mentioned as the one man who can now achieve peace. Of course, it was not long ago that President Roosevelt's efforts to serve as peacemaker got short shrift here. But things look different now. And so does the President's role. I think we may hear more on this subject in the coming days.

In the meantime, here in Berlin the lightning war against Poland begins already to slip back into memories. Almost every day in front of my hotel I see long columns of troops with their tanks and guns drive by from the East and head off to the West. There is no cheering, no victory celebration. The people stop to watch, and then the column disappears off towards the West, and the people in the streets go on their business, if they have any business left. Sometimes a few of the officers put up in the hotel for a day or two. Mostly young airmen, and you're amazed at their youthfulness, boys of eighteen, nineteen, twenty, and they talk sometimes of their achievements in Poland, the destruction they wrought, just like a youth of nineteen or twenty at home might talk of that touchdown he made last Saturday.

Of course there is another side to war too, even for the winners. In the *Völkischer Beobachter* today there is a full page of death notices inserted by families who lost relatives in the war. A good many of them now talk of the person concerned not as having been killed in action, but of having died from his wounds. Reading these notices this morning I was struck by how many only sons there were. Here is a typical notice this morning: "In a hero's death for Führer, *Volk* and *Vaterland*, there died on September 18, in the fighting in Poland, my beloved only son, aged twenty-two." And next to it this notice: "For his beloved Fatherland, there fell on September 20 in the battle around Kutno, my only son, aged twenty-five."

Every day for weeks now such notices.

[On October 9 Shirer left Berlin to spend a few days with his family in Switzerland.]

Geneva October 13, 1939 12.47

Good Evening. This is William L. Shirer in Geneva.

I hardly need to tell you that after two months in Poland and Germany, it feels good to get back to a neutral country for a few days. I arrived here Tuesday night and leave for Berlin tomorrow morning. When I left the German capital Monday evening, the Germans assured me I was making a mistake because they felt confident that Herr Hitler's peace proposals would be accepted, and I'd miss the story. I guess, I'll have plenty of time still to be in on the story when peace comes.

Now, when you step out of a belligerent country into a neutral one, you enter an entirely different world. I felt that Tuesday afternoon at Basle, a Swiss town bordering on both France and Germany. For one thing, you're almost dazed when you pick up a Swiss newspaper and see both sides of the conflict being reported. And believe me, you're no less dazed when you sit down for your first meal and find that you don't have to shell out breadcards or that even if your meatcard is all used up for the week, it doesn't make any difference. In the restaurant in the railroad station in Basle I thought I was dreaming as I gazed at the unlimited quantities of butter, eggs, cheese and cakes, and the big steak that was soon decorating my table.

Coming down from Basle on the evening train to Geneva I got another shock. We had ridden all night in Germany in a darkened train, hardly being able to make out the stations or the blacked-out towns. For six weeks I had not seen an illuminated store window, or a street light. And suddenly, here in Switzerland, the lights went on full force in our train, blinding you. And when I stepped off the train in Geneva, there were a million lights of the city and all the store windows blazing. It was a wonderful sight.

Of course, I don't mean to say that the war is any fun for the Swiss, or that life is normal and going on like it did when I left here two months ago. The war has dealt this democratic little country a heavy blow. Shut off by two of the warring nations on two-thirds of its frontier, its only free access to the outside world is through Italy. Most of its heavy imports used to come up the Rhine. Now that trade-route has been closed.

During the first month of the war, Switzerland's exports have been cut in half, her imports by a third. The second month's figures will be worse. Germany and France were her best customers–until the war started. The tourist trade was one of her great industries, but where will the tourists come from now? Switzerland must import raw materials, especially oil, and above all else, food. The blockade and the chaos of transport make that difficult.

You might have thought that the Swiss, facing ruin from a war they had no part in causing, would have been bitter at France and Britain for turning down Herr Hitler's peace proposals, incomplete and vague though they might have considered them to be. But nothing of the kind. The Swiss press, which in its news columns presents both sides, in its editorial columns today approved Mr. Chamberlain and M. Daladier in rejecting the Nazi peace offerings. The Swiss are not peace-at-any-price people.

Berlin October 15, 1939 01.15

Good Evening. This is William L. Shirer in Berlin.

After four days in Switzerland, I returned to Berlin this morning. I was a little dazed the first day or two in a neutral country, after five weeks of the war in Poland and Germany. I guess I'm a little dazed still tonight getting back to a country at war.

But here I am tonight back in my job in Berlin, and it seems to me that the blackout has become blacker than when I left a few days ago. At least I hung up a new record on my way up here to the studio in the number of lamp-posts and fire-hydrants I bumped into tonight. I suppose it takes a few days for your eyes to get used to it.

And yet, come to think of it, the physical changes in Berlin since the war began are not so great as you might suspect. Judging from the photographs I've seen, Berlin has done less to protect itself against aerial attack than have London or Paris. I noticed today in the Wilhelmstrasse and the Unter den Linden – the one a street with government ministries and the Chancellery of Herr Hitler, the other with stores and the big hotels – I noticed how few sandbag precautions had been taken. Most of the buildings in the Wilhelmstrasse had no sandbags at all, a few had five or six measly little ones piled up to protect half of the cellar windows. Same thing on the Unter den Linden. A few windows were protected by a handful of sand-bags. But nowhere were they piled more than three or four bags high.

There are no sandbag shelters here. All shelters are underground. Great yellow arrows in the streets point to them. One of the biggest open to the public is in the basement of the Führer's Chancellery.

There has been no mass evacuation of the women and children such as, I believe, London and Paris have experienced. Today it so happened that we had good evidence of that. It was the first sunny, fairly warm Sunday since the war started, after a month of raw, winter weather. Except during the Olympic Games, or the visit of Mussolini, when the city was all decked out, I've never seen so many people on the streets, especially women, children, and babies. They were all out sunning themselves, and except for the large number of men in uniform and the sight of people stopping to gaze at an anti-aircraft gun on some roof, there was little to indicate that a war was on.

Last night the inhabitants had a scare. The anti-aircraft batteries around Berlin started going off and searchlights scanned the skies. That was the first time the people of Berlin had heard any gun actually firing in this war, and many of them went out into the streets to listen. Some expected an air-raid alarm, but none was given. The High Command's communiqué today speaks of the sound of an airplane's motor having provoked some anti-aircraft fire. And tonight we're officially informed that it was a German plane which had got lost, and that it was shot down, but that the pilot escaped by parachute.

One aspect of the Berlin streets has changed since the war began. That is the almost total absence of motorcars in the streets. Because of the lack of gasoline, the great majority of people have had to store their cars. Even if you have a permit to run your car, you can only use it for important business. I can drive my car from my hotel to the studio here – a distance of five miles – because it's already past 1 a.m. in Berlin, the subways have stopped running, and it's the only way I can get home. But it's a strange sight to walk through the streets of the capital and sometimes not see a single automobile. But don't think the streets are any safer for pedestrians. Just the opposite. They are full of swarms of bicycles. As a pedestrian fighting for my life in the street, I'd take my chances with a car anytime to a bicycle. I still have a mark on my knee where the last bicycle hit me.

As to news here in Berlin, the papers still play up the sinking of the *Royal Oak*. For reasons not clear to me, the Monday morning papers play up America's reaction to the success of the German submarine, a reaction which we're told here was terrific. *Der Montag,* for instance has the following three-line banner-head on its front page: END OF THE ROYAL OAK – SENSATION IN USA – AMERICA SAYS ENGLAND'S SUPERIORITY AT SEA GREATLY ENDANGERED.

Berlin October 16, 1939 24.47

Good Evening. This is William L. Shirer in Berlin.

All the German papers play up tonight an official communiqué of the High Command announcing that the same German U-boat which sank the *Royal Oak* also torpedoed the British battleship *Repulse*. A few minutes ago I heard the British radio deny that the *Repulse* had been hit, but the German authorities stick to their story that it was.

Now, we had two official versions of the submarine attack on the *Repulse* here in Berlin today. The early afternoon papers which come out about 2 p.m. carried an official announcement from the High Command saying that the same submarine which sank the *Royal Oak* also torpedoed the battleship *Repulse*, severely damaged it, and put it out of action.

That was the first story. Then in the later editions, which came out in Berlin about 5 p.m., the High Command's communiqué was worded a bit differently. It said that the German U-boat attacked the *Repulse* and torpedoed it. But no more word about it having damaged the British ship or put it out of action.

We asked about this discrepancy in the Wilhelmstrasse tonight and were told that the second communiqué speaks for itself. In other words, that the German Naval Command insists that the *Repulse* was torpedoed, and you know what usually happens when a boat stops a torpedo.

Well, there the matter stands. It isn't very clear to me, but I give you the German version. Tomorrow, I'm told, the thing will be more fully explained.

The Germans also announce the shooting-down of one French and one British plane on the West Front. That reminds me that I traveled along the Rhine where it forms the border between Germany and France for several hours last week on my way to and from Switzerland, and I didn't see a single plane in the air. For hours we sped along within easy range of the French artillery, and often in view of French machine-gun nests, but not a shot. In fact, travelers told me there hadn't been a shot fired over the Rhine since the war began.

Berlin October 17, 1939 24.47

Good Evening. This is William L. Shirer in Berlin.

The hero of Germany tonight is one Lieutenant-Captain Prien, a typical, dare-devil German submarine commander, who returned with his U-boat to Germany today and recounted to his fellow countrymen the almost unbelievable story of how he got into the British naval base at

Scapa Flow and shot his torpedoes at some of Britain's greatest battleships.

A World War German submarine commander told me tonight that the Germans tried twice to get a U-boat into Scapa Flow during the last war, but both attempts failed and the submarines were lost.

Even German naval circles appear to have believed that a submarine had only one chance in a hundred of getting into Scapa Flow. But that one could get into it, blow up a battleship, and fire a torpedo at a second – as the Germans claim – and then get safely out of that formidable naval base, protected as it is by steel nets and mines, not to mention torpedo boats – why the Germans themselves didn't believe it possible.

That's why up in the German naval bases and also in Berlin tonight there's more of a feeling of victorious elation than you noticed when the German army walked over Poland.

The hero himself – Admiral Raeder, the German naval chief went up to the seaport himself to welcome him back and decorate him and his crew with Iron Crosses – the hero himself is a dark-blond, stocky little fellow just over thirty, married and father of one child. A few minutes ago he broadcast an account of his exploit and this is what he said –

That he sighted the boom protecting the entrance to Scapa Flow, studied it, then edged his submarine through it without mishap. Once inside he went to work immediately, he said. He took a quick glance around with his periscope, noticed a battleship in front of him and one behind, both lying at anchor, and loosed his torpedoes at once. Before he could dive to get away, he goes on, he saw by the battleship to the north of him a great fountain of water, followed by a fountain of flame. In the meantime, in the opposite direction, he observed that the ship to the south of him had exploded – he speaks of three explosions one after another and then the bridge, masts, guns and all went up in the air. "The ship burst to pieces like atoms," was the way he put it. This, he surmised, was the *Royal Oak*. As to the first ship, which he thinks was the *Repulse*, he says he observed as he was stealing out of the base, that the forward part was sinking into the water. And that's why he reported that the *Repulse* was, in his opinion, put out of action.

Having seen the damage, he says, he lost no time in edging his way through the boom and out into the open sea. The English, he said, apparently thought he was still in the harbor, as he could hear depth bomb discharges at a distance. Apparently no attempt was made to pursue him, and he got safely back to Germany this morning.

I understand photographs were taken this afternoon when German bombers raided Scapa Flow. Anyway, we've been promised a look at them shortly.

Berlin October 18, 1939 24.47

Good Evening. This is William L. Shirer in Berlin.

Berlin today gave a great welcome to Germany's latest heroes – the officers and crew of the submarine that stole into Scapa Flow and sank the British battleship, *Royal Oak.*

A bigger crowd than gathered before Herr Hitler's Chancellery the day the war began congregated there this morning to see them arrive. Herr Hitler himself dropped his other work and spent the noon hour entertaining the men of the submarine. He gave them a little talk, praising their blowing up of the *Royal Oak* as the greatest achievement in the history of German U-boats. When he had finished, he decorated the submarine commander, Captain Prien, with the highest decoration that Germany can give its military men – the Grand Cross of the Iron Cross. Yesterday officers and crew had been awarded the Iron Cross.

This afternoon, we foreign correspondents met the officers and men of the submarine after they'd lunched with the Führer. They marched into our afternoon press conference in the Wilhelmstrasse, and Captain Prien told us the story of his exploit, which was essentially that which I gave you last night.

I was struck by the extreme youth of the members of this crew who are certainly engaged in one of the world's most dangerous jobs. Most of them were boys of eighteen, nineteen, twenty – and though the comparison is not a good one, they reminded me of a college football team being banqueted after an unexpected defeat of a much more powerful opponent. They walked nonchalantly out of the room. They seemed to be youngsters without the shadow of fear and I suppose will set off on their next errand as nonchalantly as they left us today.

Dr. Diettrich, the Nazi press chief, introduced the crew to us in a speech in which he continually referred to Mr. Churchill as a liar. No mention was made of Mr. Churchill's tribute to the daring and the bravery of this German submarine crew and some of us wondered whether they had by any chance heard of this tribute from the enemy.

Berlin October 19, 1939 24.47

Good Evening. This is William L. Shirer in Berlin.

For the first time since the war began, the German High Command today made public a detailed report about just what has been happening on that strange and mysterious Western Front.

I know it doesn't agree exactly with what you've heard from the other side. But so that you may hear both sides, I give you the German version.

First of all, the report contends that nothing much at all has happened on the Western Front. Since September 9, says the communiqué, when the French opened their attack with outposts along a line running from Luxemburg to the Rhine, there has been no serious fighting anywhere. With one exception, the fighting on both sides was limited to small groups, usually less than a company strong.

The German report then explains that the French occupied German territory at three places: between Luxemburg and the town of Saarlautern, then south-west of Saarbrücken in the Warndt Forest, and finally south-east of Saarbrücken. Only in the last two sectors, according to the Germans, did the French penetrate as much as two to three miles. And with the exception of the area in front of Saarbrücken, close to the frontier, the French never really got close to the German West Wall fortifications, the report declares.

As to artillery fire, the communiqué goes on, it was as restricted as infantry action. And along the Rhine River where it forms the Franco-German border from Karlsruhe to Basle, there has been absolute quiet. I saw that sector myself last week, watched the French and German troops going about their business in full sight and range of each other, and I didn't hear a shot exchanged.

The German communiqué closes with a laconic paragraph that no British troops could be identified in the front line.

In other words, according to the Germans, all has been quiet on the Western Front.

Berlin October 29, 1939 01.01

Good Evening. This is William L. Shirer in Berlin.

Let's forget the war on the West Front and even the war in the North Sea – I really haven't any news tonight on these matters anyway – and take a peep into the lives of the people of Germany to see, for example, what they're reading and seeing and hearing nowadays.

Take books. What kind of books are they reading? You remember, a few years ago they burned some books in this country, and those books naturally are not to be found. But the bookstore windows are still full of books. I browsed around in some of those stores yesterday, and well, what do you think the best-selling novel is in Germany today?

You'll hardly believe me, because it's the very same book that was a best-seller in America not so long ago, *Gone With The Wind*. It's been translated into German under the title: *Vom Winde Verweht*, or if you translated absolutely literally in the peculiar German word-order: *From The Wind Blown About.* This American novel is almost as popular here as it was at home.

I asked a representative group of young Germans tonight what other novels were selling well, and they named two. The first one will also be familiar to you. It's Cronin's *Citadel,* and the fact that the author is an Englishman does not appear to have affected his popularity. The other novel is by a Norwegian author and is called: *The Worlds Sing Eternally.*

Note that all three novels are by foreign authors. As to non-fiction, these same Germans named five books very much in demand now:

The Colored Front – I give you the English translation of the German titles – an anonymous study of the white versus negro problem.

Look Up The Subject Of England – a propaganda book about England.

Der Totale Krieg – Ludendorff's famous book about Total War – very timely now.

Fifty Years Of Germany by Sven Hedin, the Swedish explorer and friend of Hitler.

That Is Poland by von Oertzen. Data on Poland and first published in 1928.

Three anti-Soviet books, I'm told, are still best-sellers, one especially which is called *Socialism Betrayed,* by a former German communist named Albrecht. Detective stories are also very popular in Germany just now, as are books about submarine and aerial warfare. And a friend told me that the only American magazine he could find at his news-stand today was one called *True Love Stories* – or something like that – October issue.

As to movies, two of the most popular new ones are: *Dawn,* a story about the German U-boats, and *D388,* a film about the German air force. Emil Jannings is playing in a picture called *Robert Koch.* Another popular German film is *Gold In New Frisco.* I notice Clark Gable in a picture called here *Adventure in China,* which is packing them in for the fourth week at the Marmorhaus.

The Berlin theaters, which seem to be doing a land-office business since the war started, feature a good many classical plays – Shakespeare, Goethe, and so on. Gerhard Hauptmann's new play, *The Daughter Of The Cathedral* and a play called *The Traitor* are among the season's hits.

At the State Opera tonight they played Wagner's *Valkyrie,* at the German Opera House *Il Trovatore,* and one theater is doing well with Johann Strauss's *Fledermaus.* The concert of the Philharmonic Orchestra under Furtwängler this morning was sold out a week in advance, and a repeat concert tomorrow is also sold out.

I can't quite make up my mind whether people are flocking to opera, plays, concerts as an escape. I only know they're flocking to them as never before.

117

Berlin October 30, 1939 02.05

Good Morning. This is William L. Shirer in Berlin.

My subject today – to begin with anyway – is soap, overshoes, and gasoline.

I bring the subject up not because I think you at home are especially interested in soap or overshoes or even gasoline, but because those things are big subjects right now here in Berlin, and I want to keep you informed on the big subjects.

First, about soap. The newspapers this morning tell me what I may expect in the way of soap for the month of November. I was just reading, for example, that the Reich's department for industrial fat supplies made known through Decree Number 24 which was published in the Official Gazette Number 251 on October 26, 1939, just what soap supplies might be available during November and later in return for the ration soap cards.

On November 1, I'm informed, I can take a section of my soap card on which are printed the words "One Piece of Uniform Soap B" and exchange it for a cake of so-called Uniform Soap weighing 80 grammes. For my laundry next month, I see I get 250 grammes of soap flakes or a double package of washing material, which undoubtedly is some kind of laundry soap. If I haven't drawn my big tube of shaving cream which must last me for four months, I can do it now, or get an equivalent amount of shaving soap.

The men of this country must either have put a little extra shaving soap away, or have taken to electric razors, because you see very few new beards around. In my own case, some kind listeners abroad have taken care of me very nicely in this connection.

About overshoes and rubbers. It's turned very cold and rainy here now, and a lot of people ordinarily wear them. Today we're officially informed that until the end of the year, just five persons in a hundred may buy new rubbers or overshoes, and the other ninety-five must either go without or use what they have on hand. As is only just, postmen, messengerboys, and newsboys will get the first call for rubbers and overshoes. No mention is made of professors being near the top of the list, though they're probably well up on it.

As to gasoline, I see that ration cards, Series M, are no longer good after tomorrow and we must get some new ones, which will be Series N. These, the newspapers say, will be issued only for those operating cars for "life-important needs". We're warned that even if we get the cards, we must not use our cars for private purposes, and especially not for driving to the movies or theaters or restaurants or to pay social visits. Even when you're on "life-important business", says the report, you must only use your car when it's impossible to get to where you're going by street-cars, buses, elevated or subways.

As to news, it seems very scarce here this morning. I was listening to the London radio a few minutes ago *[foreign correspondents in Germany were still allowed to listen to the BBC]* and heard reports of various air-raid alarms in England. I don't know how it is in the provinces, but we haven't had an alarm here in Berlin since the first week of the war. Some bombers flew over my window this morning, but they were German.

One German paper, and only one, the *Frankfurter Zeitung,* reports demonstrations in Prague Saturday on the occasion of the former Czech national holiday which commemorated the founding of the late republic. The report speaks of a few hundred people assembling on the chief square of Prague and says the crowd was broken up by Czech police. A few arrests, it adds, were made.

Berlin October 30, 1939 24.47

Good Evening. This is William L. Shirer in Berlin.

After a weekend of dead silence, two Berlin newspapers found space today to comment about the United States Senate's action in voting the lifting of the Embargo Bill. Two newspapers are a small minority of Berlin's press, but now that they've broken the ice, no doubt the others will follow.

Despite the undoubted importance of the repeal of our embargo law to Germany, the German press, in its news columns, published the Senate's action on it as a wholly unimportant little item of news, and no Berlin editorial writer ventured to touch it until today.

Now, the Nazi editorial comment is interesting, because it is at once bitter and yet – for these times – restrained. Also interesting is the fact that the editorial reaction of the Bolshevik press in Moscow to the Senate vote was published in the Berlin newspapers before their own comment. And as a matter of fact, the reaction of Berlin and Moscow is strikingly similar.

They both tell their readers that it is the so-called American cannon-kings and war-profiteers who've really been responsible for the first step in the lifting of the arms embargo. And that the great mass of the American people were against it.

A German reading his newspaper today, not only the German editorial comment but the quotations from the Moscow *Pravda* and *Isvestia,* which are prominently displayed, would certainly get the idea that our Senate had acted against the will of the majority of our people and that our naughty capitalists were mainly responsible for it. I find that German officials of the Wilhelmstrasse have no illusions about American opinion in regard to this war, but that the man in the street simply has no idea.

The bitter note is struck in an editorial in the *Börsen Zeitung*. It quotes an old speech of Senator Pittman in which he is reported to have spoken of the tragedy of America having lost its sons in the World War. The paper asks whether Senator Pittman, in pushing through the President's Neutrality Bill, has thought of the sons of another people who "must pay with their blood and their lives, which are still full of hope, as a result of the false prophets of the American munition makers."

The German press makes strange reading these days. There is no news of the war. Every day the High Command reports "All Quiet on the Western Front."

Berlin November 1, 1939 24.47

Good Evening. This is William L. Shirer in Berlin.

I'm afraid I can't arouse much interest by going through the German press with you tonight. When I bought a paper on the street tonight, the newsboy was almost apologetic. "No news tonight," he assured me.

"What about the war? There's a war on," I insisted.

"Strange kind of war, mister. No news," he said, but handed me the paper anyway.

As a matter of fact the German press tonight – and this holds for tomorrow morning's editions which I've just seen – continues to make the most of Mr. Molotov's speech in Moscow yesterday. Russia's moral support of Nazi Germany is certainly played for all it's worth here, as is of course the Soviet economic support which has been promised.

The two countries apparently are getting down to business on trade matters. In my hotel there must be fifty Soviet Russian gentlemen who are here to see what kind of German wares can be bought in return for all the fodder and raw materials which Moscow has promised Germany.

The Berlin press gives its readers the impression that Mr. Molotov's speech has had a terrific echo throughout the world and the very headlines which foreign papers put over the story this morning are taken here as editorial comment. For instance, one Copenhagen paper reported that Molotov emphasized that he considered the Western Powers as the aggressors. In the German press the reaction of Copenhagen is reported as: "The Western Powers Are the Aggressors" and you get the impression that that's what the Danes think, whereas it was merely what Mr. Molotov thought.

On the diplomatic front, it's worth mentioning that the German

Ambassadors in both Moscow and Rome are now on their way back to Berlin for consultations.

There is no mention in today's communiqué of the German High Command of a report I heard from outside today that the big German guns had at last opened fire today from the Siegfried Line. The German communiqué speaks merely of local artillery fire and scouting activities and, in a few places, a little action by shock-troops.

Yesterday we correspondents were assured here in Berlin that the German High Command does not consider what is now taking place on the Western Front as anything more than scouting activity, that is, keeping in contact with the enemy through patrols. A German spokesman emphasized that nothing serious had happened in the West yet.

No foreign correspondents are permitted at the front, though we're promised permission if the war really starts there. We hear about our colleagues on the other side all decked out in new uniforms, but we haven't had to buy any yet, fortunately, and we were allowed to cover what little we saw of the Polish war in our street clothes, which was all right with us.

Berlin November 2, 1939 24.47

Good Evening. This is William L. Shirer in Berlin.

The German High Command reports nothing doing on the Western Front except a little weak artillery fire. The German press reports sharp attacks in London against Chamberlain and that French workers and peasants are protesting against the war.

So perhaps it would be better if I reported on something which has not appeared in the German press yet – for instance, on the sudden death of the Anti-Comintern movement. Because so far as I can learn it is dead, and it died the day that Nazi Germany and Bolshevik Russia decided to bury the hatchet and actively cooperate. That was, as you know, just the other day.

The Anti-Comintern, though an international movement, was, in the main, a German Nazi movement. It had its headquarters here. It published a monthly magazine in German called the *Contra-Komintern*, it issued a great deal of anti-communist publicity in many languages, and here in Berlin it also maintained an Anti-Comintern museum to show you the horrors of international Bolshevism. I don't think you'd find that museum open if you visited Berlin today.

Of course, in one sense, the Anti-Comintern organization has not really gone out of business, it has merely changed enemies. Because we're informed here that the organization will remain intact, only from now on it will be directed not against World-Bolshevism, but against the Jews.

Its magazine, the *Contra-Komintern*, which did not appear in September, as scheduled, is slated to come out this month under a new title, the editors having ascertained that Germany's real enemies are not after all the Bolsheviks, but Jews.

I understand that the editors have explained this little change in a letter to the subscribers. They say: "Behind all the enemies of Germany's ascendancy stand those who demand our encirclement, the oldest enemies of the German people and of all healthy, rising nations – the Jews."

The editors further declare that they will continue to have the support of the highest government circles, as they did when they were fighting the Bolsheviks, and that the new magazine will strive "To lead our foreign friends and co-workers in the service of this common goal." That is to say, anti-semitism.

I have here a copy of the August number of *Contra-Komintern,* which came out about the time Herr von Ribbentrop made his first journey to Moscow. Its leading article is entitled: "The Bolshevik Offensive against the World" and it attacks the Western countries for considering an alliance with Russia and thereby allowing Communism to penetrate into Western Europe.

Another article in the same number reviews a book just published in Berlin, called *Can Soviet Russia Evolve into a National State?* And the reviewer heartily agrees with the answer of the author when he gives an "unconditional No" to his own question.

But of course that was all published in August, and it's November now.

Berlin November 3, 1939 24.47

Good Evening. This is William L. Shirer in Berlin.

Don't think that the House action on the Embargo Bill, with all its consequences for Germany, is the big story from America in Berlin today. I thought it would be, but it's not.

The news that gets the big headlines in Germany tonight is not the voting in the lower house of Congress yesterday but a New York dispatch about the British liner *Culmore.*

Tomorrow morning Berlin papers will appear with great headlines over the story, running like this: AMERICAN PRESS VICTIMS OF BRITISH SWINDLE – SOS CALL OF THE BRITISH STEAMER CULMORE – FAIRY STORY ABOUT ATTACK BY GERMAN U-BOAT.

122

As a matter of fact the German government issued an official statement today denying that a German submarine was in the vicinity and calling the whole affair a "shameful falsification of the British Ministry of Lies" – as the British Ministry of Information is always referred to.

And then after this sensational story, if you looked hard, or had some magnifying glasses, you might find a tiny item in the German papers headed: ARMS EMBARGO LIFTED – VOTE OF THE HOUSE OF REPRESENTATIVES – UNNEUTRAL AND SHABBY.

Unneutral and shabby. That headline which will appear in tomorrow's *Völkischer Beobachter* is the only editorial slant which will appear in the German press tomorrow morning. No editorial will be published, and it will probably be some days before the German people are given a chance to realize that, just as in 1914, the great industrial resources of the United States are to be put at the disposal of Great Britain and France.

That it is a blow to Germany, no one in the Wilhelmstrasse denies. But for some reason it is not today, at least, being presented to the German people as such, which explains perhaps why a comparatively unimportant story about the steamer *Culmore* is played up as the really important news from America tonight.

It is only fair to add that from the very beginning I found that the Wilhelmstrasse had no illusions about the lifting of our arms embargo. However little Berlin may have thought about it on September 1, when the so-called counter-attack against Poland began, in recent weeks it has accepted what our Congress has now done as a foregone conclusion. It has tried to discount, or at least face the consequences, and this was one of the reasons why Russia was pressured for all the economic help it could give.

The other night in Berlin a man took advantage of the blackout to snatch a lady's handbag containing ten dollars. Today he was tried. He got a death sentence.

Berlin November 5, 1939 15.01

Good Morning. This is William L. Shirer in Berlin.

The war gets into its third month today and the people of this country have pretty well given up the idea, I think, that it's to be a short war. It wasn't very long ago when almost every German I know not only hoped, but really thought that the war would be over by Christmas. That hope has proved unfounded, and so now the people seem to be settling down grimly for a long struggle, though just what kind of a war it's to be, and how and where it's to be fought, still puzzles most people.

This morning, if you'd been in Berlin, you'd have noticed that every man, woman and child in the streets carried on his coat a little miniature Germanic dagger or sword. It was a sign of charity – a proof that they had given a dime or a quarter or even more to the Wartime Winter Relief Fund. All day yesterday and today, swarms of uniformed S.S. and S.A. men circulated through the streets, confronting pedestrians with a little tin collection box. You put in your 50 pfennigs or a mark, and the young, uniformed men pinned a dagger on your coat lapel.

I looked around to see how the women would take to the idea of having a little dagger pinned on their coat, but they took to it the same as the men. And in the *D.A.Z.* this morning, I see in the account of yesterday's collections that the German reporter remarks: "The women also quite voluntarily decorated themselves with these weapons."

On the big squares military bands played to help drum up pfennigs for the collection. On some of the squares you saw exhibits of captured Polish guns. If you took a close look, you were expected to put a few extra pfennigs into the collection box.

On my way here to the studio I noticed some enthusiasts had their coat lapels covered with daggers, but I did not see a man, woman or child, without at least one. And one newspaper reminded its readers this Sabbath morning that in the early days of German history, the dagger was a very useful weapon and that not only German men carried them in those days, but German women too.

There is absolutely no news about the war in the Berlin newspapers this morning. As a matter of fact there hasn't been for some ten days now. Instead, the German press has concentrated on telling its readers about the bad state of affairs in France and Great Britain. This morning, the press takes a little bit different line. With one accord every single Berlin newspaper today bannerlines on its front page an identically worded story stating that England shamefully violated every tenet of international law by jailing staff members of the German consulate at Glasgow when the war broke out, even twenty hours before it broke out.

This story admits that the Germans jailed officers of the British Consulate in Hamburg, including two women, but says it was only as a counter-measure to what the British had done, and that the arrested English people were treated nicely anyway.

Berlin November 7, 1939 24.47

Good Evening. This is William L. Shirer in Berlin.

I had a chat with Field Marshal Göring tonight. I just happened to run into him, with some of my American colleagues, but you'd never guess where.

At the Soviet Embassy of all places, and the occasion was the annual reception in celebration of the Bolshevik Revolution. There, amidst the glittering decorations and furniture left over from Czarist Russia, but with the portrait of Lenin smiling down upon us, General Göring stood sipping a beer and smoking a long, stogey cigar, and chatted informally with us.

I thought he'd be pretty peeved at America selling thousands of airplanes to the Allies, and so we asked him about that. But he didn't act peeved. Instead, he kidded us about our capacity to build them.

"Can Germany build as many planes per month as America?" we asked him.

"If we could only make them at your rate of production, we'd be very weak," he retorted, and added: "I mean that seriously." He thought our planes were good, but that we didn't make them fast enough.

"Well, will Germany deliver a mass attack in the air before these thousands of American planes are delivered to the Allies?" we asked. He laughed, as if to say no, and then said:

"You build your planes, and our enemies theirs, and we'll build ours, and maybe one day you'll see who's been building the best and the most planes."

And then the conversation went on like this:

Question: What do you think of the general situation?

Answer: Very favorable to Germany.

Question: So far your air force has only attacked British warships. Why?

Answer: Warships are very important objects, and they give us good practice.

Question: Are you going to begin bombing enemy ports?

Answer: We're humane.

For some reason that drew a hearty laugh, to which General Göring retorted: "You shouldn't laugh. I'm serious. I *am* humane."

Then a question: The French say they're shooting down a lot of your planes . . .

Answer: We don't deny we lose a plane now and then. But if they're shooting down as many as they say, I know they're not ours.

So much for my talk with Field Marshal Göring.

Berlin November 8, 1939 24.47

Good Evening. This is William L. Shirer in Berlin.

That tiny fragment of hope for peace which was held out yesterday by the offer of the sovereigns of the Netherlands and Belgium to mediate appears hopelessly lost and forgotten in Europe tonight.

Adolf Hitler, in an unexpected speech in a Munich beerhouse tonight on the anniversary of his 1923 beerhouse Putsch, did not even mention it. But he did reveal to the German people that on that tense Sunday two months ago when Great Britain declared war, he ordered Field Marshal Göring to prepare for *five years* of conflict.

It was a sudden, unadvertised speech. Not a line had appeared in the papers about it, and officials in the Wilhemstrasse only knew about it an hour before it took place. It was broadcast by all German radio stations, but it was not transmitted abroad by the German short-wave stations or offered, as is usually the case, for transmission to America. That indicated it was for home consumption. After Hitler finished, it was announced that the nation-wide broadcast which Rudolf Hess, his deputy, was scheduled to make tomorrow in Munich, had been canceled.

A long war, perhaps. A war to the bitter end until Germany wins. And a savage, biting attack on Britain. That was Hitler's message tonight. I have heard nearly all his speeches in recent years, but never one so bitter against England as tonight. Said the Führer: "The British think they're Rome and we Carthage. We'll show them it's the reverse!"

You get the point? You remember how Carthage – the greatest naval and commercial power of the ancient world – was utterly destroyed by Rome?

"I can assure you," Hitler said, "that England will never win this second war against us." Here, his audience in the Munich beer cellar interrupted him with delirious yells of applause.

"England is now up against a different Germany," he went on, "and will soon realize it. England doesn't want peace. We heard that from Lord Halifax yesterday. We will now speak to England in terms which she understands."

You get those words "soon" and "now"? Because Hitler seemed to confirm an impression we're all getting here in Berlin – that something is going to break in this war soon. And that it'll be something directed against England. Without saying so exactly, Field Marshal Göring when he talked to a few of us American correspondents last night, gave us the same impression. He seemed to hint that Germany might strike before all those American planes ever get to England and France.

People in the street seem to feel that here. One said to me tonight: "We'll all be living in the cellars soon."

126

After promising Germany certain victory, Hitler closed on a strange note. He said he thought that Providence was on Germany's side. He thought it had been in Poland. Without the help of Providence – I think he was referring to the perfect weather – Germany never could have conquered Poland so fast.

Berlin November 9, 1939 14.03

Good Morning. This is William L. Shirer in Berlin.

Who tried to get Herr Hitler last night when he made an unexpected appearance in a Munich beerhouse to celebrate the anniversary of his 1923 Munich beerhouse Putsch? Who planted the bomb that missed him by only fifteen minutes, and killed eight of his faithful Old Guard party members, and wounded more than fifty others?

The German Secret Police, under the orders of Heinrich Himmler, have been working all night to find out, but so far there is no information that they've found the perpetrator of last night's bombing – the first officially ever reported in Germany against Chancellor Hitler – or are even on his trail.

At any rate, the unprecedented reward of half a million marks has been offered to anyone who can find the assassin.

Herr Hitler himself returned to Berlin today from Munich by special train. When I passed the Chancellery this morning, I thought there were more guards there than usual, but you could still walk along the sidewalk which passes the building where Hitler lives. At night, during the blackout, of course, you have to take the other side of the street.

The list of dead and injured was kept secret throughout the night, but this noon was made known. There are no prominent Nazi officials among the dead or wounded. Apparently, most of them left the Bürgerbräu beercellar with Hitler last night when he hurried away to board his Berlin-bound train.

That was about 9:10 p.m., and the explosion, so far as we can learn, occurred at 9:21. Hitler himself had quite unexpectedly gone to Munich yesterday, and at 8 o'clock had addressed the Old Guard of the Party in the historic Munich beerhouse where his 1923 Putsch began. So sudden was the decision, that the Wilhelmstrasse only knew of the speech an hour before it took place. It was broadcast throughout Germany, and I remember looking at my watch as I sat in my hotel room listening to the broadcast. It was just 9:05 when Hitler finished his speech, a biting attack on England, a revelation that it might be a five years war, and hints that something would start to break soon in this war.

Usually Hitler sits around at this anniversary meeting far into the night and chats with his old comrades of the early days, over the beers. Last night, for the first time, he decided not to remain but to hurry back to Berlin where he has been having a series of conferences with his military advisers.

The bomb that went off at 9:21 had been planted in the empty attic of the Bürgerbräu Keller. I've drunk beer there often. It's a rambling old building, with the main beer hall some 150 feet by a hundred feet. It was a heavy bomb, because it ripped open the ceiling, and most of the people were killed or injured, I believe, not by the force of the explosion or by splinters, but by the ceiling which collapsed on them. You must picture that this small hall was jammed by nearly a thousand people. Apparently there was no panic, and part of the hall which was not damaged remained lighted, so that those not hurt could immediately begin helping rescue the injured who lay moaning under the smoking debris.

Actually, the very spot where Hitler had been standing when he made his hour long speech was buried in six feet of debris, the bomb having been planted in the attic directly above the rostrum. Had it taken place fifteen minutes earlier, officials here believe, the Führer would almost certainly have been killed.

The Nazi press promises a terrible vengeance to those who were responsible for the attempt on Hitler's life. As the *Völkischer Beobachter* puts it, these enemies of the state will henceforth receive no mercy. They will be ruthlessly done away with.

The papers admit that the perpetrators have not yet been found, but already are assuring the German public that the deed was of course the work of the famous British Secret Service, and that the enemies of the state who did it were only agents in British pay. And behind them, state the papers with one accord, were the British war agitators, and "their criminal helpers, the Jews".

The Jewish people in Germany already suffered terrible repression last year as the result of the killing of a German diplomat in Paris. Will they get it now?

Berlin November 9, 1939 24.47

Good Evening. This is William L. Shirer in Berlin.

The men who planted the bomb that missed killing Adolf Hitler and most of the other Nazi leaders by just twelve minutes in a Munich beerhouse last night have not yet been found.

Arrests of suspects are going on, and this afternoon, Heinrich

128

Himmler, chief of the Secret Police, who returned to Berlin last night with Herr Hitler, went back to Munich to lead the investigation.

The newspapers admit that the perpetrators are not yet known. And yet in the same breath – and with one accord – they tell the German people tonight, in a language more inflamed than any I've seen in this war yet, that whoever did the actual deed, the real perpetrator was England. Britain herself is blamed for this attempt on Hitler's life.

As the *Nachtausgabe* puts it, "The explosion in Munich was an attack by England on the German people."

And then the German papers quote Mr. Chamberlain as having stated in Parliament on the day war was declared that he hoped to live to see the day that Hitler was destroyed. But did Mr. Chamberlain ever say that? Not according to the American press. I looked up that speech tonight in the *Herald Tribune* and what Mr. Chamberlain said, according to that paper, was that he hoped to see the day that Hitler-*ism* was destroyed. What a difference! But the fact that every Berlin paper omits that little syllable "ism", and thus makes it out that Mr. Chamberlain preached the destruction of Herr Hitler personally – as almost happened last night – will give you an idea of the tone of the German press tonight.

And now, conclude the German newspapers tonight, England will receive the answer she deserves, and it will be given without mercy. In neutral circles it was asked tonight: Does that mean that Germany is about to launch a mass air-attack against England? No one knows the answer, but we all have the feeling here that something is in the air.

As the official statement today put it, Hitler last night escaped by a miracle. It now seems clear that the bomb was hidden in a pillar directly back of the rostrum from which he spoke. The pillar, a balcony, and the ceiling collapsed just where he had been standing and buried the spot in nine feet of debris.

And it was only through a last minute change of plans that he was not standing there orating when the bomb burst. In past years, he had begun his speech at 8:30 and finished at 10. Last night, desiring to hurry back to Berlin for important talks, he began at 8 and finished at 9:05. At 9:21 the bomb went off. I might add that the radio announcer I'd heard describing the meeting just before Hitler entered was killed.

It was the third bombing in Germany since the war started. A month ago, one was thrown into the Air Ministry and a second into Secret Police headquarters in Berlin.

Among the diplomats who called at the Chancellery today and signed the book, was the American chargé d'affaires, Mr. Alexander Kirk.

Berlin November 11, 1939 14.05

Good Morning. This is William L. Shirer in Berlin.

Armistice morning – can you remember that morning twenty-one years ago? If you were at the front – the relief, the bewildered relief. And if you were home, the almost insane joy, the dancing in the streets, the feeling that we all were witnessing the dawn of a new day in which, after the bloody war to end war, there would be no more armed conflict.

We were wrong. After only twenty-one years, most of the world is at war again, with even finer instruments of destruction than we had the last time, and with new hates threatening to outdo those we knew two decades ago.

There is no mention in the German press this morning of this twenty-first anniversary of the Armistice. As you know, this day was never celebrated as a holiday in Germany. Just the opposite. It was a day to be forgotten, to be ignored, a day that recalled the great defeat, and the black days of foreign occupation and semi-starvation that followed.

I suppose at that, that many Germans when they noticed this morning, glancing at their calendar or newspapers, that it was November 11, remembered the day, and perhaps wondered what the next Armistice would bring. Peace certainly – but victory or defeat? Judging from my talks with Germans – and yesterday I spent the entire day in the country talking with farmers in the field – most Germans hope and think – and who doesn't – that this time they will win. Herr Hitler has told them so, has told them that victory is certain, and many believe it.

Three hours ago – at 11:00 a.m. German time – the state funeral for the victims of the explosion that almost killed Herr Hitler in the Bürgerbräu beer cellar in Munich Wednesday night, was held. The Führer himself journeyed back to Munich for the ceremony which took place at the Feldherrnhalle, the very spot where sixteen years ago the first followers of Hitler lost their lives, when the police put down his so-called Beer House Putsch.

I've just been listening to the nationwide broadcast of the state funeral. Herr Hitler, though he was present, did not speak. The funeral oration was delivered by Rudolf Hess, his deputy, and it was one of the most bitter funeral orations I've ever heard. When it was over, the Führer paused to speak a word with the mourning families of the dead.

The German secret police – the Gestapo as it's known here – have not yet found the perpetrators of the bombing that missed snuffing out Hitler's life Wednesday evening by a few minutes.

And yet, as you know, England is already being accused of the deed in a newspaper campaign the like of which I've never seen before, even in this country. To a neutral observer here not the slightest proof has yet been published to suggest how England could have been responsible for what happened. And yet the *12-Uhr Blatt* smears all over its front page this noon a personal accusation against Mr. Chamberlain. The paper contends that the British Prime Minister is not only the spiritual author of the deed but the direct instigator of it. And just to give you an idea of the tone of the articles which the German people are given to read today, I'll quote the first paragraph of the piece:

"Herr Chamberlain! You are today invited before the forum of World Opinion to answer the most frightful accusation ever made against a European statesman." Then Mr. Chamberlain is accused of the crime, and then follow what the paper terms thirty points in evidence. One of the points is an alleged quotation from Mr. Chamberlain's speech on September 3 in which he's quoted as saying that he wished to live to see the day when Hitler was destroyed. As I already pointed out Thursday night, I looked that speech up in our own American papers and found that Mr. Chamberlain said not that he wished to see Hitler destroyed, but Hitler-*ism*. Quite a difference. Another of the thirty points is an alleged quotation from a Reuter dispatch after the explosion in which the official British agency is quoted as saying: "The first bomb against the German dictator has exploded, but many more will follow." Now I heard that dispatch over the radio from London, and the statement came not from Reuter, but was merely a Reuter quotation of a broadcast said to have been made by the so-called Freedom transmitter. The words were those of the transmitter, not of Reuter's.

Well, so it goes, and there's no doubt that this press campaign is stirring up terrific hatred of England. The police announced that more than 1,000 depositions have been made by people claiming to know something about the origin of the explosion.

Berlin November 12, 1939 15.01

Good Morning. This is William L. Shirer.

Today in Germany is another one of those One-Pot Sundays, or as the Germans call it, *Eintopfsonntag*. That is, for lunch today everybody had to eat a one-pot meal – a sort of a stew – and give the difference between the cost of that and a regular Sunday dinner to the Winter Relief Fund.

I notice today, though, that the newspapers no longer call it One-Pot Sunday, but the Sunday of Sacrifice, or in German, *Opfersonntag* – *Opfer* meaning sacrifice. I assume that's what it's to be called while the war lasts.

Speaking of food – and you're reminded of it after you've consumed your one-pot lunch – you see, over here it's just 3 p.m. now and we've all just finished lunch – the German government has certainly taken care of the foreign correspondents nicely. If the way to a foreign correspondent's heart leads through his stomach – well, anyway, here's the way it is:

Besides the regular ration cards which entitle the correspondents to the same amount of food as is given the average German citizen – a pound of meat, a quarter of a pound of butter per week, and so on, the foreign journalists also receive from the government extra cards which in fact double their ration of food every week. Thus they get two pounds of meat a week, a half pound of butter, and so on. As a matter of fact, the correspondents now get as much to eat as those few Germans who get extra rations because of heavy labor. And if you kid the correspondents about their extra food cards, they'll tell you that they are performing heavy labor these days, and I agree with them. If long hours – sometimes sixteen hours a day – and nerve-wracking work constitute heavy labor, then they're doing it.

As for news, the German press still continues to play up today the explosion in Munich that occurred so soon after Herr Hitler and the other Nazi leaders left their Munich beer cellar last Wednesday night. Most of the papers headline the announcement of the Secret Police last night that preparations for the bombing began last August and that suspicion points to a worker who was doing repair work on the premises. And foreign allegations that maybe the Nazis did the deed themselves are refuted in the newspapers as a gross insult to the German people. Further, as you know by this time, England and the famous British Secret Service, and even Mr. Chamberlain, are held to be really responsible for what happened.

One story that is not in the Berlin newspapers these days is that about German troop concentrations on the Dutch border and the special defense measures which the Dutch have been taking.

The foreign correspondents yesterday, and especially those from the Amsterdam newspapers, did their best yesterday at the press conference in the Wilhelmstrasse to obtain a categorical denial from the German government about the alleged situation on the Dutch border. It may be significant that a categorical denial could not be obtained here. The Wilhelmstrasse declined to give it. It did point out that Germany had promised to respect the neutrality of the Netherlands, but it added that information on military matters was not the business of the Wilhelmstrasse and therefore that no comment on military measures could be given. No wonder then that the correspondents left the press conference considerably disturbed, especially the Dutch newspaperman.

And then there was an article in the *Deutsche Allgemeine Zeitung* which hinted that Germany did not consider the invasion of England as impossible by any means. "The future will teach," said the article, "whether an island denuded of much of its military striking power cannot be taken."

We may be wrong, but most of us observers here in Berlin feel that something is in the wind, and that this present calm may well be only the well-known calm before the storm.

Berlin November 13, 1939 24.47

Good Evening. This is William L. Shirer in Berlin.

However puzzling this war may be to the German people, it's going to be brought home to them in a very personal way before this month is up. Within the next couple of weeks they will receive their ration cards for clothes and textiles. I suspect quite a few people are going to get a shock.

I have one of these cards here before me now. It's good for just a year. Let's take a look at it, and see how a person like myself can make out in the way of new clothing during the next twelve months.

I have quite a choice, and here's one I could make. From December 1st until next April 1st, I could buy: two pairs of socks, two handkerchiefs, one muffler, and a pair of gloves. Then from April 1st until September 1st, I could obtain one shirt, two collars and a suit of underwear. And for the rest of the year until December 1st, I could buy just two neckties and one undershirt.

You might wonder if two pairs of socks are enough for a man for a whole year, and I wonder myself, but I see here that if you really need more socks, you can get as many as five pairs, by saving on, say, underwear, or neckties, though of course it would be hard going without that one suit of underwear every year.

Fortunately, I bought a new overcoat last year, but supposing I hadn't. Well, I see here if you give up three-fifths of your year's card, you can have an overcoat, but then you've got to give up a lot of other things. With only two-fifths of your card left, you can only buy during the next twelve months, one vest, a muffler, a pair of gloves, a necktie, two handkerchiefs, and a couple of pairs of socks. I guess if you get an overcoat, you'll have to do without underwear. You see, you have a nice big choice, but there are a lot of things you'll have to do without.

Well, I do hope we have a nice, warm winter over here in Germany.

I see there are separate cards for men, for women, for boys, for girls, and for tots between two and three. Except for the babies, the cards are divided into one hundred units – the babies get only seventy-five. Socks or stockings, for example, cost you five units each. But five pairs are all you can have in one year – I imagine that'll be a little hard on the women, and if you, in fact, buy more than three pairs annually you are penalized for the last two pairs – you have to give eight units for each instead of five units. A pair of pyjamas costs you thirty units alone – almost a third of your year's card – but you can save five units if you buy a night-gown instead. I can picture 80 million Germans going back to night-gowns. That saves them a total of 400 million units.

These ration cards for clothing fascinate me, and I wish I had more time to go into them with you. They make a wonderful argument to stay out of war, if one were needed. I might add that if you lose your card you're out of luck. We are warned there will be no replacements. According to Nazi officials, these cards entitle Germans to about as much clothing as the average German worker could buy in a year.

This leaves me no time for other news, but there is none. We're still guessing about the much advertised German offensive, when it'll begin, where it'll strike. But the German High Command keeps its secret well, and not more than a dozen men in Germany know what the next move will be, and where. The only thing that everyone seems to agree on, is that some move is coming soon.

Berlin November 14, 1939 24.47

Good Evening. This is William L. Shirer in Berlin.

Adolf Hitler has answered the Queen of the Netherlands and the King of the Belgians. The text of his reply to their offer of mediation was given to the diplomatic representatives of the two countries in Berlin at noon today. The formal note itself will be handed over to the respective sovereigns in Brussels and The Hague by the German envoys in those two capitals late tonight or tomorrow.

What's in the German reply we don't yet know. But it's assumed in well-informed quarters in Berlin that it will be negative, that Herr Hitler will point out that his conditions for peace were made known in his Reichstag speech, and that this speech was rejected in London and Paris.

It seems pretty evident here that, given the present mood of the belligerents, there is not a chance of coaxing them to the peace table. For example, I can find no evidence at all in Nazi circles that they would give up Austria, the Czech Protectorate, and a big slice of Poland for the sake of peace by Christmas. Not this Germany.

The Berlin papers play up tonight the German air-raid on the Shetland Islands. No mention is made that bombs fell on British soil for the first time. The Germans merely claim that their planes sank two British seaplanes and may have hit a British cruiser. As usual, the Germans report no losses of their own.

This morning, all Berlin papers published a list of twenty-eight British and five French passenger liners which they claim had been armed. Among the ships were the *Queen Mary,* the *Aquitania,* the *Mauretania,* the *Georgic,* and the *De Grasse.*

Now, why was this list suddenly published? We made inquiries in official quarters today, and the answer seems to be that in the future German U-boats will adopt more rigorous methods in sinking enemy shipping. The Germans deny that they've given orders to sink vessels without warning, but they claim that arming merchant vessels is against international law and that Germany is therefore justified in sharpening its U-boat methods. We couldn't get any German authority today to define what "sharpening" meant – but maybe we'll soon see. As one German in high quarters put it to me today: "We would recommend neutral citizens not to travel on the armed passenger ships in that list."

Berlin November 18, 1939 14.00

Good Morning. This is William L. Shirer in Berlin.

This war is getting grim.

Yesterday nine young Czechs, students in the University of Prague, were lined up before a German firing squad and executed. This piece of news was the first intimation we had here last night that there had been any special trouble in Prague at all. The German dispatch that told of the summary execution of the nine young Czech university students – from the German version it appears as though they were shot without trial – mentioned that there had been student demonstrations, and that those demonstrators who had not been shot, had been arrested, and that Prague University had been closed for three years.

The German University in Prague, which only a fortnight ago was taken over by the Reich government though it lies in the capital of the Protectorate, of course will remain open. Germans in the Protectorate will continue to get a university education in Prague, but not Czech students.

Commenting on the executions, authoritative circles this noon stated that special measures were necessary in wartime, and that there could be "no joking in wartime".

We have no details of the student demonstrations in Prague. One can only assume that they must have been serious for the German authorities to immediately shoot nine of the student leaders. It would be interesting to know, incidentally, if, in the twenty odd years that the three million Sudeten Germans lived under Czech rule after the World War, a single German was shot for taking part in a demonstration.

There have been further executions in Germany itself of men who are described in the German press as traitors, and even of some who were not accused of treason but of acting contrary to state interests. Yesterday two young Germans, aged twenty-six and twenty-nine, were executed for treason, the charge being that they gave information to a foreign power. They were both workers. One of their comrades, it was stated, had already been executed.

And then at Augsburg yesterday, two youths aged nineteen were sentenced to death for having committed a theft in the home of a soldier. As you know, theft during the blackout at night is punishable by death, as is any action these days calculated to hinder Germany's war effort.

And now let's turn to Poland. It's announced that Dr. Frank, the German civil governor of occupied Poland – that is the part of Poland which the Germans have not actually incorporated into the territories of the Reich – has issued a decree making labor obligatory for all Poles capable of doing any work.

Any Pole who refuses to work or tries to prevent other Poles from working will be severely punished. An inspired German statement today claims that in the past, under their old government, the Polish people really never knew what work is. But that now that the Germans are masters, the Polish people will be taught how to work. The statement explains that the Poles will be put to work, quote, "doing away with the traces of the war for which they shared the guilt with the English."

Yesterday, the small neutral countries, especially Belgium, received a sharp warning in the German press against playing England's game by submitting to its contraband control. Today, the United States of America receives in the German press – well it's not exactly a warning, because you don't warn the big fellows – but let's say a rebuke for permitting our airplanes to be flown over the line into Canada. The *Lokal Anzeiger* not only scores what it terms our war-profiteers but also our government for permitting what it calls the smuggling of American war planes over the Canadian border.

"Dirty smuggling," cries the paper, "is doubly dirty when the Government itself engages in it."

This reminds me of a newsreel I saw here this week depicting an American-style show of new hats. I'm no judge but I thought the hats looked rather nice. The German announcer, however, thought he discerned Jewish influence and moreover he thought these new American hats showed the bad taste of Americans.

Berlin November 18, 1939 24.46

Good Evening. This is William L Shirer in Berlin.

The executions of Czechs in the Protectorate of Bohemia and Moravia continue. Today, the Germans announce that they have shot three more Czechs, two of them policemen. The offense? They are accused of having attacked a German. That brings the number of Czechs executed in the last two days up to twelve.

In the Wilhelmstrasse today Nazi circles informed us quite bluntly that now that Germany was at war and fighting for its existence, it would, as a matter of course, take stern measures not only with the Czechs but also with the Poles if there was the slightest attempt to break down "law and order", as the expression goes.

As I mentioned this morning, a new German decree makes labor obligatory for all Poles in occupied Poland. We're told here this means that all Poles not actually working will be put to work, mostly restoring the devastated areas. Jews, it was added, regardless of what they're doing now, will be put to work at manual jobs. One of the familiar sights when you drive through Poland now is road-gangs made up of Polish Jews, laboring away on the roads or at nearby rock piles, and guarded by Nazi police.

Meantime, we understand here, plans are going ahead for the establishment of a great ghetto area around Lublin, in Poland, to which not only Polish Jews but also German Jews will be sent. The first contingents already have been sent there. How these Jews are to exist, we don't know, but the government promises us information on the whole subject one of these days.

As to war news, the High Command reports today that three British planes tried to attack Wilhelmshaven, the great German naval base, but were driven off before they could drop any bombs. I heard the British report that the planes were merely scouting machines, and had taken photographs, but we have no information on that here. The High Command also announces that German planes flew over the entire area of France yesterday. No losses are mentioned.

Everyone in Berlin continues to speculate as to where and when the German offensive in the West will start. Herr Hitler and Field Marshal Göring continue to confer with their generals and admirals every day, but their conferences are not public and the truth is that we don't know where the next blow will fall and when, or even if it's been decided upon. All we know is that something seems likely to break before long.

You may be interested to know how the decision of the Allied Supreme War Council yesterday to pool the economic resources of France and Britain is being presented in the German press tonight. The papers tell their readers it's simply a move to put France entirely under the control of Great Britain. It's painted as a catastrophe for France, almost as though France had lost her independence.

I'd like to mention that Mr. Beach Conger, Berlin correspondent to the *New York Herald Tribune*, left this country today, about a month after arriving. The Nazi government alleged that a recent dispatch of his was misleading and not factual. Mr. Conger stuck by what he had written. Result: his facilities for getting his story to his paper were withdrawn and he had no other choice but to leave, which he did today. Most of his American colleagues saw him off at the station today, and there were flowers for Mrs. Conger, his wife.

Berlin November 19, 1939 15.01

Good Morning. This is William L. Shirer in Berlin.

Today we go into the twelfth week of the war, and in Germany, as I suppose elsewhere, the people are wondering what the winter will bring. In Berlin the rumors fly thick and fast about a coming offensive in the West, or about a mass air attack on England, or about other possible moves. We've had them for a month now, these rumors, and yet nothing has happened so far.

For almost two months there has been practically no military action on land, on the sea or in the air. That puzzles people in this country who, with their wonderful, mechanized army, see war largely as a measuring of military power. The last few days, though, I notice that the German press refers more often to the fact that this too is a gigantic economic struggle. The argument is used to convince the people of the necessity of working harder and rationing the available supplies of food, clothing, and fuel.

It would be a mistake, however, to think that Germany will accept the Allied challenge to fight this war largely on the economic front. Certainly, that is just the kind of a war in which the Reich would be at a disadvantage, and that's one of the reasons why most people here expect military action of some kind very soon now. And yet I think the German people are now becoming reconciled to a long war. I remember most of the Germans I know were quite sure two months ago that the war would be over by Christmas. Now they are sure it won't be.

And to harden the people to it, the papers keep repeating what Great Britain would do to Germany and Germans in case of victory. In a front-page editorial this morning the *Völkischer Beobachter*, official Nazi organ, tells its readers that England's aim is not only the destruction of Germany, but the enslavement of the German people. And the

138

Frankfurter Zeitung, also in a front-page editorial this morning, tells its public that Britain's only wish is to inflict a peace treaty much worse than Versailles.

I think that line will be played up a great deal here. And, as the Führer has said, if you repeat a thing often enough, people end up by believing it.

The Berlin press plays up today a second list of twenty-nine British and three French passenger ships which have been armed, and warns that passengers on such boats are playing with their lives. The arming of those ships, it is stated, has made necessary the sharpening of Germany's U-boat war. The fact that British armed merchant vessels have fired on German submarines greatly angers the German press. The German view – if I understand it correctly – is that for an armed merchant vessel to fire on a German U-boat is a deceitful thing, and that the correct and legal thing for them to do is not to fire, but to submit to the submarines without resistance.

It was interesting last night to hear the German short-wave stations, which blanket the earth for twenty-four hours a day with their powerful transmitters, enlisting in their service none other than Mr. Bernard Shaw. The most recent of his letters was read by a German speaker and what Mr. Shaw had to say about this war sounded very good to German ears.

Berlin November 20, 1939 01.15

Good Evening. This is William L. Shirer in Berlin.

For the first time since this strange war began, the German High Command today reports lively machine-gun and rifle fire at one place on the Upper Rhine Front. That may turn out to be more important than it sounds.

The so-called Upper Rhine Front is that section where the River Rhine forms the border between France and Germany. It runs roughly for about 110 miles from Karlsruhe down to the Swiss frontier at Basle. Though not very wide, the Rhine is swift and deep in this part and would be very difficult for a big army to cross if it had any opposition at all. It is this natural barrier which forms just about half of the present Western Front. On one side the Maginot Line, on the other the Siegfried Line.

Until yesterday, so far as I can find out, there has not been a shot fired along this 110 miles front. A few weeks ago, going to and from Switzerland, I traveled the entire length of it. Our German train proceeded for four hours up the Rhine, much of the time in full view of the French fortifications on the other side of the river. I didn't feel particularly happy about it, but the French were very nice. You could see them digging in, but they weren't firing, neither were the German troops on my side of the river. My wife made the same trip a few days ago, and didn't hear a shot.

I guess that train isn't running any more. Yesterday afternoon, according to the Germans, the French suddenly opened fire with machine-guns and rifles on a spot along the Rhine between Kehl and Fristett. Kehl is the town across the river from Strasburg. The Germans say they answered the fire, and that it was a lively exchange. It looks then as if the armies, deadlocked along the front from Karlsruhe to Luxemburg, where until now what fighting there was has taken place, may feel each other out along the Rhine. But I imagine it will be a long time before any army crosses that mighty river.

It is now evident that the Nazis intend to act towards the Jews of conquered Poland exactly as they have towards the Jews in Germany. I mentioned yesterday that the Germans were putting the Polish Jews to work at manual tasks – largely road-building and clearing up the devastated areas. Today the German governor-general of occupied Poland, Herr Frank, decreed that the Jewish ghetto in Warsaw must be henceforth shut off from the rest of the capital by barricades, and placed under sharp police control. The Germans declare it is necessary to keep the Aryans in Warsaw strictly separated from the Jews.

According to a German semi-official statement issued in Berlin, this new decree has been warmly welcomed by the population of Warsaw, though I think that angle would stand checking on the spot. The Nazi statement adds that the decree will benefit the Aryan Poles as the Jews "not only took advantage of the plight of Poles in Warsaw, but also were dangerous carriers of disease and contagious germs." The diseases and germs are not named.

One American who arrived from Warsaw tonight told me that the Germans intended to divide Warsaw into four parts, one for the Jews, one for the Germans, one for the Poles and one for a mixed population of Poles and Germans. He said the devastation in the city from German bombs and shells was indescribable.

As for other news: tomorrow morning's papers in Berlin will headline the four bomb explosions in London. We've only had two in Berlin since the war started, and there are no Irish here. The sinking of the Dutch liner *Simon Bolivar* also gets a big play, and the Germans insist it hit an English mine, not a German. For the seventh time in the last two months, a German sentenced to jail for a crime has been shot "while resisting state authority", as the expression goes. The man got ten years yesterday for setting fire to some houses, but he won't have to serve them now. And a shoe dealer and his wife have just been given four years in the penitentiary for selling shoes to someone without a ration card.

Someone in New York has asked whether there's anything but war news in the German papers. If there is, I can't find it. At the local zoo all seems quiet. A lady was murdered in Berlin the other day, and it looked like we might have a big murder story, but the perpetrator couldn't be found, and the papers dropped it. I may be wrong, but it seems to me that when the mass slaughter of wartime is going on, and almost every newspaper tells of an execution for one reason or another, you lose interest in an old-fashioned murder story.

The newspapers here are timidly beginning to run stories about Christmas shopping, but when you're rationing clothing and sweets and a lot of other things, it makes sad reading, and probably, like the murder stories, the papers will soon drop it.

Berlin November 20, 1939 24.47

Good Evening. This is William L. Shirer in Berlin.

I can tell you a little tonight about the Hohenzollerns, that resourceful Prussian family which produced Frederick the Great and Kaiser Wilhelm II, and raised first Prussia and then Germany to the rank of a world power, only to step aside in 1918 when the war had been lost.

The Germans tell me that enemy propaganda has been saying things about the Hohenzollerns, reporting them, or some of them, as having been murdered by the Nazis – though this was news to me.

At any rate, at our regular press conference this afternoon, who should appear but Prince August Wilhelm, fourth son of the Kaiser. He denied that he had been murdered, or that his brother, the Crown Prince, had been bumped off, and then gave us quite a talk.

Prince August Wilhelm – or "Auwi", as he's popularly known – is the only Hohenzollern who was an active Nazi before Hitler came to power. He's been a Storm Trooper for years, and today was introduced to us by his official S.A. title – *Obergruppenführer*. He has the typical Hohenzollern face, and today he wore civilian clothes.

There's no mystery about the activities of the Hohenzollerns, he told us. Ten members of the House have been at the front, he said, one son of the Kaiser, and nine grandsons. One of the nine, Prince Oscar, was killed in Poland.

As to his father, he emphasized that after the Munich explosion, the former Kaiser immediately conveyed to Herr Hitler, through the German Minister at The Hague, his joy at the Führer's escape, and Herr Hitler thanked him for his message.

"It is unthinkable," said the Prince, "that our House could take part in

141

any action whatsoever against Germany. And all who are not behind the Führer," he added, "are against Germany."

As to the Crown Prince, he laughed at the stories of his murder. "Why, I talked with him on the phone this morning," he said. "The Crown Prince manages our property, and you can see him every morning on the Unter den Linden."

Since I live on that street, I'll keep an eye out for him.

The prince explained that he himself had never been a professional soldier but a government official, and was now working in that capacity in Potsdam. He then spoke with some enthusiasm of his work, how in Potsdam they'd built a new fish market, and hoped to build a new vegetable market to make the people there independent of Berlin.

He declared that he had many friends in America, that these friendships had not been affected by the war and that he continued to correspond with them. And then with a salute and a "Heil Hitler", Prince August Wilhelm sat down. So much for the Hohenzollerns.

I wish I could tell you more of what's been going on in Prague, but we're too shut-off from there, and you know much more than we do. Herr von Neurath *[the former German Foreign Minister and now Reich Protector of Bohemia and Moravia]* is still here conferring with the Führer over the situation there.

Berlin November 21, 1939 Berlin 24.47

Good Evening. This is William L. Shirer in Berlin.

Two very sensational stories have just broken here.

First, Heinrich Himmler, chief of the Gestapo, announces that he has arrested the man who planted the bomb that exploded in the Bürgerbräu Keller in Munich on the night of November 8th, twelve minutes after Herr Hitler and all the Nazi leaders left it.

Secondly, it's officially announced that the alleged leader of the British Intelligence Service for Western Europe, a certain Mr. Best, and his accomplice, a certain Captain Stevens, were nabbed by the Gestapo on November 9th, as they were trying to cross the Dutch frontier into Germany. It is added – and this is puzzling – that a dispute as to whether they were captured on German or Dutch soil is still being discussed. Could this refer to that alleged kidnapping case on the Dutch frontier we heard about the other day?

Well, the man who Herr Himmler says planted the Munich bomb is Georg Elser, aged thirty-six. Furthermore, the Gestapo chief announces that behind Elser was the British Intelligence Service, and that the chief

142

organizer of the crime was none other than Otto Strasser, once a leading Nazi himself and then later a bitter enemy of Nazism, who escaped abroad sometime before the 1934 purge which cost his brother, Gregor Strasser, also a former top-notch Nazi, his life.

Elser, according to the Secret Police, confessed his crime on November 14th, six days after the explosion. He had been arrested, the German account says, on the night of the bombing as he tried to escape over the German border at Konstanz into Switzerland. It would be difficult to get to Konstanz from Munich in one night, but it's explained that Elser left for there the morning of the explosion. It's stated he'd already got as far as Stuttgart after planting his bomb two days before it went off, but that for certain reasons not revealed, he returned to Munich on the afternoon of the 7th, got into the beer cellar that night and by listening to the clockwork of the bomb convinced himself that all was well. He even padded the clockwork a little more, it is stated, so that it wouldn't make so much noise.

The time mechanism, the police announced, was good for six days. Elser, it's explained, tried twice to get into the beer cellar without success, once seven days before the explosion and then five days before. Finally, four nights before it went off, he succeeded in getting in and planting the time-fuse. The bomb itself, it's added, was planted in the pillar on the 7th.

The Gestapo chief ends his statement by asking anyone who knew Elser or anything about him to volunteer information to the police.

As to the other story, about the arrest of the alleged British Secret Service chief, I've time for only a word. The Germans say the British headquarters for Western Europe were at The Hague and that the English were trying to get in touch with German opposition parties and launch a revolution. Gestapo agents, it's explained, were sent to The Hague disguised as opposition men, and made contact with the British, who the Germans say even gave them a secret wireless transmitter by means of which the German secret police to this day are in contact with the British government.

Then followed the arrests on the Dutch border.

Berlin November 23, 1939 24.47

Good Evening. This is William L. Shirer in Berlin.

The war seems to be getting a little livelier – at least in the air and on the sea.

The German newspapers tonight report great victories in the air, over both the French and British. I know that the war communiqués of the two sides don't agree at all, but I only get one side here, and that's all I can give you. The High Command, for instance, today states that yesterday and the day before the Germans destroyed six enemy planes, and lost only one of their own. The one loss, they explain, took part in a series of air battles with the French in which four French chasers were shot down. On Tuesday, say the Germans, nine German planes were attacked by seven French fighters and drove off the enemy without any losses at all.

Moreover, the Germans claim that enemy planes trying to fly over Germany actually penetrated only a few miles over the border.

Now compare that with the news my colleagues from other points tell you tonight.

What with air activity over Great Britain increasing and the mines along the English coast creating some havoc with shipping in British waters, the Germans tonight are talking of carrying the war into British territory. The *Deutsche Allgemeine Zeitung* tonight heads its front-page editorial: WAR ON ENGLAND'S COAST.

Whether in fact the German admiralty has been planting some new secret, perhaps magnetic, mine off the coast of England and whether they're doing it with submarines or airplanes is of course a closely-guarded secret here. The Germans so far content themselves with observing that laying mines in British territorial waters is definitely in accord with the Hague Convention of 1907 as long as British warships operate in those waters.

There's a great deal of resentment here about Britain's reprisals in stopping Germany's exports in neutral ships. Counter-measures are promised, but we don't know yet their nature.

At any rate, we do know that Hitler today conferred with 120 of his leading generals, admirals and party men, and laid down to them directions for the campaign based, it is explained, on the experience of the Polish war.

The Germans claim today that American patrol boats off the North American coast are helping British warships to capture German merchant ships. They cite the alleged example of an American Coast-Guard cutter having spotted a German vessel off the coast of Mexico. The Germans claim the American boat followed the German ship all day long and finally signaled its presence to a British warship. This story is published in the *Nachtausgabe* under the headline: USA PATROL BOAT HELPS ENGLAND – STRANGE KIND OF NEUTRALITY.

Well, today was Thanksgiving, and despite the war and the fact that in Germany it was just like any other Thursday, the small American colony here celebrated it as best it could. Most of the Americans in town, about a hundred I should say, spent the afternoon at the home of Mr. Alexander Kirk, the American chargé d'affaires, where turkey, with dressing and cranberry sauce, and all the other things that you yourself have had today, including mince and pumpkin pie, were served. I won't say where Mr. Kirk got his turkeys – and they were very hard to get – because that's his secret.

Myself, I've just come this minute from a very delightful Thanksgiving Dinner. My host was Mrs. Dorothy Oechsner, wife of the United Press correspondent in Berlin. We didn't have turkey, but I better let my host tell you about that.

DOROTHY: I did try to get a turkey. Only, I was 857th on the Poultry List. Two weeks after the war started, I put in my bid for a Thanksgiving turkey.

SHIRER: What happened?

DOROTHY: Nothing much. There just weren't any turkeys, but I did get a nice goose.

SHIRER: Well, I can vouch for that. Now, how did you get all those other wonderful things we had?

DOROTHY: Well, I can explain the beet soup and the pumpkin pie very easily. You don't need ration cards for beets or pumpkins. So, that part was simple.

SHIRER: I must say I've never tasted better pumpkin pie. But where did you get the whipped cream?

DOROTHY: I made that from Danish butter.

SHIRER: From Danish butter?

DOROTHY: You see, ordinary cream is not obtainable, and even skimmed milk is being rationed now. But I have a wonderful machine which makes cream from butter. That explains your whipped cream tonight. The one thing I really regret tonight was the Waldorf Salad. Didn't you notice there were no nuts or mayonnaise?

SHIRER: Well, now that you mention it . . .

DOROTHY: You see, I had no eggs nor oil. The three eggs I get on my ration card, I had already used in the pumpkin pie. So we had Waldorf Salad without the dressing.

SHIRER: I might mention that all of us four guests tonight brought our food cards for fats and butter.

DOROTHY: Yes, that's one of the requests we have to make of our guests. No food cards, no food for the guests, as our own ration cards only provide enough for my husband and myself. Bill, I felt a little badly about that coffee.

SHIRER: Why so?

DOROTHY: I did my best to bring in two pounds of coffee from Budapest yesterday, but Hungary, like most of the small neutral countries, doesn't like you to take out food. So, I had to give it up.

SHIRER: Was it expensive?

DOROTHY: It cost about five dollars a pound. Later, I found that I could have taken it out with a special permit from the Hungarian National Bank.

SHIRER: Well, Dorothy, it was a wonderful Thanksgiving Dinner, and I want to thank you for it, also for coming here to the microphone this evening.

DOROTHY: Thank you, Bill, for coming to dinner. And tomorrow, I'm going to put in my bid for next year's turkey. Maybe we'll have one then.

SHIRER: Well, I wish you luck, and thanks again.

I might add that during the dinner, we were interrupted by the police who discovered my car parked in the street without lights. I didn't think it needed lights tonight, because on my way to the Oechsners another policeman had stopped me for having my lights too bright for a blackout.

And so it went. And on the whole, it was a very American and a very pleasant Thanksgiving Day.

Berlin November 25, 1939 14.05

Good Morning. This is William L. Shirer in Berlin.

As you know, I'm not supposed to talk about the weather. The British and French are able to pick up these broadcasts and I might give valuable information about the weather to their flyers. But I think they'll let me say that last night we had our first snowfall. It reminded us all that winter had come, and that the war was going on in spite of it, and I think it made people realize more than before that no end to the war was in sight and that it would be a hard winter. It made them realize too that millions of men on the Western Front were standing out there in the snow, and that was no joke for them.

Another reminder that this war is not going to be over soon was the official announcement, played up in the newspapers today, that the

Winter Olympic Games at Garmisch had been called off. The Germans had done a tremendous job there. I saw the Olympic Games there three years ago and marveled at the ski-stadium and the ice-stadium, but the games this year were to be even bigger and better, and the Germans had torn down the old stadiums, which were made of wood, and erected gigantic new ones, built with concrete. The ice-stadium, with a 400 meter artificial ice-rink for speed skating, will be the largest in the world, but it'll have to wait until the days of peace are restored.

Human beings in Germany are not the only objects to have their food rationed. After December 1st, horses, cows, and pigs which are not kept on regular farms, are to have food cards too.

Yesterday, a woman who sold meat, butter, and clothing without ration cards got ten years in the penitentiary.

And it's just announced that when you buy a shirt, you must be given one collar for your twenty points – a year's clothing card gives you 100 points – but if you insist on two collars with your shirt, you've got to give up three points extra.

And to close on a more cheery note – the first Christmas trees arrived in Berlin this morning.

Berlin November 26, 1939 15.01

Good Morning. This is William L. Shirer in Berlin.

Today is the German Memorial Day. The Germans call it *Totensonntag* – or the Sunday of the Dead.

It's a day when most Germans visit the graves of their relatives, and decorate them with flowers and pine-branches. I remember when I was stationed here some years ago, it was a day above all to commemorate the *two million* German lives lost in the World War, and there were few families which did not have a father or a son or a brother in this tragic list of two million names.

And now there is a new war, and the emphasis today is no longer on the dead of 1914-1918, but on the dead of 1939 – those who lost their lives in the attack on Poland. The papers this morning talk of the rows of "heroes' graves" in Poland and the High Command announces that due to the impossibility of relatives visiting them, the army has arranged that each of the graves today will be strewn with flowers and pine-branches.

You cannot forget that there are also the graves of Polish soldiers – more numerous than those of Germans – but they will not be strewn with flowers or evergreens today.

Honor the dead today – especially those who fell in battle – but the war, with its daily toll of lives goes on. Tomorrow will not that toll increase? Will not the war grow sharper in intensity? The *Frankfurter Zeitung* in a front-page editorial this morning hints that it will. It hints that the flights of German airplanes last week over France and England may have been nothing less than a dress-rehearsal. And then: "What happened last week may have been only a presentiment (*Vorahnung*). We know that it will not stop with that . . . It meant a sharpening of the war. We know that this sharpening will not be the end."

And then the *Frankfurter Zeitung* adds this: "We do not point this out with a light heart. No people knows better than the German people how bitter war is, and that it spares none of the people taking part."

And the paper concludes: "We Germans must fight with all the hardness we have until victory – or we must go under. This is the naked truth."

Gradually it seems to be dawning on people who only a short time ago believed that the war would be over by Christmas, that this struggle is a fight to the finish. And there are many who believe that regardless of who wins, all will be finished.

The Olympic Stadium, which is a stone's throw from where I'm talking, has been packed this afternoon with 100,000 fans rooting for the home team against Italy in the biggest football game Berlin has seen since the war started. The game is almost over now, and so far no enemy planes have appeared to stop the contest or endanger the lives of 100,000 packed so tightly in such a small place. I take it one of the rules of this strange war is not to disturb the other fellow's football games. Well, that's something anyway.

One night, my friend Bill White of Emporia, Kansas, and I, in search of information for this report, spent the evening in various cafés and night places. They were all jammed. It was almost impossible to get a table.

No one dresses up any more at night here. You go dancing in your everyday street-clothes, both women and men. For the first three weeks of the war, dancing was prohibited, then the ban was lifted, and it became more popular than ever. English dance tunes are still played, but new German words have been written for the singers. What the Germans call American hot jazz is *verboten.*

The large places like the *Haus Vaterland*, where there are several halls and floor shows in each, and where you can spend the evening, including the cost of drinks, for fifty cents or a dollar, are very popular. The floor shows feature everything from dancing acts to acrobats and weightlifters, and the local inhabitants go wild about them.

Most of the night places used to stay open until 4 a.m. Now they must close promptly at 1. An exception is the Taverne, hang-out of the American correspondents and – since the war – artists from the theaters.

Press pass issued by the Nazi Party for the 1937 Nuremberg Rally, one of Shirer's first *nments* after joining CBS.

e: Your correspondent with a muffin: William Shirer on a street in Berlin, 1940.

Shirer with his daughter, Inga, on one of his frequent visits to Switzerlan

Above and inset: Theresa Stiberitz, Shirer's Austrian-born wife, in Geneva, where she ran the sm CBS office and where they also made their home.

Right: In the RRG (Reichs Rundfunk Gesellschaft) studio in Berlin preparing to broadcast. The canister contained a gas-mask.

Tom Grandin of the CBS Paris office, Ed Murrow, European Director of CBS Radio News, and William Shirer arriving in Paris.

At Compiègne, working on the text of his broadcast on the French capitulation, June, 1940.

ctory or Bolshevism" – a Nazi
ter. The official and virulent anti-
l campaign came to a sudden end
ugust, 1939, when the Nazis and
Communists signed their non-
ression pact.

"All Germany Listens to the
Führer with the People's Radio" –
the state-subsidized
Volksempfänger, a low-priced radio
with a limited range. Listening to
foreign broadcasts was a criminal
offence.

Below: "Youth in Service to the Führer." Willingly or not, millions of boys aged ten and over joined the paramilitary Hitler Youth, there to be "educated physically, intellectually and morally in the spirit of National Socialism."

Above: High above the crowd, standing apart even from their aides and officials, Adolf Hitler (left) and Benito Mussolini gaze down upon a 1938 Fascist rally in Rome.

Left: Mussolini and Hitler review Italian troops in Rome.

Schoolgirls and teachers giving the Nazi salute at a rally in Coburg. aged ten to fourteen were recruited into the *Jungemädel,* and then he *Bund Deutscher Mädel.*

Dr Josef Goebbels, Minister of Popular Enlightenment and Propaganda, and absolute master of the press and radio in Nazi Germany. Foreign reporters were closely monitored and subject to imprisonment or expulsion.

Below: A brown-shirted storm-trooper on guard outside a Jewish-owned fabric shop with a bi-lingual sign in the window.

Deutsche, verteidigt Euch gegen die jüdische Greuelpropaganda, kauft **nur bei Deutschen!**

Germans defend yourselves against jewish atrocity propaganda buy only at German shops!

Deutsche! Wehrt Euch! Kauft nicht bei Juden!

But to get in there after 1 a.m. we have to show a special government pass.

Why night-life is booming is an interesting question, but I'll have to save that for another evening.

[On November 27 Shirer once again left Berlin to visit his wife and infant daughter in Geneva. While he was there, the Soviet Union launched its sudden invasion of Finland.]

Berlin December 5, 1939 24.47

Good Evening. This is William L. Shirer in Berlin.

About two months ago, after the Polish war was over, and I had been down to the Western Front and couldn't find much to report about, a neutral diplomat took me aside and said:

"You see this war as a stalemate on the Western Front – as a war without a front. But be patient. It will spread. Soon there will be plenty of fronts. And more nations will be drawn in."

I remembered his words last week when Soviet Russia attacked little Finland. I remembered them on returning to Berlin this morning when the first thing I noticed in the local papers was a two-column editorial on the front page of the *Völkischer Beobachter*, official organ of the Nazi party, assessing the chances of Russia and Turkey in a war on what the paper termed the Caucasus Front.

This authoritative organ of Nazi thought spoke as if war was almost imminent there. It reported French troop movements in Syria, British troop movements in Egypt, Turkish troop movements in the Caucasus and, finally, Russian reinforcements to meet these alleged threats.

"Those are serious signs," said the paper. And then, for three columns, was an exposition of the military situation there which tended to prove that Russia would win over a Turkey backed by England and France.

The Caucasus may seem a far-away front to start worrying about now, but who, a month ago, would have dreamed that today the Red Army would be attacking Finnish guards on a snow-swept front within the Arctic Circle? And the Caucasus are even more important because, as this German survey points out, a Red Army victory would bring the Russians down to the great Allied oilfields at Mosul, in Irak, yes even bring them within striking distance of Persia, from which the British navy now gets a large part of its oil.

Germany appears to approve wholeheartedly Russia's snub of the League of Nations, and the Bolshevik argument that Russia is not at war with Finland but on the most peaceful terms with the so-called

"Democratic Finnish Republic" is given great prominence in the Berlin press today. The Russian claims that their troops are advancing all along the line, also are published in Berlin newspapers.

England is again blamed for Finland's plight, and the other little neutral countries are warned as to the consequences when they get too friendly with the Western Democracies.

I was surprised to find the German press telling its readers that Italy has no sympathy for Finland in its struggle against Russia, because my information from Rome was just the opposite.

General Franco, according to a *DNB* dispatch from Madrid, has now come out publicly in favor of a German victory in this war. The statement was said to have been made by the General yesterday.

And I just learn that Dr. Schacht *[the former German Minister of Economics]* has had a talk with the Führer, the first for a long time.

Berlin December 6, 1939 24.47

Good Evening. This is William L. Shirer in Berlin.

We've just been told here that this evening what is described as a strong detachment of British planes flew over the Frisian Islands and north Germany. According to the German communiqué, they dropped no bombs. The score seems to have been even because the German account makes no mention of any British planes having been brought down.

The aircraft were first sighted early this evening over the ring of islands which protects Germany's northwest coast. German anti-aircraft guns on the islands went into action.

The British planes were next seen over the extreme northern tip of Germany in Schleswig-Holstein. Anti-aircraft batteries on the German mainland went into action, and though they did not bring any British craft down, the Germans claim they drove them northward and that they actually made over the border at Flensberg, flying over Danish territory.

From this report and others recently, it would appear that the British air force is becoming a little more active, and plans to return the visits which the German air force has been making to Scotland.

The Germans also report the loss of a small patrol boat – apparently it hit a mine – but on the Western Front all was quiet. I traveled up half of the Western Front yesterday, about 150 miles from Basle to Karlsruhe along the Rhine and I can certainly vouch for that sector being quiet. Along the entire front I didn't hear a single shot, nor was there any aerial activity of any kind.

Today was the birthday of Germany's greatest living commander from the World War, Field Marshal von Mackensen, the strategist who rode roughshod through the Russian and Romanian armies back in 1915, 1916, and 1917. Herr Hitler forsook his work in the Wilhelmstrasse and drove down to the Marshal's farm a short distance from Berlin. He congratulated him on his 90th birthday and gave him, according to the official announcement, not only his own best wishes but those of the German people. The Marshal responded, according to the official account, that he was indeed happy to be living in these days, and that his greatest wish now was for a German victory in this war.

It's interesting to note in closing that the German press today began treating the Russo-Finnish war very objectively. I was surprised to see that the Finnish war communiqués were printed in full, and even placed over the Russian communiqués. The German press headlined that the Finns had occupied the Åland Islands with strong detachments and spoke of heavy fighting on the Karelian Front.

The German press also did not fail to report from Moscow that the Russian government had not yet given the Finnish diplomatic staff there, their passports. This new German attitude is worth noting.

Berlin December 7, 1939 24.47

Good Evening. This is William L. Shirer in Berlin.

I guess we ought to be glad – you and I – that we don't belong to one of these small neutral countries. Most of them over here seem to be suffering more than the belligerents. They're losing a lot of ships. They're forced to keep most of their able-bodied men under arms – at terrific cost. And though they strive to keep neutral, they're blamed by the belligerents for sympathy with the enemy, and they all wonder whether they'll wake up tomorrow to find themselves getting what Finland got last week.

Now there's no doubt about it, Germany is using increasingly strong language against her small neutral neighbors. This morning in the German press there were not very friendly references to Switzerland for allowing the League of Nations to meet there this weekend. There was an editorial warning to Holland – not the first by any means – for not fighting the British blockade more stubbornly. And tonight we have a semi-official statement severely taking the Scandinavian states to task and telling them in effect that they must choose between friendship with Britain and friendship with Germany.

In the German view, so far as I can make it out, a neutral country hasn't the right to be friendly with both.

Tonight's German statement is an attempt to explain Germany's

151

position in the Russo-Finnish war, but it really is a warning to Norway, Sweden, and Denmark. The Germans claim – and this will be disputed by many – that the Scandinavian countries have been consistently unfriendly to Germany since the World War, but especially so since the advent of Adolf Hitler and Nazism. Moreover, say the Germans, the Scandinavian countries have in recent years allowed themselves to become tools of the British. Since the outbreak of this war, continues the German accusation, the northern countries have been all but friendly toward Germany. This will be news to many Germans who've been told in their newspapers dozens of times that Scandinavia really backed the German case.

This German semi-official statement ends with this warning: "It is to be hoped that the responsible Scandinavian statesmen will think over once more whether it is better to deal with the English warmongers or serve the natural interests of their people by befriending the German people."

Apparently, the Scandinavians must choose or – .

The executioner claimed three more victims here today. Two men, one a Jew, were accused of working for the British Secret Service. The other was accused of distributing leaflets against the regime. All three were tried by the People's Court, sentenced yesterday, and executed today. A fourth man was sentenced to death for setting fire to a barn full of cows.

Joint Shirer-Murrow CBS broadcast Sunday night December 7-8, 1939 01.00

[Since telephone lines between London and Berlin had been cut at the beginning of the war, Murrow's and Shirer's voices were routed to each other via New York on short-wave radio. As always, Shirer's text had to be submitted to the German censor before the broadcast.]

SHIRER: A few minutes ago, I heard my colleague, Ed Murrow, speaking from London. You still there, Ed?

MURROW: Yes, Bill. Right here. And it's good to hear your voice again.

SHIRER: Good to hear yours too, Ed. We don't see as much of each other as we used to. But I suppose there are some reasons for that.

MURROW: (Laughs) Probably some reasons.

SHIRER: How's the war affecting your everyday existence, Ed? I mean, besides piling up the work?

MURROW: Wartime existence now seems normal. It's hard to remember what it was like in peacetime. I spend about sixteen hours a day reading, talking, looking, listening – also a certain amount of time bouncing off lamp-posts, sandbags, etcetera. I'm thinking of asking New York for football pads. I still have plenty of food, clothes, heat, and patience. And how about you? What's your life like, wartime model?

SHIRER: It could be worse, I guess. After all, we haven't seen much of the war here in Berlin. In Poland, the battles were over, with one exception, before we could get to them. And so far, we haven't been allowed to go to the Western Front. So we sit around here waiting for something to happen. There's the blackout of course. I thought I'd memorized the location of every lamp-post in the town – in Berlin they put them in the middle of the sidewalk – but last night, hurrying to a broadcast, I met one head-on. Result: a bump on my head the size of a billiard ball. The food situation is not too bad. The government classifies us as heavy laborers and gives us double rations. And about every third week my weekly box of bacon, eggs, butter, and cheese from Denmark gets through, and that helps. I do miss good coffee, but they say a new substitute is coming out soon which will take care of that . . . Oh yes, and my shoes need half-soling, as I discovered when the snow piled up on the streets last week, but I hope to remedy that the next time I go out to Switzerland. Of course, this enforced absence from your wife and children is no particular fun. Another thing, we miss American mail and papers and magazines. If the people where you are, Ed, could speed our mail up, that would be fine.

Ed, over here we hear on the radio most of your official pronounce-ments and speeches. But we're curious about the man in the street. What does the average man think about such things as the length of the war, the prospect of activity before spring, and that sort of thing?

MURROW: Britain's man in the street doesn't talk much about the duration of the war. He still seems confident that Britain will win, but uncertain as to how and when. The working-men here are a patient lot. The war has caused many dislocations but thousands of people unemployed for ten or twelve years are now working in the shipyards in the Tyne and Clyde, the coal mines in Rhondda and in munition factories. Most people probably believe what the papers tell them, which is that the Germans contemplate a big attack in the spring. But the British don't propose to waste men in a premature attack on the Siegfried Line. Many believe that the navy and air force will provide the economic stranglehold which will cause Germany to collapse.

Bill, what does your average man say and think these days about that?

SHIRER: Well, he's been told, and I think he believes, that this is going to be the decisive year and that the war will be over before next New Year's, if not sooner. The average fellow you talk to here thinks that there's going to be a lot of action early in the spring, probably in the air, probably against England, and he thinks Germany will come out on top.

I understand, Ed, that later in this program, Columbia's going to hear from Finland. What seems to be the English attitude regarding the Finnish war?

MURROW: British sympathy is overwhelmingly with the Finns. The papers, radio, newsreels denounce the Russian invasion in the strongest possible terms, and express great admiration for the Finnish resistance. The general attitude seems to be that Britain should assist the Finns in every possible way without handicapping her own effort. There's an increasing tendency to speak of Germany and Russia in the same breath as opponents, but the majority of the London papers emphasize that one war at a time is sufficient. Everybody is watching Allied assistance for Finland, speculating whether another front will be created in Scandinavia and hoping that the war in Finland will prevent Russia from sending promised supplies to Germany. But the outstanding question mark is whether Germany will invade Sweden in the event the Allies tranship large supplies of arms through Sweden to Finland.

How does Germany feel regarding all the shooting northward?

SHIRER: Well, officially Germany's neutral, and of course the people haven't forgotten that it was German help which enabled Finland to win its independence from Russia in 1918-1919. But now things are different, so to say; Germany is lined up with Russia, and Berlin is not pleased at the prospect of Britain and France sending military aid to Finland. The Germans say they have a feeling that Britain and France are giving aid to Finland more to gain a foothold in Scandinavia against Germany than against Russia. It's a very curious situation.

Well, Ed, it's been nice to hear your voice again, and all the best for the New Year, and don't work yourself completely to death.

Berlin December 8, 1939 14.05.30

Good Morning. This is William L. Shirer in Berlin.

Returning to Berlin after a few days spent outside in a neutral country, where you hear both sides of this war, I'm rather struck by the appearance of the German newspapers. Almost all the headlines these days are given over to telling you how bad conditions are in the enemy countries, especially in England.

The Berlin newspaper, *Börsen Zeitung*, which came out at noon today, has these three banner-lines on its front page: ENGLAND GROANS UNDER

THE CHAOS – COMPLETE CONFUSION OF BRITISH ECONOMY. And then, a third line: FRENCH AGRICULTURE IN BAD WAY.

Now day after day, Germans read this sort of stuff in their newspapers. There is very little news of actual events. What local news there is, is always favorable and heartening. But conditions in the enemy lands are painted in the blackest of colors.

And then it's interesting to note that England is always depicted as the mortal enemy. France is treated in the German press as merely the unfortunate tool of perfidious Albion. Do the German people follow their press in this? Well, a lot of them certainly. A couple of days ago, I sat in a German train. We were going down the Rhine, and a couple of hundreds yards to the left of us we could look over into France. You could see the French pill-boxes and occasionally a French soldier. On the German side, troops were working on new fortifications. A German businessman in my compartment glanced over towards France. "Why do they want to fight us?" he asked me. "We have nothing against them. We want nothing from France." But when he started to talk of England as the cause of all of Germany's troubles, he foamed in the mouth and I could hardly follow him.

In this morning's papers, for instance, all of Germany's wrath is directed against Britain. Field Marshal Göring's newspaper, the *Essen National Zeitung*, has this banner line today: NEW PROVOCATION OF THE PIRATES. "Pirates" is the term usually used for the English in Germany nowadays. And the complaint is that the British are again committing a crime against international law by arming 1,000 new merchant-men with depth-bomb apparatuses. Every other paper in Germany this morning plays up the same story with the same charges against Britain.

One piece of news which may be escaping your attention these days – because somehow it does not sound sensational – is the mass movement of populations now going on in Poland. Jews are being moved out of Germany into a gigantic ghetto settlement at Lublin – and one of these days, I'd like to take some time and go into that matter in detail with you. And now this week the Russians and Germans are meeting in Cracow to settle the details of a mass exchange of populations.

About 100,000 Germans now living in that part of Poland occupied by the Red Army are to be sent back to Germany. And three-quarters of a million Ukrainians and White Russians in the German-occupied section of Poland are to be sent back to the Bolsheviks. These 100,000 Germans will eventually be settled in Western Poland, just as the 130,000 Germans hastily recalled from the Baltic states are now being settled there. And in a short time, Western Poland, which even under the rule of Bismarck always had a Polish majority, will be predominantly German in population.

155

It is no mean task to transport these 100,000 Germans. An official told us yesterday how most of them would have to walk as far as 100 miles in the snow until they reach a railroad station or even a main automobile highway, from which they'll be transported westward. But the Germans are sending doctors to accompany them so they won't be victims of epidemics. Once back in Western Poland, they'll be placed in quarantine camps, and only next spring will they be settled on the land which the German army conquered from Poland.

The High Command's war communiqué this morning reports yesterday's patrol flights over the North Sea which London mentioned last night. According to this official German version, strong units of the German air force carried out patrol flights over the North Sea and skirted the coast of Scotland, flying low.

East of the Firth of Forth, says the communiqué, the German planes were attacked by British flyers, but, add the Germans, without success. One German plane, it is admitted, was forced to land on the sea, but this, it is claimed, was due to motor trouble. The crew took to its collapsible boat and German seaplanes have been sent out this morning to try and pick up the crew.

Berlin December 8, 1939 24.47

Good Evening. This is William L. Shirer in Berlin.

Germany's warning last night to the Scandinavian countries about the danger of being unfriendly to Germany was meant as a lesson, we're told tonight in German political circles.

In other words, Germany is telling the small neutral countries to stop playing ball with Great Britain and begin playing ball with Germany, or they may be in for trouble, and not only the Scandinavian countries were meant. I'm told on good authority that the Germans mean that the other neutrals – I mean the small neutrals, because you don't pick on the big fellows – countries like little Switzerland, Belgium, and Holland must also mend their ways if they are not to incur Nazi displeasure.

Well, what if these small countries don't mend their ways to suit Berlin? One inspired statement from the Wilhelmstrasse tonight spoke of the risks involved if they don't.

I understand that a good deal of nervousness was created in the small neutral countries today by Germany's warning. Well, that's exactly, I'm told here, what Berlin expected and desired.

It may well be that one of these days the small neutral states may have to choose between the belligerents. But from what I know of them, they'll be just as ready to defend their independence as were the Finns.

We get very little news of the Finnish war here. It's rather a painful subject in Germany, though the press publishes the war communiqués of both sides. But I was on the phone to Stockholm a few minutes ago and was told by a friend who'd just been talking with Helsinki that though the Finns were putting up a very brave fight, they could not hold out indefinitely without foreign aid. The Italians have sent fifty airplanes, and the British are sending thirty, but, of course, this is not enough against the huge war machine which the Bolsheviks are now unloosing.

The Germans, as part of their campaign to impress the neutrals, tonight report that one Norwegian and one Finnish ship, which were being convoyed across the North Sea by the British navy did not hit mines, as first reported, but were torpedoed in the midst of the convoy by German U-boats. The Germans point out they hope this will be a further lesson to the neutrals.

The German press tonight makes quite a bit of a dispatch from Ankara reporting that the Turkish President left suddenly for Erzerum, an important Turkish military base near the Russian frontier. Last week, you remember, the Nazi press claimed that both Russians and Turks were massing troops on the Caucasus frontier. Some people think the next phase of the war may break out there. Few persons over here doubt that this war is spreading.

The German radio reports tonight with some satisfaction that the latest Gallup Poll in America shows $96\frac{1}{2}$ percent of the American people against a war with Germany. The radio commented that this showed what a failure the English propagandists are in our country. I was just wondering if there were any other questions in that poll.

Berlin December 9, 1939 24.46.

Good Evening. This is William L. Shirer in Berlin.

The catch-word of the German press tonight is that it's been a dark day for Mr. Churchill. Actually, the Germans don't call him *Mr.* Churchill – they refer to him tonight as "Lying Lord" Churchill, using the German expression "*Lügenlord.*" "*Lügen*" means "lie".

Well, the "Lügenlord", that is, Mr. Churchill, is stated by the Germans to have had a hard day because he lost two new destroyers and eight merchant ships, according to the German count. That will be the big story in the Sunday morning newspapers tomorrow, and no doubt, since this is wartime, will make a lot of Germans feel better when they observe the One-Pot Sunday lunch as a sort of national sacrifice tomorrow.

I gather that the Germans are rather pleased with the success of their mine warfare. But don't think they're surprised. Probably most of us have forgotten that in the last World War, the mine was a very deadly instrument, and today a retired German admiral reveals that between 1914 and 1918 10 percent of the Allied shipping losses were due to mines. But more than that, he says, one-fourth of the Allied *naval* losses in the last war were due to mines. They sank battleships, cruisers, and destroyers. How big a business this mine war is may be gathered from the fact that in the 1914 war, according to this German admiral, the belligerents laid a total of 300,000 mines. One hundred thousand English mines, and 60,000 American mines were distributed in the North Sea alone.

The German Admiralty is still keeping very mum about the nature of its mines and how it sows them. It still can't be learned here whether the Germans are dropping them from airplanes. But the Germans laugh at the stories abroad about their mysterious new magnetic mines. Magnetic mines, they point out, were invented and first developed by the British.

America's note to London about the British blockading Germany's exports to the United States – there haven't been very many the last few years – gets a good press in Germany, as you might imagine. It isn't often that we get a good press here, so it's worth noting. And if Britain continues to stop Germany's exports to America, the Germans express the hope that we'll do something about it.

Well, Christmas is approaching, and the citizens of Berlin are certainly doing what shopping is possible under wartime ration conditions, early. I found the stores crowded today. With candies, soaps, perfumes, and clothing-ware on strict rations, the people were buying mostly books, radios, gramophones, and such things.

The government is loosening up a little on rations for Christmas. Thus everyone will get a quarter of a pound of butter extra for Christmas, also four eggs Christmas week instead of one, and an extra 100 grammes of meat.

I was surprised, though, today to find at my tobacco shop a sign saying no cigars were being sold. The proprietor didn't know when he'd be allowed to sell cigars again. He had no ordinary matches either, which for a pipe smoker like myself is a hardship. For 15 cents, however, I was able to get 100 fancy colored matches, and they worked all right.

Berlin December 10, 1939 01.00

Good Evening. This is William L. Shirer in Berlin.

Here's an item from a German concentration camp I think will interest you. Heinrich Himmler, chief of the S.S. secret police, announces that on November 25th, two prisoners in a concentration camp attacked an S.S. guard and knocked him down. The men fled, but shortly they were caught. They were brought back to the concentration camp, and yesterday were both hanged.

No mention of any trial. I guess in wartime they don't have trials in such cases, and it's the first time I've heard of a man in Germany being executed by hanging. Usually a guillotine is used.

There have been persistent reports the last few days that Germany has been secretly sending arms to Finland. Moreover, that those fifty Italian bombing planes that landed in Finland last week flew there by way of Germany, which would of course be the shortest route for the Axis partner to use.

Tonight, we have an official denial from the German government of both of these reports. The statement declares that Germany has neither sent arms to Finland, nor allowed foreign planes to land in Germany on their way to Helsinki. Such reports, says the communiqué, are pure inventions and have been spread with the object of injuring German-Russian relations.

You will remember that Germany furnished the arms which enabled the Finns to win their independence from the Bolsheviks after the last war.

Nazi Germany is also sticking up for Soviet Russia in connection with the special meeting of the League of Nations convoked by Finland. Tonight the Berlin press, obviously inspired by the Wilhelmstrasse, attacks Switzerland for even allowing the League to meet on its neutral soil.

The German case is that for the League, dominated as it is by Great Britain and France, to meet on Swiss territory is incompatible with Swiss neutrality. Thus these small neutrals – yesterday it was the turn of the Scandinavian states, and last week of the Netherlands – seem more and more to be the object of attack from Germany. The language used toward them seems to grow a little more threatening every day.

And the newspapers tonight, in inspired editorials, again warn the neutrals of the danger of lining up at Geneva with the two Western Democracies.

And here's an item of another sort. The war is booming marriages. Fifty percent more Germans married during the first month of the war than in the same month a year ago when there was still peace. I wonder why.

159

Berlin December 14, 1939 24.47

Good Evening. This is William L. Shirer.

The Germans are celebrating tonight what is hailed in Berlin as a great sea-victory of the pocket-battleship *Graf Spee* over three British cruisers off Montevideo.

I know very well that in London it is hailed as an equally great British victory, and I have no intention of passing any personal judgements or arguing the case. I remember when I used to work in London, the Battle of Jutland was celebrated every year as a British victory. When I was later stationed in Berlin, I found the Germans celebrated the same battle as a great German victory.

But since I'm in Berlin, all I can do is tell you how the Germans see it. The papers play it up as a victory for the *Graf Spee*, and there are long accounts of how the one German ship fought off three British men of war, and badly damaged them. The emphasis is on the number of ships and superior speed of the British cruisers, and not on the size of the guns engaged.

All German papers headline the sensational report that the British used mustard gas shells, and explain that the main reason why the *Graf Spee* put into harbor was because its food-stores had been spoiled by the gas.

But note that the official communiqué of the German High Command on the battle does not mention poison gas, and we were in fact advised in official circles tonight that it would be well to wait for more authoritative news on the subject. The story about gas, it was emphasized, did not come from the German Admiralty. We were told that the German losses, given as thirty-six dead and sixty wounded, were only based on newspaper reports, and not on any official German information.

Now as to who won this first open naval battle of the war – this is the German case as put to me in naval circles tonight:

The task of the *Graf Spee* was not to engage an English fleet, but to destroy enemy merchant ships. This it has done unhindered for three months. The task of the British navy was to sink the *Graf Spee* before it could do any damage. Well, the pocket-battleship is still afloat, and it's already done plenty of damage. That's the German view. As to the charge that the *Graf Spee* fled, German naval circles said tonight – how could it flee from three cruisers that were faster than it?

There was a big air battle just off the German coast tonight. I heard the London radio announce a few minutes ago that the Germans lost four planes, the British three. But that's not how the German radio has it. The Germans say their Messerschmitt fighters shot down *six* British bombers and lost only *one*.

Don't ask me who's right.

Berlin December 15, 1939 14.00

Good Morning. This is William L. Shirer.

This war seems to be picking up.

Not on land, where most people thought it would be fought, but on the sea, and in the air. What are described as great German victories in both these spheres are being celebrated by the German press this morning.

The naval battle off Montevideo between the pocket-battleship *Graf Spee* and three British cruisers still gets a lot of attention here, but it runs second place on the front pages today to the air battle that took place yesterday on the North Sea coast of Germany between British bombers and German Messerschmitt fighters.

As you already know, the British and German figures on their respective losses in this air fight do not agree at all. The Germans first reported last night six British bombers down and only one German fighter, and later in the evening Berlin said that a further check-up had established the British losses as eight, with the German still at only one.

It certainly is amazing the way this German air force always outscores the enemy seven or eight to one.

There has still not been a good report of the sea battle off the mouth of the Plata River in the German press. By far the best report was a short-wave broadcast from the scene. But the press makes up for its lack of a good report by its praise of the *Graf Spee,* and all the accounts here play up that the German pocket-battleship was outnumbered three to one. The idea is that the German navy once again has won a tremendous victory over a vastly superior force. I mentioned last night that the papers were keeping mum about the guns in this battle. But today the *12-Uhr Blatt* breaks the silence to say that it was a case of twelve German cannons against twenty-two English.

But that there were 11-inch guns against 8- and 6-inch guns is not emphasized. However, German naval circles remind you that it was not the purpose of the German raider to take on the British fleet, but to sink British merchant vessels and avoid capture or destruction – which they say it's done.

The first prize courts to sit publicly in Germany have just disposed of their first cases in Hamburg, and you will be interested to know that out of three cases of neutral ships accused of carrying contraband to the enemy which came up, the German Prize Court in all three decisions found that the cargoes were indeed contraband and therefore awarded them to the Reich. But more than that, this German Prize Court decided that Germany should seize two of the three ships.

Thus the neutrals – the two ships belonged to Sweden – not only lose their cargoes, but they lose their valuable ships as well. It would be interesting to know if all those vessels which the British seize and lay up for contraband search – if the ships themselves are grabbed by the British government in case contraband is found aboard them.

And now for some little items that reflect life in this country these days. Next Thursday, there is to be a national collection of old gunny sacks. With no jute coming in from India, gunny sacks have become very valuable property in Germany.

Another man – this time from Nuremberg – has been beheaded for stealing during a blackout.

A new decree counsels German employers against working their men ten or twelve hours a day, unless it is absolutely necessary for prosecuting the war. Probably most men in Germany today are laboring ten hours a day, and many twelve. For two of the extra hours, they get no pay; the employer pays it, but the State takes it.

In this connection I see two workers got prison sentences for declining to work the required number of hours.

Apparently food is still plentiful in Poland. Germans there are invited to send food packages home to the Reich for Christmas. I wish I knew a German in Poland.

Berlin December 17, 1939 15.03

Good Morning. This is William L. Shirer in Berlin.

Wandering around the streets of Berlin this fine Sabbath morning, it was difficult to believe that a world war was on. Before this war started, a lot of us over here thought we'd have to live our lives largely underground, spending our days and nights crouching in damp, dark, chilly cellars praying that the bombs from the airplanes missed us.

But it hasn't turned out that way. We've only been driven to the cellars twice since September 1st. I realize that in the western part of the country, and along the north-west coast, the air-raid alarms are more frequent. But in Berlin the British and French air forces have left us very tranquil.

And so this morning thousands of Berliners were out in the streets. Tens of thousands of very young boys – youngsters in the pre-Hitler Youth, aged eight to twelve – swarmed the streets, shaking collection boxes for the Winter Charity Fund. You put a dime in their box, and they gave you a miniature figure cut out of wood, and painted up to look like Mr. Chamberlain with his umbrella, or Mr. Churchill, without an umbrella. These youngsters, like everyone else in Germany, wear uniforms – a sort of a ski suit.

All the stores were open, as they always are in Germany the three

Sundays before Christmas. Those which did not sell goods which are rationed appeared to me to be doing a whacking good business. The first wartime Christmas since 1917 is of course hard on some of the stores which in the years of peace used to do very well at this time of year. The clothing stores, for example, have dressed up their windows very attractively in Christmas style, but the only drawback is you can't buy any Christmas presents in them. People stand before the windows to admire the things, but inside the shops are deserted.

However, the state has made two small concessions. It was always a custom in German families that the menfolk received a necktie for Christmas. So the authorities have announced that every man can have a necktie now, without subtracting points from his clothing card. You have no idea how happy this – it probably seems trifling to you at home – has made a lot of people. And the women of Germany are all to get one extra pair of stockings this week, which won't count on their ration card, which entitles them to four per year.

The shops that sell radios, gramophones, and above all, gramophone records, were jammed this morning, I noticed. But I found one drawback to buying records. Because of the shortage of raw materials, for every record you buy, you have to turn in an old one. But since my home isn't here, I don't have any old ones. Result: I can't buy any new records, even to give as Christmas presents.

There has been a great raid on the toy shops, which indicates that the children in Germany are to have the same old Christmas this year regardless of the war. This morning it was almost impossible to buy a doll for your youngsters, so heavy has been the buying. And the stocks of toy soldiers, tanks, guns etc., always so popular, have almost been exhausted. I noticed that a lot of these things were made out of wood instead of metal this year. I suppose the metal is saved for the real thing.

Biggest business of all is undoubtedly being done by the book-stores. Books are not rationed, and they will form the bulk of the Christmas presents in Germany this year. This morning, it was practically impossible to get inside a bookstore, they were so crowded. I don't know whether American authors can collect their royalties in dollars, but judging by the way German translations of American novels are selling, they'll all have at least a lot of marks to their credit.

It has always been very difficult to get accurate figures on the exodus of the Jews from Germany. Today, for the first time, we're given some figures from Vienna on what has happened to the Jews who lived in former Austria.

There were some 300,000 Jews in old Austria, last March. We're now informed that 70,000 of them have emigrated. Some 15,000 fled without permission or papers. The rest were handled by a control office in Vienna,

163

and, as the Germans say, left "legally". How many were sent to the new Jewish National Ghetto in Lublin, in south eastern Poland, is not stated, but there were certainly several thousands. Some time I would like to go to Lublin, if I can get permission, and make you a report on how they're getting along there.

Berlin December 18, 1939 01.05

Good Evening. This is William L. Shirer in Berlin.

Berlin is following breathlessly the fortunes of the pocket-battleship *Graf Spee* as she steams up the Plata tonight to Buenos Aires. The Western Front, where millions of men stand deadlocked, has been forgotten, also the British air attacks which have been taking place daily now, even the German air attacks on England – all this has been forgotten.

What the people in Berlin want to know is – what will happen to the *Graf Spee*?

German news on it has been scarce tonight. What little we have, we've picked up from foreign sources. At home you may know the fate of the ship by this time.

The news from Montevideo that the *Graf Spee* had transferred most of her crew and stores to a German merchant vessel seemed to indicate that the Germans had decided to scuttle the pocket-battleship rather than to intern her.

The German press tonight published an official statement which seemed to indicate that the usefulness of the *Graf Spee* was considered here to be about over. "The pocket-battleship", said the statement, "has wonderfully fulfilled her task."

It then pointed out how the *Graf Spee* had roamed the seas unhindered for three months, and had sunk 50,000 tons of enemy shipping, and finally won a great sea battle over an overwhelming enemy. The German case was, and is, that the *Graf Spee* was outnumbered three to one, and yet won, and apparently the fact that it carried battleship guns against the smaller guns of the cruisers doesn't count.

The last paragraph of the statement apparently was meant to prepare the public for what may happen. It said, "After the *Graf Spee* entered La Plata, the enemy concentrated every possible craft, airplane-carriers, battleships, heavy and light cruisers, destroyers and submarines, for the moment that they thought they could fall on a German warship which they could not conquer in an open sea battle." That sounded a little like a swan song.

164

It's a curious thing about this war that Germany, with its magnificent land army, which is now mostly idle, is being forced to fight this strange war mostly at sea, where it is weaker than it was in 1914.

And yet the newspapers tonight play up the success of the war on enemy shipping. The Germans claim that from the beginning of the war until last Thursday – that is, until December 14 – the British lost a total of 1,050,864 tons of shipping. This figure, say the Germans, includes 74,000 tons belonging to the British navy, that is, warships. Losses for the first two weeks of December alone, according to the German figures, amounted to 241,000 tons.

The Germans point out in this connection that many new submarines will shortly be ready for action. How many the Germans are building is of course a military secret, but it's no secret that they have been straining every resource to rush a large number of U-boats to completion. Of course, in the last few weeks, German mines have been almost more deadly than German submarines.

I mentioned the other day that marriages had increased by 50 percent since the war began. One of the most popular is marriage by proxy. That is, the bride and bridegroom do not have to be together when the marriage is performed. Thus a man at the front can marry his sweetheart at home, by correspondence so to speak. It takes about two months to complete this kind of marriage, as the necessary papers have to go to and fro by mail. And the woman has an advantage. When the man signs the marriage document, he is definitely married. But for the woman it is only binding two months after she has signed. Many men at the front are getting married in this way.

Berlin December 18, 1939 24.47

Good Evening. This is William L. Shirer in Berlin.

I think by the time the morning papers get out tomorrow, the Germans will have pretty well forgotten the sinking of the *Graf Spee* on the orders of Herr Hitler, and their attention will be focused on the story of the big air battle off the German coast today.

That will be the big story in the German press tomorrow. According to German reports, it was easily the biggest air battle of the war so far. The German account says forty-four British bombers were met north of Helgoland shortly after noon today by a large number of the crack Messerschmitt chasers. According to the official German version, thirty-four of the forty-four British planes were shot down and indeed this account says it is doubted if the other ten got safely home. The Germans give their own losses as two planes down, with the crews escaping in parachutes.

The official report says that a few of the enemy planes succeeded in getting through to Wilhelmshaven, the great German naval base. According to the account that was read to us in the Wilhelmstrasse this afternoon, these planes dropped three bombs near Wilhelmshaven but there was no damage. Later, the official German news agency in describing this action said that the anti-aircraft fire was so hot that the British never had the opportunity for dropping any bombs.

As to the *Graf Spee*, the German view is that the pocket-battleship met a proud and glorious end. As you know, the German government has lodged a sharp protest with the government of Uruguay for refusing to allow the *Graf Spee* to remain in Montevideo long enough to make necessary repairs. The Berlin newspapers tonight angrily attack Uruguay, charging it with flagrantly violating international law and claiming that it acted under pressure from Britain and France.

In this connection, you will recall that though the German Admiralty never made any statement about the damage suffered by the *Graf Spee*, the German press reported continually that it had been only slightly damaged and had only steamed into Montevideo to take on stores. I understand that the decision to scuttle the ship was taken here Sunday morning, after a lengthy report had been received from the German minister in Montevideo giving a full account of the state of the vessel.

The German Official News Agency tonight lists three men who have been sentenced to prison for listening to foreign radio stations and telling their neighbors what they heard. These cases are a warning, it says, and gives notice that the sharpest measures will be taken against those who listen to foreign radio reports.

Coal is the latest product to be rationed in Germany. Henceforth every household will receive seventy pounds of coal a week, about enough, if you use stoves, as most people still do over here, to heat one room. If you rent just one room, say, you'll have to warm yourself in your landlord's parlor.

Berlin December 19, 1939 24.47

Good Evening. This is William L. Shirer in Berlin.

A couple of hours ago, the German Propaganda Ministry called us in to see five or six of the flyers who yesterday took part in the greatest air battle ever fought. You remember that, according to the German version, a large number of British bombers – last night we were told forty-four of them, but the High Command put the figure today at fifty-two – well

166

anyway, there were a lot of them, and they came over yesterday and the Germans said they shot down thirty-four and only lost two themselves.

Lieutenant-Colonel Karl Schumacher, leader of the squadron which did the job, turned out to be a broad-shouldered man of forty-three, who served in the last war in both the army and navy, but not in the air force. He joined the German air force five years ago, and saw service in Poland before being transferred to the German coast.

He had some interesting things to say about yesterday's battle. In the first place, he didn't understand why the British came over yesterday in such large numbers, because there was a clear sky, therefore no ceiling, and it was easy for his fighting planes to get above the British bombers. Last Thursday, when Colonel Schumacher's squadron was credited by the Germans with bagging ten out of twenty British bombers, there had been a low ceiling, he said, and it was difficult to get over the British planes.

Another thing. I wondered how the German chasers got into the air so quickly yesterday. Colonel Schumacher told us how. He said that because of the clear weather, German patrols had sighted the British far out at sea, giving him plenty of time to prepare for them. When the enemy planes arrived, a whole swarm of Messerschmitt fighters were in the air waiting for them.

The Colonel told us he sent up two types of planes to bag the British. Pursuit planes and so-called "destroyer" planes. The latter are heavier and slower than the Messerschmitt pursuers, but they carry more machine-guns.

Colonel Schumacher said it was a real hot battle, and at one time the line of dodging, warring planes stretched 150 miles from north of Heligoland to down near the Dutch islands. Many planes were shot down as far as 80 miles out at sea. He paid tribute to the skill and bravery of the British airmen, but said their bombers were naturally outclassed by the German fighters.

The German airman gave his own losses as two dead and three wounded, and estimated that the British must have lost 170 men – five in each of the thirty-four planes which he said were brought down.

The Papal Nuncio had a long talk with Herr von Ribbentrop today. The conversation gave rise to rumors that the Pope intends to make an appeal for peace at Christmas.

Berlin December 22, 1939 14.00

Good Morning. This is William L. Shirer in Berlin.

Three days until Christmas – and the war goes on.

I remember last September, with the German army victorious every-where in Poland and the Allies doing little in the West, almost every German I know bet me that the war would be over by Christmas. People really believed it here.

That belief – perhaps it was more of a hope – died. Night before last, I went to a dinner party where I had a chance to chat with a large number of Germans. More than one said to me: "I'll bet you we have peace by next Christmas." I think that represents the feelings of very many people in this country.

In the meantime, the Germans are planning to celebrate this Christmas as fully as the rigors of war permit. In no other land in Europe that I know, is Christmas such a deeply felt holiday among all classes of people as in Germany. There are few houses in the land that do not have their Christmas tree, with real candles burning on Christmas Eve – the Germans have never taken to electric candles as have we at home. And everything is being done to give the troops at the front and in the camps, and also the sailors in their ships, what is called here a real German Christmas.

The illustrated weeklies which appeared yesterday – the German equivalents of *Life* magazine – all featured photographs of Christmas at the front or in the warships. The soldiers on the Siegfried Line who spend their days and nights in concrete dugouts far underground were photographed gathering around a candle-lit tree in their cramped bunker quarters and opening their presents from home. Other photographs showed sailors on a warship similarly celebrating Christmas.

It's been hard to buy Christmas presents this year, because of the shortage of goods. But in the end, everyone found something, and though presents and food will be restricted, the Yuletide will be celebrated throughout the land.

Berlin December 24, 1939 15.02

Good Morning. This is William L. Shirer in Berlin.

It's just a couple minutes after three o'clock in the afternoon in Berlin. The stores, which have been open since ten o'clock this morning for last-minute Christmas shopping, have just closed down. When I drove to the studio a few minutes ago through half of Berlin, the streets were thronged with people hurrying home, with parcels dangled from their arms, and some carried sizeable Christmas trees. Because of the shortage of gasoline, you could get few deliveries on your Christmas things this year. People carried their purchases home themselves.

The days are very short here at this time of year. In an hour it'll be dark, and then soon the Christmas trees will be lit in the millions of German homes, and also in the underground dugouts at the front, and on the warships.

The Germans – children and grown-ups alike – always have their Christmas celebration on Christmas Eve, that is this evening, instead of on Christmas Day itself. In Paris, I remember, during the years I was stationed there, we always went to a café at midnight on Christmas Eve and made merry over a sumptuous feast, but here the Germans celebrate the Yuletide at home in a closed family circle.

In an hour or two now, the streets of Berlin will be quite dead, and in the blackout the city will seem all the more deserted. All the theaters and movies will be closed tonight. All the cafés also, after about 8 p.m. If you haven't a home to go to tonight, you're going to be a very lonely person. A few of the small number of Americans here have been invited to German homes for the Christmas Eve festivities. Most of them, however, will foregather in the few American homes in Berlin where the womenfolk have still remained, and celebrate an old-fashioned American Christmas around the tree. As you know, most of the Americans here, on the advice of Washington, have sent their wives and children home to the States. They're a little sad about Christmas this year, with their loved ones so far away. But they're not completely cut off, at that. Most of my American friends here have been saving their marks this month so that they can telephone their families in New York or Boston or Chicago.

Because of the fear of espionage, you have to get special permission to telephone abroad, and it costs a lot of money, but it's certainly worth it.

As to news, all the papers this morning report the return of the celebrated U-boat commander Captain Prien, who, it is revealed, made his way back to a German port on December 20. According to an official statement, the Captain confirmed his earlier wireless report that he had torpedoed a British cruiser. At the time, I believe, this was denied in London. The official statement adds that Captain Prien also sank during his last trip 26,159 tons of enemy shipping. He and his crew have been given Christmas leave with their families.

The papers give a big play to Captain Prien's return, and with good reason, I think, because there had been a persistent rumor in circulation here for the last two weeks that he was long overdue and that he and his crew were feared lost. The admiralty does not make public each U-boat loss, and it was impossible to get any information about Captain Prien until today.

The German people later today are to hear two Christmas-Eve broadcasts from their leaders. The first, at 7:30 p.m., will be given by General von Brauchitsch, the Commander-in-Chief of the German army, speaking from his headquarters on the Western Front. His speech will be mainly for those millions of men now in uniform who will not be with their families at Christmas time, but no doubt most of the civilian population will also gather around their loudspeakers to hear him. In the last war, a commander-in-chief could not speak to his troops so intimately. But now, with a radio receiver in every German unit, no matter whether it's in a dugout or in a camp, practically every soldier in the army will be able to hear this personal message from General von Brauchitsch.

Rudolf Hess, Herr Hitler's deputy, will also broadcast to the nation at 9:20 p.m. from Wilhelmshaven, the great naval base. In former years, he always spoke over the radio on Christmas Eve to the Germans living abroad.

There is no news published as to how Herr Hitler will spend his Christmas, but I would not be surprised if he spent it at the Western Front – that same front where he spent four long years as a soldier in the mud and snow of the trenches.

Kiel December 25, 1939 22.22

Hello CBS and Merry Christmas. William L. Shirer calling you from one of the great German naval bases somewhere in Germany.

(*Ships' bells sound.*)

I'm speaking to you on this Christmas night from the pitch-dark, lonely deck of a German warship. Across the water I can see the dim outlines of other warships. Up here on deck, it's cold and dark, and there's a wind whipping across the water.

Let's go below deck and see what it looks like there on this Christmas night.

(*Songs of sailors . . . Accordion*)

That's what it sounds like below deck on a submarine supply ship in a German naval port on Christmas night. All these men you heard singing are members of submarine crews back for a few days from their dangerous work.

I've spent this entire Christmas Day with the German navy. So far, this has been mainly a sea war, and I wanted to see what the German navy looked like, and then – it being Christmas – how the men spent Christmas. I left Berlin long before dawn this morning and have meandered through some of Germany's best-known warships today in two big naval ports, which for obvious reasons must go unnamed. A word about that experience before we join these sailors here in their Christmas celebration.

170

The German sailors certainly enjoyed a real Christmas on their ships. I sat with them in their quarters first in the heavy cruiser *Admiral Hipper* in one port, and then later in the big battleship *Gneisenau* in another port. The crews' quarters shone with the candles from the Christmas trees, and at the foot of each tree was a present for every single man. The sailors had rigged up most ingenious exhibits, one a miniature of the Western Front true to the last detail, another an electrically-operated model of the battle with the *Rawalpindi* which was very realistic; another of the famous Christmas carnival in Hamburg, with toy merry-go-rounds, roller-coasters, all working just like the real ones. I noticed, too, many cartoons the men had painted and hung up on the walls. They mostly harpooned Mr. Churchill.

Incidentally, at one port I saw what I was told was the cruiser *Leipzig*, which I believe was reported abroad as sunk. It was in dry-dock being repaired.

A little while ago, I looked over the bay and could see the outlines of two big battleships, one pocket-battleship, two cruisers of the Cologne class, and Hitler's yacht, not to mention many submarines. And on all of them Christmas was being celebrated.

Well, let's look at the celebration on this ship. I think the boys want to sing.

(*Songs ... Few words describing scene ... Ask them to sing "Stille Nacht"*)

I return you now to America.

Berlin December 27, 1939 24.47

Good Evening. This is William L. Shirer in Berlin.

Now that Christmas is over and the New Year is almost upon us, people here – and I suppose elsewhere too – are asking: What's next? Most Germans I know agree that it has been a weird sort of war so far, and that it won't continue that way very much longer. But when you ask them what the new phase is going to be – well, that's more puzzling, they don't know. And if the German High Command knows, it naturally isn't going to advertise it.

Everyone realizes that an offensive against the short Maginot Line would be staggering in its cost of human lives. The Germans deny that they have any intention of a flank movement through the neutral countries, which is about the only other possibility for an offensive in the West.

Of course, there's the sea, where the war has been mostly fought so far.

171

But there Britain and France have too much of a superiority for a decisive sea-offensive to be possible.

There remains the air, in which Germany is certainly very strong. And most people you talk to here think that the offensive, if and when it comes, will be in the air, and that it will be directed against England. That's the talk here, but so far it's only talk. But the man in the street in Germany for some reason is now beginning to think that it will be a short war after all, that it will be over by summer and, naturally, that Germany will win.

The Christmas speeches of the King of England and M. Daladier were not reported here. But the official reaction is naturally negative and one inspired statement I saw tonight said, "The German people listened to these Christmas speeches with fine nerves."

But there is one important new development in German propaganda. Heretofore, it has been directed almost exclusively against England. Today, I notice for the first time, the propaganda guns are opening up against France too.

Herr Himmler, the Gestapo chief, today decreed that New Year's celebrations in Germany must end by 1 a.m., and he withdrew permission for cafés and night-clubs to remain open all night New Year's Eve, which he had given last week. The seriousness of the hour is given as the reason, and Herr Himmler warns that the excessive use of alcohol, in view of the blackout, must be avoided. The sharpest measures, he adds, will be taken against drunkenness on New Year's Eve.

The papers play up a story that a German woman has been given ten years in the penitentiary for having an affair with a Polish prisoner. The press comments, "Let this be a warning!"

Berlin December 30, 1939 24.46

Good Evening. This is William L. Shirer in Berlin.

We're a little ahead of you in time over here, so in Berlin it's already the last day of the year. It's going to be a relatively quiet, sober New Year in Germany this time, and on account of the war and the blackout, the police have decided to close all cafés, restaurants, and bars at 1 a.m., that is just an hour after the people have seen the New Year in.

It being the last day of the year, I can give you the substance of Herr Hitler's two New Year proclamations, which will be published in a few hours in the morning papers. There are numerous other proclamations from all the other Nazi leaders, but we'll have time only for those of Herr Hitler, one to the armed forces, the other to the Nazi party.

One thing stands out in the German Führer's New Year message to his soldiers and people. He thinks that the coming year will bring the decision in this strange war. He says so twice in his proclamation to the party.

"United within the country," Herr Hitler says, "economically prepared and militarily armed to the highest degree, we enter this most decisive year in German history." And a little later, he remarks:

"May the year 1940 bring the decision. It will be, whatever happens, our victory."

And what have been the outstanding events of 1939 for Germany? Herr Hitler, in his proclamation, names four.

First, the inclusion of what the Führer calls the "age-old German districts of Bohemia and Moravia as a Protectorate in the German Reich". This, Herr Hitler explains, pacified Central Europe and secured Germany's living room, or *Lebensraum*, and he adds that Czechs and Germans will, as a result, henceforth live peacefully together.

The second outstanding event of 1939, says Herr Hitler, was the return of Memel.

The third I better quote: "Through the destruction of the former Polish state, there followed the restoration of the old German frontier."

In these three cases, adds the Führer, the unnatural constructions of the Versailles Treaty were done away with.

The fourth outstanding event of 1939 for Herr Hitler, he says, was the pact with Soviet Russia which, he points out, killed the attempt of what he calls the "plutocratic statesmen of the West" to force the two nations to shed blood against one another and also encircle Germany.

Herr Hitler tells his people in this New Year's proclamation that what he terms "the Jewish international capitalism in league with the reactionaries" is really responsible for this war. Says he, and I quote, "The German people did not want this war. I tried up to the last minute to keep peace with England ... But the Jewish and reactionary warmongers waited for this minute to carry out their plans to destroy Germany. These war-gentlemen wanted the war, and now they'll get it."

The proclamation is a bitter indictment of England. France is not mentioned. And finally, Herr Hitler tells his people that what the Allies really want is not his – Hitler's – destruction, but the destruction of the German nation and the German people.

In his New Year's proclamation to the armed forces, Herr Hitler is much briefer. He tells the soldiers that before them lies the great struggle as to whether Germany is to be or not to be. Field Marshal Göring in his New Year's proclamation concludes that the slogan for 1940 will be: "The Führer Commands. We Follow."

Berlin January 1, 1940 24.47

Good Evening. And Happy New Year.

If this New Year has started with any sensational developments, we haven't heard of them in Berlin yet. No newspapers are published in Germany today, and the German radio has been very sparse with its news this evening.

Berlin itself took on today almost the normal appearance of peace-time, except for the almost total absence of motorcars in the streets. Thousands of citizens strolled through the snow in the Tiergarten, Berlin's Central Park, and this afternoon the streets were thronged. Except for the number of men in uniform you would hardly have known that a great war was on.

Last night's New Year's celebrations passed off quietly, compared to other years. Because the capital's transportation system closed down shortly after 2 a.m., thousands of people had to walk home in the cold. There were a few taxis about, but the police wouldn't let you get into them on the grounds that the new gasoline restrictions only permit you to ride in a taxi when you have urgent business of importance to the state, and it was hard proving that you had urgent state business at 2:30 a.m. on New Year's Eve, though a lot of us tried to.

Herr Hitler himself, though nothing is published about it, is under-stood to have changed his New Year's plans and spent the evening not in Berlin, but with the German fleet.

The Germans announced tonight that the last of five big Hamburg-America Line steamers, which in peacetime ply between here and New York, slipped safely past the British blockade into a German port today. It was the 16,000-ton liner *St. Louis*. Like the *Bremen*, I believe, it had recently been in Murmansk.

Reports from Budapest and Belgrade say that the Danube River, Central and Eastern Europe's most important waterway, is frozen over and all ship-ping tied up. Now, it is the Danube which right now brings the bulk of Germany's imports of precious oil from Romania and wheat from Romania and the other Balkan states. Formerly, most of the oil was brought around by sea, but that route is now closed by the blockade, and except for railroad lines, the Danube is the only other route left. If the Danube remains frozen over for two months, as I remember it did in 1930, for I was stationed in Vienna then, the consequences will not be very pleasant.

The snow and cold also hamper rail-transport in Eastern Europe, and with most of the Baltic ports now freezing over this will affect the transport of Russia's raw materials to Germany. These Russian materials are now scheduled to begin arriving here in large quantities, and it will be interesting to see if they do arrive.

As for other news, it's very scarce in the newspapers this morning. The noon paper, just out, the *Börsen Zeitung Am Mittag,* devotes its front page banner-line to a Moscow report that the Bolsheviks have been arresting British Secret Service agents in Russia who, it is alleged, posed as German businessmen. This report, like many nowadays, comes in a roundabout way from Copenhagen.

And then Hamilton Fish, certainly the most frequently quoted Congressman of all in the Nazi press, makes the front pages again today. He's quoted as having taken a stand against British propagandists in the United States and for having demanded that Washington send an ambassador to Berlin. Needless to say, Mr. Fish's stand is warmly approved in Berlin.

The official daily communiqué of the German High command reports all quiet on the Western Front except for slight harassing artillery fire. It then reports that the British airplanes which tried to approach the German coast on December 31st, are now established to have made their return to England over Dutch territory.

Then the High Command gives its version of yesterday's flight of German planes to the Shetland and Orkney Islands. One hundred and fifty miles from the Scottish coast, says the German communiqué, the German planes were met by an overwhelming British force. One of the German planes, it explains, had already developed some motor trouble and lost most of its fighting efficiency, and during the battle was forced to alight on the sea. One British plane, claims the High Command, was also damaged, so that the Germans say they consider it improbable that it regained its base.

Berlin January 2, 1940 14.05

Good Morning. This is William L. Shirer in Berlin.

As you know, we're not allowed to broadcast the weather, because if we did, we might give the enemy valuable information. But perhaps I can mention the temperature without giving aid and comfort to the other side. It's very cold here, and the papers this morning – the first we've had since Sunday morning – are full of pictures of the Berlin populace out skating on the numerous lakes that surround Berlin and which are now frozen over.

It looks as though we may be in for a very cold winter – Europe usually has one in seven-year cycles, and a really severe winter is overdue. The last one I remember over here was the winter of 1929-30, which was the coldest Europe had seen for a century.

Why all this talk about the weather? Well, because aside from the fact that a prolonged cold spell will make military operations well nigh impossible for many weeks, it will also freeze over the rivers and canals, upon which Central Europe, especially, depends to a larger extent than most people realize.

Take Germany. She has a magnificent system of water transportation on her rivers and canals. And now that war demands on the German state railways have taxed their capacity so fully that some of the transport for civilian needs is in a bad way, the inland water transportation system is more important than ever. Should the canals and rivers freeze over for the next six weeks or two months, Germany's transport problems would certainly increase. Already, it is difficult to get coal and many other things, not because there is not a sufficient supply on hand, but because there is no means of transporting the supply on hand to the customers.

But a cold spell such as we had over here in 1930, when all the principal waterways in Europe were blocked by ice for two months, is also a matter of concern for this country in relation to its importation of vital raw materials – especially oil and food from south-east Europe and the Balkans.

A German remarked to me today that the reason Germany was recalling all its ships was because it needed them to transport troops when the invasion of Great Britain began. I'm not sure he knew what he was talking about – it was New Year's morning – but I pass the remark along to you for what it is worth.

The High Command reports today that all was quiet on the Western Front. It adds that enemy planes tried to approach the German coast yesterday afternoon, but were driven off. For the first time in a long while it does not mention any enemy losses.

Reports from Hungary and the Balkans that the Danube is freezing over, tying up shipping, are being closely followed here. Now that the sea-route has been cut by the blockade, the Danube is a very vital artery for German imports of oil from Romania and food from the Balkans.

Berlin January 3, 1940 24.47

Good Evening. This is William L. Shirer in Berlin.

President Roosevelt's message to Congress was read too late for any German reaction to be available in Berlin tonight. It was already 8 p.m. our time when the President started speaking.

The speech, of course, was not broadcast in Germany. You at home hear Herr Hitler every time he makes an important speech, but the

German people do not hear Mr. Roosevelt, ever. As a matter of fact, they could have picked him up by short-wave, but that would have been against the law prohibiting tuning in on a foreign station in war-time. We correspondents, who are permitted to listen to foreign broadcasts, tuned in, but reception was poor tonight because of local atmospherics, and the first ten minutes of the speech were hardly audible.

I think we can take it for granted though that that part of the President's message about dictators and freedom and aggression against small powers did not make the Wilhelmstrasse feel any happier about the United States. But the President's reiteration about our keeping out of the war will no doubt be welcomed here. That's all Germany hopes for so far as we're concerned, but they really do hope for that, and indeed, I think, count on our staying out.

Incidentally, Washington's protest to Great Britain over the stopping of American mail gets a good press in Germany today, as you might expect. I see that mail from home posted early in October and held up in Britain is now being delivered to us here. Mail sent on the Clippers is the only mail we get from home regularly and within a reasonable time.

The German press today begins to publish warnings to Scandinavia about conniving with Britain and France to help Finland. A quotation from a Moscow paper about England and France having instigated little Finland to attack Russia is reprinted here with warm approval.

Berlin January 5, 1940 14.00

Good Morning. This is William L. Shirer in Berlin.

The story in the newspapers that catches the eye of the German public this morning is the announcement that Field Marshal Göring has become absolute wartime economic dictator of Germany. From now on, all the economic power of Germany is to be concentrated in his strong hands.

"What does it mean?" the people are asking today. And the economic writers in the newspapers tell them it means still more unification in the economic sphere, but with one powerful man at the top whose decisions will be the law of the land and whose well-known ruthless energy will force the German economy on to a still faster pace.

As the *Deutsche Allgemeine Zeitung* puts it: "Everyone knows what it means when Göring takes something into his hands . . . He's an economic program in himself, as the world learnt when he directed the Four Year Plan."

Well, everyone here certainly knows that world wars cost money. And yesterday the German press broke the news to the people that war taxation, already very heavy, would have to be increased still more to finance the struggle. Judged by talk in German business circles, not only are general taxes going up, but a super-tax on luxuries will also be imposed. You see, when you're on the ration system, and can only buy a relatively small amount of such necessities as food, clothing, and fuel, you're liable, as the Minister of Economics, Dr. Funk said in a speech at Salzburg the other day, you're liable to spend your surplus money on luxuries – he mentioned deluxe bathtubs and bathing gowns. The state naturally does not want a lot of the people's money squandered on luxuries. Hence it will no doubt see that a good share of the money spent on deluxe goods henceforth goes into the coffers of the treasury.

If people cannot buy luxuries or necessities beyond a limited measure, they're obviously going to have some spare change lying around. Dr. Funk and his Nazi colleagues think this ought to be put in the bank as savings, where the government could then use it as capital to help finance the war. But to make sure that the money is deposited in savings accounts, and not hoarded or thrown away on luxuries, business circles are discussing the possibility of the state instituting compulsory savings. Thus everyone, say, who earned more than $100 a month would have to deposit so much per month in the savings banks. Most people think that will come soon.

President Roosevelt's message to Congress day before yesterday finally gets four paragraphs on page four of Germany's leading newspaper, the *Völkischer Beobachter*. The official Nazi organ also comments editorially, stating that Mr. Roosevelt reminds it of the late President Wilson, and contending that when the President speaks of dictatorships and force and threats against the independence of small nations, he shouldn't overlook Britain, which, the paper thinks, is using dictatorial methods and force, and really threatens the independence of the little countries.

Listening to Mr. Roosevelt the other evening by short-wave, I wondered if any Germans were listening in, because they're not supposed to listen to any foreign stations. And I see in the papers this morning that a restaurant proprietor in Hamburg got three years in the penitentiary for tuning in on foreign stations, mainly, it seems, on the French station at Toulouse. The court said the sentence was so mild because it had not been proved that the fellow passed on what he heard. He just kept it to himself.

In that connection, the restaurant and café proprietors are complaining here that their clients don't seem to listen properly to the news broadcasts from the German stations. The complaint is they go on chatting and thus prevent those who do want to hear the news from getting it. It's therefore suggested that signs be put up in all cafés and restaurants asking the customers to observe silence when the German news bulletins are being read.

Berlin January 8, 1940 01.00

Good Evening. This is William L. Shirer in Berlin.

Here by my side is Germany's greatest living World-War ace, a famous member of the Richthofen Squadron who himself shot down sixty-two Allied planes. At the moment he's the key man of Germany's new air force, being responsible for the designing and production of German war planes. He's here to say a few words about his work – Lieutenant-General Ernst Udet.

GENERAL ERNST UDET: It is a great pleasure for me to speak to my friends today. I still remember the wonderful and happy time which I had when I was invited to the National Air Races in Cleveland in 1931 and those in 1935 in Los Angeles, Chicago, and New York. There I learned what American hospitality and friendliness really were. Therefore, I am especially glad to be able to say a word to you about the technical state of the German air force today.

After I returned from the States in 1933, my old comrade and last commander of the Richthofen Squadron, General Field Marshal Göring, entrusted me with my present task. My job, as chief of the technical and supply department of the Air Ministry, makes me responsible for the technical level of the German air force and aircraft industry.

The Field Marshal gave me powers, with clear aims and demands, in the very field where he is most expert, the air force. This allowed me to put into practice my personal experiences during the World War as well as my post-war experiences both in airplane production and in flying. I have not been hampered by any red tape. I have received special aid from my good friends, Messerschmitt, Junkers, Heinkel, Tank, and Dornier, who are among the most important constructors and industrialists in Germany.

For the first time in 1937, the German air force successfully met on neutral ground in Zürich the air forces of the other countries. It was clearly shown there that the young German air force had not only kept pace with the others, but that it was good enough to win all the military races which it entered. We subsequently began to clear up the actual top performances by establishing a series of speed records, one after the other – records which so far have not even been approximately attained by our neighbors.

I dislike exaggeration, but I can say I feel all right about the future. And I'm positively convinced that the actual airfights in this war will continue to confirm the correctness of our development and production. I think we're on the right line.

I can assure you that we shall be very quick on the trigger in our decisions. And we can adjust our actions and our production to whatever demands the air war may bring. No experiences will be neglected which may come out of this war, which we feel has been forced on us.

Personally, I have a very good opinion of American aircraft production, as I know most of your leading manufacturers.

I am therefore not surprised that England and France have chosen the easy way of brushing-up their air forces by getting valuable airplane material in the United States.

I thank you. Happy New Year to all my friends.

SHIRER: And thank you, General Udet, for coming to the microphone, especially as I know you're a very busy man these days.

Berlin January 9, 1940 14.00

Good Morning. This is William L. Shirer in Berlin.

With Herr Hitler back in Berlin to resume contact with his military advisers, it is taken for granted here that plans are now being drawn up for the resumption – or perhaps it would be more correct to say for the *beginning* – of war operations in the West.

It is still much too cold over here for much to be done immediately, but no one in Berlin thinks that the war can continue indefinitely as it has the last four months. The watchword here is: "Action in the Spring". But what kind of action and where it will be, still remains a mystery.

In the meantime, the German press makes strange reading these days, and I often wonder what the mass of the German people make out of their newspapers. For many days now, there has not been one single big spot news story. This being so, the propagandists have had a field day. They have had to fill the papers with some kind of print.

Hence a few days ago, one of the leading Berlin newspapers devoted its two-line banner-headline stretching clear across the front page to a letter which some Englishman had written to a London illustrated weekly. Last night and this morning, almost the only front-page story in Germany has been an account, written in Berlin, of the Nazi version of why Mr. Hore-Belisha, the British war minister, resigned. Perhaps you'd like to hear it. According to the Nazis, the real reason for Mr. Hore-Belisha's resignation was that World Jewry considered that he had compromised the Jewish race by not entirely succeeding in his post, and that the international Jews, who can do what they like with Mr. Chamberlain, decided to retire Mr. Hore-Belisha behind the scenes for the time being. That's the Nazi explanation given to the German people, and I merely pass it on to you.

More and more, the Nazis train their anti-semitic guns on foreign Jews. Mr. Hore-Belisha was continually attacked as being a, quote, "Moroccan ghetto Jew".

This morning, another foreign Jewish leader, Léon Blum, former French Premier, gets the headlines, though in this case M. Blum is quoted approvingly in the German press. M. Blum is quoted as having written that in this war, France has much less money than she had in 1914 and that the financial burden will be much more onerous. M. Blum is then cited as recalling that the old World War slogan that "the Boche will pay" in the end, has no more meaning for present-day Frenchmen.

To which item the German press adds a common editorial statement, in part, as follows: "Herr Blum sees, with the sure instinct of his race, the problem only from the financial side."

Berlin January 9, 1940 24.47

Good Evening.

The war in the air livened up a bit today. According to an official statement issued in Berlin tonight, German war planes destroyed several British patrol boats and also some merchant ships which were being convoyed by naval vessels. The action, says the Berlin account, took place off the coast of Scotland and England, while German planes were engaged in reconnaissance flights. The statement adds that all the German planes returned safely to their base.

There are two interesting points in this German communiqué. First, that German planes are now being used to attack merchant convoys. And second, that no mention is made of British fighters engaging the more ponderous long-range German aircraft. How is it, Germans are asking tonight, that we can send our bombers clear to the coast of Scotland – a distance of some 500 miles – and no English pursuit planes come out to meet them? Perhaps Ed Murrow will answer that one from London tonight.

The most interesting and important development in German propaganda on the home-front is its increasing anti-semitism. The new line here, for home consumption – and mark this – is that this is not only a war against the hated British but a war against the Jews.

Dr. Robert Ley, one of the most important members of the Nazi régime, states it clearly in the *Angriff* tonight. Says he: "We know that this war is an ideological struggle against world Jewry. England is allied with the Jews against Germany. How low must the English people have fallen to have had as war minister a parasitical and profiteering Jew of the worst kind . . . England is spiritually, politically and economically at one with the Jews . . . For us, England and the Jews remain the common foe . . . Germany has won the first battle. Hore-Belisha has fallen." All this from Dr. Ley.

I'm betraying no military secrets when I tell you that this has been one of the coldest days I've experienced in fourteen years in Europe. Luckily, the coal situation began to improve today. More train-loads of coal arrived, and thousands of volunteers, many of them students, went to work to unload it. This afternoon, you saw the precious coal being hauled through the streets in every imaginable kind of vehicle – street-cars, private autos, horse-carts, hand-carts, even in wheel-barrows. The coal was there, and if you could fetch it yourself, you were sure to have warmth in your house.

Berlin January 13, 1940 24.46

Good Evening. This is William L. Shirer in Berlin.

On my way to the studio tonight, I bought a copy of the early Sunday morning edition of one of Berlin's leading newspapers – the *Lokal Anzeiger*. I'd like to read you its front-page bannerline: BRITISH BOMBARD ARAB VILLAGES – FRIGHTFUL BLOOD BATH, 240 DEAD – HALF THE VICTIMS WOMEN AND CHILDREN. The headline was based on a Rome dispatch quoting travelers returning from Baghdad.

This will give you an idea of the news that we get in the German press in the very midst of a European war. Of the progress of the war, we hear very little – a few skirmishes in the air always ending in victory for the home side, and that's about all.

For example, the High Command reported that yesterday all was quiet on the Western Front. We, on this side, are not allowed to go to the front, and it's difficult to get even a picture of what the situation is there. But today, I did pick up a few scraps.

For one thing, the roads and the trenches on the Western Front the last few days have been covered with ice and snow, making movement very difficult. Yesterday, it seems, French artillery opened up a little more actively than usual, and shelled the German positions south of Perl and Schneeberg. German artillery replied by bombarding the road behind the French lines between Apach and Milchen. Berlin now admits that the engagements between various patrols have been livelier the last few days, but of course there has been no fighting on any scale. The largest unit used this week, say the Germans, was a company of infantry, and it was a French company. It's interesting that the Germans mention for the first time today the presence of Polish troops on the Western Front.

As I've frequently reported, special German courts are busy all over Poland grinding out sentences against Poles accused of having had a hand in the slaying of German civilians. The latest sentences of the special court at Bromberg are as follows: one Pole condemned to death, an eighteen-year-old Polish youth sentenced to fifteen years in prison, two other Poles to five years in prison. In the cases where the Poles escaped with their lives, no German life was lost.

The Wilhelmstrasse today denies that Germany has offered to effect a compromise settlement in the Russo-Finnish war. According to the Wilhelmstrasse, there never would have been a war had not Finland been badly advised by Great Britain – in other words, if Finland had given in to *all* the Russian demands, since, as is known, it had given in to most of them.

In this connection, there's an interesting article in the Berlin paper, *Nachtausgabe*, today, stating that Russia's goal is an outlet on the North Atlantic, that this is a vital necessity for the Soviet Union, and that Germany appreciates this.

I talked so much about the weather this week, that I think I ought to tell you that it suddenly turned warmer today. And if you live in Berlin and are still without coal, as many are, it isn't so uncomfortable tonight as it was.

You remember reading about the famous catchword in Germany during the last war – *Gott strafe England* [God punish England]. I'm told that in some of the schools in Berlin, the teachers now greet their pupils with a *Gott strafe England*, whereupon the youngsters are supposed to answer – "He will."

Berlin January 14, 1940 01.02

Good Evening. This is William L. Shirer in Berlin.

The last sentence of the official daily communiqué of the German High Command, issued in Berlin about noon today, reads as follows: "A Dutch airplane flew over the German border near Nordhorn during the afternoon and violated German territory."

Note that the communiqué does not specify whether the Dutch plane was a military or a civil machine. It merely says it was a Dutch plane and that it violated German territory.

Nordhorn, over which the Dutch plane is alleged to have flown, is a German town lying close to the border where it juts out into Holland, forming a salient of German territory. If you flew north or south along the Dutch frontier, and missed the salient because of bad visibility, you'd probably come very close to the town of Nordhorn.

We get news from outside very late in this country, and this morning, when I pointed out this item in the High Command's communiqué, I had not heard of the special military measures taken in Belgium and the Netherlands. I learned of those only this evening.

Being a Sunday, it was difficult to contact officials in the Wilhelm-strasse. Those we did contact could only speak privately. They said they were surprised that the two countries to the west of Germany should take any such additional military measures as were reported from Brussels and The Hague. And they said they thought it was a mere coincidence that the High Command happened to report a Dutch violation of German territory on the day that the Dutch and Belgian armies were suddenly canceling all military leave.

The official position here is, as you know, that all this talk about the German army contemplating marching through the Netherlands or Belgium is merely Allied propaganda. Neutral observers here are skeptical about any big military operations starting now in the West because of the bad state of the roads due to the snow and ice, which is now melting.

At any rate, I wasn't the only one struck by the last sentence in the High Command's report today. The early edition of the Berlin newspaper, *Der Montag*, carries a banner front-page headline saying DUTCH AIRPLANE VIOLATES GERMAN TERRITORY.

At any rate, the German press tonight does not play up the new military measures taken in The Netherlands and Belgium. From The Hague there is no news at all. From Brussels a four-line dispatch buried in the inside of the papers saying merely, "The Belgian Defense Ministry announces that all troops of all units now on leave must return immediately to their posts."

The cry of "colonies for Germany" was raised in this country today for the first time since the war began. Speaking in the province of Lippe, Dr. Frick, the German Minister of the Interior, told a large Nazi audience, "Germany has 360,000 more births a year than France and Britain combined. With such a population we can demand a more fair distribution of the wealth of this world. We have a right to demand our colonies back. And we'll see this demand through. But today, there's no use of talking about it. Arms will have to decide."

Dr. Frick said that the Nazi régime would strive to end the war as quickly as possible. But he told his audience that the aim of the Führer was to fight the war through with as small losses as possible. This is the first time I've heard a Nazi leader state that. Dr. Frick also reiterated the new Nazi line, which is that England is ruled by Jews and therefore Germany is fighting against the Jews.

Through a typographical error, one Berlin newspaper quoted the minister as saying that Germany also was ruled by Jews, but of course I need not insist on the fact that Dr. Frick certainly said no such thing.

I note in the speeches here lately that the hopes of an early end to this war are no longer emphasized. Said Dr. Ley, one of the most important men in the régime, today, "No one knows how long this war will last."

We now have the text of an order issued by the German police putting all Jews in German-occupied Poland under forced labor. I quote in part:

"All Jews from fourteen to sixty years of age are subject to forced labor. The length of forced labor is two years, but it will be prolonged if its educational purpose is not considered fulfilled.

"Jews called up for forced labor must report promptly, and must bring food for two days and their bedding. Skilled Jewish workers must report with their tools. Those who don't are subject to sentences running to ten years in the penitentiary."

Murrow-Shirer Joint Broadcast Amsterdam January 18, 1940

[Shirer and Ed Murrow, who had become close friends, met in Holland for a few days in January 1940, when Murrow was on his way from London to Paris.]

MURROW: Did you have a nice trip, Bill?

SHIRER: Not bad. In peacetime we used to fly from Berlin to Amsterdam in a couple of hours. Now you have to take the train. Takes about thirteen hours. All trains now are late – and cold. But it's all right when you get here. But you flew over, didn't you?

MURROW: I think so. It was more like being swung around in a barrel at the end of a long rope than flying. The plane was painted bright orange, and all the windows were blacked out.

SHIRER: Why do they black the windows out?

MURROW: Just so curious reporters can't see anything while flying over England and the Channel.

SHIRER: How long did it take you from London to Amsterdam?

MURROW: Do you mean flying time, or total time?

SHIRER: I mean altogether.

MURROW: I left London at seven in the morning, traveled on a cold train

185

to a little place you are not supposed to know about, spent about three hours doing things with little bits of paper and books, and got to Amsterdam about half past three in the afternoon.

SHIRER: It's not so simple getting out of these countries, is it?

MURROW: Six months ago, I could have traveled around the world with fewer papers and documents than were required for this trip.

SHIRER: Well, I'm glad to hear that, because I thought that the place where I work had a monopoly on that sort of thing.

MURROW: You know, Bill, this conversation isn't going very well. Maybe it's because we both want to talk about the same thing.

SHIRER: Listen, Ed, I want to talk to you about the lights I saw last night in this town.

MURROW: All right, go ahead and get it over with.

SHIRER: You've got no idea what it is like to get into a city and see the streets all lighted up.

MURROW: What do you mean, I've got no idea? I saw street lights, automobiles with real headlights, and light pouring out of windows tonight for the first time in five months. It's a shock, it seems almost indecent to have all this light about. As soon as we finish here, I'm going out to look at those lights again.

SHIRER: Maybe you think I'm not too. You know, Ed, it sounds childish to say so, but when I got in last night and emerged from the station and saw all these lights, I dropped my bags in the snow and just wandered about the streets for half an hour, just looking at the lights. I kept studying the position of every lamp-post and fire hydrant, making a mental note of their location so I wouldn't run into them if the blackout comes.

MURROW: Let's hope it doesn't come. Right now, Holland seems to me just about the nicest country in Europe. There's light, heat, –

SHIRER: And don't forget food and coffee – and oranges.

MURROW: It's been snowing all day, people have been skating on the canals and everybody is as calm, courteous and considerate as ever.

SHIRER: Just taking a quick look at this country, you'd hardly know there was a war. Like in Switzerland, you see quite a few soldiers in the stations, but that's about all.

MURROW: I'd like to forget there's a war on for a few days, but I suppose since this is the first time we've been together since the war started, we'd better compare a few notes, remembering three things: first, that we're talking from a neutral country, second, that you've got to go back to Berlin and third, that I've got to go back to London. The question most people are asking in England these days is, "Will the Germans attack in the spring?"

SHIRER: I don't know a single German who isn't sure that there will be plenty of action in the spring. But what kind it will be, and where, no one knows or is likely to know until the blow falls.

MURROW: Does that mean that the Germans have pretty well given up hope for the success of the so-called "peace offensive"?

SHIRER: Absolutely. You hear no more talk of peace in Berlin. As Dr. Frick, the Minister of the Interior, told the people last Sunday, the decision now must come by force of arms, and the German people seem reconciled to that.

MURROW: Well, when you say "action in the spring" do you mean a general offensive?

SHIRER: Not exactly. Dr. Frick promised the people the other day that no lives would be thrown away in this war. Most people took that to mean that there would be no large-scale offensive against the Maginot Line, which would be a very costly proceeding. In Germany, when people talk of action in the spring, they seem to have in mind something else, say a great air offensive directed against the country where you're stationed. Of course, the truth is, when you come right down to it, that German generals, like British and French generals, are not giving away their plans in advance. Therefore, whatever happens is likely to be in the nature of a surprise. But that something will happen, and soon, every last person in Germany is sure. Well, Ed, what sort of action, if any, do the people on your side expect as soon as the snow melts?

MURROW: Oh, we get a different theory every twenty-four hours, but on the whole the British think they are doing pretty well as things are.

SHIRER: You mean they expect the war to continue as it has, for the next few years? Because the Germans don't.

MURROW: Well, put it this way. The British think their blockade is squeezing Germany pretty hard; they aren't losing many men; they're trying to equal Germany's rate of airplane production, and a considerable number of people have some sort of vague idea that if they just keep the pressure on the Germans, they'll finally crack without a major military action. The real difficulty of course is that there is no "front".

SHIRER: You can almost say that this is a war in search of a front.

MURROW: Well, as it looks from London, the Germans still have the initiative and can pick whatever front they like for this move you expect in the spring.

SHIRER: That's interesting, because the Germans think that the Allies have already taken the initiative in their quest for new fronts, say in Scandinavia or in south-east Europe, or in both places. Strategically, it's to the advantage of the Germans to keep that front as small as possible, and of course, if it's to be widened, to pick the new front themselves.

MURROW: Of course, the British are looking about for new fronts, but the map is all cluttered up with neutrals and the British assert that they don't propose to violate anybody's neutrality; but there's always the possibility that some neutral may invite them to come in to prevent the house from being robbed.

SHIRER: Here's a question I'd like to put to you, Ed. Is there any talk in your country of a possibility of a negotiated peace before the war really gets serious?

MURROW: Plenty. You see, the official British position is this: they say they're going to negotiate peace at the end of this war even if they have to beat the Germans first. Of course, those ideas may change when the time comes to make the peace. For the time being, British propaganda is trying to convince the Germans that they can have a reasonable peace if they'll only get rid of their present rulers.

SHIRER: In all frankness, I must say that I don't think this propaganda is getting very far in Germany. The average German you talk to, regardless of whether he is a supporter of the régime or not, will tell you that he remembers very well the Allied propaganda in 1917-1918, in which America also had a part, and which promised him that if only he would get rid of the Kaiser, the German people would be given a just peace. Somehow, this Allied talk about getting rid of the present régime and then getting a fair peace strikes him as no more sincere than the similar propaganda in the last war.

MURROW: Does that mean that the Germans take the view that it's all or nothing, that they must win the war or be smashed completely?

SHIRER: Exactly. Every day it's hammered into them that they have only two alternatives: either to win the war, in which case they have a bright future, or to lose the war, in which case, their present leaders assure them, there will be such a peace as will make Versailles look like an ideal instrument of justice and fair dealing. Don't underestimate the sacrifices any German will make in order to avoid another Versailles, or worse.

MURROW: And I'm very much afraid that on that particular point, the German leaders are right. As you know, there has been a lot of discussion in London of liberal peace terms for an equal and self-respecting Germany. During the early months, the distinction was constantly drawn between the German government and the German people. That's changing. People are beginning to get mad. The bombing and machine-gunning of trawlers hasn't helped and don't forget that the French have their ideas about what's to be done with Germany when and if the Allies win this war. And from all we hear in London, those ideas, if put into practice, would pretty well pulverize Germany and probably pave the way for another war, if not in twenty years' time, then in forty. There isn't quite as much talk of a federated Europe after this war as there was during the first few months. There is more talk of a complete union between Britain and France. I think maybe we agree, Bill, that whoever wins this war is going to impose a peace that will make Versailles and Brest-Litovsk *[the treaty of March 1918 in which Germany imposed harsh terms on defeated Russia]* look like a polite exchange between friends.

SHIRER: That's one thing on which we agree anyway.

MURROW: Let's talk about more pleasant things.

SHIRER: About food?

MURROW: All right, about food and drink. First, let's record the fact that the food in Amsterdam is excellent.

SHIRER: Agreed. Especially the oysters and butter and coffee and oranges.

MURROW: What about the food in Germany? You look pretty well fed.

SHIRER: You're no advertisement for the British diet yourself.

MURROW: That's not the fault of the Controller of Food. There's still plenty of everything to eat and drink in London except bacon, butter, sugar, and ham. What about Berlin?

SHIRER: I don't do so badly myself. You'll laugh at this maybe, but in Berlin for some reason, they classify me as a heavy laborer.

MURROW: I am laughing.

SHIRER: It's no joke, Ed, because it means that as a heavy laborer I get double rations. On top of that, we foreigners are allowed to import a little butter, a few eggs, and some bacon from Denmark. Naturally, we're better off than the German people. But it's wrong to think the German people are starving. They're getting enough to eat, only personally I don't find it a very balanced diet, if you get what I mean.

MURROW: How's the beer?

SHIRER: Good. It's a little weaker than in peacetime, but it tastes all right. The beverage you miss most in Berlin is good coffee.

MURROW: What about the theater in Germany now?

SHIRER: Well, they're all open and they're all full. The war has brought them a prosperity they never knew in peacetime.

MURROW: What are they playing?

SHIRER: You probably won't believe me, but the most popular play now on in Berlin is by a British author. He's been packing them in since the war started, and his name is George Bernard Shaw. The play is *Pygmalion.*

MURROW: When I get back to London, I shall ask Mr. Shaw if he's getting his royalties.

SHIRER: How about the theater in London, Ed?

MURROW: They were all closed during the first few weeks. But most of them are open again now and doing a fair business. Most of the stuff is light, and the audiences are not too critical. Incidentally, dozens and dozens of new bottle clubs – a sort of combination nightclub and speakeasy – have opened in London during the last two months.

SHIRER: I must say they don't allow any speakeasies in Berlin. All the regular nightclubs are open and doing well, but they have to close at 1 a.m.

MURROW: What's the most popular song in Berlin now?

SHIRER: A little piece, written soon after the outbreak of the war, called *We March Against England.* It's a very catchy tune, the sentiment is popular, and everybody's singing it. Have you any popular war songs over there?

MURROW: The best effort so far is a tune called *We're Going to Hang Out the Washing on the Siegfried Line.* Another popular tune has a good strong Teutonic flavor. You may remember it was popular in Prague when you were there during the Czech crisis. It's called *The Beer Barrel Polka.* But the messenger-boys and street sweepers are whistling and humming *Franklin D. Roosevelt Jones.* That's probably the most popular tune in England today. Are there any women wearing uniforms in Germany?

SHIRER: Only the Labor Service girls, but they were in uniform in peacetime. Why? Are the women wearing uniforms in England?

MURROW: Plenty of them. But not too successfully. One of the big newspapers took a poll the other day asking Englishmen to state their pet peeve or grouse. Women in uniform led the list by miles.

SHIRER: Well, we don't have that problem in Germany. But there's another, and that is clothes in general. The Germans, men and women, get only 100 points of clothing per year, and if you're a woman and buy four pairs of stockings and one or two other odds and ends, you haven't any points left over for new dresses. That I suppose would create a problem, but I'm no expert and we'd better leave that.

MURROW: All right, let's leave it. Bill, how are you getting along with your censors these days?

SHIRER: Well, we haven't come to blows yet. They're really not bad fellows, though of course they have an unfortunate job. The worst thing is not the actual censorship of what you want to say, but the censorship of news at its source. Every day you have to scratch harder to find any news, and I imagine that's not only true of Germany but of the Allied countries too.

MURROW: It's certainly true in London. The censors over there stick to the rules and so far haven't cut out anything except things that might be legitimately called military information. My censors are a literary lot. One of them had a play of his produced in a West End theater the other night. Probably the best example of how news can be completely scuttled was the Hore-Belisha affair. That's going to be an interesting study in political maneuvring for the post-war historians. If you sum up all the public pronouncements, it just comes to this: the Prime Minister said to his War Minister, "I like you so much I think you ought to go." And he then said, to the House of Commons, "The reasons were good enough for me and they've got to be good enough for you." Of course, that's one side of things we have to watch in London, which you miss in Berlin.

SHIRER: As a matter of fact, it sounds a good deal like Berlin to me.

MURROW: Well, maybe. But don't forget the Prime Minister said something to the effect that he held his office by the will of the House of Commons and they could throw him out any time they wanted to. And that didn't sound like Berlin.

SHIRER: Well, to change the subject, let's talk about the weather. At least we're in a country where talking about the weather isn't military treason. It's still snowing and it's cold. It's midnight. The lights are turned on.

191

MURROW: And tonight is the first time in nearly five months that we haven't fumbled around in the darkness with a flashlight, pulled blackout curtains over the windows and really felt the pressure of the darkness. The fact that there is light, great oceans of it, in Holland is something you at home just don't appreciate because you've got it all the time.

SHIRER: Well, Ed, I propose that we go out under a big arc light and throw snowballs.

MURROW: I'm with you, and maybe, if we're lucky, we'll be back in Holland again at tulip time.

Berlin January 24, 1940 24.47

Good Evening.

I suppose the world looked a little brighter to Germans tonight. In the first place, it was much warmer – above freezing – so that even if you didn't have any coal for heating when you got home, or any hot water, you at least didn't literally freeze. After all, there's nothing that gets you down so much as freezing – in your home and in your office.

On top of that, if you were a German riding home on the subway tonight and wondering why more victories weren't coming in, you would have been cheered to see plastered all over your evening paper the news that another British destroyer had been sunk. The headline in the leading evening paper, the *Nachtausgabe*, said NEW BLOW TO ENGLAND – ANOTHER DESTROYER SUNK. And below the headlines was a large picture of the British destroyer *Exmouth*.

The other big story in Germany tonight, judging by the headlines, is about the Führer. I don't remember seeing a line in the papers about Herr Hitler since Christmas. But tonight the papers inform us that he went to the Sport Palace today to address 7,000 soldiers who are about to become officers. We haven't the text of his speech. We're merely told the Führer spoke about the goal and necessity of the struggle of the German people and about the duties and the tasks of the officers in the Nazi army. He pointed, the official statement says, to Frederick the Great as the ideal for German soldiers. At the end of the speech, concludes the official account, Field Marshal Göring proposed three rousing cheers for the Führer.

I said it had turned warm here in Berlin. But I notice the burgomaster today calls on the populace to stop using gas for heating rooms or water. Water can only be heated on Saturdays and Sundays, but rooms are not to be heated by gas under any circumstances.

Which reminds me that yesterday an American correspondent came to my room to get warm – we still have heat in my hotel. He said he'd kept dipping his hands all morning in a pan of warm water on his kitchen stove. It was the only way he could keep his fingers warm enough to typewrite his dispatch. He didn't realize you're not supposed to heat water except on weekends.

The Foreign Office, I'm informed, promises a reply to the accusations about German mistreatment of Poles reported to have been made yesterday by the Vatican radio station. I say "reported" because the Wilhelmstrasse claims the accusations were made, not by the Vatican radio station, but by the British Broadcasting Corporation purporting to quote the Vatican. But you probably know much more about that than I do. I just pass along what the Wilhelmstrasse says.

I regret that we correspondents in Berlin can't give you much first-hand information about what is going on in Poland, because we're not allowed to go there. Even Mr. James Thomas Nicholson, the American Red Cross representative who arrived here some weeks ago on his way to Poland to observe the distribution of medical supplies supplied by you at home for the Poles, is still here in Berlin.

Here are some court items which may interest you. In Nuremberg, a special court sentenced to death two men. Their offense? Stealing four bicycles during the blackout.

At Stuttgart, a special court sentenced a 58-year-old German to two years in the penitentiary for having listened to a foreign radio station and then passed on the news to his friends where he worked. Some of the Berlin papers are moved to publish editorials tonight praising the sentence.

In this connection, I was informed today of a case in which the British Broadcasting Corporation some time ago broadcast the names of German prisoners taken. Eight people wrote to one woman they knew to tell her that they'd just heard her son was safe. But this story has an unexpected sequel. She denounced them to the police, and all were arrested. [*This last paragraph was deleted by the censor.*]

Berlin January 27, 1940 24.46

Good Evening. This is William L. Shirer in Berlin.

It's disclosed in Berlin today that at two places on the Western Front where the Rhine forms a no-man's land between the two armies, the French yesterday bombarded the German lines with loud-speakers. The Germans themselves have been carrying on a loud-speaker war on the Western Front for some time, but this is the first time we've heard here of the French doing it.

Actually, in the end, this French loudspeaker attack degenerated into a lively machine-gun battle, which almost spoils the story – or maybe not.

It seems, or at least the German account says, that the French loudspeakers, posted on the banks of the Rhine, thundered out propaganda which the Germans didn't think was fair. The Germans say the magnified French voice, of course speaking perfect German, bellowed out low and mean things about the Führer. And as the German official news agency puts it, the French did not realize that any attack on the Führer would be immediately rejected by the German troops.

So, according to the German account, the troops of Herr Hitler gave the French a warning to desist in their remarks about the Führer, but apparently the French loudspeakers went right on, because the Germans say that at two places, Altentheim, where the Rhine forms an elbow, and near the town of Breisach, they had to open fire not only with rifles but with machine-guns. From what I've seen of that front, it must have been an extraordinary occasion to hear machine-guns going off – heretofore the war in that sector has been exclusively an affair of the loudspeakers – but the Germans claim their machine-guns finally silenced the loudspeakers and thus brought the verbal attack on Herr Hitler to an abrupt stop.

It certainly is a strange war on that Western Front. One German paper described tonight how the French send cattle out straying in no-man's land in order to set off the German mines. But the Germans retort by capturing the cattle, or killing them, and anyway getting them back to their own lines, where they make a good barbecue. Well, if slaughter there must be in no-man's land, better cattle than men.

The German people today were told in a broadcast over their own stations of the pitfalls and penalties that await those found guilty of listening to foreign radio stations. It was explained that in Germany you must not only not listen to enemy stations but must avoid neutral radio programs as well. Not only are you not allowed to listen to foreign news, but you cannot hear musical programs emanating from non-German stations. Neutral citizens sojourning in the Reich are placed in the same category as Germans in this regard, though I'm informed we correspondents are not.

It was also explained that any person overhearing a foreign broadcast must either have it stopped at once, or immediately report the matter to the police. If you don't, you're liable to punishment. The ordinary penalty for listening to an outside broadcast is a penitentiary sentence, but in extreme cases, you get a death sentence. "Extreme" cases, it was pointed out, are those in which a person listens regularly to a foreign station, or who organizes or attends a regular meeting to hear a foreign broadcast.

The announcement in the communiqué of the German High Command today that a U-boat had torpedoed two ships in a British convoy is being played for all it's worth here in Berlin tonight. All evening papers devote their front page bannerlines to it.

And they do not neglect to point a lesson to the neutrals who allow their ships to join the Allied convoys. The *Nachtausgabe* tonight devotes half of its front page to the torpedoing of the two ships in the convoy and the other half to counting neutral shipping losses. In ships of over 800 tons, the Germans say the Danes have lost thirteen, the Swedes twenty-seven, and the Norwegians thirty-two.

How many neutral ships have been torpedoed in convoys is not mentioned, nor, for that matter, how many that were just going their way alone.

Berlin January 29, 1940 01.02

Good Evening. This is William L. Shirer in Berlin.

The daily communiqué of the German High Command stated today that there was nothing special to report. As these communiqués report about events the day before, that means that yesterday there was nothing doing on the Western Front, on the sea or even in the air.

The last ten days have been the quietest of the war. Whether it's the calm before the storm – well, if I knew, that would be a military secret and I couldn't report it. But I don't know, nor can you find anyone here who does.

If you'd been here in Berlin today, you would have found it difficult to believe that a great war was on. We even had hot water over the weekend like the people used to have every day in peacetime. The streets and parks are covered deep with snow now, and in the Tiergarten, Berlin's Central Park, which is near my hotel, there were thousands of people this afternoon, old and young, tobogganing on the knolls and skating on the ponds. The place was a paradise for children, and they were in the park in droves. Do children think about the war? And if so, what? I don't know. This afternoon, they seemed to be thinking only of their sleds and skates and the snow and the ice – a much more healthy thing to think about than the war, anyway.

Berlin is surrounded by forests, and here and there amongst them is a slight hill. Tens of thousands of adults from the city spent the day in them, fooling around on skis, a sport which has swept Germany the last few years. Great ski races were also organized, but I was surprised to read in the newspapers tonight that they had to be called off because of what the sports editors called the "unsporting conduct" of the public. It isn't often that you read of a German public misbehaving, especially in these spartan war days, and so I read the news stories rather carefully. It seems that the public, for whom this war is certainly no picnic, got so frolicsome, being out there in the snow, that they tore up the signs which indicated the course of the ski race – it was a marathon – with the result that all the skiers got hopelessly lost in the woods, and the judges, very much chagrined, had to declare it no race. And they only hold the race about every ten years, because it only snows hard enough once a decade here.

If there had been peace, we would have been celebrating in a few days the Winter Olympic Games at Garmisch. With a war on, the Germans have organized their own winter games there, with skiers, skaters, and hockey teams from Italy, Hungary, Yugoslavia, Slovakia, the Protectorate, and Germany. Opening the games, Herr Tchammer und Osten, the German Sports Führer, blamed England and France for the fact that there were no Winter Olympic Games this year. They should have accepted Herr Hitler's peace proposals, he said.

I would be giving you a false impression, however, if I made you think that the German people were actually forgetting the war. The propaganda on the home front the last few days has reminded them time and again of the fatal consequences of an Allied victory. The idea is to drive home that as hard as life may be in wartime, a peace dictated by a victorious enemy would be a terrible thing. As if Versailles were not bad enough, the newspapers have been reminding the people of that other bad peace for Germany, the Peace of Westphalia in 1648 after the end of the Thirty Years War, when Germany was split up into 300 states and principalities. The newspaper, *Angriff*, publishes a map of that peace, showing how Germany was broken up, and underneath it another map showing what is purported to be the peace the French would like to make after this war is ended. According to this map, the French take the left bank of the Rhine, as Marshal Foch advised in 1919, the Poles are given eastern Germany up to the banks of the River Oder, Czechoslovakia is restored and given Saxony to boot, and Bavaria goes to a new Austrian Hapsburg state.

I'm told this kind of propaganda is very effective among the German people.

Day after tomorrow will mark the seventh anniversary of the Nazis coming to power in Germany. Because of the war there will be no celebrations, as in other years. Schools will remain open as usual and the traditional torchlight parade of the storm troopers down the Wilhelmstrasse before Herr Hitler will not take place. The Minister of Public Enlightenment and Propaganda, Dr. Goebbels, was to have made a nationwide broadcast, but tonight it's announced that this too has been called off.

With weather conditions unfavorable for military action on the front or in the air, attention in Berlin this week will be concentrated on the diplomatic front. There are two active ones just now, Scandinavia, where the Germans are trying to convince the neutral northern lands that it doesn't pay to try and trade with the British – you lose too many ships. And in the Balkans, where on Friday the Balkan Entente meets at Belgrade in a conference which may be of very great importance concerning the future of this war.

Berlin January 30, 1940 24.47

Good Evening. This is William L. Shirer in Berlin.

At about 3 o'clock this afternoon, our time, the Berlin afternoon newspapers suddenly appeared on the street with this announcement, in huge type: "The Führer will speak tonight at 8 o'clock to the German people. The speech will be broadcast over all German stations."

That was all. No mention of from where he would speak, from what hall, even from what city. The newspapermen soon found out, but they were not allowed to say so before the meeting.

Mary Marvin Breckinridge, of Columbia's foreign staff, who had arrived in Berlin barely twenty-four hours before, rushed off to the meeting. She had never seen Herr Hitler before, nor attended a Nazi meeting. She's here now to tell you about it.

BRECKINRIDGE: It was my first Nazi mass-meeting. As I walked across the beaten-down snow to the doors of the Sportpalast, the vague moonlight showed up groups of men with a lot of flags standing and knocking their feet together in the cold night, and outside the doors two lines of men in black uniforms and caps with shiny visors – the noted S.S. men.

Inside, men in the brown uniforms of storm troopers directed me to my place, where I looked down on rows of bald heads with a smattering of solid-looking women. The hall was packed with fifteen thousand people half an hour ahead of time. A band played and suggested to my mind the prelude to the greatest show on earth. The audience rose and held the Nazi salute when the flags were borne in solemnly and settled on the red and gold draped platform, marked by stark swastikas. A German behind me was pointing out Hess and other dignitaries on the platform to his girl.

Suddenly, the band's efforts stopped, and a large band of men in uniform walked rapidly down the center aisle. The third man, and only one without a cap, was Adolf Hitler. He looked small among his stalwart bodyguard, and just like his pictures, forelock and all. He received a

197

tremendous ovation of *Heils!*, given loudly and rhythmically, from everyone except the foreigners in the press gallery. Dr. Goebbels introduced him in a brief speech ending with "The Führer speaks." Another round of regular cheering, and the Führer began. While he was talking, a photographer in uniform photographed him from all angles. The Führer paid no attention to anything except his notes and performance, which had variety of tempo, tone, and gesture. He aroused derisive laughter more than once when talking about the English, and cheers and stamping when he described Germany's might and determination to help herself. His climax was well given with a fine crescendo and the audience was delighted with the picture of their power which he presented to them. Then, the striding procession marched out and the audience sang their national anthem and the popular new tune *We March Against England*, and some of them kept on whistling it as they went home.

SHIRER: Thank you, Miss Breckinridge.

It was the first time that Herr Hitler had made a public speech since a bomb exploded in the Munich beer cellar 14 minutes after he had left it last November.

He was both bitter and ironic about two of the three men I had seen him sitting around the conference table with at Munich a year before, Mr. Chamberlain and M. Daladier. He referred to the French premier as "Monsieur" Daladier and attacked him for wanting to detach his homeland, Austria, from the Reich. The British Prime Minister he referred to as "old Mr. Chamberlain who proclaims his war aims, Bible in hand".

In 1938, after Munich, Herr Hitler said he recognized that the anti-German elements in the Western capitals were gaining the upper hand. "Finally," he said, "they declared war on us. I gave them my hand. They preferred war. Well, I can assure England and France they shall have it."

The main part of his attack on the Allies was directed against Britain which he accused of planning to bomb German women and children. "When did Britain ever refrain from making war on women and children?" he cried. "Look at the Boer War, at the blockade." These remarks were met by a roar of jeers from his audience.

But when he remarked that Poland had been wiped off the map in eighteen days, the crowd roared with applause.

As to his agreement with Stalin, Herr Hitler said: "Chamberlain tried to get it and failed. If it was good for him, why was it bad for me?"

He then ironized about the London radio stations and their anti-German propaganda, though of course Germans do not listen to the London broadcasts.

The biggest applause came when he said: "Germany is a Great Power. The German army is the first in the world."

Garmisch-Partenkirchen, Germany February 1, 1940 24.47

Good Evening. This is William L. Shirer. I'm speaking to you from Garmisch-Partenkirchen, Germany.

It's a curious place to be speaking from, really. I'm sitting in the press coop in the hockey-stadium, because this is the only place where I could find a microphone. It's almost 1 a.m., everyone's gone home, and the stadium is dark. But three hours ago it was a very lively place with several thousand fans applauding a hockey game between Germany and Yugoslavia and applauding even more some very graceful figure-skaters assembled here from various countries in Central Europe.

I feel almost sentimental being here tonight, because just exactly four years ago, I sat on this same bench, surrounded by Paul Gallico, Westbrook Pegler, and a host of other American writers. At that time – and it seems a long time ago – there was peace, and we sat here watching the athletes of the world perform in the Winter Olympic Games. The idea seemed all right to us then – the idea of keeping the nations competing peacefully in sports. The Winter Olympics were to be held here again this year, and I had planned to come down. And I have – only it's different than we expected when we made our first plans last summer. What's going on here in place of the Olympics is a series of winter games, but only a handful of nations are represented – Italy, Yugoslavia, Romania, Hungary, Slovakia, the Protectorate, and Germany.

And I'm here because practically all of the foreign correspondents were transported down here yesterday, and our press conferences have taken place here today instead of in Berlin. Actually, I must say there was very little news in our press conference here tonight, so I telephoned to Berlin for more news, but Berlin didn't have any either. A lull seems to have set in here after Hitler's speech, and when it is broken, it will probably be only by the beginning of the serious prosecution of this war in the West.

The German press itself is still talking about the Hitler speech. It records today that, as it puts it, the "world has understood Hitler" and it says the foreign countries were deeply impressed by the Führer's words, especially his attack on France, his assurance of Germany's huge armaments and the fact that two big powers, Russia and Italy, remain Germany's friends.

There is practically no reaction here to Mr. Chamberlain's speech; little about it is published; and editorially it's hailed as an unjustified attempt to put pressure on the neutrals.

The German Foreign Office let it be known that it is following closely the proceedings of the Balkan conference which opens in Belgrade tomorrow, but actually the Germans say they do not expect any unpleasant – for them – fireworks there.

It's announced that the one-mark nickel pieces are to be withdrawn from circulation by March 1. They're already being replaced by paper notes. The 50 pfennig pieces of nickel already have given away to new pieces made of aluminum.

And it's also announced that henceforth babies must have clothing ration cards. Heretofore they were exempt and could have as many clothes as their parents could buy.

Berlin and most of Germany is still suffering from the intense cold, made worse by the coal shortage, but here in the Alps – strangely enough – it's quite warm. I return you now from Garmisch to CBS in New York.

A few days later Shirer joined his family in Geneva for a couple of weeks. While there he wrote to Ed Klauber, the top CBS newsman in New York:

A line to thank you for the Christmas bonus and the raise. I didn't want to write about them from Berlin, because the Germans, ever on the watch-out for a spare dollar of foreign exchange, would have devised some way of relieving me of both of them, as soon as they had read my letter.

I note that you, White and Murrow, still think I am doing a useful job in Berlin, though personally I sometimes doubt it. To be sure, I gather our censorship is not quite as fantastic as the French; still, it is bad enough. And we have not only political and military censorship of the radio script, but, what is often worse, censorship of news at its source. We are not only rarely told anything truthful, but are prevented from getting news ourselves. For instance, we cannot go to Poland to check up on the reports we get from there of German sadism, murder, repression. We indeed have done a bad job on both Poland and Czechoslovakia. Organized German murder in both is one of the most disgusting chapters in this war so far.

It's interesting that the people where I am are also getting very touchy about the Leader. When I left a fortnight ago, Otto Tolischus [of *The New York Times*] was in hot water for having written almost a banal sentence about people shivering and hungering while Hitler spoke at the Sportpalast.

On the whole, I think that if the German offensive develops in the next few weeks, we will be allowed to say very little, if anything. If it doesn't develop, censorship will tighten more gradually, but it will not be long before Berlin will put a "*Verbot*" on anything "likely to cause a bad impression in America" – an excuse which has been increasingly used for slashing my scripts by the Propaganda Ministry lately . . .

Berlin February 23, 1940 24.47

Good Evening. This is William L. Shirer in Berlin.

Returning here after a fortnight's bout with the flu in Switzerland, I find things a little changed. For one thing, it's warmer in Berlin than when I left it two weeks ago. You don't see that frozen look in people's faces. The coal situation is still far from normal. But as one man told me today, you don't notice it so much when the thermometer outside registers ten degrees above freezing.

The sidewalks are still lined with piles of scooped-up snow as high as your head. In peacetime, this snow is carted away in trucks. Now, because trucks are needed for other things, it is left to melt.

Traveling in wartime Europe is becoming a little more complicated. Yesterday, as I was about to cross into Germany from Switzerland, the Swiss relieved me of a good part of my luggage. They said it was verboten to take out supplies. They took my laundry soap, my toilet soap, my six bars of chocolate, and all my food except enough for my dinner. When they started to take some of my clothing and my two pairs of extra shoes, I protested, and in the end, I kept them.

On the German side, they search you carefully for letters they suspect might come from spies, but they leave you your clothes.

As for news, the Germans report much heavier artillery fire on the Western Front between the Moselle River and the Westphalian woods. The Germans say this active French artillery fire is directed not so much against their troops as against parties of workers busy strengthening fortifications behind the lines. The fact that the weather has cleared, say the Germans, has also allowed the enemy to site his artillery better.

I find the Germans more concerned with our American neutrality – especially with that revelation that 114 American ships have changed flags since the war began – and more especially with the sale of eight of our vessels to a new Belgian line. The Germans suspect the ships acquired by the Belgians will be used by the British. They maintain this is a violation of our Neutrality Act, and they warn that they will take sharp measures against such ships.

As for other news, a Berlin court today sentenced a man to death for stealing chickens and pigeons during the blackout.

Another court sentenced a German to four months in prison for giving a sweater and a cake to a Polish prisoner. Another German got one month for giving a Polish prisoner a package of cigarettes. A third was given four months for helping a Polish prisoner get letters home to his relatives.

And then there's a dispatch from Bucharest stating that the British are getting all the pilots of the Danube boats laid off by paying them double their salary if they won't pilot ships up the Danube to Germany. It's a curious war.

Berlin February 24, 1940 14.00

Good Morning. This is William L. Shirer in Berlin.

The *Völkischer Beobachter*, official organ of the Nazi party, has a sensational story plastered all over its front page today. In a dispatch from Amsterdam, it claims that the *Nelson*, the most powerful battleship afloat, hit a mine some time about the middle of December, and was badly damaged. According to this German account, it was towed into a small harbor – it would have to be a deep one to accommodate such a big warship – so that the matter could be kept secret. The dispatch then says the British battleship was patched up and later taken to a naval yard where it is now being repaired.

Returning to Berlin after a fortnight abroad, I find that, for one thing, the weather is no longer the principal topic of conversation here, and for good reason. It's finally turned warm and even if you don't have any coal to heat your house, you no longer freeze. There was no heat in my room today; but I hardly noticed it.

So the minds of the people are turning to other things. It takes a little time to get used to the German press again. The news pages are given over not only to news items such as you're used to in your own newspapers, but as often as not to articles and editorials pointing out the perfidy of the enemy and attacking him roundly. These latter are usually in the form of essays more than of straight news stories with a slant, such as you get in other countries. And above all, it is drummed into the minds of the readers that this is a war which has been forced upon Germany by Britain and France. And that it is not the Allies but the Reich which is fighting for freedom. It's useful to keep that in mind, when you think about what is going on in Germany.

The German press hails today the twentieth birthday of the Nazi party. It seems that on February 24th, twenty years ago, Adolf Hitler, then a very little known man indeed, proclaimed the twenty-five points of his party. I don't think many German papers published that party program at the time, but they have since. I haven't time to enumerate the twenty-five points now, but they're interesting, and if you have time, I recommend that you look them up.

While outside this country the last couple of weeks, I heard much talk about the big German offensive in the West breaking any day now. But I see in the papers this morning that the Commander-in-Chief of the German army, General von Brauchitsch, has been in Cracow after an inspection of the German army in Poland which lasted several days. Perhaps you could conclude that if the commander of the German army were planning a big breakthrough in the West today or tomorrow, he wouldn't be spending his time in Poland the last few days.

A new decree published here forbids all new building for the duration of the war, except that in the interest of the prosecution of the war. When the war began, Germany was engaged in a tremendous building program, but that must now wait until peace comes.

There are several articles in the German press today defending the torpedoing of neutral ships. In the case of the Danish ship *Martin Goldschmidt,* the *12-Uhr Blatt* blames the loss of that vessel on the Danish captain. The German explanation is that the submarine which accosted it ordered the crew to the lifeboats, and then dived. When it dived, say the Germans, the Danish boat tried to get away and because of this was then torpedoed.

And finally, here's an item from the *Völkischer Beobachter* which makes the discovery that Mr. Churchill is partly Jewish. The report comes from Sweden.

Berlin February 25-26, 1940 01.02

Good Evening. This is William L. Shirer in Berlin.

I know perfectly well that the Germans and the British never agree on how many ships have been sunk in this war. But I happen to be in Berlin and part of my job is to tell you what we're told here.

Now, today the German High Command published in its daily communiqué some very interesting figures on Allied and neutral shipping lost in this war. According to the High Command, during the first five months of the war until February 20th – that would make it almost six months, of course – 496 enemy and neutral ships with contraband for England, totaling 1,810,315 registered tons, were sunk by – as the statement puts it – "sea-war methods".

Presumably, this means by submarines, by mines, and by airplanes.

Note the wording used by the German High Command in specifying neutral ships which have been lost. It emphasizes that they were all loaded with contraband for England.

Presumably then in that figure of nearly 500 ships totaling 2,000,000 tons, you cannot count those neutral ships whose own governments have officially stated were bound from one neutral state to another – that is, without contraband goods for England, but which were nevertheless sunk.

With better weather now prevailing on the Western Front, activity in the air is increasing. Today, the German High Command spoke of some activity of reconnaissance and fighter planes on the Franco-German border and over the German Bight. It reported one French and one British plane shot down but said the Germans themselves suffered no losses.

It seems plain that with a big thaw setting in on both sides of the Western Front, no action worthy of more than bare mention can set in there for at least a fortnight. But whether it'll come, and how and when – is anyone's guess.

The newspapers here in Berlin tonight are still given over largely to Herr Hitler's speech in Munich. Commenting on it last night, I ventured a prediction, something I rarely do, because we're all bad prophets. But I thought we'd hear more in this country of one argument which Herr Hitler advanced. It was this, that in his opinion, England every twenty years tried to tell Germany what to do, threatening to blockade her if she didn't do it. Herr Hitler called this an "insupportable terror".

Now, whereas the press this morning played up that the Führer had promised Germany victory, the papers tonight emphasize the terror angle. The *Montag,* for instance, headlines the speech GERMANY WILL BREAK THE TERROR OF THE WORLD PLUTOCRACY.

A struggle of Germany to free itself from the terror of Britain and France. A struggle against world-plutocracy and the world-Jews for freedom. That's the way this war is being presented to the people of Germany.

One thing certainly seemed plain after the speeches of Mr. Chamberlain and Herr Hitler yesterday, and that is that any hopes for a negotiated settlement now, before the horrors of real war break over Europe, are vain. I noticed that the foreign ministers of Norway, Sweden, and Denmark still expressed that hope in the meeting which they held today at Copenhagen. But it really seems a forlorn hope.

Not that you'd notice it here. Today was the first sunny, warm Sabbath that Berlin has seen since the cold spell began. And tens of thousands of people thronged the avenues. In the Unter den Linden, they were so thick that the sidewalk wouldn't hold them, so they walked in the street, on the sunny side, until the traffic police shooed them back on the sidewalk. I thought they were an awfully good-natured crowd. It was difficult watching them even to believe that a terrible war was on.

Berlin February 27, 1940 00.05

Good Morning. This is William L. Shirer in Berlin.

You couldn't exactly say that the German people are waiting breathlessly for the arrival of Mr. Sumner Welles *[Under-Secretary of State and President Roosevelt's special envoy]*, who is due here Wednesday night or Thursday morning from Rome. That would be true, say, of the American correspondents here and our Embassy, but not of anyone else.

So far, there has been nothing in the newspapers here to indicate that Mr. Welles had even arrived in Europe except a few lines last weekend saying that the boat on which he traveled to Europe had been held up in Gibraltar and a few hundred sacks of mail destined for Germany taken off by the British authorities.

Nothing has been published on his visit to Rome, and no doubt, since the visit is private and unofficial, little will be published on his stay here. So far as we know, Mr. Welles will be received by the German Foreign Secretary, Herr von Ribbentrop, and also by Herr Hitler.

The newspaper reports this morning further losses of enemy and neutral shipping. They include the English tanker *British Endeavour* of 4,500 tons sunk off Funchal, which would seem to show that German submarines are now operating pretty far from home. The sinking of more Norwegian, Swedish, and Danish ships is also reported.

Yesterday's High Command communiqué mentioned that Lieutenant-Captain Herbert Schultze, the U-boat commander who is making quite a name for himself, has returned home after sinking 34,000 tons of shipping. This brings his total up to sixteen ships totaling 114,000 tons, since the war began. Naval circles here say that's about as much as the successful German submarine commanders bagged during the first two years of the World War.

I happen to know Schultze personally, and some of you may remember a radio interview I had with him after he returned from his first voyage. He's a young fellow, as are all these German U-boat commanders, and he's a daredevil of the first order. If he fears anything, I don't know what it would be. He loves his job, and the only time he seems to be nervous is when he's home, waiting for his ship to be overhauled. He's always impatient to get away again against those British ships.

205

Here's some bad news, or maybe good news, depending on your attitude towards the imbibing of beer. I understand that beginning March 1st, beer production in Germany as a whole is to be cut by 25 percent. Worse than that, Pilsner beer, the best in the world, I think you'll admit, is to be cut down 50 percent. Cutting down on beer saves grain and also releases workers for more important tasks. I understand there's more water in the beer now than in peacetime, but I can report that it's still very good indeed.

For the first time, I believe, since the World War, Germany is going to have summer-time. Clocks will be moved forward an hour April 1st and will stay that way until October 6th. That will certainly make the blackout easier to bear, as it'll come an hour later, which is something. During the winter, it used to get dark here shortly after 4 p.m., that is before office and factory workers could get to their homes. It's better now, as spring approaches, but summer-time will help.

As to the prosecution of the war, the German High Command's communiqué reports – "No Special Happenings".

Berlin February 28, 1940 24. 47

Good Evening. This is William L. Shirer in Berlin.

Mr. Sumner Welles, who arrived in Zürich today, is due in Berlin Friday morning. His talks with Herr von Ribbentrop, the Foreign Minister, and with Herr Hitler will presumably take place Friday and Saturday.

I noticed across the hall from my room in the Hotel Adlon tonight considerable activity in the neighborhood of the suite which Mr. Welles will occupy. He'll certainly have a nice view. Whereas we more or less permanent guests are quartered in inside rooms on a court, because, I suppose they're considered safer if the bombs should ever start falling, Mr. Welles gets an outside suite on the Unter den Linden, with a view of the Brandenburg Gate and the new American Embassy.

The German press broke its silence on Mr. Welles' European visit today, though it made no mention of his arrival Friday in Berlin. The German press was angry over what it termed the misuse of Mr. Welles' trip by the British and French press. In particular, it was angry at a report in the *Daily Telegraph* in which it was alleged that Herr Hitler, with the full approval of Mussolini, would offer Mr. Welles a four-part peace plan. The four points were: establishment of a new Polish state, self-government for the Protectorate, the maintenance of the status-quo in Austria and the return of German colonies.

The Wilhelmstrasse termed this a clumsy maneuvre by British propagandists and a pure invention. As a matter of fact, with the exception of the point about self-government for the Protectorate, it more or less *is* the peace plan offered by Herr Hitler after his smashing victory over Poland.

Will Herr Hitler offer Mr. Welles a plan for peace? Most observers here doubt it. Herr Hitler believes, as he told us last Saturday, that he can win by force of arms. I don't think I'm giving away any secrets when I say that the Wilhelmstrasse, as it was put to me there today, does not expect anything special to result from Mr. Welles' visit.

I'm curious about those British airplanes which London says have been cruising over Berlin on recent nights. Because of the difference in time, this broadcast keeps me up most of the night, and somehow you always keep an ear cocked for a plane at night, but this week I haven't heard any, nor seen any. That doesn't necessarily prove anything, of course. A German air force officer told me today that the British on these night flights keep three or four miles high, and that you can't hear or spot a plane that high with your naked ears and eyes. He also denied that reconnaissance flights at such a height over a blacked-out country have any military value. At any rate, we didn't have any air-raid alarm and, as a matter of fact, the Germans say the British planes didn't get east of the Elbe.

Dr. Goebbels made a speech in Münster, in Westphalia, tonight. Before speaking, he visited the room in the City Hall where the Treaty of Westphalia was signed 300 years ago. That was, you may remember, after the Thirty Years War.

Berlin March 1, 1940 14.05

Good Morning. This is William L. Shirer in Berlin.

Mr. Sumner Welles arrived here bright and early this morning from Zürich, for his conferences with the German leaders. He was met at the station by his opposite number in the German Foreign Office, Baron von Weizsäcker, the German Secretary of State, by Dr. Dörnberg, Chief of Protocol, and various other officials of the Wilhelmstrasse. These officials were all in the special uniform which members of the German Foreign Office now wear.

Most of the members of the American Embassy staff were also out to greet Mr. Welles and a large corps of American foreign correspondents was also there.

It was a very informal affair. Had Mr. Welles been paying an official visit, there would have been a company of troops presenting arms as the train rolled in. But as it is not an official visit, all this was dispensed with. As Mr. Welles, looking as though he were quite recovered from his recent attack of flu, stepped off the train, he was greeted by the American chargé d'affaires, Mr. Alexander Kirk, who introduced him to the waiting German officials. A few pleasantries were exchanged and then the whole party drove up the Wilhelmstrasse, past the Chancellery where Mr. Welles later will undoubtedly confer with Herr Hitler, then past the Foreign Office, where he'll be seeing Herr von Ribbentrop, to the Hotel Adlon, where he is stopping during his stay in Berlin. Later, Mr. Welles, in a silk hat, strolled over to the American Embassy, which is just around the corner, to confer with our Embassy officials.

At noon, still in his silk hat, the first I've seen in the Wilhelmstrasse for some time, Mr. Welles arrived at the German Foreign Office and was immediately ushered in to see Herr von Ribbentrop for his first conversation in Berlin. This conference was still on when I left the Wilhelmstrasse about a half hour ago, so that it appears to have been a pretty comprehensive talk.

Some people wondered why the American flag didn't go up on the Hotel Adlon after Mr. Welles arrived. I noticed that the Slovak flag was up, but not the Stars and Stripes. This, I understand, is because of the non-official character of Mr. Welles' visit. The flag goes up only when it's official.

All the Berlin newspapers today carried on their front pages a two and a half line story that Mr. Welles would be arriving in the capital today. There has still been no mention of his schedule, but it's obvious that he will see not only the German Foreign Minister but also the Führer and get from them both firsthand their point of view about this war and the chances for peace, if any. So far as I can see, Berlin is in no more of a mood for peace than Paris or London. This morning, for instance, the papers play up Field Marshal Göring's Order of the Day to the air force on the occasion of its fifth anniversary. The air force, says the Field Marshal, is a weapon of destruction against all who criminally break the peace. In other words, according to this German view, it is England and France who are the criminals guilty of breaking the peace. And Göring calls on his air force to fight until the final victory is achieved. That doesn't sound much like peace, does it?

But of course, what Mr. Welles will be told here, we don't know.

The air-raid sirens went off in Berlin today, but it's pleasant – pleasant at least for me – to record that it was not because of any British planes over the capital. It was just a try-out to see how the sirens had stood the winter. Judging by their sound, they had stood it very well.

208

Berlin March 1, 1940 24.55

Good Evening. This is William L. Shirer in Berlin.

Mr. Sumner Welles, who arrived in Berlin this morning, just six months to a day after the war started, will see Chancellor Hitler at 11 o'clock tomorrow morning.

Today, Mr. Welles had two important conferences. Two hours after he arrived, that is at noon, he went to see the German Foreign Minister, Herr von Ribbentrop, and was closeted with him for two and a half hours. Afterwards, the American Under-Secretary of State told us the talk had been "extremely interesting".

At 6 p.m., he again called at the Foreign Office and had a long talk with the German Secretary of State, Baron von Weizsäcker. We asked Mr. Welles whether he would be seeing Field Marshal Göring. He said he hoped to, and indeed I understand a meeting has been arranged at the Field Marshal's country estate near Berlin for Sunday morning.

So much for the schedule. How about the talks themselves, especially the one with Herr von Ribbentrop today, which lasted two and a half hours? Mr. Welles told the American correspondents afterwards that he naturally could say nothing about it.

But in well-informed German circles tonight I get the impression that the German position, as no doubt was explained to Mr. Welles, is that there can be no peace until Germany has been left secure in its living space which it demands in Central Europe and until British control of the seas has been broken. Now, since it's clear to everyone that you couldn't possibly negotiate a peace like that with the Allies now, there's no chance at all of stopping the war. There seems no doubt that this line of thinking was made clear to Mr. Welles today. With the additional point that Germany is determined to prosecute the war to the bitter end.

Indeed, it's significant that coincident with Mr. Welles' arrival here today, a semi-official statement was issued not only defining Germany's position more clearly than it has ever been defined before but adding that the German army now awaits the word of command for the "decisive stroke" – and here I'm quoting – "the decisive stroke which one can be assured will put into the shade all previous conceptions of breaking through by sheer military force".

That sounded to neutral observers in Berlin tonight very much like the heralding of the long-awaited offensive. At any rate, it did not sound like a gesture of peace, for which Mr. Welles may have been looking when he came to Europe.

"Conscious of its military superiority," the statement says, "and of its economic invulnerability, Germany faces after six months of war the final decision. The war will be carried through to a meaningful end, which can only result in the final achievement of the German *Lebensraum*, and in the guarantee of the freedom of the seas." And it adds that it must be a condition of peace that England must never again be left in a position to threaten other people whom she believes to be disturbing her interests.

There you have, as undoubtedly Mr. Welles has tonight, the German point of view about this war. This semi-official statement, incidentally, begins by remarking that Mr. Welles arrived in Berlin just six months after the outbreak of war. And it concludes that the first six months of the conflict have been very favorable to Germany, and that England and France now realize they can neither defeat Germany militarily nor economically.

Herr von Ribbentrop, as you know, speaks perfect English. But when he saw Mr. Welles today, he spoke in German, which had to be translated to his American visitor. I was told tonight that Herr von Ribbentrop has not spoken English since the war began.

Berlin March 3, 1940 01.02

Good Evening. This is Berlin.

The visit of Mr. Sumner Welles to Berlin is over. He left the capital just four hours ago for Switzerland after a final busy day largely given over to talks with Field Marshal Göring, Germany's most important man next to the Führer, and with Herr Hess, the Führer's deputy.

They met at the Field Marshal's country home, Karin Hall, at Schorfheide, about an hour's drive from the capital. It's a picturesque house, part of it built like a hunter's lodge, and lying in a thick forest which today was blanketed in snow. An official communiqué afterward said they held a long talk. Actually, Mr. Welles arrived shortly after noon, had his conference with General Göring, stayed for lunch and returned to the Embassy at 4:30 p.m.

The walls of the study in which the conversations took place were hung, I understand, with great war maps and enlarged photographs of enemy positions and harbors, taken by General Göring's air force. But the talk itself, I gather, was mostly about economic matters, the Field Marshal also being, as you know, the economic czar of wartime Germany. The economic strength of the Reich, despite the blockade, was emphasized.

And so, Mr. Welles leaves Germany, not with – so far as we know – a proposal for peace from Hitler, as some prophets had it the other day, but, as I said last night, with the formal assurances of Germany's leaders that they're determined to fight the war through to a finish, and they're sure they'll win. It seems obvious here that things have gone much too far

210

now in Europe for there to be any possibility of a negotiated peace now. Neutral observers here believe that that's about the message which Mr. Welles will take back to Washington with him when he returns.

Berlin Special Broadcast Sunday March 3, 1940 24.55

Perhaps you'd like to have some idea of what it's like to broadcast under wartime conditions. Though my daily talk at 6:45 p.m., New York time, doesn't actually take place in Berlin until a quarter to one the following morning, because of the difference in time, getting to the studio on the dot is one of my major headaches.

I have a car to get around in, but the last six weeks I haven't used it because it was almost impossible to get gasoline, nor could I get any anti-freeze during the long cold spell. And even when I did use it, I continually found myself during the blackout driving on sidewalks or plunging into snowdrifts or contacting telephone poles.

So at night, getting to the studio for a broadcast, I use the subway. But first, I have to negotiate a long stretch down the Wilhelmstrasse in the pitch dark in order to reach the subway station. Unfortunately, I have a bad memory, so it took me three months to memorize the exact position of fourteen lamp-posts, four fire hydrants, three traffic light posts, and three sets of projecting stairways lying between my hotel and the station.

I never can get it into my head that, in Berlin, the lamp-posts are in the middle of the sidewalk, instead of on the curb where they ought to be. For about six weeks, the piles of snow on the sidewalks left only a narrow lane for pedestrians, and it was a rare night when your correspondent didn't flop headlong into the snow-piles, say three or four times. So just getting to this studio, which by car takes twelve minutes, became a matter of an hour.

Since ordinary pockets hardly hold all the passes we've been issued since the war began, I sometimes arrive at the broadcasting-house without my radio pass, which is no laughing matter, and causes further delay until I can get it properly identified.

Identification over here in Europe, as you know, invariably includes giving the date and place of birth of your parents, which I can never remember, hence more delay.

Arrived finally at the broadcasting house and in your right mind, you must wait an hour for the censors to battle with your script. But you're not finished even after the censors get through with you. In order to reach the studio and microphone, I must dash through winding corridors in the broadcasting house, down many stairs, out into a pitch-dark vacant lot, in the middle of which, for some reason, is a hidden stairs – being careful not to bump into several sheds lurking in the way, or fall into a snowdrift. In the course of this journey, I must get past at least three helmeted guards who demand a look at my pass. Searching for a pass on a dark, sub-zero night with frozen fingers usually causes you to empty your pockets, and like as not the script gets lost in the snow, and you arrive at the studio without your script, your teeth chattering, thoroughly sore at the world, and New York expecting you to chat easily and intelligently about high politics.

Personally, I found it difficult to discuss politics and the war during my recent broadcasts from Garmisch, where the only microphone in town was situated in the ice-stadium. It was a job arousing the night-watchman at a quarter to one in the morning, and even more of a job convincing him of the purpose of my visit. I didn't find it any fun trying to concentrate on serious matters standing in a tiny box in the darkened stadium which was so cold that both the engineer and myself, throughout the broadcast, kept stamping our feet and blowing our fingers in order to keep going.

Timing broadcasts sometimes is a headache. Christmas night, broadcasting from a German warship, I smashed my stopwatch to smithereens sliding down a hatch from the upper-deck after the first part of our broadcast – I guess I'm a poor sailor – and had no idea when it was time to stop. In the end, I had to guess. And so it goes, but I see my time is up.

Berlin March 7, 1940 24.47

Good Evening. This is William L. Shirer in Berlin.

Don't think the arrival of the *Queen Elizabeth* in New York today isn't a big story in Germany. It is – probably almost as big as in New York or London, if not exactly for the same reasons.

Let a flaming three-line banner-headline all over the front page of Berlin's leading afternoon paper, the *Nachtausgabe*, give you the German slant. It says – THE *QUEEN ELIZABETH* FLEES FROM ENGLAND TO THE USA – THE BRITISH CONSIDER THEIR PORTS NO LONGER SAFE!

And the German papers, with considerable glee, tell their readers that the reason the *Queen Elizabeth* got off in such a hurry and so secretly to New York even before she was finished was because her owners feared the German air force would destroy her. That shows, the Berlin press is not slow to point out tonight, the respect which Britain has for Germany's flyers and how vulnerable the British really feel their ports to be.

The German radio tonight cited the New York newspapers as backing up this German view. The American press, it said, emphasized above all that the surprise trip of the new British liner proved how really frightened the Allies were of German air-bombs. So you see, the story of the *Queen Elizabeth* is for Germany just another proof of its might, and I can find no mention of the angle that the giant ship did after all elude the U-boat blockade.

Herr von Ribbentrop, the German Foreign Minister, we learn today, has just stated that Germany is armed and economically prepared for a war lasting five years, or even more, though it must be added he expressed his personal view that the war would be over this year. This is not the first time I've heard that view expressed in the Wilhelmstrasse. The men at the head of this government apparently are convinced that the war will be over before the year is up, and that Germany will win it.

That renews interest in the much-discussed German offensive, but I'm afraid I haven't any information on that – I hear only rumors. The latest rumor, which I heard tonight, is that the Germans have a secret new gun so powerful that it will pulverize the Maginot Line, and thus enable the Germans to break through with little loss of life. But I repeat, it's only a rumor.

Berlin March 8, 1940 14.00

Good Morning. This is William L. Shirer in Berlin.

Diplomatic circles here are buzzing with talk of a secret peace parley in Stockholm to end the Russo-Finnish war. You have to treat this report with great reserve, but the talk is that something is on in Stockholm.

The visit of the Swedish explorer, Sven Hedin, to Berlin this week – he had long talks with both Herr Hitler and Field Marshal Göring – is coupled with the reported Stockholm peace move. Mr. Hedin has been very close to Herr Hitler for years.

There is no official information that Germany is mixed up with this reported attempt for peace, but neutral observers consider that it would be a reasonable thing were the Germans to play the role of intermediaries between the Russians and the Finns. Besides the two Finnish political envoys, Mr. Paasikivi, who led the ill-fated negotiations in Moscow just before the war broke out, and Mr. Svenhufvud, the former Finnish president, who are both reported to be in Stockholm, Field Marshal Mannerheim is understood here to have sent General Rosenbroyer to Stockholm. Diplomatic circles here believe the Finnish envoys saw the German minister in Helsinki before they left for Sweden.

There is very little spot news here today. So the flaming headlines on the front pages are devoted to other types of stories. For instance, the *Börsen Zeitung* runs this three-line banner headline today: BRITISH SADISM KNOWS NO LIMITS – GERMANS MAY BE PUT IN ENGLISH CAMPS UNDER THE WATCH OF POLES. And the *12-Uhr Blatt* has its main headline devoted to the German report that a London MP, Sir Thomas Moore, demanded in the House of Commons that German sailors who scuttle their ship be left to drown. To which the German radio comments today, "The true face of Churchill, the proved liar, the proved murderer, is thereby plainly shown up."

I've always felt that one of the biggest successes of the Third Reich was the way it went after the youth of the country to turn them into good national socialists. Today, it's announced that the Defense Council has entrusted Alfred Rosenberg with the spiritual education of the youth of Germany during the war. He will see to it that the leading men in the state, party and army make frequent addresses to the young people over the radio, continually explaining to them the meaning and the reasons for Germany's present war.

A decree issued today orders all persons and firms who possess old metal or scrap-iron to deliver it to the state. And there's good news for growing children. Because they outgrow their clothes faster than they are allowed to purchase them under the strict rationing system, they're to be given extra cards with sixty additional points each year.

Berlin March 10, 1940 15.02

Good Morning. This is William L. Shirer in Berlin.

Today is Memorial Day in Germany – a day to remember the dead who've been slain in all the wars. In past years, I remember, it was a day to remember the two million Germans who lost their lives in the World War.

But now, there's a new war being fought, and there are new dead to mourn. And the German newspapers emphasize this morning that this Memorial Day is different than those in the recent past because the thoughts of the people will be not so much on those killed between 1914 and 1918, as on those killed since September last, and on those millions of young men who, at this moment, stand out in the trenches ready too to make the last sacrifice a man can make in this life.

Indeed, the emphasis of the editorials and special articles in the German press this morning – many of them written by leading generals in the German army – is on the fact that today millions of German men stand ready once more to die for the Fatherland. As a front-page article in the *Lokal Anzeiger* this morning puts it, "This is no time for being sentimental. Men are dying for Germany, day and night. On the West Front, our infantry and artillery men stand ready to destroy the enemy. Day after day, our flyers soar through the heavens filled with bursting shrapnel. Week after week, our U-boat crews battle with the seas and with death, and that is only a beginning. In this war too, the guns must decide . . . One's personal fate now is unimportant. There is no asking 'Why?' if one falls or is broken."

And in the *Völkischer Beobachter*, General von Rundstedt, one of the leading military figures in the German army, writes: "Memorial Day – 1940: Certainly we think earnestly of the dead, but we do not mourn. The sacrifices that so many Germans have made for the Fatherland teach us that heroism lives in our people, and that it is determined to march forward."

And the banner line in red ink across the front page of the *Völkischer Beobachter* puts the Memorial Day idea this way, THE BEQUEST OF OUR FALLEN DEAD – OVER THE GRAVES FORWARD! And a front-page editorial in the same paper takes its title from words of Adolf Hitler: "Who wants to live, must also fight."

In Berlin today, the services for this Memorial Day, which the Germans call *Heldengedenktag*, or "Heroes' Memorial Day", were held at the War Museum. They finished about an hour ago, and there amidst this great collection of arms and weapons which have been used by the soldiers of Europe in century after century of war, Adolf Hitler addressed the nation, his words going to every last hamlet in the country by radio.

Mary Marvin Breckinridge, of Columbia's foreign staff, was present at this ceremony and at the laying of a wreath on the War Memorial, which followed. She's here now.

BRECKINRIDGE: Red German flags with swastikas on them were flying from every door and roof along the wide boulevard of Unter den Linden this morning and storm troopers, S.S. men and policemen lined the sidewalks from the Chancellery on the Wilhelmstrasse to the old Military Museum as I walked down to attend the service. Inside the museum, I went by planes from the last war, ancient cannons, old uniforms, and coats of mail, to a window on the second floor where the press representatives were allowed. In the big glass-roofed hall stood a gathering of high officers on either side of a wide red matting and behind them stood about 200 soldiers who were wounded in Poland in the most recent of Germany's wars. The only civilians on the floor were Sven Hedin, the Swedish explorer who is visiting here, and a couple of Cabinet Ministers. The atmosphere was solemn.

Someone called out, "Attention! The Führer!" and Hitler walked in accompanied by his three heads of military strength, Göring, Raeder, and von Brauchitsch, while everyone stood at salute. They stood quietly in the front row while the military orchestra played Beethoven's *Eroica*. Then Hitler took his place behind the rostrum, in front of a large model of the Nazi Iron Cross dated 1939, flanked by twenty flags on each side. He wore a military-looking uniform which he has designed for himself. He spoke without gestures and without excitement, but it was difficult to understand because of the echo in the building. At the end, there was no applause, and he stepped back to the front row while a simple soldier, without decorations or insignia, a living Unknown Soldier, took the rostrum and received the salute while the band played two national anthems. The feeling was one of paying tribute to the spirit of Germany rather than to the Nazi Party.

The officers all strolled out to the War Memorial next door, and I watched from a window, next to the stuffed horse of Frederick the Great. Troops were drawn up in line before the partly-open building, and Hitler and Göring and about half a dozen other high officials followed a wreath borne by four soldiers into it; no one else. When they came out, the soldiers passed in review, one company each from the army, the navy and the air force, goose-stepping. "This is the best of all," said the wrinkled little museum guard beside me. Then Hitler got down from the pedestal which he had been on, and climbed into the front seat of a glass-enclosed car, and drove off, followed by other cars full of guards and officers, along the street which is about 150 feet wide. No one except guards were allowed on the memorial side, but on the far side of the street the public stood behind the S.S. men, watching the fine ceremony in the bright sunshine. It was really a genuine tribute to a dominant part of German life throughout history.

As I left the museum, I went into the Memorial. Inside, the only symbol on the wall was a cross, Christian, not Iron, behind the monument, which was surrounded by wreaths. The biggest one was of white lilies and tulips, and the red ribbon on it said simply "Adolf Hitler".

Berlin March 11, 1940 00.02

Good Evening. This is Berlin.

The first editions of the Monday morning newspapers in Berlin appear on the streets about 5 p.m., our time. As is natural, they are given over this evening largely to an account of today's Memorial Day ceremonies and the address of Chancellor Hitler at the celebration in the War Museum in Berlin.

There are two items of important news which I miss in these Berlin newspapers this evening. The first is that Herr von Ribbentrop will be received by the Pope in Rome tomorrow. The second is that Great Britain, for reasons so obvious that they caused wide smiles in diplomatic circles here today, has given in to Italy's demands and released all eleven of her ships with their valuable cargoes of German coal.

For reasons that I do not pretend to know, these two stories have not yet found their way into the German press.

The visit of the German Foreign Minister to the Pope tomorrow nevertheless is considered in well-informed circles here to be a very important matter. While we have no official information on the subject, it's believed that recent negotiations between the Reich government and the Vatican have gone so far that a new concordat will be signed when Herr von Ribbentrop goes to the Vatican. No doubt about it, this would certainly please the Catholics of Germany, who now form more than half the population of this once Protestant country. And no doubt it would enhance Germany's prestige in a large part of the world. For it will be remembered that not only have relations between Berlin and the Vatican not been very cordial of late, but Germany was taken to task by Rome for certain things that happened in Poland.

The arrival of Herr von Ribbentrop in Rome is reported at some length in the Berlin press tonight, but no inkling is given as to the scope or subject of the talks. Yesterday, we understood that Italy's differences with Britain over the transport of German coal would be one thing taken up – the German papers have given that story a great play of late – but now apparently there will be no need to talk about that. Italy's general position in the Rome-Berlin Axis, especially in view of the coming months, which the German papers stress will be critical and decisive for the outcome of this war, will undoubtedly be gone into thoroughly.

As to the mysterious secret negotiations for peace in Finland, we're still in the dark here. I was told yesterday that the former President of Finland, Mr. Svenhufvud, who flew here Friday left yesterday for Rome. Tonight, I'm told by those who should know that he's still here, but that he hasn't seen Hitler or any other important Germans. My own efforts and that of my colleagues to locate Mr. Svenhufvud have so far proved unavailing. We only know he's supposed to be stopping at the Finnish legation.

But the German press again tonight warns Norway and Sweden about the dangers of permitting the Allies to send troops and arms to Finland. The papers take exception to a Swedish viewpoint expressed today by a leading Stockholm paper that the sending of 50,000 British troops through Sweden is certainly no threat of danger to Germany. The German position is that it is. And there seems no doubt that Germany

217

would react energetically should any such action take place. The attitude of the German press seems to be that by continuing the fight against Russia, Finland is only fighting for the Allies, and therefore apparently not for its independence.

The High Command reports today a little more activity on the Western Front. It says there was quite a little doing on some sectors, with considerable artillery fire and action by patrols. It also tells of an air battle over the front yesterday between seven German Messerschmitts and ten French fighters – Curtiss and Morane planes. The Germans say they shot down one French Morane, but mention no losses of their own.

The German High Command also gives us today a report on their war against enemy tankers and those neutral tankers which it says ventured to England. The total number of tankers sunk, the High Command gives as forty-six, of which thirty-two were English with a total tonnage of 230,000 tons. This, say the Germans, amounts to 10 percent of the total tanker tonnage owned by Britain.

That means of course that the neutrals, largely Norway, lost fourteen tankers, and it's interesting that the High Command lumps them with the ships belonging to the enemy.

As you know, Germany has now adopted what amounts to unrestricted warfare against ships of any kind that sail to England or are taken into British harbors for contraband control. A neutral ship in the neighborhood of the British Isles is considered to be an object of attack.

Berlin March 12, 1940 24.47

Good Evening. This is Berlin.

Official quarters in Berlin tonight do not hide their deep satisfaction at the news that the Russians and Finns have concluded peace. You may wonder why the Germans, involved in a great war themselves, feel so good about the achievement of peace in Finland.

There are two main reasons. First, with Russia at peace and not concentrating all its energies and its material wealth on the war in Finland, Germany will once more be able to draw on the Soviet Union for economic aid, especially for Russian oil and manganese and grain, which the Reich needs.

The Finnish war had become so serious for Russia, that her ability to furnish raw materials to anyone became doubtful. Her great fleet of airplanes, her thousands of tanks and tens of thousands of trucks that were engaged in the Finnish war used up, for instance, a tremendous amount of oil – oil that in peacetime might have been exported to

Germany. Russia's transport system, already in difficulties, was also unlikely to improve as long as the armies in the north came first.

So, from an economic standpoint, Germany stands to gain by the peace.

There's a second reason peace is popular here. It removes the danger of Germany having to fight on a new front, many times longer than the Western Front. For Berlin made it clear some time ago that it would not stand idly by were the Allies to send an expeditionary force over Scandinavia to Finland, as M. Daladier said today the Allies were ready to do. Rightly or wrongly, the Nazis felt that that Allied army would be used mainly against Germany. For one thing, it would probably have been able to shut off Germany from the Swedish iron mines. Without that Swedish iron, Germany is in a bad way. And to have had to fight over a thousand-mile front in Scandinavia would have weakened Germany's military strength in the West, where she hopes to strike the knock-out blow.

For these reasons, then, Berlin welcomes peace in Finland. Moreover, the Wilhelmstrasse hardly conceals its feeling that the Allies have sustained a heavy blow.

Herr von Ribbentrop arrived back from Rome late tonight and will report on his talks to Herr Hitler tomorrow. However, Berlin was mainly interested tonight in Finland.

Beginning April 20th, all German youngsters between ten and eighteen are compelled to join the Hitler Youth Organization. Conscription of Germany's youth was laid down in a law dated 1936, but will only go into effect now. Boys between seventeen and eighteen will receive preliminary military training.

And here's an item from the Western Front. The Germans report that along the Upper Rhine, which separates the two front lines, the French yesterday put up a big sign which read "Down With Hitler". The Germans, says the report, warned the French to take it down. The French failed to take it down. Result: The Germans opened fire on it. What happened to the sign is not stated, but the Germans say one Frenchman was hit.

Berlin March 14, 1940 24.47

Good Evening. This is Berlin.

Field Marshal Göring, who besides running the German air force and looking after the forests is also a sort of economic czar, has just issued a new proclamation to the German people.

Tonight, he calls upon them to give up to the nation any spare copper, bronze, brass, tin, lead, or nickel they may have around the house.

Thus Germany, cut off by the blockade from the source of many of these metals, so necessary in the making of cannon and other war machines, calls on its households to help in its drive for raw materials.

"Comrades," says Göring, "in millions of German homes and places of business, there are a large number of objects made out of these metals. In the possession of individuals, they have no value for this war. But for the defense of the Reich, they're of the greatest worth."

The Field Marshal calls on the German people to help collect this old metal as a birthday gift for the Führer, whose birthday falls on April 20th. And Göring adds, "It will make the most beautiful birthday gift for the Führer. Let every comrade give his portion and thereby help the Führer in his battle for Germany's freedom."

A year ago tonight, Herr Hitler and Dr. Hacha, then President of Czechoslovakia, had their dramatic meeting in Berlin, and the next day, the German army entered Prague. On the first anniversary of this event, I'm just informed, the President of the Protectorate, Dr. Hacha, has sent a telegram to Herr Hitler thanking him for his full understanding of the position that Czechoslovakia was then in, and expressing again appreciation for Herr Hitler having taken over the protection of the Czech people. President Hacha closes with a wish that German arms may win victory in this war.

To which Herr Hitler answers that he has been deeply moved by the president's wire. And he assures President Hacha that Germany has no desire to load the Czech people with the burdens of this war. Herr Hitler thanks him for his wish for a German victory and concludes with the hope that this victory will benefit the Czechs as well as the Germans.

Berlin March 16, 1940 24.46

Good Evening. This is Berlin.

The story about the American ambassador in London falling out with the British government which, we hear here, Mr. Hull *[American Secretary of State]* as well as Mr. Kennedy *[American ambassador to Great Britain]* sharply denied today, apparently is the one issued by the German Official News Agency, the *DNB*.

The *DNB* report was actually dated from The Hague, and incidentally it was not published in the German newspapers. It seems to have been used only abroad. This *DNB* dispatch gave its source as a trusted neutral personage who had connections with London business circles.

And the dispatch indirectly quoted him, as you no doubt know by this time, as saying that Mr. Kennedy was in disfavor among members of the British government because of an alleged report he made in Washington recently. This report, according to the German dispatch, pointed out many mistakes made by Mr. Chamberlain's government and took a dark view of the position the Allies are in.

As I said, this story, though issued by the German Official News Agency, has not yet been published, so far as I can ascertain, in any German newspaper.

Of course, German propaganda, as is natural, does paint the situation of the Allies as bad indeed, and almost every German I speak to believes the Allies are in a bad way, especially since Finland made peace. Quite often, the German press cites neutral newspapers to back them up in this. For instance, today a leading Washington newspaper is quoted widely in Berlin as saying that the British blockade has not affected Germany in the least, in fact has even helped the Reich, whereas the Allies, as a result of the Nazi sea war, are in a bad position. "Time," the Washington paper is quoted as saying, "now works for Germany." I need hardly add that such a report from such a source makes very pleasant reading for the people of this country.

No leader in Europe has shown more ability to "strike while the iron is hot" than Chancellor Hitler. Feeling that Allied prestige has been lowered by Finland having given up the fight, Germany, probably in league with Russia and Italy – though these latter two would appear to make strange bed-fellows – is reported to be intensifying its economic and political drive in the Balkans. No doubt it will be pointed out to these wealthy little lands in south-eastern Europe that it doesn't pay to play ball with Britain and France, and that a benevolent neutrality, with increased trade with Germany, is the best policy to follow.

There even appear to be hopes in Berlin that in the end Turkey may be detached from her pact with the Allies. But the report that Germany will guarantee Romania's frontiers is denied today in the Wilhelmstrasse. That obviously would be too much for Russia. King Carol's rapprochement with the Romanian Iron Guard is welcomed here. The Iron Guard people have always been friends of Germany, and now they are to be set free and taken into King Carol's party.

Mr. James Nicholson and Mr. Wayne Taylor of the American Red Cross have returned here after distributing ten carloads of American hospital supplies in Poland. They personally saw to it that this American help went to Polish Jews as well as to others.

Berlin March 17, 1940 15.02

Good Morning. This is William L. Shirer in Berlin.

It may well be that this early spring Sabbath day of March 17th, 1940, Palm Sunday, will be a date to remember, a date that marked the turning point in the strange war in the west of Europe where for seven months great armies and massed air forces have stood facing each other – without fighting.

This morning in Berlin, the regular radio program was abruptly broken off and we heard a special communiqué from the High Command of the German defense forces. It contained something new that we had never heard before; a new type of action by the German air force which seems obvious enough when you stop to think that they're fighting a war after all, but withal the sort of action which the air forces of both sides heretofore have shrunk from beginning.

I'll just quote the High Command's communiqué as I heard it over the radio here in Berlin this morning:

"During the evening hours of March 16" – that is, last night – "the German air force attacked with strong forces British naval units anchored at Scapa Flow. At least four British warships, among them three battleships, and a cruiser were hit by bombs and severely damaged. Hits on two other British warships are probable. The British air bases at Stromness and Earthouse-Kirkwall and a British anti-aircraft position were successfully bombed. Despite strong reaction by British chaser planes and anti-aircraft artillery, the German planes successfully carried out their instructions and returned to their base without loss."

So much for the German communiqué. A few minutes ago, I picked up from London the communiqué of the British Admiralty which certainly differs from the one I've just read you. But at least you have both sides.

It seems to me, though, that the question of the number of British battleships hit, though important – after all it would mean, if the German version is substantiated, that a fifth of the British battleship tonnage had been damaged – it seems to me that this is not so important as the other event mentioned in this German communiqué.

For the first time since the war in the West began, the German High Command reports that its air force has bombed British airbases and anti-aircraft positions. Until now, as you know, this half-hearted aerial feud between Great Britain and Germany has been confined to bombing ships and naval harbors. Airfields and even anti-aircraft positions have been spared, apparently because neither side wanted to risk reprisals and start that unrestricted air warfare which, once begun, would end in the bombing of the cities and the slaughter of civilians.

Does the fact that the Germans for the first time last night attacked

British airbases mean that at last the war is to begin in earnest? Obviously, we'll have to wait a few days to see, but neutral observers in Berlin were very impressed this morning when they heard the German communiqué. They wondered, for instance, if those British planes which have been flying nights over Germany dropping their leaflets might not start bringing over more deadly loads.

Curiously enough, a few minutes before I heard the German radio give its account of the attack on Scapa Flow, I was reading an article on the war situation by the editor of the *Frankfurter Zeitung*, Rudolf Kircher, one of the best-informed journalists in this country. I was struck by one paragraph in his article. It was about the question we've all been asking here, namely, *why*, if the German air force was superior to that of the Allies when the war began, has it not used this superiority, why does it still not take advantage of it before the Allies, with their own production plus what they buy in America, catch up?

This is Editor Kircher's answer:

"No one can really think that Germany's war leaders are so dumb that they would sacrifice their established air superiority and remain inactive until the others were able to catch up with us." In the last half year, Editor Kircher goes on, "something quite different was taking place. We were actually increasing our superiority over the others. That will become evident."

In other words, according to this German view, while the Allies have undoubtedly been building and buying a lot of airplanes, Germany, which already had a headstart, has been building even more. Hence as long as this position was being maintained, it was of no advantage to Germany to begin the air war.

One more quote from Editor Kircher: "The gaining of time was therefore advantageous to us in every respect. Although it undoubtedly permitted our opponents to fill up some holes, it allowed us, thanks to our greater labor power and organization, to still increase our lead over the others." And he concludes: "Whenever or wherever we attack, on land, sea, or in the air, it will be not because we're forced to, but because our strength advises us. It will be offensive, not defensive."

There's little other news in Germany this morning.

The Berlin papers give quite a bit of space and comment to an order of the Dutch navy ordering all Netherlands ships to remain in harbor until further notice. The German press naturally interprets this as recognition by the Dutch of the deadly danger in sending its ships to England's shores, and recommends that all other neutrals follow a similar course. Foreign circles in Berlin are wondering if the Dutch acted on secret information that perhaps the air war between the warring powers was about to begin, as today's communiqué would seem to indicate. The Dutch are sometimes very well informed.

Here in Berlin, spring seems to be at last threatening to arrive, though it is having a hard time. As late as yesterday, we had a snow-fall. The coal shortage is still felt, and some of my American colleagues who live in apartments have been complaining to me today that despite the fact that it was a weekend – and a weekend here means that you can legally have warm water and a bath – there was no warm water. And they've been lining up in my room for baths, for in the hotels we have both heat and warm water. If it were not for the fact that the coming season promises an intensification of the war, with all its horrors, a lot of people I know here would be very glad about the fact that spring is almost on us, with summer not far behind.

Summer will also mean better food. Some of us are still smarting from an experience day before yesterday when we had to fork out the equivalent of one American dollar for an unappetizing dish of boiled carrots in one of the leading hotel restaurants here.

Berlin March 17, 1940 01.08

Good Evening. This is Berlin.

Events move rapidly over here tonight, heading either for peace, or for a war that is a war – the kind of war which the Germans signaled last night when, besides bombing British battleships at Scapa Flow, they bombed British landing-fields for the first time since the conflict began.

Tonight, Hitler is speeding south and Mussolini north and it has just been officially announced here that they will meet tomorrow morning at the Brenner Pass, on the Italian side of the border.

What the two fascist chiefs plan to do when they do meet is being kept a strict secret here in Berlin. We did not even get an admission that the Führer had left town until hours after Rome had announced Mussolini's departure. Actually, Herr Hitler left this afternoon in his special train and presumably the meeting will take place in either his train or the Duce's. The Führer was accompanied by the German Foreign Minister, Herr von Ribbentrop, his experts and adjutants.

No word was given out here that the sudden meeting of the two leaders had anything to do with the presence in Rome of Mr. Sumner Welles or the report from Italy that the sailing of the *Conte di Savoia*, on which Mr. Welles was to have sailed for home, had been postponed, in connection with it.

The official German statement merely said that the meeting of the Duce and the Führer had been arranged by Herr von Ribbentrop when he was in Rome last week, and that in fact it had been planned for some time.

Some neutral circles here, instead of taking the view that the two men were meeting to talk peace, seemed to think tonight that the purpose of the conference was to line up Italy behind Germany for whatever might happen in this war during the next few days or weeks. They apparently had heard nothing about the possible role for peace that Mr. Welles might be playing in the whole thing. And the official German statement shed no light on the matter.

At noon today, I picked up on the radio from London the report of the British Admiralty on the attack on Scapa Flow, which certainly differs from the account we've been given here. A couple of hours ago, we were convoked to a special press conference in the Wilhelmstrasse. There we met three of the flyers who had led the attack on Scapa Flow and they swore to us that they saw with their own eyes how four big British ships were hit. I'd like to tell you just a little of what they said.

You could sum it up this way – their story. First, that they took both the British fleet and the British air force completely by surprise. Secondly, that because of the surprise, the anti-aircraft fire, while hot at times, was too hastily organized to be effective, and third, that not enough British fighters took to the air to either ward them off or to bring them down after they'd unloaded their bombs and were scooting into the blackening eastern sky for home.

Major Fritz Doensch, who commanded the group of planes which did the actual bombing of the battleships – there were two other groups which attacked nearby airfields – told us that the attack on Scapa Flow had been carefully planned for several days; in fact, ever since a German reconnaissance plane came back the other day with the news that the British Grand Fleet was assembling once again at Scapa Flow.

For some days, said the Major, the German bombers stood on their landing fields, bombs loaded, ready to take off. But the weather was not favorable and so they waited. I judged from what he said that the kind of weather for an attack like that has to consist of plenty of heavy clouds along your way, so that the enemy won't know you're coming, but there must be no clouds over your objective. Yesterday morning, he said, they learned that the weather was just right for the undertaking, and they took off, timing their arrival at Scapa Flow for late dusk. The attack took place just before 8 p.m., but he said it was light enough to spot his objectives.

The Major insisted that, to his complete surprise, the English were caught completely off guard. He said both the ships and the shore-batteries gave the impression of everyone being off to dinner. There were also more ships in the bay than the Germans had expected, he said. It was impossible to identify the ships, he told us. The Germans just picked on the four biggest ones, three of which he took to be battleships and one a heavy cruiser, and swept down and bombed them. He said they hit all four.

Squadron Leader Magnusson, a youth of twenty-six, who handled the bombs on one of the machines, also described how one of his bombs hit the fore-deck of a battleship.

It was news to me that the man who releases the bombs actually guides the plane down to its objective, the pilot merely following his orders which are shouted through a telephone. Magnusson said he remembered leaning in the nose of the machine and shouting, "Right . . . a little left" and so on until suddenly he cried "Attention Zero!" which apparently is the signal to the pilot to hold it, and the bombs, as Magnusson put it, go off on their beautiful journey.

Major Doensch revealed that the *Hood, Renown* and *Repulse* were among the ships he thinks he got.

Questions were discouraged by the member of the Propaganda Ministry when the flyers had finished telling their story, but someone got in one question. He asked how a pilot could be sure of his hits, especially in the dark, to which the Major replied, "I can guarantee that each of the four ships got one heavy bomb on the deck, while several bombs fell very close."

Berlin March 18, 1940 24.47

Good Evening. This is Berlin.

For two and a half hours this morning, while a snowstorm raged, Hitler and Mussolini conferred in the Duce's private train parked on a siding in the Brenner Pass just over the frontier. Tonight, the German Chancellor is speeding back to Berlin. He should arrive here tomorrow morning.

And after that – well, the word here is that we are in for still more surprises, and that this Holy Easter week is going to be one long remembered.

Officially, all we've been told is that the two dictators had a cordial conversation. Unofficially, it is hinted that the conversation was not only cordial but historic, and that from it will come a "New Order" in Europe, as the German press phrases it this evening.

You may be interested to know what this "New Order" in Europe is to be like, as Berlin envisages it. Well, nothing less, so we're told here, than a Europe in which the three great dictatorships, Germany, Soviet Russia, and Italy shall call the tune – a Europe, as the German newspapers put it, freed from the "brutal domination of England and France".

Thus the purpose of the meeting on the Brenner today was, from the

226

German side, to win over Mussolini to the idea of joining Germany and Russia in an all-powerful tri-part bloc. Political circles here take it for granted that the Duce, who, like the Führer, only a short time ago was shipping his legionnaires to battle Bolshevism and Russian flyers in Spain, has been won over. What Italy gets out of it is not quite clear, but apparently a certain position in the Balkans plus of course the backing which such a bloc could give against Britain and France. It is assumed that the little Balkan powers would fall in with the new bloc, and that, in the end, Turkey also would see the light and drop its English and French friends.

It's indeed rumored here that this bloc of the dictatorships may be launched before Easter.

Well, that's the way Berlin sees today's meeting between Hitler and Mussolini. Nothing is said here of peace having been talked, and if Mr. Sumner Welles postponed his sailing on account of the meeting, then Berlin interprets that as meaning that the Duce merely wanted to inform him about the new turn of things, as agreed upon by the two dictators.

Incidentally, not a word of President Roosevelt's speech has been published here. When asked about that today, the Wilhelmstrasse said that the full text of the President's speech had not yet been received. But you got the feeling that Mr. Roosevelt's remarks on the kind of peace he believes in had not made a very good impression here.

The German press this evening still gives most of its space to the attack on Scapa Flow, which is hailed as the greatest military blow struck at Britain yet. And the German press is not pleased at the British version of the affair. Though the High Command did not say so in its communiqué, the press tonight announced that one of the British battleships hit was as good as destroyed. The High Command had said merely that it was badly damaged.

Berlin March 19, 1940

Good Evening. This is Berlin.

The British air force has given its first answer to the German air-raid on Scapa Flow. About an hour ago, we were informed that British bombers made three raids on the German base on the island of Sylt tonight, the first at 7:57, the second at 8:58, the third at 9:16 p.m. Sylt Island is just off the German coast where it borders on Denmark and is mainly a seaplane base.

According to the German communiqué, one house was set on fire, but no other damage was caused because of the effective German anti-aircraft measures. One English plane, it is stated here, was shot down.

227

Three days after the raid on Scapa Flow, the German papers are still banner-lining the event. Today, they headline a report in the *New York Times* which they say reached that newspaper from neutral sources in Washington and which they say confirms the German contention that six big British ships were hit at Scapa Flow.

A decree signed by General Göring today orders that all bells made of bronze be given up to help swell the reserve of metals. Payment will be made after the war and nothing is said about exempting any churches from the order.

Berlin March 20, 1940 14.00

Good Morning. This is William L. Shirer in Berlin.

The three attacks by British bombers last night on the German sea-plane base on the island of Sylt is certainly not treated sensationally by the German press this morning. All papers print the seven and a half line German statement, and the big newspapers, like the official Nazi organ *Völkischer Beobachter*, bury the story at the bottom of page two.

As I reported last night, the Germans say that with the exception of one house set on fire, no damage was done by the British planes, thanks to the German anti-aircraft fire, and one plane was shot down. No estimate is given out here as to how many planes took part in the attack, nor are the eyewitness reports from nearby neutral Denmark published.

But the High Command in its daily communiqué this morning does accuse the British of having violated Danish neutrality in their attack on the island of Sylt. The High Command does not say how, but you can assume it means that the British planes flew over Denmark and Holland. The High Command also reveals that the attack lasted from 8 p.m. last night until 2:40 a.m. this morning. The fact that in an attack lasting almost seven hours only one house was set on fire, is certainly remarkable.

The Wilhelmstrasse was considering this morning flying some neutral correspondents to Sylt this afternoon to see for themselves that the only damage was one house set afire. If the correspondents go, perhaps I can give you their story in my broadcast tonight.

An official statement just issued here in Berlin asserts that not only did the British planes last night fly over Denmark, but over Holmslands Klit and at Lyngvig, both in Danish Jutland, four incendiary bombs were dropped around midnight.

As a matter of fact, much more space is still given this Wednesday morning to the German raid on Scapa Flow, which took place Saturday evening. Berlin professes to be astounded at Mr. Chamberlain's assertion in the House of Commons yesterday that the German attack on Scapa Flow failed and that not a single British capital ship was hit. American newspapers in New York and Washington are cited to back up the German claim that six British ships were damaged at Scapa Flow. And, add the Germans, how could our attack have failed when the British admit that all our planes reached their objectives?

The Berlin papers which appear at noon have not yet carried the story of the resignation of the French cabinet. First reactions in the Wilhelmstrasse are that it's just another proof of the weakness of France in particular and the parliamentary system in general. And that it proves, if proofs were needed, the discontent in France over the Allied fiasco in Scandinavia.

As a matter of fact, the Wilhelmstrasse said, Germany was completely indifferent to cabinet changes in France, but felt it was bound to point out that for any country to change its cabinet in wartime is a sign of weakness. Asked about the German attitude towards a possible peace were a man like Laval to be named premier, the Wilhelmstrasse said that would make no difference. Germany was out to win the war, not make peace.

I just learned that about an hour ago the Russian Ambassador in Berlin hopped off to Moscow by plane. His departure is believed to be in connection with the Brenner interview of Hitler and Mussolini. There is even talk that he may return with a high Russian figure for the inauguration of a new tripart Russo-German-Italian bloc.

Mr. Chamberlain's speech in Parliament yesterday gets the leading play in all Berlin newspapers this morning, or rather editorial answers to the speech, because a straight news account of the speeches of enemy statesmen is never published in the press here. One knows what Mr. Chamberlain said only from references to his speech in the front-page editorials. I'll just give you an idea of them. The *Völkischer Beobachter* has this headline over its editorial which, as I said, is published as its leading front-page news story of the day: A WAR CRIMINAL – meaning Mr. Chamberlain – UNMASKS HIMSELF – NEW PROOF OF THE BRUTAL PLAN OF VIOLENCE AGAINST THE NEUTRALS.

The headline in the *12-Uhr Blatt* describes the session of the House of Commons yesterday as follows: HOLIDAY OF LIES IN LOWER HOUSE – THE PIRATES CONFESS THEIR CRIME AGAINST THE NEUTRALS. And the paper in its account of the debate says: "One knows Herr Chamberlain, and one laughs at him. Even in the Lower House, there is hardly anyone that takes him seriously. The old hypocrite with the umbrella thinks he can pour out his driveling mockery on the meeting of the two statesmen of Germany and Italy on the Brenner. The old gentleman will yet lose his sight and hearing. German arms will bring this weak-minded gentleman to reason and show him that Germans will not let him get by with this sort

229

of low, common crime in connection with the meeting of the Duce and the Führer. The Liar Neville will soon meet some energetic resistance. With these gentlemen, we will speak German. And that means: 'Only so far, Herr Chamberlain! You have raised the indignation of the German people to its boiling point.'"

Berlin March 20, 1940 24.47

Good Evening. This is Berlin.

The war in the air between Germany and Britain apparently is getting started. Scapa Flow last Saturday, the British reply on the island of Sylt last night. And this evening, about 9 o'clock, the following communiqué was given out in Berlin: "Near Scapa Flow this evening, a British convoy, strongly protected by cruisers and destroyers, was attacked by German flyers and broken up. Several ships were sunk, or badly hit. Our heroic flyers are now on their way back."

Note how fast these new air attacks are being reported – before the flyers even get back. Last night, the British airmen apparently did the same – reported by radio before they returned – a fact that the press here criticized.

I picked up my evening papers tonight expecting to read the German account of the British attack on Sylt last night. Here is what I read – I mean the headlines. *Nachtausgabe*, Berlin's leading evening paper: BRITISH DROP BOMBS ON DENMARK. The *Angriff*: BRITISH FLYERS AGAIN BOMBARD DANISH TERRITORY. The *Börsen Zeitung*: BRITISH BOMBS ON DANISH LAND. The *Deutsche Allgemeine Zeitung*: DANISH WARSHIP BOMBED BY ENGLISH FLYERS. BOMBS ON DANISH ISLANDS.

And there were columns of dispatches from Copenhagen describing in great detail how British bombs had fallen on Danish territory, even wrecking Danish houses. As to the attack on the German sea-plane base on the island of Sylt, there were six lines – the paragraph in the daily communiqué of the German High Command which said that in an attack on Sylt lasting from 8 p.m. yesterday until 2:40 a.m. today, the only damage done, thanks to German defense measures, was one house set on fire.

Tonight at 7 o'clock, the German News Agency informed us that it was an unoccupied house at that, and that the fire was quickly put out. Whereas the High Command had reported that one British plane had been shot down, tonight the German News Agency put the number at three.

Germany, as is natural, is closely following the cabinet change in France, though the Wilhelmstrasse said today it made no difference to

Germany who was in power in Paris. Berlin political circles interpret the naming of M. Reynaud as premier as meaning a sharpening of France's war effort. The German radio tonight described M. Reynaud as a big war agitator, a worse warmonger than M. Daladier.

Berlin March 21, 1940 24.47

Good Evening. This is Berlin.

It would seem almost too much to expect that the Easter holidays which begin here tomorrow should bring a lull in the air war which has flared up the last few days between Germany and Britain. But at least so far tonight, there has been no news of fresh air attacks either given or received.

The German newspapers are still celebrating the attack of their air force on a British convoy last night when, according to the German version, 42,000 tons of war and merchant ships were sunk, and another 11,000 tons damaged.

Tomorrow morning's newspapers will play up the story of a visit to the island of Sylt today by some neutral – chiefly American – correspondents. The Americans were shown one sea-plane base, the one at Hoernum, on the south end of the island, and reported little damage there outside of a military hospital whose roof had been caved in by a bomb. They reported the airplane hangars as untouched, but several bomb craters were observed nearby. There was a lot of smashed window glass, they said.

On the political front, interest seems to have shifted to Moscow, where the Kremlin is reported considering the German project for a tripart bloc consisting of Germany, Russia, and Italy. Whether the Russian Ambassador in Berlin who flew suddenly back to Moscow yesterday will return with Mr. Molotov to launch the bloc, as was thought likely here yesterday, seems more doubtful today. However, Berlin feels sure this powerful bloc of the dictatorships will soon become a reality.

In the meantime, Germany continues its campaign to build up its metal reserve, which has been affected by the blockade. All church bells made of bronze are to come and be melted up for more martial purposes. Next week begins a nationwide house-to-house drive for every available scrap of tin, nickel, copper, bronze and such metals which the German people are being asked to give up as a birthday present for the Führer.

Today, the army ordered all car-owners whose automobiles are laid up by the wartime ban – which means 90 percent of them – to surrender their batteries. Payment will be given – from 35 cents to 3 dollars, depending on the condition of the batteries.

231

People here, you see, certainly are kept reminded of the hardships of war, but I think you could say tonight that their thoughts are also on Easter. In the days of peace, the Germans loved to travel for Easter, visiting relatives, or driving to the mountains or the country. This year the population has been requested to stay at home for Easter and not to tax the capacity of the railroads. No extra trains will be run, and the police have issued strict orders that no private motor cars are to be used for Easter outings. A police control will see to it that the order is enforced.

The traditional Easter egg – well, I don't know what the people are going to do about that, seeing that our ration allows us only one egg a week. In the streets today, I noticed long lines of patient people standing at the entrance of candy shops, waiting for their ration of Easter candy.

And from Posen comes the news that three more Poles were sentenced to death today, the charge being the murder of a German during the Polish war.

Berlin March 22, 1940 14.00

Good Morning. This is William L. Shirer in Berlin.

This Good Friday of course is a holiday in Germany, and coming up to the broadcasting house a few minutes ago I saw more people thronging the streets than I've seen in my life in Berlin. There seemed to be a real holiday atmosphere about them, almost as if the war had been forgotten – at least for the Easter weekend.

Maybe, too, it was because many persons thought that it was the last quiet they could enjoy before the storm – before, as many people think, the war, with all its horrors, really breaks out.

If the sidewalks were thronged with people this morning, the actual streets were terribly deserted. Hardly a car in the whole stretch of five miles of boulevard along which I came to reach this studio. And those cars, army vehicles or official ones. For the police had given warning yesterday that even those who had special permission to use their automobiles during wartime – only about 10 percent – must not be caught out for an Easter joy-ride. All along the avenues, traffic policemen were posted this morning to see to it that the order was enforced.

The populace also was asked not to travel on trains over Easter, so that the railroads could devote their energies to carrying coal and other freight. And one paper this morning, the *Lokal Anzeiger*, tells its readers that the railroads are now very busy transporting fertilizer for the spring planting. And that therefore people must not burn any more coal than is necessary, so that the railroads can concentrate on transporting fertilizer instead of coal. The same paper publishes a new appeal to German housewives not to waste food or buy any more than they absolutely need.

There is no news here of the torpedoing of a German ship by a British submarine east of Denmark, as reported from London. If the news is confirmed, it would be the first time that British submarines had been active in these waters, through which most of the Swedish iron ore for Germany must pass.

The High Command reports this morning all quiet on the Western Front, with some reconnaissance activity over the North Sea by the air force. It gives the figures of enemy and neutral shipping sunk in the last three days as 32,000.

Yesterday, you will remember, the Germans reported 42,000 tons sunk on the previous evening alone by the air force.

Berlin March 24, 1940 01.02

Good Evening. This is Berlin.

Well, today was Easter and a cold, grey day it was, at least in Berlin. And here is Mrs. Dorothy Oechsner, wife of Mr. Frederick Oechsner, United Press correspondent in Berlin, to tell you about it.

DOROTHY OECHSNER: Easter this year in Berlin is unusual for various reasons. We are just emerging from the coldest and longest winter in over one hundred years. So there hasn't been much of an incentive to think of spring clothes or Easter finery. Women who have wanted to splurge on new outfits remembered that whatever they bought had to come off their clothing or so-called *Punkt* cards of one hundred points a year.

SHIRER: Mrs. Oechsner – How about hats?

MRS. OECHSNER: Hats have played an important role because they are among the few things one may buy without benefit of cards. A few shops are showing pancake-like trifles in straw plus a swirl of voile but, with an eye to the future, the women consider felt hats the smart thing to wear this season as they can be remodeled in the fall. Being limited to 100 points a year makes you practical. Considering that a suit or a wool dress takes sixty points, stockings four points a pair, undies anything from four to sixteen points, it wouldn't be at all difficult to throw the whole 100 points on something suitable for an Easter parade but not for year-round use.

The chocolate shops did a rushing business, since many people decided to spend their whole ration of half a pound per month on Easter. Even so, chocolate Easter eggs and rabbits were almost impossible to find and most children were reconciled to the lack of sweets. Many shopkeepers jokingly said that the reason they did not have more Easter goods was that the bunny froze in January. Candies could be had, one-half pound for the month after a special card had been properly stamped. One of the largest candy shops in Berlin has a most inviting window. Beautiful boxes tied with pink and blue ribbons, woolly lambs with boxes of chocolates tied on their backs, but a sign makes it clear that this is all for display and not for sale.

SHIRER: What about the kids? Did they have colored Easter eggs as usual?

MRS. OECHSNER: The food authorities were more generous this month, and for Easter week we were allowed three eggs per person, making a total of seven for the month. The ones I got came from Holland and were nice and fresh. Most people that I've talked to did not color the eggs; this was even true of some friends of ours in the country with whom I exchanged Easter greetings by long-distance. They had invited us to spend the weekend with them as they had a turkey for their Easter dinner. Here at our house we had some lamb, which I had reserved in advance. We also had a tin of string beans, a special treat which the shopkeeper gave me for the occasion. This is the first time that the food authorities have released canned goods since the war began.

SHIRER: Thank you, Mrs. Oechsner.

At Easter time, German editors usually take stock of the situation. Wrote the editor of the *Lokal Anzeiger* today from Posen, in former Poland: "The East will be German, or it will be a marsh which poisons all Central Europe. There is no third possibility . . . This land cries out for Germans . . . The fact is that the only land worth looking at is that once blessed by German labor."

And Dr. Robert Ley, leader of the Workers' Front, in a speech to the men who are building the Siegfried Line and which was broadcast throughout the nation, said: "Every German is absolutely certain that Germany will win the war. The British and French are nervous. They've become hysterical, like old women. The Maginot Line is just a piece of junk."

Berlin March 27, 1940 24.47

Good Evening. This is Berlin.

For several days now, a lot of us have been struck by the fact that the German High Command, in its daily communiqués, has emphasized that

234

Allied planes have been violating the territory of the neutral states that border the Reich – Denmark, Holland, Belgium, Luxemburg, and Switzerland.

Ordinarily, the daily war communiqués are published under a small heading, but tonight all the papers jump on this accusation against the Allied flyers, and give it flaming banner-headlines. Thus the *Nacht-ausgabe*: ENEMY FLYERS CONTINUE NEUTRALITY VIOLATIONS.

It seems only reasonable to conclude that the German High Command will not remain content forever merely to record that enemy airmen are flying over neutral lands.

There's that to keep in mind when you're thinking of what the future will bring in this war. And then there's this matter of British warships trying to stop German vessels steaming down the Norwegian coast, always within the three-mile limit, with their valuable cargoes of iron for Germany's munition plants.

The Wilhelmstrasse admitted tonight that it is convinced that the present activity of the British along the Scandinavian coast is but a prelude to more intensive action. And some people here believe that the war may spread to Scandinavia yet, despite the lessening of the pressure which followed the Finnish peace.

It was reported in Berlin today, for instance, that last week a squadron of at least nine British destroyers was concentrated off the Norwegian coast and that in several instances German freighters carrying iron received warning shots to stop. Instead of stopping they fled into nearby fjords. At the Ross Fjord, say the Germans, two destroyers followed their ships in to within a mile of land.

The German press, which has not kept its public informed of Scandinavian and other neutral ships sunk recently by German submarines or mines or airplanes, advises the Scandinavians now to stick up for their rights against the British. As a matter of fact, the Wilhelmstrasse now takes the view that it is unneutral for the Scandinavians to treat armed British merchant vessels as anything but warships, and that therefore their stay in port should be limited just as it is for war vessels. I believe the United States does not accept that view for itself. [*Last sentence censored.*]

From here, it looks as if the neutrals, especially the Scandinavians, were being ground down tighter and tighter between the conflicting claims of the Allies and Germany, and that they may be drawn into the conflict after all.

I've often mused about coffee in Germany, or rather the lack of it, and how all Germans love their coffee when they can get it. I was not surprised to hear recently that there were an awful lot of doctor's prescriptions being written for coffee. But they won't be any more. The Health Führer has now forbidden doctors to write prescriptions for coffee.

I regret to announce also that beer, in the art of making which the Germans so excel, threatens to get a little short. Some of the little beer places have announced they can no longer sell beer to be carried away in jugs, but you can still get it inside the beerhouse.

In Germany, all must work where they're told to work. Today two women were given prison sentences for refusing to work on a farm, after a government labor office had ordered them to do so.

The German High Command in its daily communiqué announces that there were no special happenings on the Western Front. Stronger reconnaissance flights, it says, were carried out yesterday over the eastern part of France. This led to several air battles in which the High Command declares the German reconnaissance planes shot down two French chaser planes, one of them a Curtiss.

This is the first time I recall a reconnaissance plane shooting down a fighter in this war.

Berlin April 8, 1940 01.46

Good Evening. This is William L. Shirer in Berlin.

The Germans tonight are calling the British desperadoes and their action in laying mines in Norwegian territorial waters as brutal, immoral and a crime against international law.

But the question you're all asking: What is Germany going to do about it? we cannot answer from Berlin – yet. That's Chancellor Hitler's secret, and he's keeping it to himself.

All the Wilhelmstrasse would say tonight was that Britain's violation of Norwegian neutrality had created a very serious situation and that Germany is watching events, as a government spokesman put it, with ice-cold determination. It was also hinted that, in the German view, Britain's action today destroys the whole conception of neutrality and that Berlin will be forced to draw the consequences. In other words, Berlin may feel no longer bound by the laws of neutrality.

Norway's reaction to the British move, as outlined in the official Norwegian statement published this afternoon, was regarded in the Wilhelmstrasse tonight as much too weak – as positively lame. Germany, it was indicated, expected something stronger. Just what, was not made clear.

Britain's swift action apparently took Berlin by surprise this morning, though it must be said that the Wilhelmstrasse for ten days had been hinting that the Allies planned a breach of Norwegian neutrality. There have been, as is natural, a whole crop of rumors racing around all day to the effect that, one, the German fleet had sailed into the Kattegat, west of Sweden, and was heading for Skagerrak, where the greatest naval battle of the World War was fought. Two, that a German expeditionary army was forming at the Baltic ports where dozens of passenger ships were waiting to carry it to Scandinavia. But so far as we're informed here, they're just rumors. As you know, the totalitarian states do not announce their next moves beforehand.

You might gather, from what I've said, and from what you yourself think of today's events in Europe, that the laying of British mines on the coast of Norway was the big story in the German press today. Not at all.

The story that led all the German newspapers and got all the headlines was another one. It was about today's revelations of the German Foreign Office which told how the Romanian authorities at the very last minute had nipped in the bud a British plot to block the Danube River, up which come valuable supplies to the Reich. A large number of British river boats, said the Foreign Office, manned by British sailors, soldiers and military officers in disguise, attempted to go up the Danube. These boats, the Germans asserted, were loaded with high explosives, depth-bombs and other ammunition, and the plan was to sink them at a narrow place in the Danube known as the Iron Gate, thus blocking the Danube. Romanian authorities learned of the plot, it's said, and seized the boats.

American newspaper offices in Berlin in touch with the correspondents in Bucharest could get no news on the matter from the Romanian capital itself, tonight.

At any rate, the Wilhelmstrasse said the German government was in touch with the Romanian government about the affair. Just what that meant – since the whole thing is alleged here to have taken place within Romanian territory – was not gone into.

Berlin April 9, 1940 15.00

Good Morning. This is William L. Shirer in Berlin.

The German government, to use the term of an official proclamation issued in Berlin, has "taken over the protection of Denmark and Norway for the duration of the war".

That is to say, at dawn this morning the Nazi army invaded the two neutral states of Denmark and Norway. The reason given – and we correspondents were given an explanation by the German Foreign Minister himself this morning – is that Norway and Denmark were unable to protect themselves from an approaching invasion by Allied troops and that Germany, in the interests of Scandinavia as well as in her own, had to provide that protection herself.

With typical lightning-like speed, the German army, navy and air force proceeded to the job of providing that protection at dawn this morning. The Danes, with practically no army, air force or navy, put up no resistance, so far as is known in Berlin. The Norwegians, also with hardly any army, air force or navy, did, according to dispatches reaching Berlin.

A special communiqué issued by the German High Command a couple of hours ago announced that Copenhagen, the capital of Denmark, had been completely occupied by German troops by 8 o'clock this morning. The Nazi forces were taken during the night in troop ships from Baltic ports, landed in the capital at dawn and first occupied the citadel and the radio station. By 8 o'clock, reported the High Command, the entire city was in German hands.

So swift and complete was the occupation of Denmark, that neutral observers have no doubt it must have been planned and prepared long ago. It took place simultaneously at several points. The High Command speaks of German motorized units crossing the Danish border at Flensburg, that is, on the mainland about fifty miles north of the Kiel Canal, at dawn. They advanced rapidly over Apenrade and Esbjerg northwards.

In the meantime, it is clear from the High Command report, German troops, protected by naval ships and airplanes, were making landings from transports at several places. In the so-called Little-Belt, just east of the Danish mainland, German troops landed at Mittelfahrt and occupied the great bridge over the Belt to the Danish island of Fyn. Further east in the Big-Belt, which separates the island on which Copenhagen is located from the island of Fyn, more German transports arrived and landed troops at Korsoer and Nyborg.

At another point, says the High Command, ferry ships from the German port of Warnemünde, carrying an armored train, disembarked at Hjedser, with their train, and proceeded northward. At the same time, say the Germans, the Vordingsberg bridge at the southern end of the island of Seeland was occupied.

The Nazi newspaper *Angriff*, commenting on these actions of the German troops, says: "The young German army has hoisted new glory to its banners . . . It is one of the most brilliant feats of all time."

Apparently the Danes offered no resistance whatsoever. It's understood the Danish minister protested in the Wilhelmstrasse at an early hour this morning but declared that Denmark was not in a position to fight Germany. It was about a year ago that Denmark, alone of the Scandinavian states, signed a non-aggression pact with Germany, in which both nations agreed to respect the independence and territorial integrity of the other.

Denmark, so far as was known here, had not been subject to any Allied mine-laying against German ships.

In memorandums to Norway and Denmark the German government said that it expected the civil population and the governing authorities to refrain from any resistance to the German army. And it added, quote: "Such resistance would be wholly useless and would be broken by every means of force."

People in the streets of Berlin took the news calmly. Few people even bothered to buy the extra papers. For several hours, Dr. Goebbels remained at the microphone reading the various memorandums, proclamations and news bulletins.

According to the German radio, the occupation of Copenhagen took place without incident. The Germans speak of the Danish government officials assuring the German commander of their fullest loyalty.

Berlin April 9, 1940 22.39

Good Afternoon. This is William L. Shirer in Berlin.

The German occupation of Norway and Denmark, which the German newspapers tell us was done to safeguard their freedom and security, continues according to schedule, according to military circles in Berlin.

Denmark, which offered no resistance at all, was said to have been almost completely occupied by night-fall, that is – about two hours ago.

The situation in Norway is more obscure. The Germans admit that the Norwegians put up quite a little resistance at two places on the south coast – at Kristiansand and Oslo, the capital. Late in the afternoon, however, Berlin announced that Nazi troops had entered the Norwegian capital.

Incidentally, most of the Americans still in Berlin, especially our diplomats, had their families in Oslo. But there was no communication with the capital today, and their fate is unknown.

It's emphasized in Berlin that the German air force, which broke the back of Poland in less than a week, took a prominent part in today's action. What the navies are doing – the German and British – we don't know yet in Berlin. There is no news of any engagement, nor have the Germans had anything to say about the report that one of their transports, the *Rio de Janeiro*, was sunk.

Incidentally, the Wilhelmstrasse denies that Germany intends to make protectorates out of Denmark and Norway. The official contention here is, as I've said, that Germany had saved the freedom and the independence of these two neutral countries, and that's what the press drums on tonight.

239

Only the Berlin press doesn't approve of the way the Norwegians have taken the German action, and sharp warnings are issued to the government and people of Norway to remember Poland and cease resisting, as Denmark did. As the official Nazi organ, the *Völkischer Beobachter,* puts it, Norway's attitude, quote, "not only shows a complete lack of a feeling for justice but borders on insanity." The paper calls on Norwegians to avoid needless sacrifice. And the *Börsen Zeitung* argues that: "Oslo ought to see that Germany's action was only done to insure Norway's freedom."

Significantly, perhaps, the German press warns tonight that the Allies may try to spread the field of operations to steal other neutral lands. It says Germany will again give the necessary answer. This warning is in a dispatch from Amsterdam, Holland.

The Berlin radio announced twenty minutes ago from Oslo that part of the Norwegian cabinet had remained in the capital and were joined by two more who returned there this afternoon. These ministers, said Berlin, were considering forming a government of their own to parley with the German army. This Oslo report followed on the Germans taking over there.

Berlin April 10, 1940 01.46

Good Evening. This is William L. Shirer in Berlin.

The invasion by Germany today of Norway and Denmark in order, as the German press puts it, to protect the freedom and independence of these two tiny neutral lands, has ended after a bare eighteen hours with the complete occupation of the whole of Denmark and – so the Germans declare – the seizure of all important military points in Norway.

Denmark did not resist, and the mighty German army, moving by land, sea, and air quickly occupied it without trouble. Neutral observers recalled that it was only a year ago that Germany signed a non-aggression treaty with Denmark.

Little Norway chose to resist, though warned by the Nazi government that opposition to the German army would be crushed by all the force at its disposal. And at two points – at Kristiansand and Oslo, the capital – the Germans themselves admit that the Norwegians offered lively resistance. But Oslo was occupied this afternoon and Kristiansand this evening.

Indeed at midnight, Berlin time, that is just an hour and forty-five minutes ago, the German High Command in a special communiqué declared that all important military bases in Norway were firmly in

240

German hands, including Narvik in the extreme north, which is the port from where the Swedish iron is shipped to Germany, and the following coastal towns: Trondheim, Bergen, Stavanger, and Kristiansand. The High Command added that wherever strong resistance had been offered, as at Kristiansand and Oslo, it had been broken. All Norwegian coastal forts, it reported, had been captured intact and were now in a position to repel enemy attacks.

The German air force, which took a prominent part in today's operations, has now established its own bases on the flying fields in southern Norway. Late tonight, according to the High Command, planes working from those bases gained a huge victory over an Allied fleet west of Bergen. The High Command maintains that two Allied battleships and two heavy cruisers were hit several times by heavy bombs.

Well, how did the Germans do it? How did they overrun Denmark and occupy not only the capital of Norway but important bases along a thousand mile coastline which was supposed by all military observers over here to be dominated by the British fleet – all in a few hours?

For the time being, I'm afraid it's a military secret. But it's obvious to a school child – and privately the Germans do not deny it – that the action was long prepared and longer planned, and actually put into operation – well, at least before this morning, and no doubt before the British mined Norwegian territorial waters. For to get to Narvik takes at least four days by sea – if the Germans got there by sea.

The German government officially informed the Norwegian government this morning that it was taking over its protection and would not interfere with its freedom or independence. Soon after the Germans occupied Oslo, the Berlin radio reported from the Norwegian capital that a new government was being formed which "wishes to avoid the fate of Finland". It was significant that the Berlin radio tonight already referred to the Norwegian government, with which only this morning it was dealing officially and which then fled to Hamar, as the "Rump Norwegian government".

To give you an idea of the state of mind in Berlin today, let me cite the German press. Its front-pages glorify today's achievements of the German army and tell the readers that Germany today, as the *Nachtausgabe* says, has merely taken steps "to safeguard the freedom and security of Norway and Denmark". The same paper blames England and France for what has happened. The *Börsen Zeitung* says, "England goes cold-bloodedly over the dead bodies of the small peoples. Germany protects the weak states from the English highway robbers." And the same paper concludes, "Norway ought to see the righteousness of Germany's action which was taken to ensure the freedom of the Norwegian people."

241

Tomorrow morning the official Nazi organ, the *Völkischer Beobachter,* will carry this bannerline in red ink on its front page: GERMANY SAVES SCANDINAVIA!

Berlin April 10, 1940 22.36

Good Evening. This is William L. Shirer in Berlin.

We have very little news here tonight about what is going on in Norway, or along its coasts. The German press tells us tonight that Norway is quiet. The German High Command says that operations at sea still continue but gives no details.

The only news published here about the naval engagement at Narvik today between German and British destroyers comes – strangely enough – from the English news agency *Reuters.* It merely says that according to *Reuters* two British warships, the *Hardy* and *Hunter*, were sunk today off Narvik. No mention is made that they were destroyers; they're referred to as warships. No mention is made either about there having been any battle there, or of any German losses.

When the German radio announced that two British warships had been sunk, the news program was broken off and the Nazi war-song *We're Marching Against England* was played.

There have been no more High Command communiqués since this noon about the progress of the German land forces. But at six o'clock tonight we were officially informed that the Norwegian town of Hamar, to which the Norwegian government fled yesterday, was occupied today by German mechanized troops. The Norwegian government, with the King, it is reported, fled further northwards with the Nazi troops in pursuit.

The German government, we were told today, is still maintaining contact with the Norwegian government, though with which one, is not clear. But I notice that the official German News Agency in a dispatch from Oslo tonight refers to the Norwegian Nazi leader, Mr. Vidkun Quisling, as the "chief of the new Norwegian government".

The Germans are still keeping secret how they managed with such lightning speed to occupy the chief ports on Norway's west coast right under the guns of the British fleet. Neutral naval attachés in particular were scratching their heads at the news, which came from London, that the Germans had been able to get two cruisers into Bergen and six destroyers into Narvik, at the extreme north of the Norwegian coast. How they got there without the British discovering them is one of those things which simply baffles the neutral experts here. And the Germans just smile and say nothing.

The world reaction to Germany appointing itself as protector to Norway and Denmark is considered by the German press today to be largely favorable. Russia and Italy, especially, the German newspapers find, showed "complete understanding". As for America, the *DAZ* says the American press refrains from taking any stand on Germany's action.

Berlin April 11, 1940 01.46

Good Evening. This is William L. Shirer in Berlin.

The news of Germany's occupation of Norway to save that country from becoming a theater of war and to protect its independence is still very meager here in Berlin tonight.

I understand that outside this country there are reports of certain sea battles having taken place in connection with the German occupation. Berlin denies them all. Berlin says it's a lie – pure invention – just British propaganda. As the German radio put it tonight, there isn't a word of truth in the English assertion that there have been battles at sea between the Allied and German navies. The only sea battle that's taken place, says Berlin, is the one at Narvik between a few destroyers, and Germany won that one.

Wilhelmstrasse quarters stated tonight that the sea communications over the 200 miles of water between Denmark and Norway, across which all German troops and supplies must be shipped, have been fully secured. Nothing is known in Berlin, we were told, about any losses of German naval ships or transports, except the two cruisers whose sinking at the hands of the Norwegians was reported the first day of the occupation.

I imagine this is all very confusing to you, as it is to me. But I'm only covering one side, and I pass on to you what I'm told here.

Since the German High Command issued its lengthy communiqué at noon today describing the battle of the destroyers at Narvik, announcing that the occupation of Norway was proceeding according to schedule and denying that the Allies had dislodged the Germans from their positions in Norway's west-coast ports, or even tried to dislodge them, there's been little news to report from Berlin.

At 6 p.m. our time, the German radio gave out two special communiqués based on the speech of Mr. Churchill. One recounted the British losses given to the House of Commons, the other Mr. Churchill's statement that no Norwegian ports had been recaptured by the Allies. At 11 p.m., Berlin time, another special communiqué informed us that German airplanes attacked British war vessels 125 miles north-west of Trondheim. A British aircraft-carrier was – to quote the German words exactly – "destructively hit by a heavy bomb". Further, an English cruiser received two direct hits. After this communiqué was read on the radio, the program was suspended, and as is always the case when an important new victory is announced, the Nazi war song, *Marching on England*, was played.

Well, that's all the military news we have in Berlin. As you see, the activities of the German fleet are not mentioned, nor is there any suggestion that the transport of troops is not proceeding normally.

Incidentally, the German communiqué quoting Mr. Churchill on British losses omitted any reference to his statement about a battle between the battle-cruisers *Renown* and *Scharnhorst*. But German naval circles wondered, if the report was true, how their ship got away, especially if it was damaged, when its speed is four and a half knots slower than the *Renown*'s.

On land, Berlin reports a victory of the German army over what is described as a vastly superior Norwegian force between Hamar and Elverum.

I note that the German press itself does not play up the actual military operations themselves tonight. It concentrates on a report from Bergen that the Germans there seized five British freighters loaded with guns and ammunition, ostensibly for Finland, but really, say the Germans, for their planned offensive against Germany through Norway.

The headlines in yesterday's papers saying that Germany had taken over the protection of Denmark and Norway and had occupied both countries evidently led many people here to conclude that the operation was as good as over and that it was just one more brilliant German military victory, like the one in Poland. After all, in a few hours, all of Denmark had been occupied and the capital of Norway and all important coastal cities likewise occupied.

The *DAZ* today warns that only now has the second phase begun. "We know," it says, "that we have to hold out against the action of the Allies. Fantastic English reports don't have to tell us that a struggle is on, and that there is no battle without losses, no military goal which is not connected with calculated risks."

Incidentally, press warnings began in Germany tonight against Sweden. That country's press was warned that its newspapers, in spreading English propaganda reports about the northern occupation, were not acting as the press of a neutral country is expected to act.

Berlin April 12, 1940 01.46

Good Evening. This is William L. Shirer in Berlin.

Government circles here reported tonight little change in the military and naval situation in Norway during the last twenty-four hours.

Tonight, according to a German communiqué issued at 10 p.m., our time, British flyers raided German air bases along the Norwegian coast but were repulsed with the loss of eight bombers. Messerschmitt chasers did the repulsing, it was stated.

There is no other news in Berlin of important engagements. The German forces which landed at Oslo appear to be spreading out, but their advance is not very rapid. They captured Drammen, twenty-five miles west of Oslo, and Eidsvold, forty-five miles to the north-east. On the west coast, the High Command says its troops are holding all points occupied Tuesday.

But apparently Berlin now expects no easy walkover in Norway, whatever the leaders here may have expected last Tuesday when the venture was launched. As a Wilhelmstrasse organ expressed it tonight, "Berlin did not count on this Anglo-German struggle to be over already. On the contrary, further fighting is to be reckoned with."

The reaction of the Norwegian government to being protected by the Reich has disappointed the Wilhelmstrasse. We were even informed tonight that Berlin has about given up hope of coming to any understanding with the old Norwegian government, though the Foreign Office maintained today its envoy in Oslo was still in touch with the King of Norway. As a matter of fact, the King's government was today openly described by the Foreign Office as a "rump" government, and Mr. Quisling was referred to in a Foreign Office organ as "the new Norwegian Prime Minister".

The Berlin press charges that the old government is out of touch with the Norwegian people who, it says, understand Germany's protective measures. As the *Börsen Zeitung* explains, "Germany wants to spare Norway from becoming the scene of war at England's dictation . . . England came to draw Norway into the war. Germany came to save it from war."

And the Wilhelmstrasse stoutly maintained today that Germany does not consider herself at war with Norway. Foreign Minister Kohts' declaration that Norway does, with Germany, was dismissed as coming from the rump government.

Questioned as to whether sovereign Denmark would maintain its legations in Paris and London, the Wilhelmstrasse thought that was doubtful because of the unfriendly attitude of the Allies towards Danish ships. Asked about Danish legations in neutral countries, Berlin thought they would be maintained since Germany has guaranteed Denmark's sovereignty.

There's considerable resentment in Berlin following the bombing of a small German railroad station near Denmark by British flyers today. Berlin says that's the first time that's happened, and if it takes place again there will be full retaliation on England. That makes it look as if the real war had begun.

Neutral diplomats are watching Sweden carefully following German press attacks on Swedish newspapers. Berlin holds they're not being neutral. But so far nothing has happened in that direction.

I understand that a large number of Americans at Oslo, mostly wives and children of Americans stationed in Europe, left there today for Sweden. They will be evacuated through Germany.

Berlin April 14, 1940 16.02

Good Morning. This is William L. Shirer in Berlin.

Almost a week has now gone by since the German army, with the lightning speed which it demonstrated so well in Austria, Czechoslovakia, and Poland, suddenly burst into Denmark and Norway. Both little countries, as well as the Allies and the rest of the world, were caught completely by surprise.

Denmark, which alone of the Scandinavian countries had accepted Herr Hitler's offer of a non-aggression treaty and actually signed one last year with Germany, had trusted in this for its safety. Of course, the Germans deny they've broken this non-aggression treaty. The official point of view here, as you know, is that Germany went into Denmark to protect it and ensure its freedom and independence.

Denmark – as Berlin fully expected – did not choose to fight, and it was completely overrun in a day by the Nazi troops.

So far as neutral observers can gauge the well-guarded Nazi plans for the occupation of Scandinavia, Berlin did not expect the Norwegians to fight either. That they did, and in so doing sank some of Germany's most valuable ships the first day, came as a surprise and complicated matters not a little. Apparently it was believed here that the lightning-like occupation of not only the Norwegian capital but all its important coast towns – and in Norway there are no important towns inland – would be a convincing enough argument for the Norwegians not to resist Herr Hitler's troops. This calculation went wrong, though no doubt the High Command took into consideration this contingency.

Well, now, how did the German troops occupy the chief Norwegian ports along a coast line stretching a thousand miles, and all in a few hours – and under the nose of the British fleet, not to mention the Norwegian authorities? Berlin naturally is very discreet on the matter. Neutral observers here piece together the story like this:

German troops with guns and supplies were transported to the west coast Norwegian ports in cargo boats which ostensibly were on their way to Narvik to fetch the Swedish iron of which Germany buys eleven million tons a year. These freighters, as they've been doing since the war, sailed within the Norwegian three-mile limit, and thus escaped discovery by the British navy. It has even been reported that these German transports were escorted to their secret destinations by Norwegian warships in order to protect them from the British.

Well, it's easy enough to understand how these freight boats could get to their destinations. But they wouldn't have been enough for Hitler's enterprise. There had to be warships at each of the Norwegian ports to protect the landing parties, and to ward off the attempts of the superior British naval forces to force their way into the fjords and recapture the vital ports.

And there were German warships there, as we know.

And unobserved by the British fleet or air force.

How did they get there? The German Admiralty keeps it a secret. But neutral naval observers here have broken their heads trying to figure it out. It seems evident, for example, from the British reports themselves that the Germans concentrated at Narvik alone seven destroyers – or one-third of the entire German destroyer strength at the beginning of this war – and one battleship, which is half of Germany's fleet of two capital ships. Narvik is three and a half days sailing at least from the nearest German port – a distance of almost a thousand miles. And seven destroyers and a battleship and a heavy cruiser are not invisible, like say rowboats.

Then again the British report their flyers as having observed two German cruisers in the fjord at Bergen. How did two cruisers slip into there unobserved? Well, those are questions which will have to wait for answers.

The German High Command, which did not give out any report last night about yesterday's naval battle at Narvik, has now come out with the German version of that engagement. It's this – I'll just quote the official communiqué: "German destroyers under the command of Commodore Bonte, which covered the landing of troops at Narvik, have in the last few days with the help of German U-boats and airplanes been engaged in a heavy fight against repeated attempts of British naval forces to break through.

"Yesterday noon the enemy began another grand attack. For this purpose, he assembled a squadron consisting of two battleships, aircraft carriers, cruisers, and several destroyers. Despite the superiority of the British forces, our destroyers attacked them. In a heavy fight, the British destroyer *Cossack* was set on fire by our naval and air forces and stranded. The destroyer *Eskimo* as well as other British destroyers were either damaged or destroyed. The complete losses of the enemy as well as our own have not yet been fully estimated."

So much for Narvik. Who holds the town, whether the British have landed, whether there are still German naval forces there offering resistance, what the German land-forces are doing – these questions, as you see, are not answered in the High Command's report.

The same German communiqué today also reports on the battle which Mr. Churchill in his speech on Wednesday mentioned as having taken place between the *Renown* and the German battleship *Scharnhorst*. The German High Command does not say it was the *Scharnhorst*. It merely says that last Tuesday – the day the Scandinavian operations began – strong British naval forces attacked a strong German contingent of ships. In this engagement, say the Germans, the *Renown* was damaged, but no damage was done to the German units.

Further, the High Command reports that yesterday a total of five enemy submarines were sunk, three by German naval vessels, two, as we already reported last night, by German planes. North of the Shetland Islands, the communiqué goes on, a German U-boat torpedoed a British cruiser of the Glasgow type. British air-attacks on Narvik, Bergen, and Stavanger are also reported, but the High Command says no military objectives were hit. Around Oslo, German troops occupied the towns of Sarpsborg and Askim. At Heidstadtoen, 1,600 Norwegian troops surrendered, says the High Command.

And that's the lot so far as military news from Berlin is concerned.

Berlin April 15, 1940 02.02

Good Evening. This is Berlin.

I have here before me the early edition of tomorrow morning's *Der Montag*, one of the three Berlin journals appearing on Monday morning. Its banner headline reads: GREAT BRITISH ATTACK ON NARVIK REPULSED. That headline stands over the text of the High Command communiqué. The official German News Agency also used the same headline over the text of the army communiqué.

The official German radio tonight summed up that communiqué as follows: "Big English attack on Narvik thrown back – the British battle-cruiser *Renown* damaged – a cruiser of the *Glasgow* type torpedoed – the

248

English murder-ship *Cossack* stranded – a total of five British submarines sunk – these and further successes of the German armed forces were reported today by the High Command."

And *Der Montag* is led to editorialize about the failure of the British attack on Narvik.

Actually, what the position in Narvik is today, we cannot learn in Berlin. Who holds the town, whether the British have landed, whether there are still German naval forces there offering resistance, what the German land forces are doing – there is no answer to those questions in Berlin, yet.

Around Oslo, the German army is spreading out fan-like in all directions, but the pace of its occupation would indicate that it has not yet assembled a very great force there.

In the meantime, the commander of the German army in Norway, General von Falkenhorst, informed the Norwegian people today that unless they ceased their resistance, the German High Command would break it by the sharpest means.

That would indicate that the Norwegians are resisting. I'll just quote part of the commander's proclamation as given in the *DNB*: "The Norwegian government has turned down several offers of cooperation. The Norwegian people must now decide the future of their Fatherland. If the proclamation is obeyed, as it was with great understanding in Denmark, which found itself in the same position, Norway will be spared the horrors of war. However, if any more resistance is offered and the hand which was held out with friendly intentions rejected, then the German High Command will feel itself forced to act with the sharpest means to break the resistance."

Last Tuesday, it will be remembered, Berlin informed Oslo that the German occupation of Norway was being made solely to preserve it from the horrors of war. [*This last paragraph was deleted by the censors.*]

Berlin April 17, 1940 15.00

Good Morning. This is Berlin.

The daily communiqué of the German High Command is just out and it declares that the Germans still hold Narvik. As a matter of fact, it states that yesterday the English made no attempt to land near the actual town. British landings, say the Germans, have been made at Harstadt and a nearby island, some thirty-five miles to the north-west of Narvik, but there has been no contact between German and Allied troops. In the meantime, the German forces at Narvik have pushed eastward on the

249

railroad line as far as the Swedish frontier. Norwegian troops which resisted, says the army, were routed with heavy losses to them.

German forces pushing eastward from Trondheim, which lies half way up the Norwegian coast, have advanced eastward on the railway and yesterday reached the Swedish frontier. That's important because it cuts Norway in two. The British air attack on Stavanger night before last caused no damage to military objects, says the German Command.

It also announces that Commodore Bonte, in charge of the German destroyer flotilla at Narvik, has been killed in action. The sailors from the destroyers, whose ammunition had been exhausted and which had been damaged – or two-thirds of the sailors – were taken ashore and have joined the German land forces.

Some, though not all, of President Roosevelt's remarks about the present goings-on in Europe which he made in his speech to the Pan-American Union are published for the first time in the Berlin press today. The President's first statement about the Scandinavian affair was not published here.

Now the German papers take issue with the President's point of view. They quote for instance his remark that the Americas have achieved an international order without hysterical outcries or powerful movements of troops, and answer to that – I'll just quote them: "In more than a century of struggle, America has achieved its present position at the cost of other nations, including the English, *with* force, *with* hysterical outcries, and *with* powerful movements of troops. We don't deny America's right to have done this, but we believe it's therefore America's duty to act with greater reserve and discretion in regard to European events . . . Events in Europe must be regarded from a European standpoint and not regulated according to American conceptions and ideas."

Actually, the Wilhelmstrasse told us yesterday that in its opinion the President must have been referring to England and France when he spoke of powers interfering in the affairs of other nations.

I mentioned the other day that several Germans I know had been watering their mouths in expectation of all those Danish supplies – butter, eggs, bacon – coming in soon. The *DNB* now reports that German wholesale grocery firms are placing huge orders in Copenhagen. The report speaks of the Danish warehouses being packed to the roof with choice bacon. Now that we have a shortage of fruit here, these Danish supplies will be rather welcome.

Berlin April 18, 1940 15.05

Good Morning. This is Berlin.

German and British land troops have at last come to grips in Norway. That's the most interesting information in today's communiqué of the German High Command which was published here an hour and a half ago. First contact between the land forces of the two countries was made at Narvik. Actually, according to the German account, it wasn't an especially decisive contact. Here's what the German Command says of it:

"In the region of Narvik for the first time yesterday a weak English force attempted to make a landing in the Herjangs Fjord near Elvegardsmoen. The attempt was repulsed by German troops."

If you consult your map, you'll see that Herjangs Fjord, where the Germans say the British tried to land, is the easternmost one of the fjords which lead in from the sea to Narvik. That would seem to indicate that the Allies were trying to establish their land forces east of Narvik town, thus cutting the German troops there off from the railway or from any German forces that may be stationed along the railway as far as the Swedish border. You'll remember that yesterday the High Command told us that that railway had been occupied as far as the Swedish frontier.

The second most interesting item in the German Command's communiqué today is the one describing the bombardment by British naval craft of the Stavanger airdrome. I'll just quote the Army Command on that: "Yesterday morning Stavanger was bombarded by British cruisers from a great distance." (Note it says Stavanger, not the Stavanger flying-field). "Four German planes were damaged by splinters. German airplanes attacked the ships taking part in the bombardment as well as others located further northward. One cruiser, as has already been reported, received a direct hit and sank immediately. Four other direct hits were scored with heavy bombs on light and heavy cruisers. Also, a destroyer received a hit from a heavy bomb. The cruisers hit were of the Suffolk and London class. One cruiser was seen to be listing."

Well, those are the most interesting items in the High Command's report today. Other items are:

A British air attack on Trondheim was made but it was unsuccessful due to German countermeasures. At Bergen, yesterday passed quietly. Over Stavanger, two British planes were shot down. Around Oslo, the German troops reached all their day's objectives. The advance of the German forces northward near Kongsvinger continued.

German planes attacked two Norwegian torpedo boats north-east of Arendal. (Arendal is on the coast about seventy miles south-west of Oslo.) One boat was set on fire and grounded, the crew fleeing; the other was further pursued. The hunt for Allied U-boats in the Skagerrak and

Kattegat continued, with what result is not reported. The carefully planned supplying of the Norwegian ports continued despite very unfavorable weather.

So much for the High Command's report. It shows that the fight for Narvik itself appears just to be beginning, and tells of the first attempt of the British fleet to bombard Norway's most important airdrome at Stavanger.

One of the most difficult problems facing the Danes and, of course, the Germans, is what to do with the highly intensified agriculture of Denmark. If it could be maintained at its present level, it would help give Germany just those products it needs: butter, eggs, bacon. But Denmark's three million cows and three million pigs and three million laying hens live on imported fodder. Grain fodder comes mostly from North and South America, and the soya bean, which is also an important fodder item, comes from Manchukuo. Both are now cut off. The most pressing problem is to keep Denmark's livestock and poultry alive. Last fall, Germany contracted for a million tons of grain fodder from Russia. Not more than a fourth has been delivered and all of it is needed for Germany's own use. It'll be interesting to see how that problem is met.

Berlin April 20, 1940 01.45

Good Evening. This is William L. Shirer in Berlin.

Today was Herr Hitler's birthday. He was fifty-one. Just a year ago today I remember flying over from London to report on the birthday celebration. Then, in peacetime, it was a public holiday, with a great military parade in the morning and a torchlight procession past the Chancellery in the evening.

Today, with the country in the midst of war, the birthday celebration was restrained. There was no holiday. Factories and schools carried on as usual. There were no parades, no torchlight procession.

The German Führer made two brief appearances on the balcony in answer to calls from the crowd that stood assembled outside the Chancellery on the Wilhelmplatz. He saluted the crowd for a minute or two and then disappeared from view. Police, through loudspeakers, then requested the crowd to disperse as the Führer wanted quiet and must continue his work.

Hitler, when he appeared on the balcony, was wearing a field-gray uniform. I was not close enough myself to get a good glimpse of him, but the photographs in this evening's papers show a very serious expression on his face as he saluted the people in the street below.

All the houses in Berlin flew flags today in honor of Herr Hitler's birthday, and I noticed the Stars and Stripes flying from the American Embassy. All other embassies and legations also flew their flags.

A number of foreign rulers and heads of state sent birthday telegrams. They included the King of Italy, the Emperor of Manchukuo, the King of the Belgians, the King of Denmark, and others. I do not find President Roosevelt's name on the list. Mussolini, in his telegram, expressed his confidence in a German victory in this war. Herr Hitler answered the Duce by saying he believed that both Germany and Italy would be victorious in this struggle for their vital rights.

This exchange of telegrams caused several eyebrows in diplomatic circles to quiver.

All three armed forces issued special Orders of the Day on the occasion of the Führer's birthday in which they again swore loyalty and obedience to the Leader. Earlier in the day the heads of the three services, General von Brauchitsch, Grand Admiral Raeder, and Field Marshal Göring, called at the Chancellery and extended birthday greetings. Göring also reported that the collection of scrap metal as a birthday present had been a great success.

Herr Hitler's deputy, Rudolf Hess, broadcasting to the Youth of the nation, said he knew their highest wish was to be fighting in Norway. He also told them that after this war Germany would have her colonies back, and that the whole world would be open to them. He listed seven commandments for the Youth, among which one was to always act as they thought the Führer would act and they'd never be wrong. "Have the courage to tell the truth," he told them, "and despise lying. Believe in God, who is with the courageous."

Berlin April 22, 1940 01.46

Good Evening. This is William L. Shirer in Berlin.

Opposition to the German forces driving northward from Oslo to Trondheim is stiffening. For the first time tonight the German High Command speaks of stubborn resistance in this sector, where most of the fighting in Norway has occurred so far.

The German Command makes no mention of any Allied troops north of Oslo. It refers only to Norwegian resistance. But that that resistance is more than just that of a few ill-armed mountaineers defending their homes, comes out clearly in a special communiqué issued in Berlin tonight that speaks of not only armored German units, that is tanks and armored cars, being used, but also airplanes in the fighting itself. The main struggle, say the Germans, took place yesterday at the town of Gjövik, ten miles west of Hamar, and about twenty miles south of Lillehammer, which the Germans say they captured yesterday. Says the communiqué: "Gjövik was taken only after a stubborn fight with the Norwegian troops. The enemy had entrenched himself in land well-suited for defense and attempted to defend the town. The employment however of strong armored units brought a quick decision. The Norwegians suffered through the attack of the armored detachments, part of which took them in the rear, heavy losses." German losses are not mentioned.

It does seem as though Germany's declared intention of saving Norway from experiencing the horrors of war was not being fulfilled.

The German Command informed us today that the two ports and railheads where the British have landed north and south of Trondheim – Namsos and Aandalsnes – are now in flames as the result of bombings by the German air force. This was confirmed in the daily communiqué of the High Command which said that towns where enemy troops were found and the nearby railways were destroyed by German bombing attacks. It also mentioned that the air force had bombed the rear railroad connections of the Norwegians north of Hamar.

At ten minutes past midnight – that is about an hour and a half ago – the High Command issued a special communiqué on the work of the German air force. It said that Aandalsnes and Namsos, where the British are concentrating, were the targets of concentrated German airattacks. Concentrations and columns of troops were attacked with bombs and machine-gun fire. Villages occupied by British troops were bombed. The important railroad junction of Dombas has been destroyed. The harbor works at Namsos and Aandalsnes have been badly damaged. According to first reports, continues the communiqué, three British transports were hit by bombs, two of which immediately sank. Two warships were hit by heavy bombs.

From here it looks as if the race which Allied and German troops are running to capture control of the two railways from Oslo to Trondheim will be decisive in this Norwegian campaign. But it'll probably be at least a fortnight before a real decision is fought. By reaching Lillehammer, the Germans are about a fourth of the way up to Trondheim, but there's still a lot of difficult country yet to get through. The Allies probably have got as far as the important junction some fifty miles north-west of Lillehammer at Dombas. There, they can block one railway. But there's a parallel one running to Trondheim some thirty-five miles to the east. And to stop the Germans they'd have to get astride that too.

The other important item revealed by the German High Command today was that they had established a land communication between Kristiansand on the south coast and Stavanger where the big airfield is. There is no railway, but there is said to be a fairly good road between the two towns, and this would be of immense help in supplying the German air base at Stavanger.

As to those air-battles on the Western Front, the Germans gave out their version tonight. They claimed five enemy planes downed, which with six more in the north made a total of eleven shot down yesterday. As is usual when the German radio announces a new important victory, this communiqué when it was read was preceded by fanfares and followed by the *March on England* song.

[From April 23 to April 29 Shirer was in Lausanne, Switzerland, for a meeting of the International Broadcasting Union.]

Berlin April 29, 1940 14.05

Good Morning. This is William L. Shirer in Berlin.

Returning this morning to the German capital after a week in neutral Switzerland, I find that people here are as confident as ever that Germany will win the Norwegian campaign hands down.

Indeed, the Nazi press and radio this morning speak already of an Allied fiasco in Norway and give the impression that British and French troops so far have offered little opposition to Germany's crack mechanized troops. The press of Germany's faithful ally, Italy, is cited to confirm the German case that the Allies have failed to save Norway.

Even that eminent American correspondent, my friend Leland Stowe of the *Chicago Daily News*, who is not particularly popular in Berlin political circles, is quoted by the German radio this morning as expressing his wonder at the speed and efficiency with which the Nazi troops are overrunning Norway.

Well, neutral observers, while they have no reason to doubt the German successes so far, will probably wait a little before they predict the final outcome. The key battle in Norway, for the junction points between Oslo and Trondheim, still remains to be fought. That battle probably will be fought this week. And after it is over, there will be time to assess the real position in Norway.

In Switzerland, where you hear both sides of the case, one did get the impression that the Allies had not yet landed sufficient tanks or artillery to seriously hold up the Germans. And their lack of suitable airbases is still giving the Nazis a tremendous advantage in the air. It's taken for granted, however, that the Allies probably have landed more guns and tanks in the last few days. Whether they can be rushed to the proper places in time is the important question.

The German High Command issued about an hour ago one of its shortest communiqués since the war in Norway started. It contains no specific information about what we all want to know, the state of the advance towards Trondheim. Here's what it says:

"Supported by the air force, which attacked land positions and communications in the rear, the operations in Norway continued according to plan. Mopping up in the interior of Norway progressed. Six batteries with twenty-four guns along with their munition were captured. On the coast of Central Norway, two British cruisers and eleven transports and supply ships with a total of 50,000 tons were hit by heavy bombs so that a portion of the vessels were destroyed. Near Lesjaskop three enemy airplanes on the ground were destroyed in a bomb attack. Two German planes are missing. In the West, all quiet."

That eleven transport and supply ships were attacked would seem to show that the British are still landing more troops and supplies, and intend to fight it out even if the situation is not very rosy for them.

Incidentally, one Berlin newspaper, the *12-Uhr Blatt*, which has sort of specialized in outlining enemy naval and shipping losses, publishes a new list of British and French ships that, according to it, have been sunk or damaged. The German High Command has never confirmed this newspaper's figures but no German paper nowadays publishes news against the will of the government. Well, the *12-Uhr Blatt* claims that the Allies have lost 59 planes and 94 naval or transport ships off Norway since April 9th. Some of the figures will perhaps surprise you. For example, seven British battleships are listed as having been damaged, some of them badly. That would account for just half of Britain's battleships, if it were proved to be true. Further, the paper claims that five cruisers have been sunk and fourteen damaged. That would be almost a third of British cruiser strength. Here are some other figures this Berlin paper gives of enemy losses: seventeen submarines, or about one-third of Britain's total; seven destroyers sunk, seven more damaged; six transports sunk, nineteen damaged.

So far as I know, Germany has only admitted the loss itself of two cruisers, sunk on the first day of operations, and several destroyers at Narvik. No news of any German transports having been sunk has been published here.

Berlin April 29, 1940 24.46

Good Evening. This is William L. Shirer in Berlin.

There is no specific news here tonight about the advance of the German army towards Trondheim. The High Command in its daily communiqué speaks in general terms and merely remarks that the operations in Norway continue according to plan.

The official German News Agency reveals that fighting is going on at several points, but does not disclose *where*.

While the war rages in Norway, all is quiet on the Western Front. For the fourth or fifth time yesterday, returning from Switzerland, I traveled along several miles of that front where the River Rhine divides the two armies. I've never seen a more peaceful sight in my life. German children were playing in a village playground in full sight of some French soldiers loitering on the other side. In an open meadow, not 200 yards from the river and in full sight of a French blockhouse, some German soldiers were frolicking about kicking an old football. Trains on both sides of the Rhine, some loaded with those very articles which are working to such deadly effect in Norway, chugged along undisturbed. Not a shot was fired. Not a single airplane could be seen in the skies.

What kind of a war, what kind of a game is this? I wondered. Why do airplanes bomb communications behind the lines in Norway, as they did in Poland, as they did everywhere in the World War, and yet here, on the Western Front, where the two greatest armies in the world stand face to face, refrain completely from such killing activity? I don't know the answer. But isn't it a baffling state of affairs?

Berlin May 1, 1940 24.47

Good Evening. This is William L. Shirer in Berlin.

Today was Labor Day in Germany, and in the main it was given over to celebrating a victory in Norway – the meeting of German columns operating from Trondheim and Oslo. In an Order of the Day to the troops in Norway, Herr Hitler stated that with this meeting, the aim of the Allies to force Germany to her knees by a tardy occupation of Norway had definitely failed.

Actual news of what has been going on today at Trondheim and the key railroad position at Dombas is difficult to obtain in Berlin today.

Last night, the High Command told us German troops had reached Dombas. In its regular communiqué this afternoon, it does not mention Dombas. It says merely that fighting is still going on around Trondheim. Neutral observers believe that the Germans must have occupied Dombas today, but the High Command has not yet confirmed that.

What does seem clear in Berlin is that the Allies have not succeeded in stopping the German drive to Trondheim. But one news organ close to

257

the Wilhelmstrasse warns tonight that yesterday's victories do not necessarily mean that the fight in Norway is over.

Though the Germans have moved northward from Lillehammer with almost incredible speed, a German correspondent at the front telegraphs back today that every mile had to be bitterly fought for. "The Norwegians," he reports, "defended every creek, every turn in the valley to the last man or the last bullet. The English sent some of their best troops. They dug themselves in well along the narrow valleys and raked the road with murderous machine-gun fire. Poland and even the Western Front were nothing compared to this," he concludes.

Note he speaks of the British using machine-guns. Where was their artillery? you are tempted to ask.

So for Germans, May Day has been a day of victory. Herr Hitler, for the first time since he came to power, did not speak or make any public appearance. His deputy, Rudolf Hess, spoke in his place from, it's interesting to note, the Krupp munitions works at Essen. In his speech he referred to the President of the Norwegian parliament, Mr. Hambro, as "Mr. Hamburger", and he attacked Jews and Democracy. He said the "blessings of Democracy mean the rise from a dirty Ghetto in Warsaw to the English Money Aristocracy". He concluded that the guarantor of a German victory was the Führer.

Berlin May 3, 1940 14.00

Good Morning. This is William L. Shirer in Berlin.

After a two-day holiday – Labor Day on May 1st and Ascension Day yesterday – the German people went back to work this morning bucked up not only by their two-day rest, but by the news of the German victory over the British in Norway.

It would be hard to exaggerate the feeling of triumph in the Third Reich today. Some of the newspapers made use of red ink in their flaming headlines about the flight of the British army to Aandalsnes and its hasty evacuation from there. As you know, the German forces occupied this British base at 3 o'clock yesterday afternoon.

But one thing is certain. The putting to flight of the British south of Trondheim and the virtual occupation of all of southern Norway, easily the most important part of the country, has given a tremendous flip to German morale and spurred the Nazi leaders on to an increased effort to win the war while things are going their way.

I was in Berlin after the completion of the smashing German victory over Poland. But somehow – at least that's the feeling I personally get –

the reaction of the people was nothing then compared to what it is today. As they see it – I do not say as I see it – as *they* see it, Germany has at last met the great British Empire in a straight fight and won hands down. Germans had little respect for the Polish army. They had considerable respect for the British army and a great deal for the British navy. And in a campaign where they fully expected the British navy to make a great fight for Norway – what have they seen? Only an engagement at Narvik way up there in the Arctic Circle. Not even an attempt to break into Trondheim or Bergen or Stavanger or Oslo by the world's most powerful fleet. They've been told that the German air force prevented that. And rightly or wrongly, they see in Mr. Chamberlain's statement yesterday that the Allied fleets have now concentrated in the Mediterranean, a proof that they did not find it wise to concentrate off Norway because of fear of German bombers.

It may be, as some think, that the hasty British evacuation from Aandalsnes, which the German press today compares to the British withdrawal at Gallipoli, is only the first round in the battle for Norway. But the Germans certainly believe that it was a very decisive round. Today, after a little more than three weeks, they are firmly entrenched in the whole southern half of Norway, with little prospect for the Allies of driving them out soon in a straight fight.

Berlin feels then that its prestige has been enormously enhanced by the victory in Norway. I notice that the German radio this morning does not fail to point out the impression made by German arms in the neutral states nearby, in Italy, and in the United States. The New York press was quoted extensively this morning in all German broadcasts.

Berlin May 3, 1940 24.46

Good Evening. This is William L. Shirer in Berlin.

Despite the German victory in the north, Norway suddenly dropped out of the German headlines tonight. Other parts of Europe where the war may break out tomorrow, or next week, or next month, claimed Berlin's attention this evening.

In the Nazi press, Mr. Chamberlain's speech, or rather his revelations that strong Allied naval forces were now concentrated in the Mediterranean, is given as the reason for Germany suddenly becoming aware of danger at other points besides Scandinavia.

You see, Great Britain, which only a few weeks ago was accused of wanting to spread the war in Scandinavia, now, suddenly this evening, is accused of wanting to spread the war elsewhere. And Berlin assures us

259

that it is ready to take on the Allies elsewhere, or anywhere. Or, as one Wilhelmstrasse source put it tonight: "We'll get there first, just as we did in Norway."

Where? Where are these places which the controlled German press tells us tonight may see new Allied action to catch Germany in a flank, now that the Reich's northern flank has been made secure in Norway? It's worth while noting them.

First is the Mediterranean, but that depends upon what Italy does. But Berlin says there are other places which more directly concern her, the Balkans, Romania – Romanian oil.

But perhaps, suggest the Berlin papers tonight with one accord, the Allies are not thinking exclusively of action in the south or south-east, but of somewhere else. Just where, the press does not say. My guess is that it is thinking of perhaps Holland.

Significant in all this new Nazi press talk, which, as I say, came very suddenly this evening, is the suggestion that the war may be even further extended, and soon. Of course, the blame is put on England. Listen to these headlines in the Berlin press tonight – the *Völkischer Beobachter*: WHICH NATION WILL ENGLAND NEXT BRING BAD LUCK TO? Or the *Deutsche Allgemeine Zeitung*: ENGLAND'S NEW AGGRESSIVE DESIGNS. Or the *Börsen Zeitung*: WHERE WILL ENGLAND ATTACK NOW?

The point is that these headlines, and other things, put people to thinking that the next days or weeks – or if you're an optimist – months, may well see this European war spreading all over the map. Well, as a policeman put it to me today, there may be one consolation in that. If the war does spread all over, it won't last so long.

I said that the German feat in driving the British out of southern Norway had been shunted to the inside pages even here. True. But you must not overlook the fact that the German military victory in Norway has greatly bucked up the morale of the people in this country, and no doubt too strengthened the determination of the leaders to win this war – if possible while things are going good. First in Poland, then in Norway, the German army has proved invincible, and that heartens the people.

Another thing, the German air force has apparently justified the confidence which Berlin had in it to keep the British fleet from operating effectively in Scandinavia. Had the British navy been able to get into Skagerrak and shut off the supplies going to Oslo, there would have been none of those tanks and artillery which made the drive to Trondheim such a walk-away.

The German radio tonight aired the report from Stockholm that the Allies were withdrawing also from Namsos, but the German High Command has not yet confirmed that.

Berlin May 4, 1940 14.00

Good Morning. This is William L. Shirer in Berlin.

Suddenly, since last night, the German press is talking of only one thing: the spreading of the war to still other parts of Europe. I don't mean to say that the Germans are saying they intend themselves to march into this or that country. What they say is that the British are planning some aggression somewhere and that of course Germany will be ready to act wherever it may be, just as it did in Denmark and Norway. The point the Germans make is that they intend to get there first, wherever it may be.

All over the Mediterranean and the Balkans, the German press professes suddenly to see the danger signs. Under a general headline ENGLAND'S NEW PLAN FOR ATTACK, the *Völkischer Beobachter*, official Nazi organ, runs dispatches from various key points with headlines such as these: ALARMING ANGLO-FRENCH REPORTS FROM EGYPT – ALLIED FLEET ORDERED TO ALEXANDRIA – WAR PANIC IN EGYPT – TURKISH TROOP MOVEMENTS NEAR THE DODECANESE – (the Dodecanese Islands are owned by Italy, remember.) Other Berlin papers play up headlines like these: NERVOUSNESS IN THE BALKANS – ATHENS TROUBLED – PANIC FEELING IN SALONIKI – SOFIA SPEAKS OF SURPRISE MOVES AND IS NERVOUS – ALEXANDRIA AWAITS REINFORCEMENTS – ALLIED PRESSURE ON ITALY. And so on. And all this only since last night.

It leaves people here wondering where the next blow is to fall. There seem to be so many possibilities.

The German High Command has just announced that a squadron of its bombers sank a British battleship off Namsos yesterday afternoon. It relates that the war vessel was attacked by dive-bombers, and that a heavy bomb hit the deck between the two fore gun-turrets. According to the German Command, a half a minute after the bomb struck, there was a tremendous column of smoke seen to belch forth 1,500 feet high. After the smoke blew away, says the communiqué, there was nothing to be seen of the ship except a bit of wreckage.

It's certainly difficult for Americans to get at the truth about these naval losses on both sides in the Norwegian campaign. The Germans admit only a fraction of the losses which the British say they've suffered, and the British do not agree with the Germans about British losses by a long way.

If you take English naval casualties as we've been given them by the German High Command since that morning on April 9th when the Nazis lit into Norway, they add up to the truly astonishing total of 135 ships, of which, according to the Germans, seventy-eight were sunk or set afire, and fifty-seven badly or slightly damaged.

If the German figures could be checked and proved to be true, then

261

about half of the battleships of the British navy, and about a third of its cruisers have been put out of action, and it is difficult to see how Britain can spare so many ships for the Mediterranean right now.

Berlin May 5, 1940 01.02

Good Evening. This is William L. Shirer in Berlin.

So far as the Germans are concerned, the Norwegian campaign is over. And people here naturally feel pretty good about it. In a little more than three weeks, the German army overran the most important part of Norway and drove an Allied army – or what there was of it – to flight. Mopping up operations will presumably take a few days more. And German forces at Narvik are being hard-pressed. But the main fight is over.

What it cost Herr Hitler in loss of life, we don't know yet. No hint of the extent of the casualties has been given up until now. Nor has Berlin yet revealed exactly how much its navy suffered, beyond the loss of two cruisers and the destroyers at Narvik.

Studying the lessons of the brief campaign, the Germans say the conquest of Norway has given them one strategic advantage, and confirmed another.

The strategic advantage is of course that it gives them airbases and submarine bases much nearer Scapa Flow and Scotland than they had before. Their north flank is protected, they say. And Great Britain is cut off from valuable Scandinavian supplies, especially timber and ore.

Probably more important to the German High Command is a certain strategic theory which Berlin feels has been confirmed by the Norwegian campaign – namely that the once all-powerful British fleet is useless in offensive operations within the radius controlled by the German air force. And since Friday, when the Germans claim that one of their dive-bombers sank a British battleship, they rather think that the old controversy about the superiority of the battleship or the airplane has been settled in favor of the latter. If the German claim that a British battleship was sunk is later confirmed, backers of the big ship against the airplane would certainly be embarrassed.

But what interests German military circles is that the fight for southern and central Norway was won, in the main, by Göring's airplanes. They performed four vital tasks. They kept the sea route to Oslo free of British warships and thus enabled the main German force to be liberally supplied with men, artillery and tanks. They apparently prevented the British navy from even attempting to attack the vital ports, such as Stavanger, Bergen

262

and Trondheim. By continually bombing the Allied ports of debarkation, they made it almost impossible for the British to land heavy artillery and tanks, as Mr. Chamberlain admitted. Last, by bombing and machine-gunning enemy positions, they made it fairly easy for the land troops to advance through difficult country.

But most important of all, was their keeping the British fleet out of the Skagerrak and away from the important ports. War in the North Sea has thus been revolutionized.

But of course, the war itself has not been decided yet merely by the German victory in Norway. The actual percentage of German troops operating in Norway – at my own guess – would not be more than five percent of the total mobilized. The vast bulk of them are still on the Western Front, as are those of the Allies. And most observers still believe that the final decision in this war, as in the last, will be fought in the West.

Of course, this time, as in 1914-1918, there may be other secondary theaters of war which will contribute to the final decision. The German press for the last three days has professed to see the danger of Allied attack at several points – the Mediterranean, the Balkans – and tonight they discover a new place – Spain. They report new British interest in Spanish iron ore, and conclude that Spain may be in the war as a result. How all this sounds like the talk of six weeks ago, when Britain was accused of designs on Scandinavia and especially Scandinavian iron!

Tonight, incidentally, the German radio gave prominence to a Havas report which it said stated that the Turks were concentrating troops on the Bulgarian frontier. A commentator added that this report should not be underestimated.

Berlin May 6, 1940 24.46

Good Evening. This is Berlin.

The Wilhelmstrasse stated tonight that relations between Germany and Sweden in regard to their respective future policies were clarified in an exchange of letters between the King of Sweden and Herr Hitler a few days ago. Apparently, Herr Hitler assured the king Germany did not intend to walk into Sweden too. It's interesting to note that Sweden for the first time in a century now has a large German army on its border.

The German press continues to devote most of its headlines to warning that the British are about to spread the war by aggressive action in the Mediterranean, in the Balkans, even in Spain. Observers here still wonder what is back of this press campaign, remembering that we had a very similar one in regard to Scandinavia six weeks ago. There's a report here tonight, which has not yet been confirmed, that Göring may go to Italy. The activities of the Vatican have not been reported here.

Herr Rust, the Minister of Education, broadcast to Germany's Youth today. He said: "God created the world as a place for work and battle. Whoever doesn't understand the laws of life's battles will be counted out, like in the boxing ring. All the good things on this earth are trophy cups. The strong win them. The weak lose them." He concluded: "The German people under Hitler did not take to arms to break into foreign lands and make other people serve them. They were forced to take arms by states which blocked their way to bread and union."

School girls today were asked to bring the combings from their hair to school. The combings will be collected to make felt.

Berlin May 8, 1940 14.05

Good Morning. This is Berlin.

Everyone here – and I suppose that goes for the rest of the world too – is waiting, not without suspense, for the answer to the question: Where will the next blow fall?

The possibilities are many, as a glance at the map will show. In the West, Holland, Belgium, the Maginot Line itself, Switzerland. Some people think the next move may come there – in the West – even though other parts of Europe figure more prominently in all the rumors and talk. But as a German officer pointed out to me this morning, the blow doesn't always fall at the places which have figured most in talk.

So far, most of the talk here is about the Mediterranean, about the Balkans, especially Romania, Greece, Turkey.

As a matter of fact, for a whole week now, the German press has been fuming, with one accord, about the danger of the war spreading. A week's press campaign is a pretty long one, even for this country, and it naturally leaves people, after the idea of the war spreading even further has been hammered into them daily for a week, with a certain tenseness. I suppose it's all part of the general war of nerves. But don't underestimate it. It's an important part of this strange war.

Everyone has his own ideas as to who are the aggressors over here. But part of my job is to keep you informed as to how Germans see the war, and I notice this morning that the press redoubles its efforts to brand England – not so much France, but England – as the aggressor, and as about to commit a new aggression out of revenge for its defeat in Norway. Take the headlines in the Berlin press. The *Börsen Zeitung Am Mittag* banner lines today: ENGLAND'S AGGRESSION SEEN THROUGH

EVERYWHERE. And in an editorial on Mr. Chamberlain's speech yesterday, it dubs him "Europe's Aggressor Number One." The *12-Uhr Blatt* heads a similar editorial: AN AGGRESSOR SEEKS NEW VICTIMS. Again, the aggressor is Mr. Chamberlain. And the same paper finds that yesterday's debate in the House of Commons "confirmed the English intention to spread the war."

With all this talk of aggressors and possible new aggressions, I thought it would interest you to see how the picture is presented in this country.

The leading story in this morning's *Völkischer Beobachter* is worth noting because it hints – as I did a minute ago – that the next blow may after all fall in the middle – that would be in the West. Curiously enough, its authority is the Rome correspondent of an American paper, the *Christian Science Monitor*, which thus provides the chief Nazi paper with its principal item of front-page news this morning. It quotes the Boston paper's Rome correspondent as saying that the Allied plan may be to draw Germany far from its bases into south-east Europe, just as the Allies drew the Germans far into the Scandinavian north – but that all this might be a screen for a big blow in the middle, that is the West.

Don't forget that the bulk of the armies on both sides are concentrated in the West.

Berlin May 8, 1940 24.47

Good Evening. This is William L. Shirer in Berlin.

We're in now, it appears, for a very brief lull in the war, following the British withdrawal from central Norway. But the war of nerves goes on full blast, with rumors flying thick and fast over this part of the world about the next move. One moment the war is about to break out in the Mediterranean, the next in the Balkans, and so on. Today, the German press is rather angry at the allegation that Hitler intends next to march into Holland. It blames the *Associated Press* for a report that two German armies, one from Bremen, one from Düsseldorf, were marching on Holland. Berlin claims that it has been able to establish that the *Associated Press*, which says it got this news from "highly dependable sources", actually received it from the Ministry of Information, in London. Berlin holds this alarm about Holland is just a maneuvre of diversion to hide the Allies' aggressive intentions in the Balkans. At any rate, the cry goes on here, as it has for a week, that the Allies are about to commit an act of aggression.

One well-informed man, however, assured me today that nothing much would happen until after the Whitsuntide holidays. That would give us until next Tuesday.

In the meantime, the fighting still goes on around Narvik where the Germans reported today that they had done some heavy bombing, hitting two British cruisers and strafing the ground forces.

Those ground forces, or at least the ones which the German land troops have been actually fighting, are, according to the German command, almost exclusively French, Norwegian, and Polish troops. The Germans say they've met so far scarcely any British units around Narvik.

Berlin May 9, 1940 24.46

Good Evening. This is William L. Shirer in Berlin.

The headlines in the Berlin press increased in size tonight, but they told the same story they've been telling for more than a week now. Namely, that England plans a big act of aggression somewhere.

If people here believe what they read in the newspapers, they must certainly be expecting an Allied blow any day now, though you couldn't exactly say that the Allies have struck many deadly blows so far in this war.

Tonight, the press is exercised about a quotation from a speech by Lord Halifax in the House of Lords yesterday. The German press quotes him as saying: "We cut our losses in Norway in order to begin operations elsewhere." To which the *Börsen Zeitung* headlines: ENGLAND'S PLANS FOR AGGRESSION CLEARLY PROVED.

Herr Hitler today ordered his commander in Norway to release all Norwegian prisoners except the professional soldiers. The latter may also go free if they agree not to fight against Germany, or if, to use Hitler's words, "The former Norwegian government takes back its call to battle against Germany."

In his order, the Führer gives us a picture of how he sees the Norwegian campaign. He begins it by saying, quote, "Against the will of the German people and its government, King Haakon of Norway and his army staff brought about war against Germany."

Herr Hitler says he's releasing the Norwegian prisoners because, unlike the Poles, they fought cleanly.

Mr. Alexander Kirk, American chargé d'affaires, left Berlin this evening en route to Italy from whence he'll sail for America – or fly – next week. He's going back to report on the situation to Washington. He didn't look very optimistic when he boarded his train tonight. As we have no ambassador here, the Embassy will be in charge of a first secretary, Mr. Donald Heath.

The big event in the Berlin theater world tonight was the premiere of a new play, called *Cavour*, and it's about the famous Italian statesman. I mention it because the author of the play happens to be named Benito Mussolini – or at least he's the co-author. The Duce let it be known that his share of the royalties tonight go to the German Red Cross. Thereafter, the Red Cross will get half of his royalties.

A small advertisement in the papers tonight said: "German Premiere of *Cavour* – A play by Mussolini and Forzano. Sold Out!"

Berlin May 10, 1940 14.05

Good Morning. This is William L. Shirer in Berlin.

The blow in the West has fallen.

After a week of accusations in the German press that the Allies intended to make an aggressive move, the Germans themselves took the initiative today and at dawn their army supported by a great air armada, moved against Holland, Belgium and Luxemburg.

As German troops moved over the three borders into these three small neutral states, German airplanes bombed airbases, according to the first report of the German High Command.

Actually, news of the military operations is almost totally lacking here in Berlin, ten hours after the German invasion began – it's now just 2 p.m. here. What sort of opposition the Dutch and Belgians are putting up we do not yet know. From the communiqué issued by the High Command, it is evident that Germany's great air-fleet is playing a decisive role, as it did in Poland and Norway. Now, presumably, for the first time in this war, it will have some effective opposition.

Hitler himself, the High Command announces, has gone to the Western Front to take charge of the entire operations of the German forces.

The Führer's decision to begin what he himself calls in a proclamation to the German troops on the Western Front "the battle which will decide the future of Germany for a thousand years", caught everyone here as usual completely by surprise. As I said a day or two ago, we all felt that the decisive struggle would come in the West, as it did in the last war, and many people, as I've tried to indicate in these talks recently, thought it would come soon. But no one picked today. Mr. Kirk, our chargé d'affaires, had left Berlin last night en route for America to report to Washington on just what might be expected from Germany. He remarked to me just before he left that he might be back sooner than expected. In fact, he was caught at Munich this morning, as his train pulled in at 8 a.m., and is flying back to Berlin now.

No one in Berlin was caught more by surprise than the ministers from Holland and Belgium. They were handed the German memorandum explaining why Germany considered it necessary to march into their countries shortly before 6 a.m., Berlin time. At that very moment, the German forces were on the march.

In the memorandum handed to them, the German government requested the two governments to issue orders that no resistance be made to German troops. "Should the German troops encounter resistance in Belgium or Holland, it will be crushed with every means. The Belgian and Dutch governments alone would bear the responsibility", concluded the German memorandum, "for the consequences and for the bloodshed which would then become unavoidable."

Whether the Dutch and Belgian ministers had time to deliver this memorandum to their governments is not known. But obviously, their governments had no time to consider it, though the Wilhelmstrasse seems to have had no doubts as to what the answer would have been.

At a hastily convoked press conference at the Foreign Office at 8 a.m., Herr von Ribbentrop read to us the memorandum in which Germany explains why she marched into the two Low Countries. The argument, summed up, is that Britain and France were about to attack Germany through the two little countries, and that Germany therefore deems it necessary to send in its own troops to safeguard the neutrality of Belgium and Holland. The memorandum also blames the two countries for not having maintained a really neutral attitude. Belgium, for instance, is blamed for having built its fortifications against Germany, not against France, though it would seem that the Belgians this morning should be glad they did.

Hitler, in a proclamation to the troops on the Western Front, gives a similar explanation. His first words are: "The hour for the decisive battle for the future of the German nation has come."

The people in Berlin, I must say, took the news of the beginning of this decisive phase of the struggle with great calm. Before the Chancellery an hour ago, I noticed that no crowd had gathered as usually happens when big events occur. Few people bothered to buy the noon papers which carried the news. There were no extras sold in the streets.

And until now, we've had no air-raid alarms.

Berlin May 11, 1940 14.05

Good Morning. This is Berlin.

It's still difficult to realize from the atmosphere in the streets of Berlin that the war has now entered its decisive phase, with Germany's powerful army sweeping into Belgium and the Netherlands.

I mean, yesterday and today have been so normal here. People going about their business just as usual. No excitement in the air. When I came up to the studio just now, I noticed that repair work on the streets was going on just as before. Workers were busy on new buildings. No excitement discernible in them.

The morning papers all headline the results after the first day of this decisive battle. These are, in the main, that in Holland the German nutcracker reached the Yssel Line, which is the first Dutch line of defense. That further south, the advancing German troops crossed at several places the River Maas, just inside the Dutch frontier. That Maastricht was captured, which means that the Dutch province of Limburg, which juts down between Belgium and Germany, was completely overrun on the first day, and that the Germans have now crossed the Albert Canal west of Maastricht.

I toured along the Albert Canal last year soon after it was completed, and it forms a fairly strong defensive line, running as it does across northern Belgium from Maastricht to Antwerp. The canal, when I saw it, was dotted with bunkers, and the Belgians thought it would be a hard piece of water to cross. German correspondents with their army report that the first two or three of these bunkers at the extreme eastern end of the canal have been taken, largely, one gathers from their dispatches, by aerial bombings.

That the Germans are using air superiority to the full became apparent shortly after yesterday's operations began. And several German correspondents with the air force report on the bombings and machine-gunnings which were carried out yesterday on Dutch, Belgian, and French airbases, and on troops and communications behind the lines. They report for the most part having met a lot of anti-aircraft fire, but little opposition from fighters.

German army engineers are also playing a prominent part in the German drive, as indeed they did in the Polish and Belgian campaigns. The German correspondents report that there has been a great deal of blowing up of bridges by the retreating Dutch and Belgians, but that German engineers are putting up emergency bridges in great haste. The same German correspondents also report – and this is interesting – that yesterday enemy airplanes certainly did not strafe the advancing German troops.

The papers take some delight in the occupation of Malmédy in eastern Belgium. It's a small strip of land which Belgium took from Germany after the World War.

Berlin May 12, 1940 04.35

Good Evening. This is Berlin.

What the High Command describes as the strongest of the Belgian forts protecting Liège, that of Eben-Emael, was captured this afternoon by the German army, according to an official communiqué issued here early this evening. The Belgian commander and 1,000 men were taken prisoners.

This is the most important piece of military news given out in Berlin tonight, just forty-eight hours after the German army marched into the Netherlands, Belgium, and Luxemburg.

The fort of Eben-Emael was of great strategic importance because it commanded the passage over the junction of the Meuse River with the Albert Canal north of Liège and just west of the Dutch town of Maastricht, which the Germans took yesterday.

But the capture of this strongly fortified position assumes even more importance because of a mysterious reference in the communiqué to the fact that the fort was actually put out of action yesterday and its defenders rendered helpless by what the German High Command terms a "new method of attack".

I wish I could tell you what that new method is, but I can't. I don't know. And the German army isn't telling. I remember that all last winter we heard rumors of a new German method of subduing the underground fortifications on the Western Front, but most of us thought it was just a rumor. This much the German High Command tells us, and the story centers around a first-lieutenant name Witzig, who was decorated by Herr Hitler yesterday with the highest military order a few hours after the new campaign started. A German communiqué yesterday stated that detachments of the air force played an important part in an attack upon a Belgian fort. It added that Lieutenant Witzig, along with a Captain Koch, had shown particular daring and pluck in the operation.

Reading that communiqué last night, we wondered just what the lieutenant and the captain had done. A communiqué today tells us what they did, but not how.

It says that the fort was put out of action yesterday by a detachment of the air force under Lieutenant Witzig by the use of a new method of attack. This new method, it is added, rendered the defenders in the fort helpless. Well then, today, the communiqué concludes, a German force attacking from the north was able, after a bitter fight, to establish contact with Lieutenant Witzig's detachment and the fort, whose defenders had already been rendered helpless, surrendered. The communiqué thus makes it plain that the lieutenant's air force detachment was on the ground, but what it was doing remains a complete mystery.

It reminds you of 1914 when this same fortress of Liège, comprising several separate forts, fell after a twelve-day resistance to a German army which then too used a new method of attack, namely the employment of 42-centimeter howitzers which caught the military experts by surprise and crushed the Belgian forts as if they'd been made out of wood.

As to the fighting elsewhere in Holland, Belgium, and Luxemburg, we're without news tonight. Nothing since the High Command reported that at the end of yesterday, the Germans on the north had reached the Yssel River along which the first Dutch defense line runs, and behind which is a flooded area, or at least there was one there when I was in that neighborhood a few months ago. By last night, the Germans had also overrun Luxemburg and taken Malmédy at the beginning of the Ardennes Forest, but what they've done in those sectors today has not been reported in Berlin. There has been no mention here yet of any contact with French or British troops.

Against the reports from Amsterdam that the Dutch had recaptured the airports at The Hague and Rotterdam, the German High Command insisted tonight that all airfields seized yesterday by the air force were still held today and had not been recaptured.

Yesterday afternoon, it was officially announced that the German town of Freiburg had been bombed and twenty-four civilians killed. Twenty-four hours later, it was officially announced that thirteen children had been killed while peacefully gathered on a playground at Freiburg, during the air-raid.

I heard a German radio commentator a few minutes ago say this: "This monstrously shameful act shows that brutality with which England and France are waging this war. Germany will know how to punish them for this."

If there have been any civilians killed on the other side, it has not been reported here.

Berlin May 13, 1940 01.16

Good Evening. This is Berlin.

The German army steamroller continues to batter its way through Holland and Belgium.

After two days of fighting, it has, according to the German High Command, occupied all of north-eastern Holland, east of the Zuider-Zee, broken through the first and second Dutch defense lines in the heart of the Netherlands, and pierced the eastern end of the Belgian line of defense along the Albert Canal.

And through all the reports of the fighting runs the emphasis on the deadly role which the German air force is playing in what promises to be the greatest battle in history.

A few minutes ago, I heard a German radio reporter broadcasting from a German position near the Albert Canal. He appeared to be impressed most by the way German planes were battering down the Belgian defenses. Half the time you could hardly hear him because of the roar of the planes. So far as you could gather from his front-line report, the German planes were having their own way, and were not being molested.

Well now, the picture as the German High Command gives it tonight is this: In Holland, the Germans claim to have broken through the first Dutch defense lines behind the Yssel River. This line runs roughly from the mouth of the river at the Zuider-Zee some twenty miles eastward to the town of Zwolle, and then eighty miles southward to the town of Arnheim. Behind it was a water-line and how the Germans got over this would be interesting to know, but they don't tell us. Some thrity-five miles to the west of this first defense line begins the first of the two main Dutch defense positions forming the so-called Fortress of Holland. This first main line is known as the Grebbe, or Ditch, Line and is composed of strong fortifications and a water line. It runs from Amersfort, just south of the Zuider-Zee, to Rhenen, thirty miles south of the lower Rhine. It was supposed to be a very strong line, but the German High Command says tonight that it's been broken through.

Further south of this, the Dutch had fortified a line of swamps known as the Peel Positions. The Germans claim to have pierced this one too.

The High Command naturally does not say how these defense lines have been pierced, or in what force, but if they have been broken through by strong forces, then that would be serious news for the Dutch.

Around Liège, the Germans are pressing the attack. Yesterday, they captured the important fort of Eben-Emael, and thus were enabled to move troops over the eastern end of the Albert Canal, Belgium's first line of defense on the north-east. The High Command today says that in front of Liège, which held out for twelve days in 1914 under the pounding of the German 42-centimeter howitzers, the Reich troops have advanced deep into the no-man's land that lies before the Belgian forts.

From all of which, you can see that the Germans are engaged in driving a wide wedge into the low-lands, through the southern half of Holland and northern Belgium.

The High Command makes no mention of any activity along the Maginot Line, but an inspired statement issued in Berlin tonight about its alleged invulnerability is worth nothing. It points out that the capture yesterday of the Liège fort of Eben-Emael, which was built by the Belgians on the principle of the Maginot Line, throws a different light "on the alleged invulnerability of the Maginot Line".

272

The German air force claimed tonight to have sunk a 15,000-ton transport ship off the Dutch coast and set fire to six others. It also states that one of its planes sank a British cruiser in the North Sea and damaged another in a Norwegian fjord. The score of the air-fighting yesterday, according to the German High Command, was sixty-four to thirty-five in favor of Germany.

The German radio warned tonight that if Germans were mistreated in Holland, there is "ample opportunity for retaliating on the numerous Dutch nationals living in Germany".

Berlin May 13, 1940 14.05

Good Morning. This is William L. Shirer in Berlin.

The daily communiqué of the German High Command is not yet out, but we've just been informed that the German army has scored sensational, astonishing victories in pushing forward in Holland and around Liège in Belgium.

The Germans do not hide their elation at what their army accomplished yesterday in smashing through the Dutch and Belgian defenses.

Again, the German air force seems to have played a great role in the operations. According to one report, there was a mass air-attack on the Dutch coast where British troops were landing. It's stated the German planes wiped out landing docks and sank many ships.

For the third day in succession, Berlin claims that another 300 Allied planes were shot down yesterday. A report speaks of twenty-five English fighters, Gladiators and Spitfires, having been shot down in one engagement by Messerschmitts. Fifty-six more, it's said, were destroyed by anti-aircraft fire.

The situation yesterday, as given out by the German Command, looked very good for Herr Hitler's army. It's claimed to have occupied all of north-eastern Holland, east of the Zuider-Zee, smashed through the first and second Dutch defense lines, and cracked the Belgian defenses at the eastern end of the Albert Canal.

Neutral observers here are still waiting for details of this German breakthrough. The Dutch line along the Yssel River was supposed to have been a strong one, and behind it lay a water line. How and where the Germans broke through is not yet clear here, but a German radio bulletin speaks of the Germans having occupied the Dutch town of Arnheim, which was at the southern tip of the Yssel Line, where it joins the lower Rhine River. That would indicate that the Germans got through by a flanking movement from the south. This would have been an obvious

273

move, as a neck of German territory stretches out into Holland to within a few miles of Arnheim, so the Germans wouldn't have had very far to go from the frontier.

What was surprising to observers here was the High Command's claim to have pierced the Grebbe, or Ditch, Line, thirty-five miles west of the Yssel Line. This Ditch Line forms the first line of defense of what is known as the Fortress of Holland protecting the four main Dutch cities – Utrecht, Amsterdam, Rotterdam, and The Hague. It was believed to be heavily fortified and was also covered by a wide water line. Somewhere between the town of Amersfort, just south of the Zuider-Zee, and the town of Rhenen, thirty miles to the south – the Grebbe Line runs between these two towns, – the Germans say they've broken through. If confirmed, this would appear to put the Dutch in a very precarious position. We still wait news here of what method the Germans use in getting over these Dutch water lines.

The High Command indicates that there is severe fighting going on along the eastern end of the Albert Canal and in no-man's land in front of the various forts protecting the key Belgian point at Liège.

A German correspondent with the Reich army here lifts the veil a little this morning on how the Germans secured the two important bridges over the Albert Canal at this point. He reveals that Captain Koch and Lieutenant Witzig, who were specially decorated on the first day of operations by Herr Hitler, landed by plane along with some shock-troops near the bridge-heads across the canal. Then, operating with machine-guns, they obtained control of the ignition chambers from which the Belgians planned to blow up the bridges. They then stormed the bridge-heads and captured them. This entire operation, according to the German correspondent, was carried out alone by the troops landed by air. And they succeeded in holding the bridge-heads all morning. It was not until afternoon that Germany infantry, fighting its way over land, arrived to find the bridges intact and in German hands.

Such is modern war, as Germany is now fighting it.

Berlin May 13, 1940 24.46

Good Evening. This is Berlin.

LIEGE FALLEN! GERMAN LAND FORCES BREAK THROUGH AND ESTABLISH CONTACT WITH AIR FORCE TROOPS NEAR ROTTERDAM!

Those were the astounding headlines in extra editions of the Berlin papers that came out about 5, our time, this afternoon. Today was a holiday in the capital – Whit Monday – and there were large crowds strolling in the streets. They bought up the extras like hot-cakes.

The announcement by the German High Command on the fourth day of the big drive that the citadel of Liège had been captured, and that German – well the Germans call them "speed troops" – had broken through the whole southern part of Holland and made contact with the air force troops who've been fighting since the first day in and around Rotterdam on the west coast, caught almost everyone by surprise. Even German military circles seemed a bit surprised. They admitted that the breakthrough to Rotterdam, as one put it, came somewhat sooner than expected.

How much of a force the Germans pushed through to Holland's chief port is not divulged. But how even a small motorized force could push through a land divided by canals and rivers so fast astounded neutral military observers here – assuming that the Dutch had time to blow up all the bridges.

The communiqué of the High Command states that the Swastika flag was hoisted on the citadel at Liège this forenoon. It admits that some of the forts around the town are still holding out. These are the ones to the east, where the Belgians naturally expected the brunt of the attack to fall.

Well, now, after four days of fighting, and basing our report only on what we know from the communiqués of the German High Command – which is all we can do from Berlin – you begin at last to get a picture of what's been going on since last Friday morning.

The story of the German advance is one of outflanking the other fellow, which of course was the story of Napoleon and Sherman and all the other successful generals of history.

Take Liège, which held out for twelve days in 1914. It appears to have been taken this time by an encircling movement from the north-west, where an attack from Germany would be least expected. The main Belgian defenses were to the east of Liège. They still hold out, but with the Germans in the city behind them, how long can they hold out?

A still bigger flanking movement seems to have been carried out in Holland. The first Dutch defenses along the Yssel River, south-east of the Zuider-Zee, if we follow the High Command's reports, were turned on the south flank. Further west lay two strong Dutch lines comprising the Fortress of Holland and protected by wide water lines. These too, if we take the German Command's communiqués, were turned on the southern flank. This is the only explanation of how the Germans could push forward so rapidly towards Rotterdam.

Indeed, judging from one bulletin tonight which speaks of a Dutch general and his staff having been captured at Tilburg, the German army swept in a wide circle through the south of Holland, *around* the main Dutch positions. Tilburg is close to the Belgian border, and some fifty miles south-east of Rotterdam. In the meantime, the German troops which had been landed at The Hague and Rotterdam by air seem to have held out there. One report in Berlin speaks of them being in control of a district which runs all the way from The Hague past Rotterdam to Noerdijk, fifteen miles south-east of that port.

It's interesting that the High Command mentions action on the Maginot Line for the first time. South of Saarbrücken and south-east of Zweibrücken, the Germans, says the High Command, advanced their lines and captured prisoners. Another report says 600 French prisoners were captured in this operation.

In answer to M. Reynaud's declaration that German parachutists not in military uniform will be shot on sight if caught, the High Command says it will shoot ten French prisoners to every German shot. It denies the parachutists are not in uniform.

Berlin May 14, 1940 24.46

Good Evening. This is Berlin.

We're all a little dazed here tonight, trying to keep up with the latest news of the German army's lightning strokes in Holland and Belgium.

At the moment, the picture as given by the German High Command is this:

An hour and a quarter ago, Berlin announced that the Dutch army had given up the struggle and capitulated. An hour before that, the German Command had given us the news of the surrender of Rotterdam. I give you the two army communiqués. The latest one says: "After the capitulation of Rotterdam and in view of the imminent threat to the Dutch capital, the Dutch Commander-in-Chief has given up resisting and ordered his troops to cease fighting."

Thus, to the amazement of the world, Holland, despite its great defense positions protected by water lines which seemed impassable, has been overrun by Hitler's steamroller army in five days.

The fall of Rotterdam was announced this evening in the following army communiqué: "Under the tremendous impression of the attacks of German dive-bombers and the imminent attack of German tanks, the city of Rotterdam has capitulated and thus saved itself from destruction."

It was the first news we had that Rotterdam was being bombed and was at the point of being destroyed.

Off the Dutch coast, the High Command added in another communiqué, German bombers sank two cruisers and damaged another, and damaged and set fire to one 25,000-ton steamer and an 8,000-ton ship.

That's the principal news from Holland tonight, as given out by the German High Command.

There is also news about Belgium, from the same source: Using tanks and planes on a scale never dreamed of before, the Germans have been hammering against the Belgian, French, and British forces defending the main Belgian line running down from Antwerp through Louvain to Wavre. This is the so-called Dyle Line, running along the Dyle River.

A communiqué just issued claims that the Germans have pierced this main line at Ligny, north-west of Namur and about twenty-one miles south-west of Brussels. It was at this town of Ligny that Napoleon defeated Blücher two days before the Battle of Waterloo.

Earlier in the day the Germans had claimed to have thrown back British, Belgian, and French forces from the River Nethe, north-east of Namur. It was here, say the Germans, that the first big tank battle of the war took place, between German and French tanks. The Germans claim to have thrown the French tank squadrons back. They speak of being greatly aided in this by the air force, which swept down and bombed the French tanks.

Indeed, the part that German bombers, fighters, and destroyers have played in the operations up to date is continually emphasized by the High Command.

Further south, in France, the High Command claims that German forces have crossed the Meuse River near Charleville. In this engagement the High Command speaks of the unbroken attacks in support of the ground troops by bombers and fighter planes. It says their annihilating work made possible the crossing of the Meuse.

Dr. Ley, one of Herr Hitler's chief lieutenants, writes in the *Angriff* tonight: "Hitler brought Germany to reason and made us happy. We're convinced we will now bring Europe to reason and make it happy. That's his God-given mission." [*This last paragraph was deleted by the Foreign Office censor on the grounds that it "gives changed meaning to article".*]

Berlin May 15, 1940 14.00

Good Morning. This is Berlin.

Having overrun Holland and forced its army to capitulate after a campaign of only five days, to the astonishment of people here as well as elsewhere, the main force of the German steamroller drive appears now to be directed against the Anglo-Belgian-French army defending a strong line that runs roughly from in front of Antwerp south-east past Louvain,

Wavre, Namur, and then down the River Meuse into France to a point some forty miles north of Verdun.

I'm tempted to qualify that statement and say that was the position, as last we knew it, but events are moving so rapidly and the German army is hurling itself forward with such terrific power, that for all I know this news may already be out of date.

Last night, for instance, we had a hard time keeping up with the High Command communiqués. We were just getting ready to tell you of an imminent German attack on Rotterdam when the news came in that it had surrendered. Then, we were about to figure the consequences of that and where the Dutch would make a last-ditch fight for Amsterdam and Utrecht, when the High Command informed us laconically that the Dutch army had capitulated.

That was the situation last night, with the German pressure on the Anglo-Belgian-French forces further south growing stronger in intensity, supported as they were by continuous massive attacks by the German air force and by German tanks on a scale never experienced before in warfare.

This morning, Berlin announced that two of the Belgian forts protecting Namur have fallen. Further eastward at Liège, which the Germans captured Sunday, two forts to the east and south of the town have fallen, it's reported here. These are the forts of Lantin and Loucien. Further, the Liège fort of Ancremont-Pepinster has been put out of action by heavy artillery fire, say the Germans.

That's the first information we have here that a Belgian fort has been reduced by heavy artillery. The first key fort at Liège was reduced in some mysterious manner not yet made clear by a handful of parachutists.

It's obvious then that a very decisive battle is being fought along the Meuse between Namur in Belgium and Sedan in northern France. By last night, the Germans say they had reached the right bank of the river all along the line and captured the towns of Dinant, south of Namur, Givet, further south still and just inside French territory, and Sedan, where Napoleon III surrendered to the Germans in 1871. Thus this territory is seeing its third major war within seventy years.

All those towns, be it noted, are on the right bank of the River Meuse, and the Allies appear to be trying to make a determined stand on the left bank. There are reports that the Germans have already broken across the river, but they're not yet confirmed.

The Wilhelmstrasse said this morning that so far as it knew, the former Kaiser was still at Doorn. Yesterday, we were told that should fighting occur in his neighborhood and he requested to return to Germany, his request would be liberally considered and he would undoubtedly be permitted to return to one of his estates here. But now that there is no danger of fighting taking place there, the plans of the Kaiser are unknown.

The German press and radio have not been slow to point out the strategic importance for a war against England which the capture of Holland now opens out to this country. Maps in the papers show the short distance now from Dutch airbases to the English coast and remind you that the flying distance is less than half an hour now for fast German bombers. The talk here is that air attacks against England from these new Dutch bases are imminent.

All Berlin papers, as you would guess, have only one set headline this morning. It reads: HOLLAND CAPITULATES – END AFTER FIVE DAYS OF A HOPELESS RESISTANCE.

Berlin May 15, 1940 24.47

Good Evening. This is Berlin.

Headlines in the early editions of the morning papers sum up the news tonight of the progress of Germany's terrific drive in the West. I give you a few:

MAGINOT LINE BROKEN THROUGH AT SEDAN – RIVER MEUSE CROSSED BY NAMUR AND SEDAN – TWO FORTS AT NAMUR AND THREE AT LIEGE FALL.

That was the main news given out by the High Command at 2 p.m. today, and for the first time since the big offensive started we've had no special communiqué tonight.

The situation, as seen from Berlin, is that a great battle is now raging along the Meuse River from north of Namur to Sedan. And it is not yet over. The *Völkischer Beobachter* tonight warns its readers that this is a very strong line and that stubborn resistance must be expected, not only because it's strongly held, but because the Allies know that to lose it means endangering the Belgian and French Channel ports and therewith the main bridge between England and its Allies on the continent.

The German Command says the line has been pierced and the Meuse crossed at several points in Belgium and France, but it does not say that the line has been smashed. The French especially, we are told, are counter-attacking, though so far, say the Germans, without success.

A word about the general strategy in this gigantic battle. The German press confirms tonight that Hitler's army is using a modified form of the famous old Schlieffen Plan, which – to put it in a sentence – called for a "swing-door" movement across the low-lands, with the hinge somewhere near Metz, and the German right-wing swinging in a great circle down past Antwerp and Brussels and eventually enclosing the French armies between Paris and the Rhine.

In 1914, the Schlieffen Plan failed, by a hair's breadth. It failed because the German right wing failed to swing around fast enough and with sufficient force. On his death-bed in 1912, Schlieffen's last words were: "Keep that right flank strong." That was what was the trouble in 1914. And the German press emphasizes that this mistake will not be made again. The occupation of Holland has secured the right-wing. And the capitulation of the Dutch now releases a sufficient German force to enable the right-wing to attempt its turning movement through northern Belgium.

The line of battle – if you glance at your map – now runs in a fairly straight line from Antwerp down through Louvain and Namur to Sedan. You might now expect to see this turn, like the spoke of a wheel, the top part – the line at Antwerp – turning left. That could come not only by a drive against Antwerp, which has not yet apparently started, but also by pressure at the lower end, where yesterday it was indeed strongest – by Sedan.

And keep in mind when you visualize what's happening that it's not a vast frontal attack that's taking place, as in the last war, but arrow-head thrusts at vital points led by tanks and airplanes.

Herr Hitler tonight issued a proclamation thanking his troops in Holland for their brave work. He mentioned especially the feats of the parachutists and airmen landed by planes for the part they played in conquering Holland in five days.

Berlin May 16, 1940 14.05

Good Morning. This is Berlin.

The daily communiqué of the German High Command is just out. It confirms that the big battle along the Meuse from Namur to Sedan is still being fought violently and that yesterday was marked principally by French counter-attacks led by heavy tanks. The German Command says they were repulsed. I quote the communiqué on the fighting here:

"In Belgium the enemy has engaged battle along the Dyle positions" – those are the ones around Louvain protecting Brussels – "and at the Fortress of Namur. South-west of Namur our divisions furthered their successes on the west bank of the Meuse and threw back renewed French tank attacks. South of Sedan, French counter-attacks, led by heavy armored units, were repulsed. Many heavy tanks were thereby destroyed. Between the Moselle and the Rhine," continues the German communiqué, "our positions west of Saarlautern and near Lauterburg were pushed forward." This, of course, is on the main Maginot Line, where a decisive battle has not yet been engaged.

In the air, the German Command gives yesterday's score as ninety-eight planes to eighteen, in their favor. Many enemy air-bases were also bombed, it says.

Further, says the High Command, during the night enemy planes bombed points in western Germany. Their attacks, however, the Army Command claims, were without plan, and did little damage and failed to hit any important military objectives. A number of civilians, however, were killed and wounded, it says. Numerous Allied naval and merchant ships were bombed and hit off the Dutch and Belgian coasts, it concludes.

The morning and noon papers play up the capitulation of Holland and Herr Hitler's congratulations to the army which smashed the Netherlands to surrender in five days. They also feature prominently last night's warning of the High Command that unless the Belgians ceased their troop movements through Brussels and stopped fortifying the city, it would be bombed.

"The German High Command," said the warning, "cannot regard Brussels as an undefended city. If the Belgian government really wants to save the city of Brussels from the horrors of war, all military movement through the capital must immediately cease and the work on fortifications stopped."

The Berlin paper calls this a last warning and recalls what happened to Warsaw. The Polish capital, as you will remember, was destroyed after the Poles had decided to try to defend it. "The example of Warsaw," comments the *Börsen Zeitung*, "ought to make the Belgians think a little."

An idea of how German leaders see the present drive through Belgium is given us today by Herr Hitler's press chief, Dr. Diettrich. Writing from the Führer's headquarters, he says: "Now the German sword is speaking. Conscious of their sacred rights, Germany's sons are marching against the hired soldiers of the plutocrats."

Dino Alfieri, Italy's new ambassador to Germany, arrived here this morning, and was given a hearty reception. A warm friend of the Third Reich since years, his coming has naturally aroused interest in diplomatic circles as to what Italy is going to do. Will Italy join its ally? And if so, just when?

Berlin May 16, 1940 24.45

Good Evening. This is Berlin.

We're on the eve tonight of a great and decisive battle – perhaps the decisive battle of this war.

The lines are formed, the battle-ground accepted by both sides. That battle-ground – very much the same one that has been fought over century after century since the time of Caesar – runs for roughly 125 miles from in front of Antwerp down through Namur to a point south of Sedan.

There the armies, with all their deadly weapons of destruction, are lined up tonight – the Belgians, British and French awaiting the onslaught, the Germans ready to make it. When the blow will fall we don't know. Perhaps tomorrow. Perhaps the day after. The Germans, being on the offensive, have the choice of time. But of course, the sooner you're ready to attack the better your chances.

Neutral military experts here tell me that what has been happening is this. For the past seven days, we've been witnessing what they call the "development stage" of the great battle. The Germans were pushing ahead in arrow-head attacks and they did this until yesterday or the day before when their arrow-heads began to hit flat upon very strong Allied resistance. It was no longer possible, or advisable, to push ahead in needle thrusts at various points. A very strong enemy defense line had been met, and it had depth over a wide front. So now, say my neutral military advisers, the conflict changes from a "development stage" to "battle-stage". The real forces of both armies have been brought up. The real battle is about to begin.

A front-page editorial in the *Lokal Anzeiger* tonight speaks of the beginning battle, calls it a very serious struggle and says the enemy should not be underestimated.

They started firing with the big guns along the Rhine tonight, a front I've visited nearly every month since last September and which has until now been so peaceful and quiet. A German communiqué says the French bombarded the German Rhine town of Rastatt with long-distance artillery. As reprisal, the Germans bombarded the French town of Hagenau across the Rhine. On the map both towns are shown as railroad junctions.

We heard President Roosevelt's message very clearly here on the short-wave tonight. We got it between 8 and 9 p.m. our time, and so far the German News Agency has only had time to issue a four-line bulletin on it stating the President declared that recent developments showed that no fortress was impregnable. It is still too early for any reaction to the message, and there is none yet.

The latest special war communiqué announces that German planes bombed 100,000 tons of Allied naval and merchant tonnage today, about half of which was destroyed.

Berlin May 17, 1940 15.35

Hello CBS. This is Berlin.

The great battle in Belgium and northern France has begun, and the German High Command, in its daily communiqué, has just claimed a major success for the Germans.

It says that the Maginot Line from south of Maubeuge, which is on the main railroad line from Paris to Brussels, to the town of Carignan, just south-east of Sedan, has been broken through by the German army on a front sixty-five miles wide. This would bring the German army to within 100 miles of Paris.

Further to the north, says the German High Command in this communiqué, the German army has broken through the Dyle Line south of Wavre, which lies half way between Namur and Louvain.

As to Namur itself, the German Command declares the north-east front of the Fortress of Namur has been taken. Apparently the rest is still holding out.

Thus, according to the German Command, you've had two serious breakthroughs in the great Allied defensive line running south from Antwerp through Louvain and Namur to Sedan. One in the center at Wavre, between Louvain and Namur, and another which appears to be the main one through the Maginot defenses which run along the Franco-Belgian border. This last, the Germans claim, is on a sixty-five-mile front, which is a pretty wide front. And if you look at your map, you'll see that Maubeuge, itself a strong fortress, just south of which the Germans say they've broken through, is at least forty miles to the west of the Meuse River Line running south from Dinant and Givet to Sedan. So, if the Germans are right, it is a very deep breakthrough and has brought the German steamroller far west of the Meuse River on which the Allies appeared to be making a strong stand.

South of Sedan, the High Command says that 12,000 prisoners have been captured, including two generals and many guns. It further speaks of strong counter-attacks on the south wing near Sedan, but says the Germans beat them back and even advanced their lines.

Again, as in all the main communiqués of the High Command, there is the emphasis on the part in this colossal drive played by Germany's air armada and its great fleet of tanks. West of Dinant there was another tank battle with French tanks. The Germans say they threw the French armored units back. South of Sedan, the work of the German tanks is also mentioned.

The air force, says the communiqué, concentrated all day yesterday on bombing enemy concentrations, marching columns, and roads and railroads. Troop columns of all kinds were wiped out by the bombings, it says.

To the surprise of many strategists, the main German attack then has come in the center of the German army, from Louvain to Sedan, and not on the famous right wing around Antwerp, as those who thought the Germans would be following the Schlieffen Plan, calculated. But if the Germans maintain their drive to Maubeuge, then the Allies' left flank, it would seem, would become untenable, and would have to be withdrawn south-west. But this opens up the Belgian coast, which is very close to England's, to the Germans.

The news I've just given to you has just been announced on the German radio to the accompaniment of fanfare and patriotic songs. Extras are just coming out on the streets.

Berlin May 17, 1940 24.46

Good Evening. This is Berlin.

Once again tonight the news the Germans give us about their terrific drive in Belgium and France almost takes your breath away.

Here is the situation so far as I can keep up with it.

At sun-down this evening, says the High Command, German troops entered Brussels. The Belgian government had already left for Ostende.

The story of the fall of the Belgian capital just eight days after Hitler unloosed his great offensive in the low-lands was told here this evening in three brief army communiqués. I'll just read them.

Number One: "In an encircling attack, Louvain has fallen."

Number Two: "After heavy fighting, German troops have broken through the Dyle positions north of Louvain and have captured Malines."

Number Three: "After the collapse of the Franco-British positions south of Louvain, German troops this evening entered Brussels."

That was one breakthrough reported today by the German High Command and it consisted of smashing the so-called Dyle Line east of Brussels. When it broke, Brussels went with it.

The other breakthrough – which may be even more important – was announced by the High Command about 3 p.m., our time. This communiqué said that on a sixty-five-mile front reaching from the two French border towns of Maubeuge and Carignan, south-east of Sedan, the German army had broken through the Maginot Line. A glance at the map seemed to indicate that after this breakthrough, the Germans were hurling their mighty war-machine head-on towards Paris over two cities you will remember from the Word War, Saint-Quentin and the cathedral town of Reims. The High Command does not tell us how far their breakthrough here has got, but one gets the impression that it has gone far, far.

And finally, the extreme right German flank which old von Schlieffen on his death-bed begged his followers in Berlin to keep strong in any battle of the low-lands, the very battle we are now witnessing, started moving today. As the center around Louvain and the southern flank by Sedan cracked, the right wing around Antwerp started to swing around. Tonight, the High Command reported that German troops have closed in around Antwerp from the north.

It would seem obvious, however, that the British and Belgian troops which have been defending Antwerp will now have to get out of there in a hurry to keep from being cut off by the troops which tonight marched into Brussels.

Berlin May 18, 1940 14.05

Good Morning. This is Berlin.

The big story in the Berlin newspapers, which have been busy headlining one victory after another ever since Hitler started his lightning strike in the West a week ago last Friday, is the entry of German troops into Brussels last night. It took them just eight days to get there. In 1914, I find, it took the Germans sixteen days to get to Brussels, or just twice as long as this time.

The fall of Brussels became a foregone conclusion yesterday when the German army, using great masses of tanks and airplanes, hurled itself against the so-called Dyle Line, strongly defended by Belgian, British, and French troops. The battle, we gather from reports here, was bitterly fought, but short. Both north of Louvain and south of it, the German machine broke through the Allies' defenses, and before nightfall they were in Brussels and Malines, to the north of it, and half way to Antwerp. In the meantime, the Germans increased their pressure on Antwerp from the north, that is from Holland, and started to close in on it. To save themselves from being cut off, it would seem as if the British and Belgian troops defending Antwerp will have to – if they already haven't – withdraw down the coast to keep from being cut off by German troops coming in from Malines and Brussels.

Well, that is the situation as pictured by the German High Command up to the present, but it's a picture of the situation as it was yesterday, and things seem to be moving so fast, that an entirely new picture may be given when the regular communiqué comes out within the next hour or so.

It seems almost incredible that within a week and one day, the German army could have overrun Holland and forced it to surrender, and broken through three great defense lines in Belgium and Holland. The three were the Albert Canal Line in northern Belgium supported by the fortress of Liège. That was broken in two days. Then, the Meuse and Dyle Lines running from Antwerp to Namur, which was cracked yesterday. And finally, the Maginot Line in north-eastern France, which the Germans say they broke through yesterday on a sixty-five-mile front.

How are they doing it? one asks. Without saying so in so many words, the German High Command indicates that it has been doing it by the mass use of airplanes and tanks on a scale never before imagined, let alone used. Yesterday's army communiqué spoke of ceaseless bombings behind the Allied lines – roads, railroads, columns of trucks and tanks, columns of marching troops – everything. That, it seems, is the explanation. Airplanes and tanks, and a masterly use of them.

It's worth noting that immediately after yesterday's great break-throughs, editorials in the German press appeared asking what point the Belgians had in continuing the fight except to protect England a little longer. The editorials thought that the goals of the three Allies had become different, and that the French would now concentrate no longer on protecting the Channel ports but on saving Paris. The effect of this on England was not overlooked.

An editorial in this morning's *Börsen Zeitung* caused some excitement in diplomatic circles here. It reported that Italy's patience with the Allies, because of the blockade, was at an end, and said that if Italy was now determined to break it, she would find herself in good company. The Wilhelmstrasse confirmed this noon that the editorial represented the views of "well-informed circles" in Berlin.

Berlin May 18, 1940 24.46

Good Evening. This is Berlin.

The fortress of Antwerp has fallen. Belgian, French, and British troops are falling back from there along the coast, pursued by German bombers and tanks. And further south, striking with endless masses of planes and tanks, a German mechanized force is driving down through north-eastern France towards Paris.

That, at least, is the picture we get here in Berlin at the end of this ninth day of Hitler's great offensive in the West.

Antwerp fell during the day. Late this afternoon, the German High Command gave out the following communiqué: "By means of a rapid attack, the fortified front of Antwerp has been broken through. German troops have penetrated to the heart of the city. The German war flag flies from the City Hall in Antwerp."

The fall of Antwerp, it's pointed out here, became a foregone conclusion yesterday after the Germans had broken through north and south of Louvain and entered Brussels and Malines, south of Antwerp. From that moment Allied troops were in danger of being trapped there, as they were in 1914.

It's hard to tell from the German army communiqués today how far the Nazi forces have penetrated towards Paris after their break through the Maginot Line between Maubeuge and Montmédy day before yesterday. The High Command communiqué, which covers operations up until last night only, speaks of German armored forces pushing the French back over the Sambre River to the upper reaches of the Oise River. This would put them in the neighborhood of Saint-Quentin.

Incidentally, military circles here in Berlin told us today that it was not accurate for the other side to speak of several German tank *divisions* having been used in the drive through the Maginot Line day before yesterday. The Germans say they used rather tank *corps*, which is a much larger unit.

Well now, there the Germans are, pushing the Allies west of Antwerp and Brussels up against the coast, and further south driving towards Paris. The main fighting, the decisive fighting, will now unfold between Brussels and Paris, which Clausewitz, Germany's great strategist, once called the solar-plexus of France. It's already been hit hard, but it still remains to be seen whether the knock-out blow will be struck.

The *Börsen Zeitung* tonight speaks of three possibilities opened up for the German army in its present position:

To strike due south and roll back the Maginot Line from the flank, to strike west against the heart of France, or north and north-west against the Channel ports, from which a further move, it points out, could be made against England. Which the Germans will do, or whether they think they are now strong enough to do two or even all three, is of course a secret of the general staff.

Judging from talk in military circles here and also from a broadcast from the front which I heard a few minutes ago, the French, Belgians, and British put up a very fierce resistance yesterday, but the sheer mass of German metal – especially tanks and airplanes – simply blew them out of their strong positions. A German radio observer near Louvain made it very clear in his broadcast that it was the deadly work of the German dive-bombers which really reduced the enemy to helplessness. When the dive-bombers and artillery got through with the Allied troops on the far side of the Dyle River, he observed that the German infantry then went forward almost without resistance. Apparently then, the Germans are using an entirely new technique of warfare. The spearhead of their attack is the bomber, especially the dive-bomber, and the tank. But they used it in Poland nine months ago, so the Allies cannot have been taken completely by surprise. Tomorrow, I plan to go to the front to see for myself, if I can, just how the Germans are doing it.

Cologne May 21, 1940 04.32

Good Evening. This is William L. Shirer in Cologne, Germany.

I followed the German army into Belgium today as far as Brussels, and drove back here during most of the night to the first microphone I could find. There are two or three things I'd like to say.

First, about *how* this Blitz Krieg is being fought. And let's face some hard truths. The tactics the Germans have used so far with such success are these: They attack Allied positions first with dive-bombers, then with tanks – and if need be, artillery – and then the mechanized infantry delivers the final blow. Judging from the ruined railroad stations, junction points and crumbled fortifications we saw today on our way to Brussels, the dive-bombers have been as accurate as artillery and much more deadly. Perhaps they are the chief reason for the amazing German advance.

Another hard truth: So far as we could observe today, the Allied air force has done very little to hamper German communications in the rear. Though we drove for fourteen hours today along roads choked with columns of troops and supplies, we did not see a single Allied plane. Along the road to Brussels, the Allies had blown up a few bridges – though others remained intact – and dynamited the road in two or three places. But German tanks and trucks were already thundering over it.

There are the British night bombings, to be sure, and I experienced one last night. But I saw no trace of any bomb-craters in the many roads we took today. I do not pretend to know what damage has been done in western Germany by these night raids, but I motored through the Ruhr yesterday, and the vast network of railroads there, so important for Germany's war effort, was functioning very well, as far as I could see. I saw hundreds of important factories. Not one hit. Tonight, I talked to six British prisoners, all that were left of a whole company. They said they were simply overwhelmed by dive-bombers and tanks.

"What about your own bombers and tanks?" I asked.

"Didn't see any," they answered.

From Aachen, we drove through the Dutch province of Limburg to Maastricht. In this province at least, the Dutch appear to have done little fighting. Almost no damage to be observed.

It was otherwise with the Belgians. They appear to have fought like lions. And the shambles of Tongres, St. Trond, and Louvain are a testament to that and to the punishment they took.

Take Louvain. That ancient university city is to a considerable extent destroyed. Here the Belgians and the English fought hard for three days before they were overwhelmed. Block on block lies in ruins. That also goes for the famous University Library, built by American donations after it was burned in 1914. The library is completely gutted, and it was still smouldering this morning. All the books went up in flames. But you could still read the inscriptions on the stones in memory of the donors. I noted a few of them: The Public Schools of the City of Philadelphia in Pennsylvania; University of Rochester; University of Illinois; The Finch School; The American Association of University Women. Those tablets still stand. The City Hall, which was used by the British army as headquarters in Louvain, is untouched; also the cathedral across the square. But the blocks of houses where many of the 41,000 inhabitants lived are a terrible sight to behold. There was intense street-fighting, and often a boulevard changed hands several times. When the German troops finally entered the town after the Allied withdrawal, not a single civilian was there. They'd fled, but today, along the road to Brussels, I saw them filtering back, dazed and bitter and sad from their experience, but trudging along in the hot sun with their belongings on their back or on a bicycle, or if they were lucky, on a cart.

On the way to Brussels, we stopped off at Steenockerzeel, the home of Otto von Hapsburg. Close to the house was a huge crater from a bomb, and a small part of the roof had been blown off. In Otto's study, I noticed a book in French entitled *The Coming War*.

Brussels we found intact. The streets were thronged with people. Their faces were bitter, but they were accepting their fate with dignity. The Belgians also said that the behavior of German troops had been correct. All Americans in Brussels are safe, and though we did not get to the Embassy, two American bankers told me that Ambassador Cudahy and his staff had remained in Brussels. For the moment, because of the breakdown in communications, they are cut off from the outside world. One party of Americans tried to get away last Thursday night by train, but twenty miles outside the capital, they were halted by a bombed bridge, and they had to return. As soon as communications are restored, the Americans probably will be evacuated through Germany.

The shops and cafés in Brussels opened today and by order of the German army gave you an exchange of ten francs for one mark. Street-cars were also running in Brussels, though no private cars were circulating. German soldiers mingled freely in the crowded streets with the civilians. Before the English retreated, they blew up all the bridges around the city. The chief concern of the womenfolk of Brussels is for news of their relatives in the Belgian army.

Tomorrow, we hope to get to the actual front and I hope to be back tomorrow night or the next day with a report on that.

Berlin May 23, 1940 04.51

Good Evening. This is William L. Shirer in Berlin.

I returned here from the front a couple of hours ago after a 450-mile drive from the Belgian border. Berlin, I must say, seems a little quiet after three days of hearing the big guns go off and the heavy bombs exploding. Yesterday, we got so accustomed to the roar of the German heavy artillery all around us that we were able to write our reports about as coherently as ever. To file them, however, we had to return to the Belgian-German border where normal communications begin. And correspondents of the three American press associations and I had quite a time of it making ourselves heard on the telephone with our reports last night because of the noise of the British bombs and the German anti-aircraft guns nearby.

Actually, the British bombers were aiming for an important military objective about 100 yards from our hotel. They kept at it all night, and were always warm, so to speak, but not hot. The nearest they hit was about four or five hundred yards from the hotel, and though the bombs jarred us, they did not jar us enough to break any windows. Tired out from three days and nights without sleep, we dozed through most of it. After what I've seen in Belgium, I've come to the conclusion that if a bomb happens to hit the building you're in, you might just as well be on the top floor as in the cellar, because the whole building goes.

During the day, at least on the Belgian front west of Brussels, where we were, the Allies do not do any bombing. And one of the things that impressed me most was the picture of the German army bringing up men, guns, and supplies, jamming the roads with them for miles and miles behind the front, without hindrance from the Allied air forces. I'm convinced that the ease with which the German Command has been able to bring up reinforcements and guns and ammunition, and at an unbelievable speed, is one of the reasons for the German success so far. I understand that this is not the case on the other side because of the deadly work of the German air force behind the Allied lines. This state of affairs gives the Germans a tremendous advantage even before the battle starts.

In a talk I had yesterday with the commander of the German army in Belgium, he emphasized that *the* decisive battle had not yet been fought and he readily admitted that it was quite possible that the German advance would be slowed up if, as he put it, General Weygand decided to make a bitter stand.

The communiqué of the German High Command today rather indicates that the German advance has slowed up and that the Allied resistance has stiffened in the last twenty-four hours. One paragraph of the army communiqué today says: "In Flanders, the enemy in covering his retreat is still putting up a stubborn resistance on the River Scheldt."

It was this battle on the Scheldt yesterday that I happened to watch from a point about a quarter of a mile in front of the German heavy artillery positions and some two or three miles back of where the infantry were actually fighting. Now, to tell the truth, I, at least, found it difficult to observe the varying fortunes of the infantry. For one thing, they were operating in wooded country near the banks of the river. For another, dense smoke from the artillery barrages laid down by both sides often hid just what was going on. We could see, though, when the German artillery advanced its barrage and peppered the roads in the rear of the Allies. This meant that the German infantry, led by tanks, was going forward. But it was hard going, and when the German artillery went back to its old range, you could figure that there had been an Allied counter-attack, and the Germans had to start all over again. This was the way the battle seemed to go all day long, though when we left at dusk the German artillery, I noticed, was moving forward to new positions, so their advance here, though slow, seemed to be going on.

But the main fighting now is in the wedge which the Germans have driven to the sea along the Somme. The Germans are now trying to enlarge it by driving north-west from the Somme; Allied resistance is strong and it may well be that this will turn out to be the decisive battle of the war.

Berlin May 23, 1940 24.46

Good Evening. This is Berlin.

The German troops which day before yesterday broke through to the sea near Abbeville, thus cutting off an Allied force of a million men in Belgium and northern France, are now fighting their way north along the French coast towards Calais.

If they get to Calais and stay there, then Great Britain will be cut off from France, with consequences for the Allies which need not be stressed.

How far the Germans have got in this decisive turn northward towards the Channel ports, we have not yet been told. English reports that fighting is already going on in and around Boulogne have not yet been officially confirmed in Berlin, though they have not caused any surprise here. German army communiqués, in the main, always refer to the previous day's achievements. And yesterday the Germans were already at Montreuil, some thirty miles south of Boulogne, and moving towards the north with their fast mechanized forces.

Yesterday, according to the High Command, German planes bombed the harbor works of Dunkirk and Dover, between which a good share of the Allied supplies and men have been passing.

It seems obvious then that the main German drive at the moment is northward from the wedge they've driven to the coast towards the Channel ports. England – and not so much Paris – appears now to be the main goal of the German drive.

Note, too, that the Germans have pulled out of the bag yet another weapon hitherto little used – the speed-boat carrying torpedoes. Today's communiqué of the German Command speaks of them operating off the French Channel port of Dunkirk where it's claimed they sank a French destroyer.

It might be a good thing to pause a moment and try to get a view of the whole military situation so far as that is possible in this swift war of movement. A German news agency, the *Dienst Aus Deutschland*, comes to the conclusion this evening that the first phase of this greatest of all battles ended yesterday with the Allied armies cut in two. It had lasted just twelve short days. The second phase, beginning today, which the agency thinks will decide the fate of the war, will be determined, in its opinion, by three factors:

1. The outcome of the fighting now progressing on both wings of the forces in Flanders and the Artois. The north wing would be that fighting along the Scheldt River in Belgium which I had the chance of watching earlier in the week. The south wing would be that now fighting to the south of Calais.

2. The outcome of the attempt of the Allies to break through the center

of this front, and thus restore their communications with the rest of France.

3. The result of a possible attempt by the French armies south of the German corridor, that is between, say, Montmédy on the Franco-Belgian frontier and Reims, to break through north and thus cut off the Germans from behind.

Those are the three factors which will prove decisive, thinks this Berlin news agency.

Probably, the Germans expect a French thrust from the south somewhere between the Meuse and the Somme. It's interesting therefore that the High Command today states that the French troops in this sector are being held on the *defensive*. As long as they can be kept on the defensive, they will be unable to attack and relieve the Allied armies now cut off. This is a familiar form of tactics dear to the Germans and was used in Poland with the Polish army around Posen. In fact, German military circles tonight compare the plight of the cut-off Allied armies to that of the Polish forces around Kutno, though they admit that in the present case the Allies are much stronger, more heavily armed and better led than were the Poles. Well, the coming days will show whether we are to have a new Kutno on a grand scale. In any case, it looks as though we'll have a definite decision.

Berlin May 24, 1940 24.47

Good Evening. This is Berlin.

It was just two weeks ago today that Hitler unloosed his terrific Blitz Krieg in the West. In that short space of time, Holland has been overrun, four-fifths of Belgium occupied, the French army hurled back towards Paris and an Allied army believed to number a million men and including the élite of the Franco-British forces, trapped and encircled.

You have to see the colossal machine, which is the German army, in action – as I did earlier in the week – to believe it. But there are the facts.

German military circles again warned us today that the war is not over yet, that the decisive action, like the short eight-hour battle which decided Napoleon's fate at Waterloo, has yet to come, and that much hard fighting remains to be done.

In the meantime, however, the German steamroller pushes on. The situation today, as outlined by the German Command, is marked by three factors:

1. The ring in which the Allied armies are cut off in Flanders and the Artois has been further narrowed.

2. The wedge that the Germans have driven through to the sea has been further widened.

3. German armored and mechanized units, pushing up the French coast, appear to be nearing their goal of seizing the Channel ports and cutting off Great Britain from France.

You might add a fourth point. The High Command speaks today of the French counter-attacks, made in an effort to break through the German gap, as weakening. In particular, it mentions that an attempt of the French to push north around Amiens was not made very strongly – was in fact weak – and, adds the High Command, was repulsed.

The High Command for some reason has been very slow the last couple of days to report the progress of the shock troops closing in on the Channel ports. For instance, the German capture of Boulogne, admitted by London, has not yet been announced here. There was a report this evening that the Germans had also entered Calais, but it's not yet confirmed.

At any rate, Saint-Omer, a key junction town lying twenty-five miles inland from the three French Channel ports of Boulogne, Calais, and Dunkirk, is now in German hands. And with its fall, it would seem that the port towns will go quickly too.

German military circles tell me it's a mistake to assume that the troops which have been moving through the gap to the sea are only small detachments of armored and motorized units. They say they've been able to rush very strong reinforcements indeed through the gap, and their rapid progress towards the Channel ports would seem to bear this out.

From my own observations at the front this week, I can tell you that, contrary to what I too first believed, these rapid German thrusts are certainly not carried out by weak forces, or by tanks and planes only. During the Scheldt River battle Tuesday, I had a chance of seeing how the Germans do it. The tanks go up first all right, but right behind them and moving just as fast are strong forces of infantry on trucks and motorcycles and very strong detachments of artillery.

When opposition is hit, the infantry and artillery deploy with amazing speed and go right into action. If you remember that, I think, you'll understand not only how the Germans go forward so fast, but how they hold on to what they get.

Berlin May 25, 1940 24.46

Good Evening. This is Berlin.

In the opinion of German military circles, the fate of the great Allied army bottled up in Flanders is sealed. The Germans believe that army, containing the flower of the French, British, and Belgian forces, cannot now escape.

In their opinion, it's another Kutno, where the bottling up of the cream of Poland's army in the second week of last September sealed the doom of Poland. Only of course a Kutno on a much greater scale, and with infinitely greater consequences for the outcome of this European war.

Hitherto the German High Command itself has been reluctant to make any predictions about the ring it was forging around the Allied army in Flanders and north-west France. But in its daily communiqué this afternoon, it stated flatly – I'll just quote it: "The ring around the Belgian army, parts of the first, seventh, and ninth French armies and the mass of the British Expeditionary Corps was yesterday considerably strengthened and thereby finally closed."

Tonight, the German Command, in giving us a general picture of the situation as it sees it, stated categorically that the Allies cut off in Flanders and the Artois now have no more possibility of breaking out of their trap. As the High Command stated it, quote: " The end of the enemy here is imminent."

How many Allied troops are cut off? German generals at the front to whom I put the question earlier in the week said about a million. Well-informed circles in Berlin think it may be a little higher than that. Roughly, they estimate the trapped armies this way: 400,000 Belgians, 500,000 French, 200,000 British.

More than that, the Germans believe they have closed in on the flower of the Allied armies: the bulk of the mechanized British Expeditionary Force, and the best part of the French army. Apparently what happened, so far as you can figure it out here, is that the Allied commanders, thinking they were up against the same old Schlieffen Plan which the Germans used in 1914, threw their strongest forces up into Belgium to hit the German right wing, which Schlieffen had planned should deliver the main blow and thus roll the Allies back on Paris. What happened is that the Germans, scrapping the Schlieffen Plan, struck their heaviest blow in the center around Maubeuge, and instead of swinging around on Paris, rolled up against the Channel ports.

Now yesterday, if we follow the German reports, and that is all I can do from here, began a new phase of the German move to close in on the encircled Allied forces in Belgium and north-west France. If you glance at your maps, you'll see how the Germans, after breaking through to the sea near Abbeville, headed northward, took Boulogne and surrounded Calais. Yesterday, in this push northward, they held a line running roughly south-east along the railroad line from Calais to Lens, just north of Arras. In doing this, incidentally, they stormed the famous Vimy

Ridge, on which the Canadians fought so hard in the last war.

On this line, the Germans have now turned north-east and are coming up behind the entrapped Allied armies from the rear. Since breaking through by Maubeuge, they have executed a completed circle and are actually moving in the opposite direction from which they were going a week ago. In the meantime, according to the German Command, the French are counter-attacking along the Somme, that is on the southern side of the German gap, but Berlin says these attacks are not very strong.

The High Command told us today that a new secret weapon might still cause some further surprises. It's still unknown, we were told, and one officer emphasized that it was not a new howitzer, nor a tank, nor gas, nor a flame-thrower, nor a speed-boat, or anything to do with parachutists, but something really new and very decisive. Hitler, we were told, knew that with this new weapon, he would win the war.

I'm as much in the fog about it as you are and I'm just passing along what I've been told. Personally, from what I could see at the front, the Germans were doing well enough without secret weapons.

Berlin May 27, 1940 01.01

Good Evening. This is Berlin.

Calais has fallen. That great French Channel port, familiar to many Americans who have crossed from London to Paris, fell into German hands today after a hard fight, according to a special war communiqué issued by the High Command late tonight.

The communiqué read: "After German troops had continued their advance to Gravelines, Calais fell today into German hands after a hard fight."

Gravelines is a small town on the coast road half-way between Calais and Dunkirk. Dunkirk, the last of the three great French Channel ports, apparently is still in the hands of the French though its harbor works, say the Germans, have been continually bombed from the air by Stukas in the last few days.

But Calais was the gateway from France to England, the port through which most of the supplies passed for the British Expeditionary Army in France. Its capture by the Germans practically completes the cutting off of Great Britain from its ally on the continent.

Moreover, Calais is only twenty-five miles across the Channel from Dover, on the English coast. The massive, mechanized German army is that close to England tonight – twenty-five miles – the first time, unless I'm mistaken, that a hostile army has been that close to England's shores since the days of Napoleon more than a century ago. Military circles in Berlin have not been slow in pointing that out. They're a little reluctant about saying that the German army has artillery which will easily shoot over that twenty-five miles of water. When we put the question tonight, the answer was: "Well, we had a gun in the last war which fired further than twenty-five miles – the gun that shelled Paris. And artillery, like all other branches, has been improved since then. Of course, that was just a lone trick gun and decided nothing."

Be that as it may, German military circles certainly believe that their heavy mobile artillery from today on will control the Channel waters in the sense that no Allied shipping will be able to get through it.

Now then. Will Hitler, now that he's got the Channel ports, and assuming for a moment that his armies will either wipe out or force to surrender those million Allied troops cut off in Flanders – will Hitler then try to invade and conquer England, a feat that has not been successfully done for almost 1,000 years, when William the Conqueror and his Normans did it?

No one here knows. But the fact that the German forces after penetrating into northern France turned abruptly north-west towards the English Channel instead of continuing on towards Paris, as in 1914, makes some people think that he will try.

I notice that the official newspaper, the *Völkischer Beobachter*, was on the streets this afternoon with an extra whose flaming headline, underlined in red ink, reads: BOMBS ON EAST AND SOUTH-EAST ENGLAND. This refers to a sentence in the daily communiqué of the German High Command today which stated: "On Friday night, the air force attacked with good results numerous landing fields in east and south-east England."

Military circles in Berlin recalled to our attention this evening in this connection that the initial step in the invasion of Holland, Belgium and France was the bombing of the airbases in these countries.

The same circles also pointed out that it is from these fields in east and south-east England that the British bombers, which have been bombing western Germany every night, take off.

Of course, if an invasion of England is not attempted, two other possibilities remain open to the Germans if and when they liquidate the Allied army they now have encircled.

One would be to strike south and attempt to take Paris. The other would be for the German armies now attacking around Montmédy to try to break through Verdun and Metz and take the old Maginot Line along the Franco-German border from behind. It's probably much easier to take from behind than from in front.

In the meantime, according to the German Command, the trap in which the Allied armies in Flanders and the Artois have been caught, is slowly but surely narrowing, though the Germans admit that their enemies are putting up a very stubborn resistance.

However, the Germans claim that their right wing has already advanced ten miles beyond the River Lys in the direction of Iseghem, which is on the road to Ostende. Further south, German forces enlarging the gap south of Lille, which is still in Allied hands, have reached the La Bassée Canal, the scene of heavy fighting in the World War. In reaching the canal, say the Germans, they have narrowed the distance between their armies converging on Lille by nearly twenty miles.

Berlin May 27, 1940 24.47

Good Evening. This is Berlin.

For the first time in this offensive, we hear today the name of Ypres, that famous world-war battlefield where the Canadians fought so hard.

The German High Command reports that the German forces in Flanders have made a breach in the Allied line north of Menin and pushed westward almost to Ypres. Menin lies directly on the Franco-Belgian border, north of the French industrial city of Lille. And if the Germans have penetrated almost to Ypres, it means that they've pushed across the Lys River, the last water defense line between the cut-off Allied armies in Flanders and the coast.

Apparently, judging from the German war communiqués, there have been three different kinds of operations in the general movement to close in on the encircled Allied forces in Flanders and force them to surrender. The first, which the Germans say was virtually completed with the capture of Calais, announced officially here last night, was designed to cut off England from France by seizure of the Channel ports. This also made it practically impossible for the British to withdraw their encircled army by sea, the only route that remained open.

The second was a general pincers movement to gradually catch the Allied army between one German force moving south-west from Belgium and a second force moving north-east from the gap to the sea.

The third seems to be a pincers movement within a pincers movement. That is, German forces, which now surround Lille from three sides, appear to be trying to close the pincers on that great city before the larger pincers movement, designed to get the whole entrapped Allied army, is brought to a conclusion.

Most of the fighting reported here in the last two days has been going on around Lille. Thus yesterday it was claimed here that the German army advancing north-eastward from the gap had taken Bethune and Lens, which lie just south of Lille. The Ypres salient reported in today's communiqué is just north of Lille.

And the German Command today told us of a French counter-attack north-east of Lens – that would be between Lens and Lille – by French colonial troops. The Germans claim it was repulsed with heavy losses for the colonials. But it's the first attempt we've heard of for some days of the French to drive south against the German gap. To drive south here and try to break through that gap, if successful, would of course free the encircled Allied army from its trap and also cut off the Germans now in possession of the Channel ports.

It was announced in Berlin today that the special treatment accorded Allied prisoners so far has ceased. Reason given: The Germans claim the Allies are no longer treating German prisoners well.

The second Hohenzollern to be killed in this war is Prince Wilhelm of Prussia, eldest son of the Crown Prince. It's announced he was killed in action May 13th. A cousin, Prince Oscar, was killed in the Polish war.

Berlin May 28, 1940 24.46

Good Evening. This is Berlin.

There's jubilation in Berlin at the unconditional capitulation of the Belgian army on the orders of King Leopold today.

A half million very sturdy Belgian soldiers, who, as I can testify from personal observation at the front, have been fighting for three weeks like lions, are removed from the field of battle.

And moreover removed from that trap in Flanders and Artois where they, with another half million British and French, had been fighting doggedly for a week in an attempt to extricate themselves from a desperate situation, surrounded on three sides by the German army and on the fourth by the sea.

The surrender of the Belgians certainly puts the encircled British and French forces in a terrible hole. The German High Command puts it even stronger than that. It holds that after the Belgian capitulation, the situation of the enclosed Allied troops is "hopeless".

But it does not yet make any definite prediction as to just what is to happen in this sector where every day the German ring around the British and French appears to be tightening. Military circles in Berlin put it this way: "Just how quickly things come to a conclusion on this battlefield cannot yet be predicted." But, they add, "The last act of the great battle of May 1940 has now begun."

Today's communiqué of the German Command gave a few details. North of Valenciennes, it said, German troops have broken through the French border defenses on a wide front, while west of Valenciennes, they have crossed the Scheldt Canal. The important French town Douai, west of Valenciennes, is in German hands, says Berlin. North-west of Douai, more French towns have been captured, including Hazebrouck and Merville, the Germans claim, thus drawing the knot tighter around the great industrial city of Lille.

Lille, the most important city in northern France and generally believed to have been general headquarters of the British Expeditionary Force, apparently is one of the immediate objectives of the German steamroller. Tonight, according to military quarters in Berlin, German forces, approaching the city from three sides, are only fifteen miles away on the south-west, and only ten miles away on the east.

To return for a moment to the Belgian surrender. The German press fully approves King Leopold's step. The German radio tonight said: "He acted like a soldier and a human being."

The Berlin papers make much of the announcement that the Führer has ordered that the King and his soldiers receive treatment worthy of the valiant fighters which they proved to be. From the Führer's headquarters, it was announced that though King Leopold had expressed no personal wishes for himself, a castle in Belgium will be put at his disposal until his final living place is decided.

A couple of hours ago, the German radio announced that Field Marshal Göring, chief of the German air force, had ordered as a reprisal against the French that all French airmen captured in the future be immediately put into chains and as prisoners be made subject to the strictest measures. It was explained that this was ordered after Göring had received information that the French were mistreating captured German airmen. Specifically, the Germans charged that one of their flyers, Colonel Lackner, had been put in chains by the French after being captured wounded.

Furthermore, Göring ordered that if he hears of a German flyer being shot by the French, he will order five French flyers shot. Further still, if he hears of a German flyer being shot while making an emergency landing, he will order fifty French prisoners shot.

This order of Göring's, it's added, does not apply to English airmen, only French.

Berlin May 29, 1940 24.47

Good Evening. This is Berlin.

Lille, Bruges, Ostende captured! Ypres stormed! Dunkirk bombarded! Fate of encircled Allied armies sealed!

The incredible headlines, as amazing to the Germans here at home as they are to you and me, went on tonight without a let-up.

And yet – tonight – still another phase of this gigantic battle, without precedent in all history, appeared – at least in Berlin – to be drawing to a conclusion.

The German High Command told the story in these words at the beginning of its daily communiqué. It said: "The fate of the French army in Artois is sealed. Its resistance south of Lille has collapsed. The English army which has been compressed into the territory around Dixmunde, Armentières, Bailleul, Bergues, west of Dunkirk, is also going to its destruction before our concentric attack."

And then this evening, the German Command announced that in rapid attacks designed to crush the British army, Ypres and Kemmel had been stormed.

Now, if you consult your map, you can see the grave situation of the trapped Allied armies, as explained to us by the German High Command. In reality, the Germans tell us, the French and British armies since yesterday have been isolated, the one from the other, and each trapped in a tiny pocket. The smaller pocket which is in the form of a square the sides of which are about twelve miles long, lies south of Lille – between there and Douai. In that small square is what is left of three French armies, and tonight the Germans are battering them from four sides.

The larger pocket runs roughly in a semi-circle around the port of Dunkirk, reaching inland for some twenty-five miles. Here the British are trapped. The Germans think they're trying to get as many men and guns and tanks away as possible by sea through Dunkirk, which today was under German artillery fire.

Well, that's the situation, and Berlin thinks that by the weekend it will all be over with the Allied army in Flanders.

What next then, if it *is* all over with the British Expeditionary Force and the northern French armies by the weekend?

Well, for one thing, England will face for the first time since 1066 the possibility of invasion. Its bases on the continent, barring a last minute miracle, are gone. The low-lands just across the Channel and the narrow southern North Sea, which it has always been a cardinal part of British policy to defend, are in enemy hands. And the French Channel ports which linked Britain with its French ally are lost.

But whether an attempted invasion of Britain will be Hitler's next step, we, of course, don't know. He doesn't advertise his next step in advance.

Some think that before attempting this, the German High Command will try to finish France. A German news agency, the *Dienst Aus Deutschland*, pointed out tonight that the French line protecting Paris – that's the line that runs along the Rivers Somme and Aisne to the Argonne Forest – is, as it put it, "improvised and drawn out not on strategic grounds, but on conditions forced on the French by the advance of the German army".

Incidentally, the German Command gave as its opinion tonight that the surrender of the Belgians did not decisively affect the fate of the Allied armies in Flanders. It claimed that fate already was settled before King Leopold made his decision. [*This paragraph was deleted by the censor.*]

One weird aspect of yesterday's decisive fighting is mentioned in the German communiqué today. It points out that in taking the French positions east of Cassel, the French were actually made to defend their strong fortifications along the Belgian frontier here from *behind*. That is, the Germans were attacking from the south-west, or French rear. The fortifications of course were built for an enemy coming in the other direction. [*This paragraph was also deleted by the censor.*]

Prince Wilhelm of Prussia, killed in action on the Western Front, was buried with military honors in Potsdam today. Present at the funeral were his parents, the former Crown Prince and Princess, and Field Marshal von Mackensen. The former Kaiser sent a wreath.

An official statement issued in Berlin tonight stated that an exact list was being made of the number of German civilians killed and also the property damaged as a result of the nightly British air-raids on Western Germany. "When the hour of reckoning comes," said the statement, "every British bomb will be repaid many times over."

Berlin May 30, 1940 24.46

Good Evening. This is Berlin.

The great Battle of Flanders, as it will probably go down in history, is rapidly nearing its end, the German High Command stated flatly today.

The first few lines from the daily High Command communiqué give the story. I quote: "The great battle in Flanders and the Artois approaches its end, with the destruction of the English and French armies still fighting there. Since yesterday, the British Expeditionary Force has been in a complete state of dissolution. Leaving behind its entire mass of war material, it is fleeing to the sea. By swimming, or on small boats, the enemy is attempting to reach the English ships lying off the shore on which our air force is falling with devastating effect. Over sixty ships have been hit by our bombs, sixteen transports and three warships sunk, and twenty-one merchant ships and ten warships damaged or set on fire." That's how the German war communiqué today described it.

Earlier in the day, a special communiqué of the German High Command told of a great air battle over Dunkirk in which the German air-armada strove to prevent the British from extricating what is left of their expeditionary force by taking them back to England in ships. This gigantic air attack, apparently on a scale never before seen even in this war, took place yesterday afternoon after German reconnaissance planes had discovered a great fleet of English transports approaching the Franco-Belgian coast between Dunkirk and Ostende. The communiqué speaks of the Germans throwing in strong detachments from two entire flying corps. This is the first time we've heard of two flying corps being used in one operation. We do not know how many German planes took part, but there were certainly hundreds of them in the air. The British too must have sent hundreds of planes into that battle because the Germans claim to have shot down sixty-eight British planes in this one engagement. The German planes were commanded by two of Germany's greatest flying officers, General von Richthofen and General Grauert.

You may ask, as I did today, how it was that the British ships, sent to take off as many of the British troops as there is room for, were lying off shore. Why weren't they in Dunkirk harbor, where it would be much easier to take on their loads?

The Germans say that the harbor works, including the docks, at Dunkirk have been completely destroyed by German bombs or artillery fire, so that they were useless as a base for embarking troops. And useless too for embarking supplies.

From Dunkirk to Ostende, the Franco-Belgian coast consists mostly of long, wide beaches. According to the Germans, it is along these beaches that the British army is congregating and then being taken out to the transports which lie a mile or two offshore.

The map of the Flanders battle looks different tonight, compared to yesterday, in one respect. Last night, we had two pockets, one south of Lille where most of the French army was reported by the Germans to be encircled, and a larger pocket consisting of a semi-circle around Dunkirk. Tonight, there appears on German maps a third pocket. The High Command reports that south of the line Poperinghe-Cassel, German troops advancing from west, south, and east met, thus cutting off further large numbers of enemy troops.

Berlin May 31, 1940 24.46

This is Berlin.

The great Battle of Flanders is as good as over and the German High Command emphasized today that most of its troops are now free for further tasks, as it put it.

Whether that means that the German Command will next strike against England or try to roll the French back to Paris, we don't know. Most of us amateur strategists here think the latter course will be adopted, and that the German steamroller will next be hurled against the French army holding the line of the Somme and the Aisne to Montmédy.

The fact that General Weygand has not felt himself strong enough to try an offensive from the Somme northward, which if successful would have saved the Franco-British-Belgian armies in Flanders, seems to have made an impression on military quarters here. The idea seems to be to strike against the French before they've recovered from the blow of losing three of their best armies and before they have time to erect a strong line of defense along the Somme and the Aisne.

It's just three weeks ago today that Hitler went seriously to war in the west. Today, German military circles took stock of the third week of the great offensive and found it had netted five results. I'll just run over them, as given to us:

1. The Belgian army surrendered. The Germans occupied the Belgian coast.

2. The First, Seventh, and Ninth French Armies were liquidated in Flanders and the Artois. The continuation of the Maginot Line from Montmédy to Dunkirk, a distance of 200 miles, has been broken through and occupied. The German army is now sixty-three miles from Paris.

3. The British Expeditionary Corps also was liquidated. The Channel ports, Calais and Boulogne, came into German hands. The air force and the German navy have obtained valuable bases for an attack on Britain.

4. The important roads and railroad lines in Belgium and northern France are in German hands, so that a provisioning of the northern wing of the German army is secured.

5. The Germans now possess the important coal mines and industrial centers in northern France and Belgium.

Well, that's certainly an impressive week's achievement. But of course, as military people here warn the over-optimistic, the war is not over yet. As one put it to me today, the Germans have certainly won a terrific first-round, but there has been no knock-out blow yet. The fight goes on.

There was little news in the High Command communiqué today. It stated that while the mass of the French army in the Artois was either wiped out or captured, scattered groups still offered resistance at a few places. The German Command told us for the first time that the British had succeeded in flooding the area around where they're evacuating their troops in the region of Dunkirk. The High Command observed that the British were trying to get as many men as possible away, but apparently not trying to save their arms or supplies. The German communiqué speaks of there having been bad flying weather yesterday, and this must have helped the British a great deal in their evacuation work. While the Germans say their planes did bomb Dunkirk harbor, they do not mention any air attack on British transports.

Military quarters tell me that the British still have a stretch along the coast between Dunkirk and Nieuport stretching about thirty miles, but that it's narrow – only six miles or so deep.

Herr Hitler today received Signor Alfieri, the Italian ambassador, but we have no hint as yet as to Italy's intentions. The first American ambulance driver to be captured by the Germans is Mr. Garibaldi Hill. The German army has offered to release him at once.

Berlin June 1, 1940 14.00

This is Berlin.

The communiqué of the German High Command is out this very minute. Here are its high points:

- The resistance of the last part of the encircled French army in northern France has been broken. At Lille alone, 26,000 prisoners have been taken.
- The attack on the remainder of the British Expeditionary Force on both sides of Dunkirk has made good progress despite stubborn resistance and the difficulties of the terrain.
- Despite difficult weather, the German air force attacked successfully around Dunkirk. Five transports were sunk and three cruisers or destroyers as well as ten transports damaged by bombs.
- A U-boat torpedoed an English warship before Ostende.
- At Cassel, sixty-five English tanks were destroyed. Near Abbeville, an enemy tank attack failed.

The newspapers here, naturally enough, give themselves over this morning to headlines about the great German victory in Flanders. The *Börsen Zeitung Am Mittag*, a paper that comes out here at noon, is typical. Its headline reads: CATASTROPHE BEFORE THE DOORS OF PARIS AND LONDON – FIVE ARMIES CUT OFF AND DESTROYED – ENGLAND'S

EXPEDITIONARY CORPS NO LONGER EXISTS – FRANCE'S FIRST SEVENTH AND NINTH ARMIES ANNIHILATED. Well, those headlines are pretty common here in Berlin today.

Some papers put their emphasis on what is still to come, on the line of yesterday's army communiqué that the mass of the German army which liquidated the Allied forces in Flanders and along the English Channel is now ready for new assignments.

The question is: What will those new assignments be? There appear to be two courses open to the German Command. To strike against England, or to concentrate on the French in an attempt to administer another crushing blow to France, capture Paris, and thus perhaps put France out of the war. As I mentioned last night, most of us amateur strategists here think the latter course will be adopted, that is, that the German juggernaut will next hurl itself against the French who have now dug in along the rivers Somme and Aisne. From Amiens to just north of Reims, the Germans are only some sixty-five to seventy miles from Paris.

General Weygand has now had ten days to strengthen this long line of defense, but Berlin, while recognizing this, seems to be confident that the German armies, flushed by their great victory in Flanders, can crack this too and eventually break through to Paris.

More and more, you begin to realize over here what a price England and France are paying for having neglected their air forces, and what an advantage Germany gained by not neglecting hers.

In three days at the front last week, I myself did not see a single Allied plane during the day, which is the best time to do accurate bombing. Only at night did the British bombers come over. I, of course, did not see the whole front, and I don't mean to say that in other sectors the Allied air force may not have bombed German communications. But certainly, it was not on a scale comparable to the German bombings.

In the last few days, I've talked to other neutral observers back from the French and British fronts and they all tell the same story of the terrible havoc wrought by the German Stuka bombers and of how few Allied planes they saw in action.

Press attacks on France continue. Said a German radio commentator: "There can be no peace in Europe until the Negro-ized and Jew-ized people of the plutocrat Reynaud are taught with a sharp sword that no crime goes unpunished." Many more statements along this line are appearing here in Berlin.

Berlin June 1, 1940 24.46

This is Berlin.

For a change, here's a piece of news about the war on sea. German military circles told us tonight they could confirm a report, apparently coming from abroad, that the battleship *Nelson*, flagship of the British Home Fleet, has been sunk.

According to the Germans, 700 out of a crew of 1,350 went down with the ship.

The same source did not state whether the ship was supposed to have been torpedoed or bombed. Unofficial sources hinted that Stuka dive-bombers had sunk the great battleship.

Germans were given the news at 10 p.m., when a news announcer merely quoted the Associated Press in New York as having reported the *Nelson* sunk.

German listeners are getting so used to long strings of German victories that I doubt if the news caused much of a sensation in most German households tonight. As a matter of fact, the announcer devoted but one short sentence to it, and then passed on to other victories.

The latest one was given out by the German High Command in a special war communiqué late this evening. It said: "The rest of the defeated British Expeditionary Force tried today to escape on small craft of all kinds to the transports and warships lying offshore near Dunkirk. The German air force frustrated this attempt through continuous attacks, especially with Junkers dive-bombers, on the British ships. According to the reports received so far, three warships and eight transports totaling 40,000 tons were sunk, and four warships and fourteen transports set on fire and damaged. Forty English fighter-planes protecting the ships were shot down. The attack is still going on, so that further successes may be reckoned." No mention of the German air losses.

As to the Flanders battle, the German communiqué declared that the resistance of the last French troops in northern France had been broken. As to the British still fighting around Dunkirk, the German Command said they were still offering a stubborn resistance, but despite this and the flooded terrain, the German attack was making progress. German army circles do not hide their admiration for the dogged defense which the British have put up in covering the evacuation of what is left of their expeditionary force. It is more than a week now since the Germans, swinging up the coast, took Calais and Gravelines, the latter only twelve miles from Dunkirk. A mere twelve miles have previously been nothing to this fast-moving army on wheels. Dunkirk has been the only exception.

The High Command communiqué mentioned today a French attack

307

on the southern front at Abbeville, led by tanks. The communiqué claimed that not only was it repulsed, but that a German counter-attack even resulted in the net gain of some ground. Curious thing. Military circles here state that in this tank attack, the French used no infantry, only tanks. That's difficult to figure out.

Herr Hitler today decreed the release of captured Dutch troops. Half of them will be freed immediately, and his decree stipulates that the first to return to their homes are farm laborers and workers in the mines and in the foodstuff industries. Dutch industry and agriculture, now cut off by the British blockade, is as rapidly as possible being drawn into the German economic picture. The Führer's decree also stipulated that individuals responsible for the arrest of German parachutists in Holland, or for their having been handed over to the British, will be made to answer for these deeds.

Interest in what Italy may do is increasing here.

Berlin June 2, 1940 15.01

This is Berlin.

Those British Tommies at Dunkirk are still fighting against the advancing German steamroller like bulldogs.

The German High Command is our authority for this in its daily communiqué which has just been given out in Berlin. Here is its account of yesterday's operations:

"In hard fighting, the strip of coast on both sides of Dunkirk, which yesterday also was stubbornly defended by the British, was further narrowed. Nieuport and the coast to the north-east are in German hands. Adinkerke, west of Furnes, and Ghyvelde, six and quarter miles east of Dunkirk, have been taken." Six and a quarter miles. That's getting very close. On the southern front, adds the German communiqué, there was nothing special to report.

But again, in the air, the great German air armada continued all day yesterday, the communiqué declares, to harass the British in their attempt to evacuate the British Expeditionary Force . It makes grim reading.

"Altogether, four warships and eleven transports with a total tonnage of 54,000 tons were sunk by our bombers. Fourteen warships, including two cruisers, two light cruisers, an anti-aircraft cruiser, 6 destroyers and two torpedo boats, as well as thirty-eight transports with a total tonnage of 160,000 were damaged by bombs. Numberless small boats, tugs, rafts were capsized and troop concentrations along the beach successfully attacked with bombs."

the 1938 *Anschluss,* Jews are forced to scrub the sidewalk in Vienna. Denied access to a
mitter in Austria, Shirer had to fly to London to broadcast his account of the Nazi takeover.

e Minister Neville Chamberlain on his return from Munich waving the document that he
ed would bring "peace in our time".

Sudeten German women and children greet Wehrmacht soldiers as they enter Czechoslovakia, October 1938. "A very peaceful occupation," Shirer wrote. "The whole thing went off like a parade."

Left: Citizens of Prague look on in dismay as motorized German troops enter their city on March 15, 1939.

Below: German troops march into Prague.

Josef Stalin and German Foreign Minister Ribbentrop look on as Soviet Foreign Commissar Molotov signs the German-Soviet non-aggression pact in Moscow, August 23, 1939. "For the German people," wrote Shirer, "the dreaded nightmare of encirclement had been destroyed."

Masked against anticipated poison-gas bombs, schoolchildren and teachers in Potsdam assemble for the first day of the school year in late August, 1939.

Above: September 1, 1939. Hitler informs the Reichstag that the "counter-attack" on Poland has begun.

Left: German infantry and tanks in Warsaw, late September, 1939.

Above: Sunken British ships and destroyed vehicles at Dunkirk, June 1940.

German 3.7 cm anti-tank gun outside La Gare de l'Est, one of the principal stations in Paris, June 14, 1940.

Right: German troops parade past the Arc de Triomphe in Paris at the height of the victory para in the French capital, June 14, 1940.

Reviewing the text of a broadcast with a censor shortly before going on the air. The steadily tightening censorship prompted Shirer to leave Germany at the end of 1940.

The communiqué adds that a speed-boat sank a 4,000-ton transport loaded with troops.

I have a little more time than usual this morning, and I'd like to take a few minutes off from the spot news which has occupied most of our time lately and look into a few things for which there has been little or no time previously.

In three weeks, Hitler's steamroller army has overrun Holland, Belgium, and northern France, pushed past the western extension of the Maginot Line on a front 200 miles wide, and liquidated three of France's best armies and most of the British Expeditionary Corps.

How do Germans at home feel about the tremendous victory?

It's manifestly impossible for one observer to ascertain how millions of people feel about anything. But you do get a rough idea, I think, living here. As a whole, the German people, I think you can say, are feeling pretty elated at the victory. For one thing, they believe they cannot now lose the war – hence the nightmare of another defeat, which their leaders have told them would be worse than Versailles, is removed. That makes them feel good. They also believe that the decisive battle has been won and that the war will certainly be over by the end of the summer. That also makes them feel good. Many Germans I've talked with have an idea that a sort of united Europe – under German leadership, to be sure – will come out of the war, and that will be a good thing. They say it will ensure a long period of peace and probably of prosperity.

Another thing, many Germans who've complained at the deprivations they've been subject to since Hitler really went to work to forge his army five years ago – the lack of butter, fruit, coffee, coal – to mention a few of the shortages – now feel, after the victories of the last three weeks, that it was not in vain. A typical remark you hear in Berlin is: "Perhaps the English and French now wish they'd had less butter and more cannon."

As to the invasion of Holland and Belgium, most Germans you meet believe the justification given by the government and the army – namely, that the Allies would have attacked Germany through Belgium and Holland if the Germans hadn't beaten them to it. Thus the German move is always referred to in the press as the "counter-thrust". Exactly the same explanation was given for the Norwegian campaign and, I think, accepted by the great majority of people. One must remember that when Germany went into Poland last September, the official communiqués described it as a "counter-attack".

One of the most amazing phenomena of this war has been the city of Berlin, from which I'm speaking. Even since the decisive offensive, which Herr Hitler said would decide the course of history for the next thousand years, began, Berlin has remained fundamentally unchanged. If you didn't read the newspapers or listen to the radio, you'd hardly know that a great and terrible war was being fought a few hundred miles away. The population appears to go about its business just as before. Last evening just before dark, I strolled down Berlin's main street, the Kurfürstendamm. It was jammed with people, strolling along pleasantly. The great sidewalk cafés on this avenue were filled with thousands, chatting quietly over their *ersatz* coffee or their ice-cream. Most of the women you saw were smartly dressed.

Life goes on here so peacefully. Every theatre in town is open and playing to packed houses. Today, being Sunday, you could observe tens of thousands of people, mostly in family groups, going out to the woods or the lakes which line the outskirts of the capital. The Tiergarten – Berlin's Central Park, where I took my walk this morning – was filled with folk. They all had that sort of lazy, idle, happy-go-lucky Sunday-morning feeling.

One reason for this state, I think, is that the war has not been brought home to the people of the capital. They read about it, or on the radio even hear the pounding of the big guns. But that's all. Paris or London may feel in danger. Berlin doesn't. The last air-raid I can recall here was early last September. And then nothing happened.

Berlin June 2, 1940 01.01

This is Berlin.

Most of the war news we have here today is about the fighting in the air.

In the last twenty-four hours, according to the German High Command, Göring's air force has made two big attacks, one on British warships and transports trying to evacuate the British army from Dunkirk, the other – and this indicates a new turn in the war – on Marseilles and the railroad line from there to the great French industrial town of Lyons.

Though the German radio tonight called what the British are doing at Dunkirk a "cowardly flight", a German war correspondent in the *Völkischer Beobachter*, describing the battle for Nieuport, says the British there fought doggedly over every inch of ground.

The unit opposite his troops was, he says, the South Lancashire Regiment. "We must admit," he writes, "that our enemy has been fighting with unusual stubbornness against our hard-hitting infantry." This man is also the first German correspondent I've read to report strong action by the British air force. As I've mentioned before, we correspondents who were at the front in Belgium, never saw an Allied plane over the front. But, reports this correspondent from near Dunkirk, "The activity of the

310

enemy in the air has been very lively. One minute it's enemy planes; the next minute, our own. British fighters attack our observer posts, but miss. We keep experiencing a fluctuating fight in the air." That's how one German correspondent saw the fighting around Dunkirk.

The bombing of Marseilles stirs interest in the big question over here as to Italy's demands in the Mediterranean. An Italian military mission – as well as a Spanish – has arrived here and is to be taken to the front to see what the Germans did in Belgium and France. Day before yesterday, the Italian Ambassador in Berlin journeyed to the Führer's headquarters and conferred with him. One gets the feeling that Italy is about to make up her mind.

The radio tonight broadcast an appeal to the Youth of Germany to join the air force. Pilots, radio operators, gunners, and parachutists – the young men were told they could take their choice of callings. Addresses of the nearest recruiting stations were given. Those who join the air force, it was stated, would be excused from having to do a year in the Labor Service.

Poland was in the news here tonight. A German court at Posen sentenced nine Poles to death. They were accused of murder. Said the German radio in giving the news, "The black and white sadists of France will also get this hard but just punishment for their treatment of harmless German prisoners."

Berlin June 4, 1940 24.46

This is Berlin.

The great battle of Flanders and Artois is over.

After a last embittered struggle, the German army today entered Dunkirk and the remaining Allied troops – about 40,000 – surrendered. A short communiqué from the German High Command gave the news to the public tonight. It said:

"The Fortress of Dunkirk has been taken after a hard fight. 40,000 prisoners and booty that cannot yet be estimated is in our hands. The entire Belgian and French Channel coast extending to the mouth of the Somme has thereby been completely occupied by German troops."

And then – just about an hour ago – the High Command gave out a résumé of the great battle which it said would go down in history as the greatest Battle of Destruction of all time.

This account traces the course of the campaign leading up to the encircling of the Allied armies in Flanders and Artois and then the final victory.

These are some of the figures given by the German Command. German losses – and I understand this means for the whole fighting since the offensive began – German losses: Dead: 10,252 men. Missing: 8,467 men. Wounded: 42,523 men. Note that the number of dead is the same as in the Polish campaign of the same length. The number of wounded and missing is somewhat higher, though not much.

German losses in airplanes are given as 432. The German navy states it did not lose a ship of any kind.

Allied prisoners, including Dutch and Belgian, are given as 1,200,000. Allied dead have not yet been estimated, says the communiqué. The arms and supplies from seventy-five to eighty divisions have been captured, it adds. It also lists numerous warships it claims the Allies lost, including five cruisers sunk and ten damaged.

The communiqué closes with this sentence: "As the enemy still declines peace, he will get a fight until he's destroyed."

All day long today the Berlin newspapers have played up the story of what happened in Paris yesterday. A typical headline is that of the *Nachtausgabe*: OUR FLYERS ACHIEVE A NEW TRIUMPH – BOMBS ON PARIS AIRBASES – 300-400 AIRPLANES DESTROYED ON THE GROUND.

The German press informs its readers that only military objectives were bombed. The *Börsen Zeitung* tells us that the French themselves admit that the German flyers endeavored to hit only military objects. "Whether they hit them," it adds, "is another question."

There is no mention in the German press of any civilians having been killed in the Paris raid.

But while the emphasis naturally is on the point that the Germans went after only the numerous airfields in and around Paris, the German press and radio cite American opinion in an endeavor to prove that the city of Paris itself is a fair object for German bombs because it is not an open city and it is not undefended.

Thus the semi-official news agency *Dienst Aus Deutschland* says: "It's recognized in American quarters that Paris is not an open city and that even France does not regard it as an undefended city . . . Of the legality of the German attack in the meaning of international law, there is therefore no doubt."

Ambassador Bullitt – often bitterly attacked personally as an arch-enemy of the Third Reich – receives some more salvoes from the German press and radio for his report on the bombing yesterday.

Thus the German radio tonight said that yesterday's bombing gave Mr. Bullitt "the opportunity of making himself the center of a laughable and transparent sensation". It then charges that Mr. Bullitt's various communications to Washington on the bombing were conflicting.

Actually, the French have not taken revenge for what happened to

Paris – yet. They didn't come over here last night. And no sign of them yet tonight, and it's nearly 1 a.m. here. Thus far it has been a very quiet evening.

Berlin June 5, 1940 24.47

This is Berlin.

Church bells have been ringing and millions of flags flying throughout Germany today.

But hardly were the Swastika banners hoisted, on the orders of Herr Hitler, to celebrate what he, himself, considers to be the greatest military victory of all time – the one that ended in the ruins of Dunkirk yesterday – when the German people were given word that a new offensive on the Western Front has started.

Hitler himself gave the public the first inkling of it this morning in the same proclamation to the people which ordered them to fly their flags and ring their bells. He ended his proclamation with these words: "This morning German divisions have renewed the battle for the freedom and future of our people."

Sometime after noon, the German High Command announced the beginning of the new offensive, which carries the war into its second decisive phase, in these laconic words: "Early this morning, new offensive operations began on the defensive front in France." That was all. And all day long, we had no news as to where the German army had struck – and with what success.

Three hours ago, the German radio issued the first army communiqué on the progress of the new offensive. It said: "Our army this morning began an attack against the army of France on a wide front. The crossing of the Somme between its mouth and Ham and over the Oise-Aisne Canal was forced and the so-called Weygand Line, which was in process of construction on the other side, fell at many points."

The German blow today then has fallen on the Allied left wing, extending from the sea near Abbeville to Soissons, some sixty miles north-east of Paris. In other words, the thrust was made by the German right wing, and thus some neutral military observers profess to see the Germans reverting to the old Schlieffen Plan, which to the surprise of the French Command they dropped in the attack two weeks ago, in favor of a breakthrough in the center at Maubeuge.

If the Germans follow a revised Schlieffen Plan now, it would appear that their right wing, pivoting on Soissons, intends to swing down in a wide circle, envelop Paris from the north-west and then continue

313

eastward in an attempt to take the old Maginot Line from behind. But we all were fooled the last time on German strategy, and I'm not going to say any more.

The press here tonight indicates that what the Germans are after now is a "Total Victory". It cites a sentence in the High Command résumé of the Flanders victory which said that the fight would continue until the complete destruction of the enemy. "That," comments the *Lokal Anzeiger*, "is no empty word."

Field Marshal Göring issued an Order of the Day to his flyers today. He said: "Now is the time to tighten your helmets and stand ready. The terrible blow that has struck our opponent makes him ripe for the plunge into his heart. We in the air force are the point of the German sword which will make this plunge and win the victory."

Berlin June 6, 1940 24.46

This is Berlin.

For the first time since the big German drive started four weeks ago tomorrow, the daily communiqué of the High Command on the progress of operations came out much later than usual today.

It was too late to catch even the late editions of the evening papers and will not appear in the German press until tomorrow morning.

As a matter of fact, it was very brief about the big offensive which started yesterday on the Somme. It said merely that "the operations begun yesterday in France continue according to plan and our troops have gained ground everywhere towards the south-west."

You will remember that yesterday the German Command reported that in the first day of the new push, the so-called Weygand Line, just south of the Somme, had been broken through at several places. How deep it was broken through, and just where, was not divulged.

Again according to the High Command, Göring's great air force was active yesterday. Besides operating with the main army in bombing and strafing Allied troops along the Somme, the German flyers, we're told, also bombed airbases in central France. And last night, it's added, they struck at British landing fields in east and south-east England.

It's from these bases that the British air force, the Germans say, is operating in the present Somme battle and it's also from these landing fields, the Germans add, that the night attacks on Western Germany are carried out.

These night attacks continue. They even seem to have increased recently. The places they attack in Germany are rarely mentioned, but today the High Command does state that two British planes were shot down last night by so-called "night chasers", over Hamburg. We're just beginning to hear about these night chasers. Formerly, the defense of the German cities at night was left largely to anti-aircraft, but lately we've heard of the night fighters going up. There's no moonlight now, so apparently they work in cooperation with ground searchlights. German military circles explain the few planes they've brought down so far as being due to the fact that the Allies come over at night with one plane at a time, hitting here and there, but never in force at one time.

One German correspondent on the Somme writes about the French colored troops encountered yesterday. Obviously, he doesn't like them – one reason is because he says they fight back with long, curved knives. Still, against flame-throwers and tanks and machine-guns, what chance has a fellow got with a long curved knife?

Berlin June 7, 1940 24.46

This is Berlin.

News is very sparse here this evening about the progress of the German offensive on the Somme.

We have only the daily communiqué of the German High Command issued early this afternoon which stated flatly that the so-called Weygand Line south of the River Somme and the Aisne-Oise Canal had been broken through by the German army on the entire front. The German Command added that the offensive was proceeding successfully, and according to plan.

Not a single place name is given. Nor any other hint which would give us a clearer picture of just what is taking place.

Not since Hitler's great offensive in the west began just four weeks ago, has there been such reserve in military quarters, so little news about how the military operations are going.

One misses those special communiqués which have brought excitement into the lives of the people at home on almost every evening since the big push began. I don't think I've ever mentioned how they were given on the radio. They received, invariably, what we at home would call a "build-up". They weren't just read as such in a program break. Instead, after a moment of silence, you would suddenly hear on your radio a loud fanfare of trumpets. After a few days, we came to know that that meant a special war communiqué, perhaps news of a decisive break in the battle. Listeners got in the habit of tuning their ears for the trumpets. When they heard the fanfare they dropped everything and gathered around the radio. After the trumpets had ceased, the announcer read slowly the special war

315

communiqué. And then, as part of the build-up, a band would strike up the war's most popular song, *Marching on England*, a catchy tune. When the band finished, a chorus struck up. Recently, another popular war song about France was added. The communiqué might take only thirty seconds to read, but the whole presentation took several minutes. I think, with the majority of Germans, it was very effective.

We had them almost every night during the past month, but we've had none since the new offensive started.

The German newspapers themselves comment on the lack of news about the big battle. The *Lokal Anzeiger* remarks: "We must maintain a reserve. The new operations have only begun." And the more official *Völkischer Beobachter* notices that the High Command mentions no place names in its communiqué and concludes that this shows the very importance of the operations now in progress.

Most German editors also point out tonight that the French had always calculated on having a British army of at least thirty divisions for its left flank. And that in this battle, the French, with the British Expeditionary Force driven off the continent, are fighting alone.

Germans, too, are going in for night bombardments. It's stated in Berlin this evening that last night German planes bombed a number of airfields in east and central France, as well as in England. Cherbourg, it's said, was also bombed. Fires and explosions were caused, it's added, on the docks. Probably, the Germans suspect that Cherbourg is now the chief port for British supplies and men reaching France.

Berlin June 8, 1940 24.46

This is Berlin.

Don't expect any startling news from me tonight about the Battle of the Somme. The German High Command simply isn't putting out any. And we get our news here from the High Command.

This great and decisive battle has now been going on for four days. The High Command's daily communiqués are always a day late, so they cover only the first three days of the new offensive. This is what we have been told so far:

First day – the Germans crossed the Somme River. Second day – the Germans broke through the so-called Weygand Line south of the Somme and south-west of the Oise-Aisne Canal all along the front. Third day – that is, the report we got today – I'll just read it: "Our operations south of the Somme and the Oise-Aisne Canal continue successfully. Also south of the lower Somme, the enemy has been pressed back."

316

And that's all. As a matter of fact, things have come to such a pretty pass that the German press has taken today to citing Allied reports about the battle. And the Berlin radio tonight, in commenting on the offensive, explained that the High Command communiqué is always laconic and short when great military operations whose end cannot yet be foreseen are in progress.

And the *Deutsche Allgemeine Zeitung* tells us this evening that the present battle is in many respects different than the one in Flanders. "Admittedly," it says, "the German successes here cannot be measured in so much gained ground, as in Flanders."

When you stop to think of it, none of those great fortified lines in Belgium or northern France held out anything like four days.

The German military experts, writing in the Berlin newspapers, also show great reserve. The main point they make today is that now the Weygand defenses south of the Somme have been captured, warfare of open movement – so dear to the Germans – has been made possible.

The German correspondents at the front continue to write a lot about the French colonial colored troops. One reporter telegraphs today that in this Somme battle, these colored soldiers have been fighting with unbelievable tenacity. The French, he reports, leave detachments of these men behind, hidden in cellars and woods, and that they then attack the German forces from behind. "Our men," he comments, "are filled with rage at these attacks from behind."

Since the big offensive started, the Führer has decorated quite a few officers and men for extraordinary bravery with the Knight's Cross of the Iron Cross. Tonight, he announced a new decoration to be given to those who've already received the Knight's Cross of the Iron Cross. It's to be called the Oak Leaves of the Knight's Cross of the Iron Cross.

The German press reports renewed interest here in the learning of foreign languages, especially English and French. One news agency reports the opening of 350 courses in English and French in Berlin alone and comments that many people here are convinced that the evolution of the war offers new possibilities to persons with a knowledge of these languages.

More American mail arrived in Berlin today. In mine was a Christmas card. It was postmarked in New Orleans December 7th.

Berlin June 9, 1940 01.01

This is Berlin.

The German High Command finally broke its silence about the

317

progress of the second great offensive of this war. For four days, you will remember, we had practically no news here of how the attack was going. And even among some Germans, I gather from the press comment tonight, there were those who thought that no news must mean bad news.

Then . . . at 2 p.m. this afternoon, the German Command lifted the veil of secrecy – or rather tore it off.

In its regular daily communiqué, it informed the German people that the attempt of the French to halt the German attack at any price had failed, that a strong enemy had been beaten and forced to retreat, that on the western flank the German steamroller was driving towards the Seine River, and that further to the east, on both sides of Soissons, it had forced a crossing of the River Aisne.

And as if that weren't enough, that a new offensive on a further part of the front had been launched at dawn this morning.

It then capped the report by divulging that Germany's only two battleships, the *Gneisenau* and the *Scharnhorst*, had gone to the relief of Narvik and that they had started off their operations in this neighborhood by sinking the British aircraft-carrier *Glorious*, of 22,500 tons, and a British destroyer.

The German navy, it was concluded here, had once more pulled a surprise move on the much more powerful British fleet. How two such large ships could slip all the way up to Narvik unobserved by the British fleet somewhat puzzled neutral observers here, already puzzled, as are we all, by the rapidity and extent of recent events all around us.

But Narvik, which once seemed so important, can only be a side-show. Interest here is concentrated on the West where the battle for France goes into its decisive stage on a scale never before imagined except in the minds of a handful of generals on the German General Staff. The battle, which appeared to be reaching its climax on a 200-mile front from the sea to the Argonne today, from all accounts puts the greatest of the World War battles far into the shade. Certainly, no offensive in the last war took place on a 200-mile front.

Now, the German Command, while fairly enlightening on the progress of the offensive, is still reserved. Note that it announces a new drive on, quote, "a further part of the front," but neglects to say where. Undoubtedly, this is the one referred to in the French communiqué today, to the east of Soissons in the neighborhood of Rethel.

Thus from the German communiqué, it is clear that at the moment there are three distinct German drives. One on the German right flank towards the lower Seine River. In this sector, the High Command speaks of the rear French lines of defense having been broken through and vast supplies captured. This would seem to refer to the tank detachments mentioned by the other side as having broken through to Forges-les-

Eaux, about half way between the Somme and the Seine on the road to Rouen. One German newspaper thinks the object of this drive is to take Rouen and Le Havre, and thus shut off Paris from one more port connecting it with England.

The same paper suggests that the drive in the neighborhood of Soissons has as its goal Paris itself. Soissons is only fifty-five miles from Paris. The German communiqué today said that German troops had forced their way across the Aisne River on both sides of Soissons.

The third German drive further east would seem to have as its purpose the breaking into the old Maginot Line from behind. That is, the German troops now driving south, if successful, would turn eastward right into the rear of the Maginot defenses. To do this, however, they would have to get past Verdun and Metz.

The Germans give us no figures on the number of troops or tanks being employed in this gigantic battle. But the High Command does emphasize the close cooperation between the infantry, the armored divisions and the air force.

In the meantime, neutral diplomatic circles here wonder if this will be the week when Italy will make its decision.

Berlin itself still strikes you as being as far removed as possible from this decisive battle before Paris. It's really a curious phenomenon. Today being Sunday and warm and bright, everyone left in Berlin seemed to be out in the woods or along the lakes that dot the outskirts. The atmosphere was so peaceful and calm. The bathing beach at Wannsee jammed with thousands. Hundreds of sailboats and canoes on the Havel. Families picnicking under the trees.

And so far not even an air-alarm here, despite certain reports recently.

Berlin June 10, 1940 24.46

This is Berlin.

At 6 o'clock this evening, our time, just as people here were tuning in on their radios to hear the latest news of the German army's onslaught on Paris, the German announcer said: "In one hour the Duce will address the Italian people and the world. All German stations will broadcast his speech."

An hour later, they did – with a German radio commentator conveniently on hand at the Piazza Venezia to describe the tumult. Thus Germany learned of Mussolini's decision to enter the war.

Berlin, as a whole, took the news calmly, as indeed it has the whole war so far. Most of the people I've talked to here this evening – waiters, policemen, businessmen – take the view that Italy's entrance into the war will only hasten the coming of peace. And, of course, a victorious peace for their side.

If the streets of Berlin remained as quiet as usual, there was one exception. Before the Italian Embassy in a little street that runs off the Tiergarten, two or three thousand Italian fascists, residents of Berlin, and a sprinkling of Nazis, staged a demonstration that was, I suppose, a minor replica of the scenes in the Piazza Venezia at Rome. They shouted themselves hoarse and cheered the Duce and the Führer.

In this demonstration, the German Foreign Minister, Herr von Ribbentrop, took part. He had hurried back from the Führer's headquarters at the front, arriving here at noon, by which time the Wilhelmstrasse obviously knew of what was to happen.

At the Italian Embassy, Herr von Ribbentrop stood on the balcony with the new Italian Ambassador, Signor Alfieri. Both acknowledged the cheers of the crowd, and both made short speeches. Said Herr von Ribbentrop: "Germany and Italy will fight together and will not lay down arms until the common enemy has been struck down."

Before he went to this little German-Italian demonstration, the German Foreign Minister convoked us to the Wilhelmstrasse where he read a formal declaration of the German government saying how deeply moved the government and the German people were at the decision just announced by the Duce.

Hardly had Mussolini's strident tones in the Piazza Venezia died down, before a lively exchange of telegrams set in between the rulers of the two countries. They were made public immediately.

The King of Italy wired Herr Hitler: "The Almighty has willed that against our own intentions we have been forced to defend the freedom and future of our people in battle against England and France." The Führer replied, sending the King his heartiest greetings and expressing his conviction that the two allies would win the war. Mussolini also wired the Führer who replied that the "World historical decision" had touched him deeply and that the fascist and Nazi revolutions would henceforth stride forward together.

Berlin June 11, 1940 04.30

This is Berlin.

Berlin, on the whole, has taken Italy's entry into the war very calmly.

Military circles in Berlin are extremely reserved tonight as to the military aspects of Italy joining the war, now that the German army is almost at the gates of Paris and appears to be doing pretty well alone. We tried to budge some sort of information out of them tonight as to just where Italy will attack, but German military men can be exasperatingly mum. They were tonight.

We know of course that Italian military missions have been here since the war began last September, and a new one arrived only a fortnight ago. Presumably, the general staffs of the two countries have worked out their plans. But we'll have to wait a few days to see what they are. Neutral observers here were surprised that Mussolini excepted Egypt from his field of operation, as they thought Egypt would be one of the first countries involved.

In the meantime, the German onslaught on Paris continues. The High Command said today that its armies were now driving towards the Seine and the Marne and that all operations were proceeding as planned – and as expected. At some points, the German claimed, the battle had turned into a rout. "Great victories have already been won; greater are developing," was the way today's war communiqué put it.

Military circles told us tonight that the German army at some point had advanced fifty-six miles, that strong armored detachments and mobile units had reached the Seine north-west of Paris, thus cutting off the French capital from the all-important port of Le Havre. And that further east, the armies which yesterday crossed the Aisne on both sides of Soissons were now nearing the Marne, where the Germans were stopped in 1914 and 1918.

President Roosevelt's speech was heard perfectly here at 1.15 in the morning, our time. It's too early for official reaction, but the first unofficial reaction I heard was that, from the German standpoint, it certainly wasn't any stronger than expected.

The prevailing opinion in Germany seems to be that the war will be won before American help for the Allies can become effective.

Berlin June 11-12, 1940 24.46

This is Berlin.

There's no news in Germany so far of any Italian military action since Italy entered the war against the Allies some twenty-five hours ago. No Italian war communiqués have been published in Berlin yet.

The Berlin press headlines other news from Italy. King Victor Emmanuel's proclamation to the armed forces; his appointment of Mussolini as commander-in-chief; the Duce's Order of the Day; and so on. And the *Völkischer Beobachter* publishes an editorial entitled "Italy's Genius".

Anyway, German interest today has gone back to the great battle in France. For responsible quarters here scarcely hide their conviction that on the outcome of this decisive battle hangs the fate of France, if not of the Allied cause.

However that may be, today's communiqué of the German High Command gives the definite impression that the tide of the battle has turned – in Germany's favor. It's true that the communiqué starts out by saying that the great battle between the coast and the Meuse River is still in full swing. But it adds: "On our right flank and in the middle the pursuit of the beaten French armies is being restlessly pursued."

Further east, the German Command admits, it's a bit different. Between Reims and the Argonne, it says, the fighting is still bitter but going successfully.

But then it makes two points. It says that at several points, enemy forces have been split up and surrounded and are going to their destruction, as it put it. Secondly, the German Command states that – and I'll just quote here – "as the result of heavy, bloody losses and also the great loss in prisoners and material, enemy resistance is visibly shrinking."

Now from military quarters in Berlin, I'm given some additional information about the situation before Paris, as they see it.

For one thing, they tell me that the Germans have now advanced to within thirty-eight miles of Paris, both north-west and north-east of the capital. The German right wing is on the north-west, the center on the north-east.

Moreover, these same German military quarters went so far as to say tonight that two entire French armies between the coast and the Champagne district – that would be somewhere near Reims – have been smashed. They use the German word *zerschlagen*, which means "smashed" or "broken-up."

In other words, the Germans think that their right wing on the western flank, which was very strong, has pretty well won the day already. Also military circles here were dead certain tonight that those French forces which the High Command mentioned today as having been split up and surrounded, were certain now to be destroyed within the next few days.

The Germans cite as a proof of their claims the reports that the government departments and most of the diplomats have left Paris. Indeed the German press tells its readers tonight that the French government, with M. Reynaud at its head, has fled from Paris. They brand as a lie the dispatch that the French premier has gone to the front.

Well now, the Germans are now getting roughly about as near to Paris as they did on September 1, 1914. This led military circles to point out to us today that really the German position is much better than it was then.

First, because their right wing is stronger and has maintained its advance *west* of Paris, whereas in 1914 it wheeled *east* of Paris. Secondly, that there is no real British army to help the French. Thirdly, that there is no Eastern Front, so that, unlike 1914, the entire German army can now be hurled against Paris.

President Roosevelt's speech yesterday is not reported in the German press or on the German radio. It was, of course, reported to the Wilhelmstrasse, and the semi-official reaction is that the President's promise of speedy delivery of supplies to the Allies has not surprised Berlin. As I said last night, Berlin still thinks American help will come too late.

Berlin June 12, 1940 24.47

This is Berlin.

The news from the front tonight is that the Germans are now only twelve and a half miles from Paris, or – as the military quarters put it here tonight – within artillery range. This is closer than they got in 1914. For the first time since 1870, a German army is literally at the gates of Paris.

The nearest point to Paris reached by the Germans, they say, is on the Oise River, north-west of the city. North of the capital, the Germans report they are on both sides of Senlis, and have reached here the first defenses of Paris itself. Further east, they are at the Marne.

You have to remember that the German High Command reports the situation as it was yesterday. Where its army is tonight we won't know till tomorrow.

Well, further east still, where the Germans have admittedly been having a harder time of it, they announce that Reims has been taken and the River Suippe crossed. While the fighting around Paris appeals more to our imagination, watch this front to the east of Reims. For here the German objective obviously is to take the Maginot Line, protecting France on the north-east, from behind.

On the west flank, the High Command said today that Rouen had been occupied some days ago, and that the Seine had now been crossed at several places. Incidentally, the German Command in announcing the capture of Compiègne added that this was the scene of the shameful armistice dictated in 1918.

A special war communiqué issued this evening announces that an entrapped French army near St. Valéry surrendered. One French corps commander, four French generals, an English general and 20,000 men were captured.

Berlin June 13, 1940 24.46

This is Berlin.

Though the German High Command in its war communiqué today did not mention the fighting around Paris, it became evident this evening that the German army is at the gates of the French capital.

In Berlin tonight, the question was being asked: What will happen to Paris, Europe's most beautiful city?

In well-informed German quarters here tonight, the answer was this: What happens to Paris depends upon the French themselves.

A German news service called the *Dienst Aus Deutschland*, which is usually very close to the German Foreign Office, attempts to render this answer a little less ambiguous. It explains that the fate of Paris depends upon whether the capital, considered as a part of the French front line, defends itself or not.

This would seem to mean that for Paris to escape bombardment, it must be eliminated as part of the French line of defense stretching across France. That is, the French army must retire south of the city so that it cannot be used either as a front or as a base for the moving of troops.

You'll remember that the Germans last month threatened to bomb Brussels on the charge that the Belgians were transporting troops through it.

Some quarters here tonight thought that the Germans would demand simply the unconditional surrender of the city – or else. The news from Washington that Ambassador Bullitt has taken steps to notify the Germans that Paris is an open city has not been published here. Indeed, we could not definitely establish up to midnight, our time, that is, an hour ago, whether the information had been delivered to the German government.

I just learned this minute that the Germans will recognize Paris as an open city.

The most important news in the official communiqué of the German High Command today was that Châlons-sur-Marne had been captured. I mentioned last night that though our interest is bound to be concentrated on the fate of Paris, we should watch this front to the east. For here, according to all accounts, the fighting has been most bitter of all. Why? Because the Germans in this sector threaten the Maginot Line which still protects the Franco-German frontier – and threaten it from behind.

Judging by the German war communiqués, something of a break-through has occurred in this Champagne sector where, incidentally, many American doughboys fought in 1918. Yesterday the Germans announced the taking of Reims. But today they say they are in Châlons, twenty-five miles to the south-east, a big jump for a day, if it was made in a day.

Further east still, between the Argonne – a place that also will not be forgotten by those who fought in the American Expeditionary Force – and the Meuse, the High Command declares that German attacks have won some ground, though how much is not stated. If they win very much in this sector, they will soon come upon Verdun, whose forts have been modernized since its great stand in the last war.

It is quite natural that names like Verdun and the Marne arouse bad memories amongst the Germans, and I note the banner headline in tonight's *Lokal Anzeiger* stresses that the German army has pushed *beyond* the Marne, which the High Command says has been crossed at several places. Total prisoners taken in this second battle number 100,000, the Germans announced today.

Dr. Goebbels addressed German women here tonight. He said: "German politics are at the moment being made by the German sword. To talk politics now is superfluous."

Berlin June 14, 1940 24.46

This is Berlin.

We heard the church bells ringing again today – ringing the tidings of the entry of German troops into Paris.

And tonight the Swastika flag of Adolf Hitler's Third Reich flutters from the Eiffel Tower there by the Seine in that Paris which so many of us knew, or hoped to know, or see before we died.

Grey-clad German troops tread the streets there, the Champs Elysées, the Grand Boulevard, the Avenue de l'Opéra, the Place de la Concorde – the same soldiers who just five weeks ago today struck over the borders of Holland, Belgium and Luxemburg in the first hours of the greatest offensive the world has ever seen.

They reached their goal early this morning. Berlin says that the last forts guarding Paris fell last evening, leaving the city open to them. The Wilhelmstrasse insisted on the point today that the taking over of the French capital was done by direct negotiations between the German and French military authorities, and it goes at some pains to point out that it was not American mediation which brought it about.

However that may be, a little after noon today loud fanfares blazed out of millions of radio sets in Germany and a voice said an important announcement was about to be made. It came at 1 p.m. It was a war communiqué from the Supreme Command. It said: "The complete collapse of the entire French front from the Channel to the Maginot Line by Montmédy destroyed the original intention of the French leaders to defend the capital of France. Paris, therefore, has been declared an open city. The victorious German troops are just beginning to march into Paris."

I was having lunch in the courtyard of my hotel. Most of the guests crowded around the loud-speaker to hear the news. They returned to their tables with wide smiles on their faces, but there was no undue excitement and everyone resumed eating.

In fact, Berlin took the capture of Paris as phlegmatically as it has taken everything else in this war. Later in the afternoon, I visited a popular bathing beach. It was crowded but I overheard no one discussing the news, and out of 500 people, only three bought an extra.

But it would be wrong to conclude that the taking of Paris has not stirred something very deep in the hearts of most Germans. "Germans Capture Paris!" They are magic words to so many here, and for one thing, they help to wipe out the bitter memories of 1918 which have lain so long – twenty-two years – in the German soul.

The *Völkischer Beobachter* editorially tonight minces no words. Paris, it writes, was a city of frivolity and corruption, of democracy and capitalism and Jews and negroes as well as of French. That Paris, says the *Völkischer Beobachter*, will never rise from its fall. Army circles tonight said that "despite the wrong done the German people from Paris, the German soldiers will avoid all unnecessary destruction and will show the French people by their conduct and discipline a picture of the German army vastly different from that shown by the French army on the Rhine."

The German Command said today that with the capture of Paris, the second phase of the campaign had ended. The third phase, it said, would be the pursuit and final destruction of the enemy.

Simultaneously, it announces that a direct onslaught on the Maginot Line had begun today in the Saar sector. Other high points of Germany's amazing drive were: the capture of Montmédy, corner-stone, according to the Germans, of the Maginot Line; the taking of Le Havre; the storming of Hill number 304, north-east of Verdun; and the reaching of Vitry-le-François, east of the Marne and Paris.

Said military circles here tonight: The French front has collapsed. The French army is in full retreat. The total defeat of France can be expected shortly.

Paris June 17, 1940

Hello CBS. This is Paris.

The Parisians – or at least those two million, out of the five million, who did not flee – are still dazed. They were dazed when the unbelievable happened, when the gray-clad German troops entered their capital last Friday morning.

Today – after two days and nights of driving from Berlin to reach here – I saw them still dazed. But not at the sight of the endless columns of German troops hurtling up the proud Champs Elysées in trucks bound for the front in the south. They're used to that by now – and they've taken it philosophically – and the friendly attitude and correct behavior of the German officers and men so far has helped.

No, today they were dazed at something much more important to them. At the broadcast of Marshal Pétain, their new prime minister – the "Savior of Verdun" – telling them that the French army could no longer hold out, and that he had asked for an armistice from the German conquerors.

They got the news by radio – mostly from loud speaker trucks set up by the Germans in the principal streets and squares of the capital. I stood in a throng of French men and women on the Place de la Concorde when the news first came over. They were almost struck dead. Before us was the Hotel Crillon – where Woodrow Wilson stayed during the Peace Conference when the terms for Germany were being drawn up. Now, it's General Headquarters for the German army. Cars raced up with high officers. Others raced away with other officers – an act performed with that cool efficiency which characterizes the German army. But the people in the square – that square without equal in Europe, where you see from one spot the Madeleine, the Louvre, Notre Dame in the distance, the Chamber of Deputies, the golden dome of the Invalides where Napoleon is buried, then the Eiffel Tower on which floats a Swastika flag and finally the Arc de Triomphe – the people in the square did not see any of these, nor the bustling in front of German headquarters in the Crillon – they looked at the ground, then at each other. And I heard them murmur – "Pétain has offered to surrender! What does it mean?" And no one appeared to have the heart for an anwer.

It was a strange and a sad and tragic Paris that I saw when I entered at noon today after driving down through the ruined cities in Belgium and northern France. For I had lived and worked in the city for many years – in the happy and joyous years that followed the war. I had loved it that way, and I did not know it otherwise. I knew the city of bright shop-windows and thronged streets, and madly driving taxi-cabs and wide shaded avenues and café terraces crowded with the rich and the poor.

But today as we drove in, the shutters on most of the shops were down – and most strange and sad of all – the streets were nearly deserted. A few people, mostly the type who are down and out at any time – in peace or in war – stood idly at the curbs watching phlegmatically the motorized

German army hurl by. I roamed through the residential quarters, where the great middle-class dwell. The shutters on their windows were drawn. I asked the concierges why. "They are gone, monsieur. They fled." This was the invariable answer. This is true of the bulk of the middle-class and the wealthy. They fled – many in great panic.

This evening, Paris is scarcely recognizable. There's a curfew at 9 p.m. – that is, before dark. The civil population, by order of the military authorities, must be indoors by that time. The streets tonight are dark and deserted. The Paris of the gay lights, the laughter and the music – there is none of that left.

It's a fact that, so far, there has been no friction between the German troops and the people of Paris. Actually – so far as one can see – they have started to fraternize. On the squares and boulevards you saw them today trying to chat with one another; the Germans asking directions or information, the Parisians giving it politely. Most of the German troops on the streets act like tourists. It seems funny, but every German soldier carries a camera. You could see them by the thousands today photographing Notre Dame, the Arc de Triomphe, and so on. Thousands of German soldiers went to the tomb of the Unknown Soldier where the flame still burns under the Arc de Triomphe. They bared their heads and stood there gazing.

Two newspapers appeared today, *Le Matin*, a familiar paper in Paris, and *La Victoire* or *The Victory* – certainly an ironical title – but that's what it was called before, and the German military authorities did not seem to mind. *La Victoire* urged Parisians no longer to refer to the Germans as Boches. Its bannerline read: "Days of Pain and Mourning." Its editorial ended: "Vive Paris! Vive la France!" Whatever has happened, and much has happened, the French, you see, are still the French.

Compiègne June 21, 1940

Hello America. Hello NBC. Hello CBS. William C. Kerker and William L. Shirer calling NBC and CBS in New York. Calling NBC and CBS from Compiègne, France.

This is William L. Shirer of CBS and with me is William C. Kerker of NBC who will be speaking to you in a moment in this joint broadcast to CBS and NBC. We've got our microphone at the edge of a little clearing in the Forest of Compiègne, four miles to the north of the town of Compiègne and about forty-five miles north of Paris, where the armistice in 1918 was signed. They're signing another armistice in the same old railroad coach now. Hello CBS. Hello NBC. We hope you're getting us, but since we have no feedback, we can't tell. Anyway, we'll keep modulating for another minute and a half, and then start with our broadcast from Compiègne, France, where they're signing the armistice.

(Repeat) Now 30 seconds of silence, and then we start.

Hello America. Hello NBC. Hello CBS. This is William L. Shirer of CBS, and William C. Kerker of NBC is also here. We're broadcasting to you from a little clearing in the Forest of Compiègne, four miles to the north of the town of Compiègne, itself some forty-five miles north of Paris.

Here a few feet from where we're standing, in the very same old *wagon-lit* railroad coach where the Armistice was signed on that chilly morning at 5 a.m. on November 11, 1918, negotiations for another armistice, the one to end the present war between France and Germany, began at 3:30 p.m., German summer time this afternoon.

What a turning back of the clock, what a reversing of history we've been watching here in this beautiful Compiègne forest this afternoon! What a contrast to that drama of twenty-two years ago! Yes, even in the weather, for we've had one of those lovely, warm June days which you get in this part of France close to Paris at this time of year.

The railroad coach – it was Marshal Foch's private car – stands a few feet away from us here, at exactly the same spot where it stood on that gray morning twenty-two years ago.

Only – and what an "only" it is, too – Adolf Hitler sat in the seat occupied that day by Marshal Foch – Hitler who, at that time, was only an unknown corporal in the German army.

And in the quaint old wartime *wagon-lit* car, another armistice is being drawn up as I speak to you. An armistice, designed, like the other that was signed on this spot, to bring armed hostilities to a halt between the ancient enemies, Germany and France.

Only everything – *everything* that we've been seeing here this afternoon in Compiègne Forest – has been so reversed. The last time, the representatives of France sat in that car dictating the terms of the Armistice. This afternoon, we peered through the windows of the car and saw Adolf Hitler laying down the terms. Thus does history reverse itself, but seldom has it done so as today, on the very same spot.

The German leader, in the preamble of the conditions which were read to the French delegates by Colonel General Keitel, chief of the German Supreme Command, told the French that he had not chosen this spot at Compiègne out of revenge, but merely to right an old wrong.

The armistice negotiations here on the same spot where the last armistice was signed in 1918 – here in Compiègne Forest – began at 3:15 p.m. our time. A warm June sun beat down on the great elm and pine trees, and cast pleasant shadows on the wooded avenues, as Herr Hitler, with the German plenipotentiaries at his side, appeared. He alighted from

329

his car in front of the French monument to Alsace-Lorraine which stands at the end of an avenue about 200 yards from the clearing here in front of us where the Armistice car stands.

That famous Alsace-Lorraine statue was covered with German war flags so that you could not see its sculptured work nor read its inscription. But I had seen it many times in the post-war years. Doubtless many of you have seen it – the large sword representing the sword of the Allies and its point sticking into a large, limp eagle, representing the old Empire of the Kaiser. And the inscription underneath in French saying: TO THE HEROIC SOLDIERS OF FRANCE . . . DEFENDERS OF THE COUNTRY AND OF RIGHT . . . GLORIOUS LIBERATORS OF ALSACE-LORRAINE.

Through our glasses, we saw the Führer stop, glance at the statue, observe the Reich war flags with their big Swastikas in the center. Then, he strode slowly toward us, toward the little clearing where the famous Armistice car stood. I thought he looked very solemn, his face was grave, but there was a certain spring in his step as he walked for the first time towards the spot where Germany's fate was sealed on that November day of 1918 – a fate which, by reason of his own deeds, was now being radically changed.

And now – if I may sort of go over my notes I made from moment to moment during the next half hour – now Hitler reaches the little opening in the Compiègne woods where the armistice was signed, and where another is about to be drawn up. He pauses and looks slowly around. The opening is in the form of a circle about 200 yards in diameter, and laid out like a park. Cypress trees line it all round – and behind them the great elms and oaks of the forest. This has been one of France's national shrines for twenty-two years.

Hitler pauses, and gazes slowly around. In a group just behind him are the other German plenipotentiaries – Field Marshal Göring, grasping his field marshal's baton in one hand. He wears the blue uniform of the air force. All the Germans are in uniform, Hitler in a double-breasted gray uniform, with the Iron Cross hanging from his left breast pocket. Next to Göring are the two German army chiefs – Colonel General Keitel, Chief of the Supreme Command, and Colonel General von Brauchitsch, Commander-in-Chief of the German army. Both are just approaching sixty, but look younger, especially General Keitel, who has a dapper appearance with his cap slightly cocked on one side.

Then, there is Erich Raeder, Grand Admiral of the German Fleet, in his blue naval uniform and the invariable up-turned stiff collar, which German naval officers usually wear. There are two non-military men in Hitler's suite – his foreign minister, Joachim von Ribbentrop, in the field-gray uniform of the Foreign Office. And Rudolf Hess, Hitler's deputy, in a gray party uniform.

The time is now – I see by my notes – 3:18 p.m. in the Forest of Compiègne. Hitler's personal flag is run up on a small standard in the center of the circular opening in the woods.

Also in the center is a great granite block which stands some three feet above the ground. Hitler, followed by the others, walks slowly over to it, steps up, and reads the inscription engraved in great high letters on that block. Many of you will remember the words of that inscription. The Führer slowly reads them. The inscription says: HERE ON THE ELEVENTH OF NOVEMBER, 1918, SUCCUMBED THE CRIMINAL PRIDE OF THE GERMAN EMPIRE . . . VANQUISHED BY THE FREE PEOPLES WHICH IT TRIED TO ENSLAVE.

Hitler reads it and Göring reads it. They all read it, standing there in the June sun and the silence. We look for the expression on Hitler's face. But it does not change. Finally, he leads his party over to another granite stone, a smaller one some fifty yards to one side. Here it was that the railroad car in which the German plenipotentiaries stayed during the 1918 Armistice negotiations, stood – from November 8th to 11th. Hitler looks down and reads the inscription which merely says: "The German Plenipotentiaries." The stone itself, I notice, is set between a pair of rusty old railroad tracks, the ones that were there twenty-two years ago.

It is now 3:23 p.m., and the German leaders stride over to the armistice car. This car of course was not standing on this spot yesterday. It was standing seventy-five yards down the rusty track in the shelter of a tiny museum, built to house it by an American citizen, Mr. Arthur Henry Fleming of Pasadena, California. Yesterday, it was removed from the museum by German army engineers, and rolled back those seventy-five yards to the spot where it stood on the morning of November 11, 1918.

The Germans stand outside the car chatting in the sunlight. This goes on for two minutes. Then Hitler steps up into the car, followed by Göring and the others. We watch them entering the drawing room in Marshal Foch's car. We can see nicely through the car windows. Hitler enters first, and takes the place occupied by Marshal Foch the morning the first armistice was signed. At his sides are Göring and General Keitel. To his right and left at the ends of the table are General von Brauchitsch and Herr Hess at one end. At the other end, Grand Admiral Raeder and Herr von Ribbentrop.

The opposite side of the table is still empty. At it stand four vacant chairs. The French have not yet appeared. But we do not wait long. Exactly at 3:30 p.m., they alight from a car. They have flown up from Bordeaux to a nearby landing field, and then driven here by car. They glance at the Alsace-Lorraine memorial, now draped with Swastikas, but it's a swift glance. Then they walk down the avenue, flanked by three German army officers. We see them now as they come into the sunlight of the clearing – General Huntziger, wearing a bleached khaki uniform, Air-General Bergeret, and Vice-Admiral Le Luc, both in their respective dark blue uniforms. And then, almost buried in the uniforms, the one single civilian of the day, M. Noël, French Ambassador to Poland when the present war broke out. The French plenipotentiaries pass the guard of honor drawn up at the entrance to the clearing. The guard snaps to attention for the French, but does not present arms.

The Frenchmen keep their eyes straight ahead. It is a grave hour in the life of France, and their faces, their bearing, show what a burden they feel on their shoulders. Their faces are solemn, drawn, but they are the picture of tragic dignity.

They walk stiffly to the car where they're met by two German officers, Lieutenant-General Tippelskirch, quarter-master-general, and Colonel Thomas, chief of the Führer's headquarters. The Germans salute. The French salute. The atmosphere is what Europeans call "correct". But you get the picture when I say that we see no handshake. Not on occasions like this.

The historic moment is now approaching. It is 3:32 p.m. by my watch. The Frenchmen enter Marshal Foch's Pullman car standing there a few feet from us in Compiègne Forest.

Now we get our picture through the dusty windows of that historic old *wagon-lit* car. Hitler and the other German leaders rise to their feet as the French enter the drawing room. Hitler gives the Nazi salute, the arm raised. The German officers give the military salute. The French do the same. I cannot see M. Noël to see whether he salutes or how.

Hitler, so far as we can see through the windows just in front of us here, does not say anything. He nods to General Keitel at his side. We see General Keitel adjusting his papers. Then, he starts to read. He is reading the preamble of the German armistice terms. The French sit there, with marble-like faces and listen intently. Hitler and Göring glance at the green table top.

This part of this historic act lasts but a few moments. At 3:42 p.m. – that is twelve minutes after the French arrive – we see Hitler stand up, salute stiffly with hand upraised. Then he strides out of the drawing room followed by Göring, General von Brauchitsch, Grand Admiral Raeder, Herr Hess and Herr von Ribbentrop. The French remain at the green-topped table in the old Pullman car. General Keitel remains with them. He is going to read them the detailed conditions of the armistice. Hitler, Göring, and the others do not wait for this. They walk down the avenue back towards the Alsace-Lorraine monument. As they pass the guard of honor, the German band strikes up the two national anthems, *Deutschland Uber Alles* and the *Horst Wessel* song.

The negotiations go on. They keep on talking. They'll undoubtedly take some time. But that's all for the moment. And William C. Kerker and William L. Shirer return you now to America.

Compiègne June 22, 1940

[This broadcast was one of the scoops of Shirer's career. All the other correspondents, German as well as foreign, had been ordered back to Berlin, where the announcement of the armistice would be made by Hitler. Wanting to be on the spot, and on the off-chance that they might be able to get a broadcast through, Shirer, along with William Kerker, a stringer for NBC, remained. Their joint broadcast was relayed by telephone line to Berlin, then sent out over short-wave radio to New York without the German military engineers at Compiègne or the censors in Berlin realizing what was happening.]

Hello America. Hello NBC. Hello CBS. William C. Kerker and William L. Shirer calling NBC and CBS. This is William L. Shirer speaking to you from the Forest of Compiègne in France.

The armistice has been signed. The armistice between France and Germany was signed exactly at 6:50 p.m., German summer time, that is, one hour and twenty-five minutes ago.

And it was signed here in the same old railroad coach in the middle of Compiègne Forest where the Armistice of November 11, 1918 was signed.

I'm standing now about thirty-five yards from that historic railroad car. We've been keeping watch here since Adolf Hitler opened the armistice negotiations here at 3:30 yesterday afternoon. These negotiations have been going very fast, faster than in 1918 when it took three days before the Germans would write their names under the terms of Armistice offered by Marshal Foch.

Well now, the armistice, though signed on the dotted line by the French and the Germans, does not go into effect yet.

We've been informed that the French delegation, which has just signed the armistice with the Germans here in Compiègne Forest, is leaving by special plane for Italy. They should arrive there this afternoon. And then Italy will lay down armistice terms for ceasing *its* war with France.

There was one touching scene in the famous old Armistice car which stands here before us. After both the French and Germans had signed, General Keitel, a pleasant looking man who appears much younger than he is, almost sixty, rose and made a short address, honoring both the German and French dead in this war which has now come to an end. German quarters accepted it as the first act of appeasement (*Versöhnung*) on the part of the German authorities. The French delegates – we were watching them through the car windows here – seemed deeply touched as the German general paid tribute to the dead warriors of both countries.

Then the plenipotentiaries stepped down the steps of the old Pullman, there were salutes, photographers snapped pictures from discreet hiding places in the bushes nearby. And then the French drove away to catch their plane for Italy, where they will go through the same thing again with the Italians.

The skies were slightly overcast, but the sun occasionally came out, transforming this beautiful forest of Compiègne into a sort of fairy land. A mile down the road, through one of the wooded avenues, you could see the refugees, slowly, tiredly filing by – on weary feet, on bicycles, on carts, a few on trucks. They were very tired and footsore and dazed, and they did not know yet that an armistice had been signed and that the fighting would soon be over. But judging from their tragic, weary, half-starved faces, they wanted it to be.

You all want to know, of course, the terms of the conditions laid down by Germany in this armistice. But we don't know them yet, and won't – so we're told here – until after the Franco-Italian armistice is signed.

Paris June 24, 1940

This is Paris. Not Berlin.

I say that. And it's a fact. This is Paris from which I'm speaking.

But for one who knew the old Paris, it is hard to believe. And of course, it is even a much different Paris than the one from which my colleague, Eric Severaid, spoke to you the other evening just before he went south with the French government.

I rub my eyes and try to get things straightened out, but it's not much use. The rapidity of events is too much for us all. The rapidity also of change.

For instance, I pick up the evening edition of *Le Matin*, an old Parisian paper. It is full of bitter attacks on Mr. Churchill – the ally of yesterday *[Churchill had become Prime Minister on May 10.]* Says *Le Matin* in a front-page editorial: "Mr. Churchill finds that there are not enough French and German bodies to satisfy him. We ask if the British Prime Minister has lost his head. If he has, what a pity that our ministers did not perceive it sooner." That from the Paris paper, *Le Matin*. Most of its news columns on the front page are devoted to extracts of Marshal Pétain's reply to Churchill, in which the aged marshal denies that he is the prisoner of anyone. And then another editorial charging Mr. Churchill with preparing a rebellion in the French Empire. And more bitter remarks about General de Gaulle in London, who, as you know, has been deprived of his rank by the French government.

That is the Paris of today, a Paris on which the beautiful June sun shone down today as it always does at this time of year, down on the tree-lined streets and the wide avenues in which gray-clad German soldiers largely replace the Parisians, most of whom fled the German occupation and are now – many of them – facing starvation along the innumerable roads that lead to the sunny south.

And here is a fact which we might as well face. You will find it hard to believe, but you know me well enough by this time to realize that I'm not putting out anybody's propaganda. The fact is that while no Parisian likes a foreign occupation, and a German one least of all, the people of Paris have been pleasantly surprised by the polite behavior of German officers and soldiers alike. Moreover, the American correspondents here notice an increasing degree of fraternizing between the soldiers and the population. I saw a little example in a small restaurant today. A German major, who spoke not bad French, admired the dog of two Frenchmen sitting at the next table. He said so, a conversation was struck up about dogs in general and in particular. Soon, the major was showing the Frenchmen photos of his dog, then of his house and family in Germany. The Frenchmen, at first cool, warmed up, the talk went from dogs to families to children and finally to peace, and in the end they all drank a toast to peace. I saw and heard this myself.

Soldiers mingle in the streets with the Parisians, strike up all sorts of conversations with them on the sidewalk terraces of the cafés, and so far as I know there have been no incidents. Strangely enough, most of the German soldiers here seem to speak French.

But Paris is largely without news. *Le Matin* comes out twice a day, and today the *Paris-Soir* appeared. They carry appeals to the population to keep up their spirits but to prepare for a hard road ahead.

The French radio, apparently still controlled by the government in the south, announced tonight that it was hoped that the fighting would stop at four tomorrow morning. Just now I learn, from the Germans here, that fighting will stop at 1:35 a.m., that is in a little more than half an hour from now. But the people of Paris haven't heard it yet. They expected after what happened at Compiègne that the armistice with Italy would go through quickly, but they haven't heard yet that it's been signed. And we've had no inkling here in Paris of the terms of either armistice.

In the meantime, most Parisians you talk to seem to have only one hope – that the armistice will save the lives of the ten million refugees facing starvation between here and Bordeaux. A few have been straggling into Paris today, and it wrings your heart to see them – gaunt, half-starved, weary, foot-sore, and bitter at the authorities who did not take better care of them, or give them better advice.

All at the American Embassy are safe and well. I've talked to Ambassador Bullitt, Counselor of Embassy Robert Murphy, Colonel Fuller, Mr. Barnes, and the others – they're all well, and carrying on at the embassy. The American Red Cross under Wayne Taylor is doing everything it can to help the refugees, but it has practically no supplies left. The American Hospital is caring for as many French wounded as can be crowded into it.

Berlin June 27, 1940 24.46

This is Berlin.

We're going through here now another one of those "calms before the storm". We had one after Poland. Another after Norway. And now this one after Holland, Belgium, and France.

The tension and excitement of the big battles relax. The troops – and, you might add, the reporters – get a little sleep. The folks at home go for outings instead of remaining glued to their radio sets. The newspapers resume publishing articles instead of news.

As a matter of fact, while people here in Germany wait for the next move against Great Britain, even the Republican Convention gets first-page play in the German newspapers. I say "even" because not one German in a thousand knows the difference between a Republican and a Democrat, or what American politics are all about.

And yet the Republican Convention in Philadelphia is front-page news in Berlin today. The reason, I think, is this: that the party program contains a pledge – or so it's reported here – to keep the United States out of the war. I need not tell you that such a pledge makes pleasant reading in this country. Germany has always hoped that we would stay out of the war for it had no illusions on which side our sympathies, for the most part, lay.

It's true that since the catastrophic defeat of the Allied armies in Flanders, Berlin – as I've constantly reported from here – thought that American intervention would come too late to decide anything. Nevertheless, one gets the impression here that the Republican party's stand on our staying out of the war anyway has been welcomed here.

The German press of course maintains a complete editorial reserve about American politics. It publishes no editorials at all. You can only get a hint of its feelings by its selection of news. Thus the *Deutsche Allgemeine Zeitung* devotes more than a column on page one today to convention news. It publishes what appears to be a fairly adequate résumé of the party program. And it – like all Berlin papers – plays up Mr. Hoover's speech, especially that part about official persons making what the former president described – according to the German dispatches – as "provocative speeches".

The *Völkischer Beobachter*, the official party paper, puts this headline over a dispatch about a statement by Senator Pittman. The headline reads: "Senator Pittman advises England to give up the struggle."

The New York correspondent of the *Nachtausgabe* reports in his paper tonight that the feeling is growing in America that "England's game," as he puts it, "is lost".

As for actual war news, the German High Command today reported that its troops, following the terms of the armistice, had reached the Dordogne region east of Bordeaux. Now that the fighting is over, the Germans appear to be taking their time. In a day or two, though, they should be at the Spanish frontier. Incidentally, a German army at the Spanish border means that Germany can now obtain important supplies of Spanish iron by rail. The rest of the High Command report deals with night air attacks on England. Last night, it's claimed, harbor works and important airplane factories were hit. The German Command also reports that British planes again flew over Germany last night, but insists no damage was done to military objectives. Several civilians, it says, were killed or wounded.

[*The following paragraph was censored by the German Foreign Office*: Not a word has come out in Berlin in either the press or on the radio about Soviet Russia's ultimatum to Romania, demanding Bessarabia, Bukovina, and the port of Constanza. The Wilhelmstrasse declines to comment on the matter. The only thing we know for sure is that Berlin, following the recent Soviet action in the Baltic states, is closely watching developments in the Balkans. But its main interest at the moment is in the West, on the action that the papers say will shortly be taken against Britain. Russia has timed her latest move well.]

Tomorrow is the 21st anniversary of the signing of the Versailles Treaty – a very dead piece of paper today. How the Germans will observe the day has not yet been told us.

Berlin June 28, 1940 24.46

This is Berlin.

Today was the 21st anniversary of the signing of the Treaty of Versailles. And the world it created appeared to be singing its swan song today as German troops reached the Spanish border, and Soviet troops marched into Bessarabia and Bukovina.

No tears – as you may guess – were shed in Germany as the doom of that post-war Versailles world seemed almost a completely accomplished fact. As a matter of fact, surprisingly little attention was paid in Germany to the anniversary.

Most of us rather thought that, seeing what had happened, the Germans would make a big day of it, hold a monster parade in Versailles or Paris, or even here to celebrate the end of the Versailles époque. But – not for the first time – we guessed wrong. As prophets, we haven't been much good recently.

No parade was held. No speeches made. The parades and the speeches will no doubt come – but later. All that happened was that a few newspapers published editorials recalling what Germans have always held to be the injustices of the Peace Treaty. All the German writers appear to think that the next Peace Treaty will not be a vindictive one, as they charge Versailles was. But, of course, only Hitler and a few of his confidants know what sort of peace is in store for Europe if and when Great Britain is beaten. The rest of us can only guess.

Everyone here is expecting the campaign against England to begin any time now. But as yet there is no indication of the date. And there won't be. Hitler, as you know, does not advertise his strokes in advance . . . I understand there's been some talk of a possible peace with Britain, but the Wilhelmstrasse denies any knowledge of it. The attitude there still is: "Let the cannons talk." It would probably be more accurate to say, "Let the Stuka bombers talk."

The Soviet Russian march into two of Romania's provinces, Bukovina and Bessarabia, gets little attention today from the German press. In fact, I can find nothing about the matter in the afternoon newspapers. Tonight, the German radio gave a brief account of the Soviet demands, how the Romanians accepted them, and how the Russian troops started marching in this afternoon.

German official reaction seems well summed up in one sentence in the radio report. It said: "Romania has chosen the reasonable way."

In fact, you get the impression in Berlin that Moscow's action did not cause any surprise here, and that the new frontier which the Soviets are pushing into the Balkans was more or less agreed upon between Berlin and Moscow when they came to an understanding about the Baltic states and the line of demarcation in Poland.

No one here expects Hungary or Bulgaria to get back their former provinces in Romania just yet. Those are matters which will be settled by the victorious big powers.

The nomination of Mr. Willkie *[Wendell Willkie, Republican candidate*

338

in the 1940 Presidential election] gets three lines in the Berlin press this evening. Incidentally, the German press refers to him as "General-Direktor," or "Director-General" Willkie, a title which Germans bestow on businessmen as a matter of habit. Thus the radio here announced that "General-Direktor Willkie had been nominated." But the German radio gave more attention to a New York dispatch saying that the Republican party program had taken a definite stand to keep the United States out of the war. Mr. Willkie's stand on foreign policy is not gone into here, in the press or on the radio.

[Shirer spent the first week of July in Geneva with his wife, Tess, who was planning to return to the United States with their infant daughter. While in Switzerland, he took advantage of the absence of Nazi censors to write to Paul White, the CBS Director of Public Affairs in New York.]

July 5, 1940

Dear Paul:

A line from Geneva where I've been getting a bit of a rest and gradually recovering (I hope) my senses.

Many thanks for trying to help Tess get away. She was all set to get away on the *Washington* from Genoa when the ship failed to show up in that port. Then she was on the point of leaving for Bordeaux from which she hoped to get to Lisbon and catch the *Clipper*. Fortunately, at the last minute, she didn't go, for which I'm glad. She would have joined the ten million French, many of whom I saw battling starvation and thirst along the roads of France. I've seen a few things in my life, but nothing quite so tragic. Present plans are for Tess to stay the summer here, and then in September catch the *Clipper*, unless the war is over. If the British hold out and can enforce the blockade, the food situation on the continent will be very critical by November. The Germans are confident however that they'll finish the British by the end of this month. Personally I have my doubts, but so did I also about Norway, Belgium, and France!

Sometime (when I take a longer rest) I'll write you about France. What I saw at Paris was a complete breakdown of French society.

As to Russell Hill *[a CBS reporter in Berlin]*, he was thrown out because of a story which Ralph Barnes wrote for the *Herald-Trib* about Russo-German relations cooling, which of course was a fact. Hill's expulsion had nothing to do with his radio work. The High Command in fact went to bat for him in order to save him for us, but the All-High could not be convinced. I may get him back later. In the meantime, I hope you can use him in the Balkans. My own status is none too high as many powerful people do not forgive me for the objective line I try to take.

As you probably know, Mary Marvin Breckinridge married Jeff Patterson, first Secretary of the American Embassy in Berlin, a fellow with many millions from National Cash Register in his pockets. I guess maybe she won't do much broadcasting now.

Glad you liked the break we got on the armistice. Like all scoops it was a combination of luck, hard work and foresight. The three Press Assoc. boys, bless them, who were at Compiègne the day before, flew back to Berlin the day the armistice was signed, thinking they'd get it first there. The two of us were the only foreign correspondents who stuck around! *DNB* and the German radio were not very pleased either at our beat. It made them look kind of funny. We did not know that we were a little ahead of the rest of the world on the story until next day when a friend of mine in Paris told us what he'd heard on the American short-wave the night before . . .

Berlin July 8, 1940 24.46

This is Berlin.

Events are moving fast over here, and there's no time to rub your eyes.

Tomorrow, France, which until a few weeks ago was regarded as the last stronghold of democracy on the continent, will shed its democracy and join the ranks of totalitarian states.

I learn this from the German newspapers today after returning from Switzerland. The sturdy Swiss, you may be interested to know, while resigned to adapting themselves to a new order in Europe, still hope to retain both their democracy and their freedom. How they can do this surrounded on all sides in their lovely mountains by three totalitarian states remains to be seen. They do not know themselves. But they hope.

The manner in which democracy will be buried in France tomorrow is described in some detail in dispatches in the Berlin newspapers tonight.

Tomorrow morning, according to these German dispatches, the French Chamber will convene in Vichy. In the afternoon the French Senate will meet. The following day – on Wednesday – the two houses will then constitute themselves as the French National Assembly. It is this assembly which will finish with the democratic business so far as France is concerned.

According to the German press, the Assembly will then give a vote of confidence to Marshal Pétain. This vote will empower the marshal and his government to draw up an authoritarian constitution which the Berlin

340

papers say will be based on the slogan: "Work, Family, Fatherland." Presumably this will replace that famous foundation-cry born in the French Revolution and which you see engraved on every French public building – you remember it: "Liberty, Equality, Fraternity".

The *Deutsche Allgemeine Zeitung* says the foundations of the new French constitution will be, and I quote: "Authority, Responsibility, Order, Discipline and Stability".

Thus, one great step in the re-forming of Europe on new lines is taken with the changeover in France. Perhaps other steps will be planned here in Berlin in the next few days when Count Ciano returns to resume his talks with Chancellor Hitler.

The historic Pullman car of Marshal Foch in which two such different armistices were signed in Compiègne Forest arrived in Berlin today. Pending final arrangements it will be placed in the Anhalter freight depot. Later, undoubtedly, it will be placed in a Berlin museum. It seems only yesterday that I stood in Compiègne Forest watching German army engineers remove the walls of another museum so that the car could be pushed out for the armistice talks, following this war.

Field Marshal Göring tonight ordered that there should be no more air-raid alarms when only single planes come over German towns. This is being done, it's explained, so as not to disturb economic activity any more than is necessary.

Berlin July 9, 1940 24.46

This is Berlin.

If France today thought that emulating her German conquerors by going totalitarian might save her from the consequences of her military capitulation, German editorial writers tonight stepped in quickly to correct any such thoughts.

"Too late," chorused the German press, commenting on M. Laval's *[Pierre Laval, pro-Nazi leader of the Pétain government]* hasty action at Vichy in scrapping democracy for a French version of totalitarianism. In fact, the German press and the German radio made it very clear that the action of the French government in Vichy in setting up a form of government resembling those of the victorious Axis powers will not influence by one iota the kind of peace which Berlin and Rome intend to set up ultimately, nor for that matter will it affect the kind of treatment which the victors will mete out to France in the end.

Let me quote a little bit on this. The German news service, *Dienst Aus Deutschland*, an organ known to be close to the Wilhelmstrasse, remarks that the changes announced in Vichy have been received with "cool reserve" in Berlin. And then it goes to the heart of the matter so far as Germany is concerned: "It is not to be supposed that the change of the former régime in France to an authoritarian form of government will influence in any way the political liquidation of the war. The fact is that Germany does not consider the Franco-German accounts as settled yet. Later they will be settled with historical realism."

This authoritative German organ gives an idea of what it means by "historical realism". The German plans, it states, and I quote, "are governed by the idea that the new Europe will be conditioned by the natural weights which its peoples exert. It is natural that in this framework of things, the special position of the Reich, politically, economically, and militarily, will find its expression in this new world. The future relations between Germany and France will be revised not only on the basis of the two decades since Versailles but will also take into account much earlier times."

And finally, this organ of German opinion remarks about something that had also struck correspondents here, namely that the German press today played up accounts of alleged mistreatment of German prisoners by the French. "This," observed the *Dienst Aus Deutschland*, "shows the degree of strain between the two countries."

The *Deutsche Allgemeine Zeitung*, commenting on France going totalitarian, is no more approving. It says: "No new names crop out at Vichy. It's the old democrats who today wish to create an authoritarian régime in France. But this experiment comes too late for the new order in Europe. Arms have decided that an equal sharing between Germany and France will not be the form of the new Europe . . . It will be another France from the old one which will find a different place assigned to it in this new Europe."

So much for Germany's reaction to France going totalitarian.

Dr. Rosenberg addressed us this evening. He also expressed some ideas about the future shape of things to come in Europe. Confining himself to the Nordic situation, he pictured a Scandinavia of the future being a great space peopled by Germanic people – in which he, of course, included the Scandinavians – and under the protection of the German Reich. He included Sweden in this new Scandinavia which would be protected by the new German Empire. It's emphasized in Berlin that these are Dr. Rosenberg's own philosophical opinions, and not those of the German government.

And it may be that some of the future of the Balkan part of Europe will be decided in Germany in the next few days. Count Teleki, the Hungarian Prime Minister, and his Foreign Minister, Count Csaky, arrive at Munich tomorrow where they will confer with Herr Hitler and Herr von

Ribbentrop. Count Ciano, returning from a visit to the battlefields, is also expected to take part in the talks. The theme of the talks will probably be the new order in the Balkans.

Prime Minister Laval is reported here to have incorporated in the proposed new French constitution which he is drafting the abolition of all traditional French parties and the establishment of a single political party along totalitarian lines.

In the territories occupied by the German army, military officials have ordered the confiscation of all agricultural products and all food of every kind. The officially announced purpose is to assure more equitable distribution in the occupied territories. In the same areas, military orders tie every worker to his job. He is forbidden to leave his place of employment, or to strike. Further, all prices are fixed at their present levels unless special permission is granted. This means that, just as has been the case here in Germany throughout the war, scarcity will not be permitted to cause any increase in prices. The old economic law of supply and demand is put out of business by official edict.

Meanwhile, Count Ciano is here for the purpose, according to the German press, of rounding up all questions of German-Italian co-operation arising from the armistice and from continuation of the war against England. Just what these questions are is what we would all like to know. The suspense is getting intense. Will it be the Mediterranean or England? And when will it come? Today's brief war communiqué doesn't throw much light on these questions. The German High Command says German planes bombed Falmouth on the south-west coast of England and claim to have damaged harbor facilities and set a merchant ship on fire. It also claims that another bombing squadron attacked a British naval squadron in the North Sea, badly damaging a 10,000-ton cruiser and two destroyers. Which means that we are still waiting for the big news.

Berlin July 10, 1940 24.46

This is Berlin.

Hungary, which, like Germany, lost territory after the last war, had her inning in court today, so to speak. With what result, we don't know yet.

All we know is that early this morning, the Prime Minister of Hungary, Count Teleki, and the Hungarian Foreign Minister, Count Csaky, arrived in Munich. So did Count Ciano, the Italian Foreign Minister who has been visiting the recent battlefields on the Western Front.

Both the Italian and Hungarian delegations were received with full

343

military honors, and greeted at the station by the German Foreign Minister. Later in the morning, Herr von Ribbentrop conducted them to Herr Hitler where a conversation lasting several hours took place.

After it was over we got an official communiqué saying that the Führer, in the presence of Foreign Ministers von Ribbentrop and Ciano, received Messrs Teleki and Csaky. "The conversation," concluded the communiqué, "took place in the spirit of the traditional friendship existent between the three nations."

More than that, we're not told. Hungary, of course, lost the rich province of Transylvania to Romania after the last war and naturally wants it back, just like Russia wanted back – and got back – Bessarabia. But today it is Germany which is deciding such matters, leading to what the whole continental press nowadays calls the "New Order in Europe." Most people, however, believe that it will not be before the peace conference that the new map of Europe will be redrawn, and no doubt states like Hungary and Romania and Bulgaria will have to wait for that before knowing what their future is to be like.

But there can be no peace conference until the issue with Great Britain is settled one way or another. If and when Germany intends to invade Great Britain is still the chief topic of conversation here. But no one knows the answer. In the meantime, the German air force continues to test daily Britain's defenses, attempts to bomb its munition factories and oil depots and get an idea of the British aerial strength.

I remember at the start of the great German offensive, General Reichenau telling me in his headquarters just behind the front line, which was then just west of Brussels, that the British in the first days of the campaign had certainly not used much of their air force. Nor apparently did they use much of it in the fighting that followed up to the collapse of France. They were, it is thought here, saving it for the defense of England.

It is that defense which the Germans are now testing. Yesterday, for instance, according to the High Command communiqué issued today, German planes dropped bombs on oil tanks at the airfields of Pembroke and Ipswich. They also bombed, says the German communiqué, British munition works at Norwich, Leeds, Tilbury, and Swansea. Last night, as every night, British planes returned the attack, dropping bombs on Holland and on spots in north and west Germany. As has been the case every single night since the British started bombing Germany, the High Command stated today that no military objectives had been hit.

A special communiqué issued tonight claimed that all seven British bombers which tried to bomb a German airfield near Amiens today were shot down by German fighters.

Another special communiqué issued in Berlin tonight claimed that in the Straits of Dover, German bombers sank a British cruiser and four

344

merchant ships and damaged another cruiser and three further freight ships. Ten British fighters were shot down in this engagement, say the Germans, who admit they themselves lost four planes.

Incidentally, the air-raid alarms in Germany have been cut down from two minutes to one minute. This is hard on heavy sleepers like myself. Usually two minutes of a screaming siren fail to wake me up. But the army says there are military reasons for the shortening of the alarm, and asks all inhabitants to wake up the comrades who, by reason of a deep sleep, fail to hear it.

Berlin July 11, 1940 24.46

This is Berlin.

The lull continues. And no man – at least no reporter – can tell when it will end.

The Hungarian Prime Minister and his Foreign Minister have gone back to Budapest after being received by Herr Hitler in Munich. It seems evident that the Hungarians are not going to attack Romania in order to get back Transylvania. Matters like that, it is believed here, can wait for the peace conference. So far as Hungary is concerned then, there will be peace in the Balkans.

There is still no indication here as to when the much-talked-of German drive on Great Britain will begin. In the meantime, according to the High Command, the daily bombing raids on England continue. Yesterday, says the German Command in its communiqué today, harbor works on the south and south-west English coast as well as munitions factories were bombed. Fires and explosions, the communiqué declares, were observed at a munitions dump at Pembroke and in the harbors of Plymouth and Swansea. Further, it reports that oil tanks at Pembroke and Portland were set on fire.

Incidentally, you'll be interested to know that for the first time – so far as I can remember – since the German offensive started in the West nearly two months ago, the High Command reported today that no British bombers came over Germany last night. Whether they returned tonight I can't yet tell you. But it's 1 a.m. here in Berlin, and I've heard no alarms so far. But we rarely get them in Berlin anyway.

The High Command also reported today that in the last six weeks, due to the favorable bases now available to U-boats, 669,000 tons of enemy shipping were sunk, or about 100,000 tons a week. That's certainly a sizeable figure, but still much below the top figures of 1917.

Incidentally, the German newspapers are telling their readers that the

British are getting very nervous as the result of the German air-raids. The banner headline in tonight's *Nachtausgabe*, for instance, says: DAY AND NIGHT ENGLAND LIVES IN FEAR OF GERMAN BOMBERS.

Certain interesting arrests by the German authorities have become known here. It's reported that the burgomaster of Prague, Dr. Klepka, has just been arrested. He's accused, it is said, of having actively supported a subversive organization.

Then in Brussels, now under German military occupation, the Berlin newspapers report two arrests: that of Colonel van der Meersch, former head of the Belgian military court in Brussels, and the former head of the Belgian secret police, M. De Foy. They are accused of being responsible for the mishandling of German and Italian subjects before the German army reached the Belgian capital.

The Commander-in-Chief of the Dutch army, General Winkelmann, has been removed from his post and made a military prisoner by the German military authorities in Holland, who have warned the Dutch against helping British flyers at night and otherwise not supporting the army of occupation.

The German press also takes up tonight the question of King Haakon of Norway, who is described here as a deserter. According to the *Lokal Anzeiger*, the Norwegian parliament will take a decision about the King before the end of July. What that decision will be, what kind of a government is in store for occupied Norway, we're not told.

Berlin July 12, 1940 24.46

This is Berlin.

The German High Command today reports further air-raids on Great Britain. Harbor works and armament factories in south and central England were the main land targets, according to the German communiqué, but ships on the east and south coasts of England were also attacked.

Specifically, the Germans claim to have scored hits on the harbor works at Plymouth and Lowestoft. In Plymouth and the industrial district around Burton-upon-Trent, it says, big fires were started after bombs had struck.

In the Channel, according to the High Command, a large tanker and four sizeable merchant ships were sunk by bombs, and nine other ships damaged.

It seems obvious that while these daily German air attacks on Britain are only a preliminary to what would come were the Germans to attempt an invasion of the British Isles, they do have certain aims: To demoralize the population of Britain, to hamper production in the British armament and aircraft industries, and, above all, to force a blockade upon England.

How far those aims are being achieved, Mr. Murrow can tell you much better than I can. The German press makes a great deal tonight of a Washington dispatch to the *New York Times* which it quotes as saying that well-informed circles in Washington believe that the German air attacks on Britain have been more effective than has been admitted in London.

The High Command did a little summing-up today and came to the conclusion that since the start of the war, 4,329,213 tons of enemy shipping had been sunk. Submarines and mines accounted for nearly two million tons, or almost half. Surface vessels and what is termed by the Germans "other sea-war means" accounted for another 1,300,000 tons, and airplanes bagged just over a million tons.

News of France's hasty transition to a totalitarian state has suddenly been shelved to the inside pages of the German newspapers, which continue to carry attacks on the French for one reason or another. But the Wilhelmstrasse makes no secret that it is watching events in France closely, and it was stated tonight that General Weygand's remarks to returning French troops that their role was not yet over had not passed unnoticed in Berlin.

The organ *Dienst Aus Deutschland*, which is close to the Foreign Office, says bluntly tonight: "The main point in Germany's attitude towards France is that the Reich demands that France voluntarily recognize Germany's leading role in Europe and give up the idea of revenge or of obtaining hegemony in Europe. For the moment . . . it is important that Germany be given full guarantees that a repetition of France's policy against the Reich will not take place."

The German radio put it this way tonight. "We expect France to recognize," it said, "that it is Germany's task to build up the New Order in Europe."

The German government has sent out a call for colonial officials. "The final victory of Germany," says the call, "makes it necessary to start recruiting officials for the colonial service at once."

The German radio again warned its listeners tonight against tuning in on foreign stations. "The war is not yet over," said the warning which emphasized that heavy sentences were in store for "radio criminals," meaning those who listen to foreign broadcasts. "Germans listen only to German news. They, alone, tell the truth," it was added.

Berlin July 14, 1940 01.01

This is Berlin.

The Berlin papers call this period of quiet we're in now "the pause between the battles". They refer constantly to the "coming attack on England", which the average man in the street in Germany thinks will be a matter of a mere few weeks.

As a matter of fact, the man in the street in Berlin today – and his family – didn't appear to be thinking much about the war, possibly less about it than you've been thinking. He was thinking about what a perfect day it was – and it was – and he and his family packed a picnic bag and betook themselves to the lakes that dot the woods around Berlin. I've never seen so many Berliners out for a Sunday outing in my life. I've never seen so many sailboats out as there were on the Wannsee today. The bathing beaches couldn't nearly accommodate the crowds. The pleasant beer-gardens along the lakes – and there are hundreds of them – were jammed, even though wartime beer isn't what beer used to be in Germany. The war – all the horrors of war that some of us have seen in Belgium and France – seemed far away. Here today was the warm sun, the cool water of the lakes, the green of the woods.

Returning to the city about sun-down, the people bought the early editions of the Monday papers. The headline in my paper read: AIR VICTORY OVER THE CHANNEL – SUPERIOR ENEMY FORCE BEATEN – BOMBS ON BRITISH CONVOY. That sort of brought the war home to you. Those headlines summarized today's communiqué of the High Command, which for the first time in many days did not mention any bombing of inland objectives in Britain. The Sunday holidayers could also read in the army communiqué the daily paragraph about British night air-raids on north and western Germany which, said the High Command, caused small damage and failed to achieve any military objectives.

If the citizens later in the evening turned on their radios, they received a picture of great distress and even panic in England.

In the English naval dockyards, said the announcer, there had been serious sabotage, holding up work on warships for many weeks. In the British armament factories, the German radio said, production was being greatly cut down because of the continual shortening of food rations for the workers.

Next, the announcer cited the *Washington Post* as stating that the situation of the British Isles had become hopeless because of the German air attacks on Britain. "All English hopes for American help are illusions," the announcer went on. "The British position is hopeless."

Finally, the announcer quoted the London correspondent of a Stockholm paper describing how the King of England last Friday got

348

caught in a German bombing attack. "The King", said the German announcer, "threw himself quickly to the ground. Among those with him there was a general panic."

If the Berliner was not too tired after his day out, he may have read the more serious editorials in this morning's press giving him further hints as to the new Europe which, as the *Börsen Zeitung* put it today, Germany and Italy have been called to form. Russia, for some reason, is not mentioned in this connection.

It seems clear from press articles and Berlin radio commentaries today that the Germans now envisage a unified Europe under German leadership – not only economically, but politically and militarily. Today's *Frankfurter Zeitung* puts it in a nutshell. It says, "We must comprehend the entire continent as a political unity organized from the center, a unity based not on outworn rivalries, but on the leadership principle and the needs of peoples. The main point is not the revision of frontiers, but the uniting of the continent under German and Italian leadership."

A Berlin radio commentator tonight thought that the small states, as he put it, were beginning to recognize that they did not lose their honor if they placed themselves under the protection of the great empires.

Berlin July15, 1940 24.46

This is Berlin.

I wish I could enter into the spirit of what most of you are probably thinking about tonight – the Democratic Convention in Chicago – and tell you what the Germans think about it.

But I can't – because the Germans aren't giving it a thought. Oh, I suppose the Wilhelmstrasse officials are following it. It's important to Berlin to know if the President is going to be renominated, and what the sentiment of the Democratic party is about the war and help for the Allies.

But I doubt if more than a handful of people in Berlin even know a convention is on. The *Deutsche Allgemeine Zeitung* did have a piece about it last Saturday from Paul Schaeffer, its New York correspondent. But there's been not a line about it in the Berlin press either yesterday or today. The Republicans got a few lines in the paper when their convention met in Philadelphia, and perhaps when the convention gets going the Democrats will creep into the columns of the German press.

Over here tonight, the press concentrates on the war and its headlines are given over to claims of new victories of the German air force over the British. Actually, the High Command communiqué was rather brief today. It told of new air attacks on British shipping, claimed that three ships were sunk and four others damaged while a destroyer and an auxiliary cruiser were also hit. It told also of bombing raids during the night on British ports, airfields and munition works. There was also the daily paragraph about the British night air-raids on north and west Germany. The High Command declared the damage was slight and that three of the British bombers were shot down. The score in the air fights over England was given as four to two in favor of the Germans.

Incidentally, the Berlin newspapers reminded their subscribers today that it must be kept in mind that, after all, there has not yet been a really big air attack on England. What's been going on in the past few days was just small stuff, they said. The purpose of these small attacks, it was explained, was two-fold. To sharpen the blockade of Britain and to curtail British military strength by destroying harbor works, airfields, military camps and munition factories.

The German press also informed its readers today that the German troops of all arms now stand ready for the attack on Britain. The date of the attack, it was added, will be decided by the Führer alone. But German bases for the attack, from Norway to the French Atlantic coast, it was said, have been fully prepared for the task. The troops themselves have been completely rested after their hasty march through France. All in all, the German papers seem to think that a quick victory over Britain is assured.

The German people were informed of Mr. Churchill's speech this afternoon by various editorials in the press which roundly attacked it. Both the press and radio referred to Mr. Churchill by a new title. They called him "All-High War-Lord of the Plutocracy". They called the speech "foolish and criminal".

German editorial writers seemed especially interested in Mr. Churchill's promise that London would be defended to the last. They immediately warned him of what happened to Warsaw and Rotterdam. Says the *Deutsche Allgemeine Zeitung*: "The unscrupulous rulers of Warsaw did not draw the consequences until their capital lay in ruins and ashes. Also in Rotterdam a timely decision was not forthcoming as it was with the other Dutch cities and also, at the last minute, with Paris."

But one thing seems certain. The German press and radio tonight accept Mr. Churchill's statement for face value, that he is determined to go on with the war.

I don't know whether it's the sign of anything, but there was one item in the Berlin press tonight that had nothing at all to do with the war. It was a dispatch from Munich and it said that the master fisherman, one Franz Friedl, caught a sea trout in the Lake of Constance that was over three feet long and weighed thirty-one pounds. That was news in Germany today, and somehow it made me feel better.

Berlin July 16, 1940 24.46

This is Berlin.

The Democratic Convention in Chicago at last broke into the columns of the Berlin press today.

The main story for the Germans, naturally enough, was a Chicago dispatch telling of a last minute change in Speaker Bankhead's speech. The paragraph about sympathy and help for Great Britain, which the dispatch says was cut out of Mr. Bankhead's speech at the last minute, is quoted in full by the German newspapers.

There is no editorial comment in the German press, but the dispatch emphasizes that what was stricken from the speech was a reference to American help for Britain. That the words were never spoken is naturally a welcome sign in Germany.

This Chicago dispatch, which the *Deutsche Allgemeine Zeitung* features in its pages this evening, also informs German readers that Senator Wheeler, considered one of the outstanding candidates for the nomination as vice-president, told the party on the eve of its convention that the Democratic program must guarantee the American people isolation from the European war. "The senator," says this German agency dispatch from Chicago, "criticized Roosevelt and said it was not enough to say that America wouldn't send any troops to the European war. The United States must make it clear that it would not take part in any way in this war."

Such things make good reading here in Berlin, though, of course, the German government is under no illusion about the material help the United States already has rendered the Allies, nor as to the increased help which probably would be given Great Britain if it holds out for very long. It is only fair to say, however, that the German view has been from the start that American aid would come too late to help the Allies. That held good for France, and Berlin still thinks it holds good for Britain.

The war communiqués here in Berlin appear to be getting shorter, as is natural during the present lull in the war.

Today's communiqué of the High Command confined itself to submarine and air attacks on British shipping, to further bomb attacks on England, and to British air attacks on Germany.

During yesterday's daylight air-raids on Britain, the German air force claims to have bombed airfields at Pembroke, St. Athan, Plymouth, and Bicester, harbor works at Cardiff and Brighton, and an airplane factory at Yeovil.

British planes, concludes the German communiqué, again dropped bombs over north and west Germany last night, and again it is stated they did no damage.

351

Tonight, the German radio advised its listeners to equip their houses with fire-extinguishers, which it said could put out most fires started by enemy flyers. Listeners were reminded that every house-owner was obligated by law to have a fire-extinguisher around. "Don't wait," the announcer concluded, "until the police force you to get one or until your house burns down."

The German radio tonight stated that British air-raids on Emden on July 14th killed five civilians and wounded sixteen. Forty bombs were dropped on the town, but it's denied that oil depots, docks, or industrial plants were hit.

Berlin July 17, 1940 24.46

This is Berlin.

It is now almost a month since France gave up the struggle and laid down her arms. And we know no more today than we did then, if and when a German attack on Great Britain is to be made.

In the meantime, the readers of the German press are given each day new accounts of what is called the desperate situation in Britain. Just to give you an idea, the *Nachtausgabe* tonight has this headline: PANIC FEELING IN ENGLAND – ANXIETY BEFORE THE DECISION – CHURCHILL WISHES TO INCREASE HIS DICTATORIAL POWER. And the story under this headline, which occupies two columns on the front page of the paper, begins with this paragraph: "In England there is taking place with unexpected speed a transition from an orderly rule by government to a chaos of measures and acts. The English people, as the London newspapers make clear, show signs of a really catastrophic anxiety over the coming military and political events. The mass of the English people have come to the conclusion that the possibility of military and political resistance to Germany is negligible."

The leading front-page article in tonight's *Börsen Zeitung* begins: "It is an open secret throughout the world that the state of mind now prevailing in England resembles helpless desperation." The leading front-page editorial in the *Deutsche Allgemeine Zeitung* begins: "Worry over an attack grows in England from day to day." The average reader over here by now must indeed have an idea that England is about to collapse. I'd like to hear what Mr. Murrow has to say about that.

The High Command has little to report today, mainly because flying weather was bad yesterday. Activity of the German air force therefore, says the High Command communiqué, was greatly reduced. The only air attacks on Britain mentioned are some on Scotland, where it's claimed harbor works at Thurso were bombed and a ship there set on fire.

The only two states in south-eastern Europe which have not more or less openly played ball with Germany are Yugoslavia and Turkey. Yesterday the German press called Yugoslavia to account for permitting anti-German pamphlets to be published there and also for the circumstance that high Yugoslavian officials attended a Fourteenth of July celebration at the French Legation.

Today the *Börsen Zeitung* takes Turkey to task for continuing, even at this late date, its pro-Ally policy. "By being bound to the Western Powers," warns the *Börsen Zeitung*, "those responsible for Turkish policy have unnecessarily begun the process of self-destruction."

One lone Berlin newspaper, the *Deutsche Allgemeine Zeitung*, continues to keep its readers informed about the Democratic Convention in Chicago. Its correspondent, Paul Schaeffer, reports today from Chicago that this year's Democratic Convention is the quietest and most uncarnival-like one which the Democrats have ever staged. The watchword from the party leaders, he says, is "Dignity", seeing the seriousness of the times.

He remarks that in contrast to the Republican Convention, the Democratic gathering in Chicago has what he terms "a lord, a boss". And Mr. Schaeffer explains that he sits in the White House.

Three hundred Germans in Berlin have started learning Swahili. Swahili is a sort of lingua-franca of the former German colony in German East Africa.

Berlin July 18, 1940 24.46

This is Berlin.

For the first time since 1871, German troops staged a victory parade through the historic Brandenburg Gate in Berlin today.

They comprised a division conscripted from Berlin itself, and nearly the whole town turned out to welcome them back. They were tanned, hard-looking fellows who had seen service first in Poland and then taken part in the storming of the Maginot Line in the last days of the war. But they goose-stepped through the famous gateway and then past the reviewing stand in the Pariserplatz, or Paris Square, and then on down the wide tree-lined Unter den Linden, with a confidence you get when you've smashed one army after the other.

The crowds, especially the women and children, threw flowers at their feet as they marched by and yelled and yelled until they were hoarse. Bands boomed away and church bells tolled and on the whole it was a very happy

353

afternoon – both for the battle-scarred soldiers and the local populace.

Some of the men, it was obvious, were also veterans of the World War. And no doubt some of them remembered – and some in the cheering, happy crowd remembered – the dismal cold day of December 10, 1918, when the Prussian Guards came home and marched down this same avenue. German newspaper writers tonight recall that day too and emphasize the difference between that day of defeat, and this of victory.

Incidentally, General Fromm, who reviewed the troops, informed them that those who had also fought in the World War would be demobilized immediately. Apparently the High Command does not think that it will need the older men anymore.

Herr Hitler himself was not present at the parade, nor was Field Marshal Göring. The speech of welcome was made by Dr. Goebbels in his capacity as party *Gauleiter [District Leader]* of Berlin.

Said Dr. Goebbels: "The war isn't yet over. The last part must still be won. Then peace will come and we'll build a greater Reich and a better Europe."

As to the lessons of the war, Dr. Goebbels said: "France, which tried to annihilate us, has been crushed. Those who set themselves up against the honor and freedom of the German Reich will be crushed like France."

The *Deutsche Allgemeine Zeitung*, which devotes more space to American news than any other Berlin newspaper, is not very pleased with the platform adopted by the Democratic Convention at Chicago. Discussing the paragraph in the platform about democratic institutions having been overthrown by those who rely on force, the paper observes: "Translated into the deadly language of facts, such a bombastic statement means a plain avowal that the revolution of the century has dethroned outworn democracy in the world." By the "revolution of the century" is meant of course the totalitarian revolution.

This German editorial mentions a reference in the Democratic platform to "material help", but does not say to who. On the whole, the paper finds that American democracy simply doesn't comprehend the great changes going on in Europe and Asia. As for the war, this Berlin paper does concede that: "American democracy now understands that the decision in Europe will fall without her." In other words, that we are too late to do anything about Europe.

Dispatches from unoccupied France tonight say there is bitterness in the Pétain government against Britain whom France accuses of having seized 260,000 tons of badly needed foodstuffs under the new blockade measures. The French, says the dispatch, urgently need this food. Incidentally, American Red Cross officials tell me that the first American food for France is now being delivered in both the occupied and unoccupied sections of France.

Berlin July 19, 1940 24.46

This is Berlin.

"In this hour I feel it to be my duty before my own conscience to appeal once more to reason and common sense – in Great Britain as much as elsewhere . . . I can see no reason why this war must go on."

A little more than four hours ago I sat in the Kroll Opera House, a great barn-like structure across the Königsplatz from the old Reichstag building, listening to Adolf Hitler saying these words and feeling the tenseness in the hall.

There was no applause, no cheering, no stamping of heavy boots as I've witnessed countless times in this same building when he reached the climax of other Reichstag speeches. There was tense silence. For it was this answer to the question: What next? – An attack on England? Or peace with England? – for which the House and indeed the entire German nation had been waiting.

There was dead silence, and he went on: "I am grieved to think of the sacrifices which it will claim. I should like to avert them, also for my own people." Millions of Germans, Hitler declared, were burning for a settling of accounts with Britain, but . . . but . . . "I also know," he continued, "that at home there are many women and mothers, who, ready as they are to sacrifice all they have in life, are yet bound to it by their very heart strings."

In other words, Hitler offers peace to Britain. On what terms, he does not say. But one thing is evident. The German people will now follow him as never before, for they will say: He offered England peace and no strings attached to it. He said he saw no reason for going on with the war. If the war goes on, it's England's fault. That's what the German people will say. And Count Ciano's presence in the Reichstag today seemed to bind Italy to Hitler's declaration.

Hitler himself seemed rather skeptical that Mr. Churchill, whom he roundly attacked, would react to what he said. Concluded Hitler: "Possibly Mr. Churchill will again brush aside this statement of mine by saying that it is merely born of fear, and of doubt in our final victory. In that case, I shall have relieved my conscience in regard to the things to come." In fact, the Führer cast out some dark hints of the terrible things to come for Britain if the war goes on.

In many ways, it was the most colorful Reichstag session I've ever attended here. There were undoubtedly more gold-braided generals and admirals than have ever congregated under one roof. Pausing in his speech, Hitler named no less than twelve of them Field Marshals. He would salute each one and the generals, who were massed in the first balcony, would rise and return the salute as he named them. Twelve Field

Marshals after one war is a record for Germany. Hitler also created a new title for Field Marshal Göring. He promoted him to be a Field Marshal of the Reich, which makes him the ranking military man in Germany. Judging by the cheering in the Reichstag and in the street outside afterward, he is also the most popular man in Germany next to Hitler himself. General Halder, Germany's brilliant chief of staff, was named a colonel general, and several other of the returning victorious generals also were promoted. General Dietl, the defender of Narvik, received the largest cheers of all when Hitler announced that he was awarding him the first Oak Leaf of the Knight's Cross of the Iron Cross, the highest German decoration.

Count Ciano, who arrived in Berlin shortly before the Reichstag session opened, occupied the place of honor in the diplomatic box. He rose and gave the fascist salute several times when Hitler made friendly references to Italy. Once Hitler paused in his speech to salute Ciano who sprang up again to return it. When Hitler named Göring Reich Marshal, he stopped his speech and strode back to the speaker's chair and handed up the insignia to Göring, who was all smiles. And so it went, a most extraordinary scene. I noticed Dr. Schacht, with his high stiff collar, on the ministers' bench – like Göring, all smiles. And in the back row of the diplomatic box, the American chargé d'affaires, Mr. Alexander Kirk.

Berlin July 20, 1940 24.46

This is Berlin.

The rapidity of British reaction to Herr Hitler's speech before the Reichstag yesterday – I remember last night I had hardly got out of the Reichstag building before I heard the British radio roundly denouncing the speech – caused, I judge, some surprise here in Berlin. But the German press lost little time in breaking the news to its readers. The Berlin newspapers frankly told them tonight, not only that the British radio and press had rejected Hitler's declaration, not only that they had belittled the whole speech – they told their German readers tonight that the British press was emphatic that the war go on to the bitter end.

I don't think the German people were expecting that answer so soon. But the way Herr Hitler put it to them yesterday, I think, does make it certain that the great mass of the people in this country will now blame Britain if the war goes on.

Count Ciano, who attended yesterday's Reichstag session, had a long talk with Herr Hitler today, and late this evening left for Rome. Presumably, they discussed the next move in the war. By the time they met, London's emphatic "no" to peace was already known in Berlin.

American reaction to Hitler's speech, incidentally, is stated by the German News Agency to be this: that America thinks his offer to England was "a logical German action", but that Britain will reject it.

Though the German press devotes pages and pages to Hitler's speech, another speech, that of President Roosevelt, has not passed entirely unnoticed here, especially in the Wilhelmstrasse. The *Diplomatic Correspondence*, organ of the German Foreign Office, remarks that Mr. Roosevelt's program, as outlined in his speech to the Chicago convention, is "based from beginning to end on a willful opposition to the reborn West." The "reborn West", means, I take it, the new Europe which Germany and Italy hope to build up.

As to Mr. Roosevelt's renomination, a *DNB* dispatch from Washington states that the methods by which it was achieved have been "sharply condemned by all eyewitnesses."

Berlin July 22, 1940 24.46

This is Berlin.

Announcement is made here tonight of a special gift from Herr Hitler to Signor Mussolini.

It's an anti-aircraft armored train of the latest German model, with sixteen potent anti-aircraft weapons mounted on it. General von Pohl presented the gift to the Duce in the name of the Führer, suggesting, according to the account given here, that it accompany Mussolini on his travels so as to protect his life which, it is added, is so valuable for the Italian and German peoples.

Lord Halifax's curt rejection of Herr Hitler's Reichstag offer to call it quits with Britain caused no surprise in the Wilhelmstrasse this evening. But the German press still expresses complete bewilderment at the British reaction. I find such expressions as this in the papers here tonight: "What on earth are the British thinking of? The expressions of opinion we've heard so far don't sound genuine." And so on.

Now tonight in the *Deutsche Allgemeine Zeitung* there's a rather remarkable article which probably sheds some light on what is behind Germany's attitude towards England. This paper reveals that Hitler's idea has been all along a division of functions between the two empires – Britain as the great oceanic empire and Germany as the continental empire. Now, a great continent without equivalent sea-power is unthinkable, the paper declares. Germany would have been content, it continues, to see Great Britain contribute the sea-power to the continent of Europe. The decision of the United States to build a two-ocean navy with thirty-five battleships must also be taken into consideration, according to this Berlin paper, which concludes that Britain alone could never have built up to the United States. Only on the basis of a division of labor with Germany, it adds, could it have given Europe the needed naval power.

On the basis, therefore, of the continent for Germany and the seven seas and a big navy for Britain, Germany would like peace.

The *Deutsche Allgemeine Zeitung* made another point that I've not seen mentioned in the German press before. It discovered that the probable reason for Britain not wanting to halt the war now was its confidence in its navy to protect it from a German invasion and also to enforce the blockade of Germany and German-controlled areas. Heretofore, the British navy hasn't received attention in the press as a factor in the much-talked-of invasion of Britain. The paper argues, of course, that air-power can triumph over the British fleet, and perhaps that is the calculation that has been made here in regard to future events.

The Wilhelmstrasse let it be known today that the German government is closely following the Havana Conference. Officially, there is great reserve about it, but judging by certain press articles, Berlin does not like the American plan for a big cartel to dispose of South American products. The plain fact is that Germany, once the war is over, hopes and expects to regain its South American trade.

A lady in Chemnitz yesterday received a letter from South Africa postmarked September 3, 1914. Seems the letter got as far as France in 1914, stayed there during the war, and then during the twenty-two years of the peace remained in a pile of old mail in a French post office in a village near Maubeuge. German soldiers found the mail and dutifully put it in the mailbox. It is now being distributed in the regular way.

Berlin July 24, 1940 24.46

This is Berlin.

Germany today gave warning that it would treat members of that Home Guard which the British are forming as *franc-tireurs [guerrillas]*. And the German short-wave station broadcast in English the following warning: "German official quarters once more warn the misled British people and remind them of the fate of Polish *franc-tireurs* and gangs of murderers. Civilians who take up arms against a German soldier are, in accordance with international law, no better than base murderers, whether they be priests or bank-clerks.

"British people, you would do well to heed our warning!" This was what the German short-wave station said.

Since the people in Britain are permitted to listen to foreign radio stations, I suppose quite a few Britons heard that German warning. It would be interesting to hear from Mr. Murrow some time as to their reaction.

Lord Halifax's "no" to Hitler's peace declaration has now been taken at its face value in the German press, and the British Foreign Secretary and Mr. Churchill and his colleagues are branded today as criminals by the German press for not making peace with Germany. Now that the Germans know that Britain will not give up the struggle, the question arises in everyone's mind: When will the attack on Britain begin? How will it be made? The Germans naturally will not advertise the date in advance, if there is a date. But I can find no evidence that there is any rush here to start the last and most difficult assignment of the war. Yesterday, Herr Hitler was in Bayreuth, listening to Wagner's stirring opera *Götterdämmerung*. The rest of the week Herr von Ribbentrop will be in Salzburg talking to the Prime Ministers and Foreign Ministers of Romania and Bulgaria, not to mention the President and the Foreign Minister of Slovakia. You almost get the impression here that there is no hurry to come to grips with the British, to get an army over that stretch of sea separating Britain from the continent – and that maybe – maybe something will turn up in the meantime to bring peace after all.

In the meantime, the German air force pecks away at Britain and its shipping from its nearby bases in France. A special communiqué this afternoon declared that this morning five British merchant ships in convoy were destroyed by German bombers and a sixth set on fire. The High Command communiqué claimed that a British submarine and three small craft were sunk by German bombers. British bombers also visited Germany last night. According to the High Command, their bombs caused no great damage.

As you know, Germany has taken a tremendous number of prisoners in this war. A report issued here today reveals that most of them have already been put to work, thus relieving Germany's labor shortage. There are 700,000 Poles working on the farms alone. Two months after the war in the West began, a quarter of a million Belgian, British and French prisoners had been put to work in German trade and industry. Thousands more are being assigned jobs as laborers every day.

Two more Germans were put to death today on the charges of damaging the people's interests in wartime. They were accused of theft during the blackout.

Berlin July 27, 1940 14.00

This is Berlin.

The strange lull in this war continues. People keep wondering when the attack on Britain will get under way. But no one knows. But most Germans I talk to are deadly sure the war will be over before the winter sets in. After what happened to France, they are confident of the next phase of the war.

The papers make as much as possible of the air-attacks on Britain and especially on British shipping in the Channel. Yesterday, for a change, German motor-torpedo boats carried out an attack on British shipping near Brighton. A special war communiqué came out last evening claiming that 34,000 tons of shipping had been sunk in this speedboat raid. The *Völkischer Beobachter* claims this morning that the Germans have sunk 100,000 tons of enemy shipping in the last two days alone.

But of course all of this is merely skirmishing. The real war with Britain, it's realized, has not begun. Probably we must wait another ten days at least – perhaps longer.

In the meantime, Germany is consolidating its position in the Balkans and giving the governments in south-eastern Europe their first inkling of the kind of "New Order" which Germany expects to set up if and when the war is over. Recently the Hungarian Prime Minister and Foreign Minister journeyed to Munich to see Herr Hitler about the matter. Hungary of course wants Transylvania back from Romania. But the German course is that such matters as this can wait until the war's end.

Yesterday, it was the turn of the Romanians, who have swung so quickly into the German camp since the collapse of France. The Romanian Prime Minister and Foreign Minister arrived in Salzburg yesterday, had a talk with Herr Hitler and Herr von Ribbentrop over the New Order, and left last night for Rome to hear Mussolini's ideas on the same subject. The Romanian minister is quoted in the German press today as stating that the foreign policy of his land has taken a new turn. Bucharest's attitude towards Britain is shown in dispatches today which say that as a reprisal for the seizure by the British of three Romanian ships at Port Said, the Romanians have confiscated eighteen British tugs on the Danube. Romania is also turning against its former ally, France. Several French oil experts and directors of Franco-Romanian oil companies, it is reported, have just been expelled from Romania.

Following the Romanians come the Bulgarians, who arrived today for talks with Herr Hitler and Herr von Ribbentrop. Tomorrow the Slovaks arrive, Dr. Tiso, their President, and Dr. Tuka, the Foreign Minister. All roads on the continent now lead to Berlin, or wherever Herr Hitler and his Foreign Minister happen to be, and Germany naturally is taking advantage of its new position as the dominant power on the continent. Incidentally, I notice by the photographs that the Romanian statesmen wore uniforms when they arrived in Salzburg yesterday, just as do the Germans and Italians. It seems to be the new mode in Europe for the civilian statesmen. The Slovaks wear uniforms too on state visits.

While the war effort lags, the press here gives a lot of attention to the opening in Munich today of the Exhibition of German Art, an annual affair. Dr. Goebbels opened it this morning with a broadcast speech. "Only one enemy remains," said the Propaganda Minister, "and no one doubts who will win in the end. The German nation," he went on, "is in its entirety a fighting nation." Herr Hess opened the exhibition in the name of the Führer saying, "I greet him as the protector of German culture."

The theme of war dominates this exhibition of German art. There are paintings of the grim bombardment of Warsaw by heavy German artillery, and I notice one painting entitled *Bombardment of the Westerplatte*. And it shows the German battleship *Schleswig Holstein* firing point-blank into this little island by Danzig where the Poles defended themselves against overpowering odds so valiantly. There is a whole room devoted to paintings of the Polish war, and three to the war in the West.

It's announced in Berlin today that on the orders of Herr Himmler, chief of the secret police, a Polish land worker has been hanged. The charge is stated to be immoral conduct.

Berlin July 28, 1940 01.06

This is Berlin.

Germany's U-boats, about which we haven't heard so much in recent months, are creeping back into the communiqués of the High Command and into the German headlines.

A special communiqué of the German command issued this afternoon states that a submarine bagged five armed merchant men with a total tonnage of 48,000 tons out of a British convoy. Among the ships, it's claimed, was an 18,000-ton auxiliary cruiser. The same U-boat also reported sinking a 6,000-ton ship on another occasion.

It isn't so difficult for the German submarines as it used to be when they were operating from German naval bases on the North Sea. Then, to get out into the Atlantic at all, they had to make a hazardous journey up through the British-patrolled North Sea, around the tip of Scotland and Ireland, and then south to the Atlantic trade routes. It was a long trip, and dangerous.

Today, as the press here does not fail to point out, German submarines are using bases in Norway, Holland, Belgium, and especially France. Look at your maps. See how near Brest and Cherbourg and Le Havre are to the south-west tip of Britain, how near to the Atlantic trade routes. It makes it much easier for the U-boat commanders.

In the air yesterday, according to today's High Command communiqué, German flyers sank a 7,000-ton auxiliary cruiser, two destroyers and a merchant ship. A further destroyer and two freighters, it is added, were badly damaged. Over land, the German communiqué says harbor works at Swansea and several airfields in Cornwall were bombed. The score of yesterday's air battles over the Channel, according to the Germans, was five to two in their favor. I wager Mr. Murrow gives a different score. British bombers were again over Germany last night, and again the High Command declares they caused no damage.

Well, all these things make ringing headlines in the German newspapers, but they don't shed much light on the question everyone's asking: "When is the big attack on Britain to begin?" Judging by the little we can go on, it is not even very imminent and I still run into people who explain this extended lull as really being due to the possibility of a peace being negotiated after all. But the fog and rain of a European autumn will be on us soon, making big-scale operations impossible, so some sort of a decision cannot be too long in coming.

But if Herr Hitler appears to wait, he is not idle. The last three days he has been mending his fences in the Balkans where, to put it mildly, the leaders of state are lending their ears to the new signs of the times. Friday, the Romanians came to Salzburg where they were received by Herr Hitler and his Foreign Minister. Since then, dispatches from Bucharest tell us that the Romanian press has been full of talk of Romania's growing friendship with Germany and of her anxiety to fit herself into the new European order which Germany is preparing. Yesterday we had the Bulgarians, who, of course, have some claims against Romania. They too – their Prime Minister and Foreign Minister – were received by Herr Hitler and his foreign minister. Today, the Slovaks came, Dr. Tiso, the President, and Dr. Tuka, the Prime Minister, and they too were received by the Führer and Herr von Ribbentrop. The Hungarians have already paid their visit to Munich, leaving only Yugoslavia and Greece. Whether they will come too in the near future, I don't know. But I believe their lands are included in the Berlin picture of the New Order in Europe.

Count Volpi of Italy is also here. I ran into him in the elevator of my hotel this afternoon. He's here for economic talks. In fact, the atmosphere in Germany today is thick with discussion over the new economic set-up for which, as Dr. Funk told us a few days ago, Germany is already drawing up plans.

362

One is reminded of the old set-up, the old order, by a small item in the press today that M. Avenol, the secretary general of the League of Nations, has resigned. How long ago, it seems, that Geneva was the center of a new order many people were trying to build up. I was in Geneva the other day. There were but twenty-five or thirty officials left in that huge new marble League building above the lake in which the hopes of so many lay. It stands there today, above the lake against the blue of the Jura mountains, a beautiful but very dead and silent building, and the idea too seems dead on this continent, a thing of the past.

Berlin July 29, 1940 24.45

This is Berlin.

There's very little of a military nature to report from here tonight. As to yesterday's air fights over the English Channel, the High Command declares that six enemy planes were shot down and only one German. In north and west Germany, it reports that the British last night dropped only a few bombs without doing any damage except at Hamburg, where it says a bomb fell in the residential district.

It's curious, isn't it, how the Germans and British still respect each other's capital. I haven't heard of any German bombers over London and I haven't heard or seen any British planes over Berlin. As a matter of fact, Berlin is so quiet right now I heard the American correspondents at the Adlon complaining tonight that they couldn't find anything to write about. Perhaps it's always quiet before a storm.

I see in the local papers that Herr Hitler has sent a birthday telegram to Signor Mussolini. And that the Führer and King Victor Emmanuel have exchanged telegrams on the occasion of the fortieth anniversary of the latter's ascension to the throne. All three men expressed confidence in their final victory. I notice too that the mouth of the Danube has been mined – the Germans say against the British. And that the Romanian Prime Minister and Foreign Minister have returned home saying they were pleased with their visit to Germany and that a great future lies ahead of their country, in cooperation with the Reich.

The Slovaks were also pleased with their visit. Said Slovak Propaganda Minister Sano Mach, on his return to Bratislava today from Salzburg: "We are grateful and happy in the expectation that the fulfillment of the Führer's ideas will bring a better tomorrow to the Slovak people. In faith and loyalty to the great creator of the new Europe, we shall make our contribution to the completion of his work. If up to now," Dr. Mach went on, "I admired the devotion of the German people to Hitler, today I

363

understand it completely and I myself am so charmed with the Führer's personality that I cannot express my feeling in words." Thus spoke Sano Mach, Slovak Propaganda Minister.

Dr. Seyss-Inquart, the German commissar for Holland, has made an interesting speech at The Hague. He explains, for one thing, why he has prohibited the Dutch people from partaking in celebrations of any kind in honor of the Queen or the House of Orange. The reason, says Dr. Seyss-Inquart, is that the Queen lent her authority to the Dutch declaration of war on Germany, that she has proven herself an enemy of Germany, and is now residing in enemy territory. The commissar promises the Dutch, however, that eventually they will be free to choose their own form of government and to settle themselves their relations to the House of Orange. He also promises that Germany does not intend to rob the Netherlands of their independence or to take their colonies.

The German commissar then remarks that certain things are happening in Holland that can cause trouble for the Dutch. For one thing, he finds that the Dutch are boycotting the German civilian population in Holland. He then warns the Dutch against insulting the German people, their flag, and above all, he says, their Führer. Every such insult will find the sharpest reaction from the Germans, he adds. " I wish to especially warn those," says Dr. Seyss-Inquart, "who are trying to fish in troubled waters and think they can prove their bravery behind the backs of the German army. Every attempt to disturb will be ruthlessly punished . . . Also, the slightest aid to the enemy will be punished by death."

Berlin July 30, 1940 24.46

This is Berlin.

I went to a movie tonight. Two items are worth mentioning. One, newsreel shots of German army engineers blowing up the French Armistice monuments in Compiègne. I will never forget that afternoon of June 21st at Compiègne when I watched Herr Hitler and Field Marshal Göring staring at the monument in the center of the clearing. On it was the famous inscription: "Here on the 11th of November, 1918, Succumbed the Criminal Pride of the German Empire, Vanquished by the Free Peoples it Tried to Enslave." Hitler and the Germans regarded that inscription as a national insult. In the film tonight I saw it blown to bits. Blown to bits also was the little museum in which the Armistice car was housed – a museum built by an American, Mr. Arthur Henry Fleming of Los Angeles.

The second item was a little propaganda comedy – a feature shown weekly at all German film houses. There are always just two characters, played by a pair of popular Berlin comedians – one an old scamp, the other a young hero. The old scamp says: "The French are a nice people and have wonderful culture. I feel sorry for them. We ought to help them back on their feet." The young hero does not agree. He says: "Yes, put them back on their feet so that in another twenty-two years they can make war on us and get their revenge. That would be smart, wouldn't it."

These little propaganda features are always supposed to have a moral, and this one seemed obvious.

The German press this morning makes a great deal of anti-American articles in the Rome newspaper *Tevere*. The title of the piece is "The Unwanted Guest", meaning the USA. It says among other things that the "Jewish lust for booty" of the American business-getter has nothing in common with that thousand-year lesson of moral and authentic culture which Europe has. Let the Americans mind their own business and stop mixing in Europe, says this Italian paper – a sentiment that finds full approval in Berlin.

The bad weather – it has been rainy and cold for a week now – is limiting the activities of the German air force, the High Command tells us today in its daily communiqué. Despite curtailed flights yesterday, however, German night-raiders, says the High Command, bombed a British aircraft factory at Filton and harbor works at Swansea and Plymouth. British night-raiders were also over Germany, but only a few this time, according to the High Command.

German military circles here, in an effort to answer questions of the correspondents as to when the war on Britain really will start, informed us today that it had started already. Their point was that the daily attacks of submarines, motor-torpedo boats and airplanes already represented a serious beginning. They compared these to the opening sword thrusts in a duel. The military people asked us to consider that besides the bombing of aircraft factories, munition works and harbors in Britain, German sea and aircraft had destroyed 1,200,000 tons of British shipping since June 25th. However, we were not let into the secret of when the big attack is to begin, or if it is to begin; and we're not likely to.

Berlin August 1, 1940 14.05

This is Berlin.

No less authoritative neutral sources than Secretary of State Hull and Secretary of War Stimson are cited today by the German radio to back up

Germany's argument that the British haven't a chance to win the coming show-down with the Reich.

No one here accuses members of the present American government with being unduly prejudiced in favor of Germany – hence the weight which their opinions carry among the people here.

The German radio first takes up the speech of Mr. Hull in Havana in which he advised his fellow American delegates that they must all reckon after the war with European markets which would be dominated by authoritarian régimes. The German radio jumps on that remark and concludes: "This shows that in the United States they count on a defeat of Britain."

According to the German radio, Secretary of War Stimson, speaking before a Congressional Committee, also held out no hope for Britain. The German radio quotes him as saying that "Britain will be overpowered in a short time and the British fleet will pass under enemy control." "This remark of the American Secretary of War," comments the local radio, "is a new sign that in the United States they hold that England hasn't a chance now."

The announcement by Great Britain that henceforth it will blockade the entire continent is scoffed at in Berlin – at least by the editorial writers. They doubt that Britain has the navy for the job. They think there will be plenty of holes in that blockade. Welcome also in Berlin are dispatches from Washington saying that President Roosevelt insists that American vessels keep the last bridge to Europe open by maintaining their voyages to Portugal and Spain.

The Supreme Council of the Soviet meets today in Moscow to deliberate on the request of the Baltic states for incorporation into the Soviet Union. There seems to be no doubt as to the Soviet decision. Already today the German radio reports that all Lithuanian ships at sea have been ordered to report to Russian ports.

Nearly every day now one or the other of the German newspapers gives us a glimpse into the New Europe which the Third Reich is now planning for this continent as soon as the war is over. Today Dr. Ernst Timm, writing in the *Börsen Zeitung*, gives us a further glimpse.

The last result of nationalism in Europe, he says, was the union of all Germans in one nation. The next phase in Europe he thinks will be known by what he terms "European Responsibility", a responsibility, he adds, which has been taken over by Germany. He finds three points in his new conception of Europe.

1. Only a nation in Europe which is conscious of its European responsibility has a right to take part in the new reconstruction. A people like the French, which he says has become mixed with Negroes and Jews, has no right to European leadership.

2. Only peoples who through their greatness and their life-force are capable of independent European contributions have the right to self-responsible action.

3. The European leader-peoples, as he puts it, carry the responsibility not only for their own national fate, but also for that of the smaller peoples who are placed in their *Lebensraum* — or living space.

He concludes that Germany and Italy are the nations to take the responsibility. He also says this will be the *last* European war. After all these centuries, nay millenniums, of wars in Europe, it will be comforting to many to know that this is the last European war.

The other day I mentioned an announcement in the German press that a Polish farm laborer had been hanged for an immoral offense on the orders of Herr Himmler, chief of the German police. The *Dienst Aus Deutschland* reports today that this case had led to rumors that Herr Himmler had been empowered by law to order hangings. This, says the German news organization, is not the case. Sentences of criminals, it explains, will follow the laws of the districts in which they're committed.

Berlin August 2, 1940 14.05

This is Berlin.

Germans this morning learned for the first time of the sea-battle in the South Atlantic between the British auxiliary cruiser, *Alcantara*, and a German armed raider. The Germans add no new details of their own, not even the name of the ship. The Wilhelmstrasse this morning let it be known it was highly pleased with Mr. Molotov's speech yesterday. Final figures on the losses of the Dutch army are given out in Berlin today. They were 2,890 killed, 7,000 wounded and twenty-nine missing.

People over here often ask what is going to happen to countries like Belgium and Holland if the Germans win the war. Today the *Völkischer Beobachter* hints that the Netherlands, at least, will become closely associated with the German Reich. "Leading German circles," it writes, "know perfectly well that the Dutchman is a part of the low-German race which in the course of history was torn from the Reich." The paper then argues that the European position of the Dutch must now be restored. It admits, however, that most Dutch do not yet understand this and moreover they are still hoping for the return of their former position. Apropos of this I notice a photograph in the *Börsen Zeitung* today showing Dutch workmen clearing away débris from the ruins of a bombed Dutch town. The Berlin paper has this caption: "Dutch clear up what was ruined by their own guilt."

367

Berlin August 4, 1940 01.01

This is Berlin.

Today has seemed very much like a London weekend in August. Nothing exciting in the newspapers, the city deserted, and everyone who has the carfare, out in the country.

Not that the city was exactly deserted. Thousands of provincials and thousands of soldiers on leave were here to rubberneck. I watched them from outside my hotel, staring at the Brandenburg Gate, the Reichstag, and snapping photographs. The Germans, I'm convinced, are the most camera-mad people in the world. I have yet to meet one on the street without a camera slung on his or her shoulder.

What about the war, the Total War, you wondered. But the multitudes in the streets and parks, the tens of thousands swimming or sailing on the Wannsee, or picnicking in the Grünewald Woods that ring the city – they didn't seem to be thinking of it. Yes, and in a short stroll through the Tiergarten, I passed six groups of people – forty or fifty in a group – clustered attentively around a squirrel whom some good soul was feeding. I wanted to address these gentle squirrel-feeders and say: "Are you the people that conquered Poland and Norway and Holland and Belgium and France?" I didn't, because they were the people.

Well, some people think the big attack on Britain is coming off soon. And some people don't. And frankly I don't know. Nor do I understand why it hasn't come off before this. Nor why it's being held up. One Sunday newspaper, the *Lokal Anzeiger*, tells us this morning that the British army isn't much good, and they all tell us that the British air force is definitely inferior to the German. So what? you ask, but the answer as to why the attempt to invade Britain has not begun is not forthcoming. One learned fellow explained to me today that the air force must first wear down the British, destroy his harbors, his oil stores, his big army camps, his shipping. When the bombers had made Britain ripe, then would come the invasion.

"When will that be?" I asked him. He said he didn't know. But the papers here tell us the real air business hasn't yet begun. The present activity is only preliminary.

On the other hand, the *Börsen Zeitung* tells us this morning in a big headline that: ENGLAND'S POSITION IS HOPELESS. The article under it then describes the week's results of the air and sea warfare against British shipping and reviews the strategic advantage Germany has in the air, not only because of its superiority in planes but because its bases are within a few minutes of British objectives.

Now actually, the most important story this coming week – barring a surprise attack on Britain, which seems most unlikely – will take place in

Bucharest. Tomorrow, a Bulgarian delegation will arrive there to ascertain whether Romania is willing to return the Dobruja, which she seized from unfortunate Bulgaria after the last war. Feeling in Berlin tonight is that Romania, without too much argument, will satisfy Bulgaria on the matter, thus further reducing its size and population in a peaceful manner, as was done in the case of Bessarabia and Bukovina.

After the Bulgarians will come the Hungarians, asking back a much bigger chunk of territory which went to Romania after the last war, namely Transylvania. This is a more serious matter for Romania and may take longer to decide, for it is a big chunk of territory and a lot of Romanians reside in it. Probably, thinks Berlin, there will be some sort of compromise, and Romania will succeed in keeping a small chunk. All of these negotiations are the result of the recent talks of the leaders of the three nations concerned with Herr Hitler.

At Salzburg, one is given to understand, the Romanians were told that they must agree to a peaceful solution of the revisionist claims of Hungary and Bulgaria – and that discussion could not wait for the war's end. Berlin wants to get the Balkans settled as soon as possible so that they can take their place in the new Axis economic order.

As to war news, the High Command today reports that German bombers last night set fire to oil tanks near Liverpool. British planes again visited Germany last night. The High Command states they dropped more bombs than on recent evenings but caused less damage.

Berlin August 5, 1940 14.05

This is Berlin.

The *Börsen Zeitung am Mittag* tells us this noon that the entire world press regards this week as a crucial one. Meaning, I take it, that the long-awaited attack on Britain may begin before the week is up. Well, it may be. And we all know by this time that Germany is pretty good at concealing its zero-hours for the big take-offs.

But I must say there is no evidence around Berlin that this is to be the crucial week. Before the Scandinavian campaign, before the big offensive in the West, there was tension in the air in Berlin. You don't feel that tension here just at the moment. An awful lot of people seem to be vacationing this week.

Some people here think that the German air force has to do a great deal more work on Britain before there is any question of an attempt at invasion by a great land army. That is to say, British harbor works, oil stores, landing fields, anti-aircraft positions, must first be pretty well liquidated before an attack by the tanks and troops is feasible. Obviously, that, as yet, has not been accomplished in Britain. No one here pretends that it has.

This strategy was outlined to us yesterday in an article in the *Völkischer Beobachter*, the official party organ, signed by "Arminius," which is Latin for "Hermann", a very well-known first-name in these parts. The author developed the idea that the first job of an air force is to gain complete superiority in the air by destroying the other fellow's airfields, hangars, planes, oil stores, and anti-aircraft nests. That over, the second phase begins when the air force can devote most of its energies to supporting the land army. This strategy was followed in Poland and in the West. Presumably, it is the strategy to be used with Britain. The only question is this: Why hasn't the German *Luftwaffe* attacked Britain on a bigger scale, since we know it is superior in numbers?

The German press itself tells us that what Britain has experienced so far has only been a taste of what will come later when the war really gets serious.

The *12-Uhr Blatt* front-pages a Washington dispatch today to the effect that Senator Lundeen is trying to start a third party which will fight the so-called interventionist policies of the two major American parties. The dispatch is published without comment, but its position on the front page is interesting. Washington dispatches in the German newspapers also pay considerable attention to the opposition in the United States to conscription. It's a subject which interests a nation which has built up the world's best army by conscription.

Berlin August 6, 1940 24.40

This is Berlin.

The German people were informed today by the German High Command that no less than five million tons – to be quite exact, 4,986,860 tons – of enemy shipping have been sunk by the German navy and air force in the first eleven months of the war. FIVE MILLION TONS IN ELEVEN MONTHS is the big banner headline in the early editions of tomorrow's morning newspapers in Berlin.

It's a big headline and it's a big figure, and I'll wager that Mr. Murrow will give you another.

But five million tons isn't the whole story, as we're given it in Berlin. The High Command adds to that another sizeable figure. It adds another million and a half tons which it says the German air force has damaged, but not sunk, since the war began.

Now if we accept this German figure of five million tons, almost all of which would be British, we come to the conclusion that Great Britain in eleven months of the war has lost nearly a third of her shipping, which amounted to some seventeen million tons last September.

The High Command breaks the figures down to show that despite all we hear about the overwhelming power of the airplane, about how the air force alone can blockade Britain, the German navy in fact has sunk twice as much as the German air force. Sinkings of enemy shipping by the German navy are given as 3,725,000 tons; by the German air force 1,260,000 tons.

The vast majority of ships sunk by the navy, it is plain from the account, have been due to submarine action. The figures given by the High Command for the last three weeks of July – from July 9 to July 31st – are truly startling. They are: 679,324 tons —or more than 200,000 tons per week.

I almost forgot to mention that this does not include, we are told by the High Command, the enemy ships sunk by mines, or ships damaged.

As to the air battles over England yesterday, I cannot give you a score tonight because the High Command gives only British losses, which it says were eight. German losses are not mentioned.

Your correspondent has been spending most of his time lately trying to ascertain from the neutral aviation experts here how the coming battle in the air between Germany and Britain is going to shape up. I keep asking, for instance, how many planes have the Germans and the British. The truth seems to be that none of them know. But most of the neutral experts here do seem to agree – and I pass the information on to you for what it's worth – that Germany has: (1) more planes than Britain, (2) bigger and more deadly explosive bombs, and (3) the strategic advantage due to the short distance between its new bases in the Lowlands and France.

General Pershing's *[Commander of the American Expeditionary Force in World War One]* proposal to sell a large number of American destroyers to Britain has not failed to attract attention here. The *Lokal Anzeiger* front-pages the story. Commenting on a suggestion it attributes to Senator Pittman, that Britain give us a few battleships in exchange, the paper concludes: "Old over-age destroyers against useable battleships – despite all the friendship, not a bad business."

Berlin August 7, 1940 24.46

This is Berlin.
Every newspaper in Berlin this evening plays up the same story on Page

One. It's not about the war. It's not about a new victory over the British. It's about a man known in this country as Dr. Krupp von Bohlen und Halbach. To you that man is known as Krupp, head of Germany's great Krupp armaments works, without which Germany could not have fought the last war nor the present one.

Why does Dr. Krupp snatch the main headlines away from war and victory in the German press today? you may ask.

Well, he had a birthday today. He was seventy years old, and no less a personage than Adolph Hitler dropped his work in Berlin and made the long journey to Essen to congratulate the armaments king on his birthday and confer upon him some of the highest honors of the Reich.

Calling on Dr. Krupp at his villa in Essen, Herr Hitler personally conveyed his birthday greetings, and then presented him with the golden Emblem of Honor of the National Socialist party. The Führer did not come by himself. With him was his economics minister, Dr. Funk, who, on behalf of the government, decorated the armaments chief with the Eagle's Shield of the Reich on which had been engraved the words: "To the German Economic Führer." Various other organizations presented Dr. Krupp with birthday gifts. Herr Hitler visited the huge munitions plant before leaving Essen.

You may have noticed that Alsace and Lorraine, that bone of contention between Germany and France for centuries, have not yet been formally incorporated into the Reich. But Berlin is not waiting on formalities. Today, on the order of the Führer, the civilian administration in the two provinces was taken from the military and handed over to German civil control.

Gau-leader Bürckel, who had been ruling Austria, becomes chief of the civil administration of Lorraine. Gau-leader Wagner takes over control in Alsace. Gau-leader Simon is put in charge of Luxemburg.

The German-appointed burgomaster of Strasbourg, welcoming Alsatian refugees from France, yesterday said: "If you do not find your home a waste-land, your thanks are due to the Führer and the German Army."

Incidentally, Baldur von Schirach, head of the Hitler Youth organization, has been appointed governor of Austria. He's thirty years old.

The German press is following very closely the debate in the United States over compulsory military service. No editorial comment is offered, but the German dispatches from Washington play up the opposition to conscription. The negative attitude of the AFL and the CIO as well as the railroad brotherhood is duly noted in the press. The resolution of the CIO seamen's union that conscription spells slavery also gets attention in the German press.

Food cards for dogs and cats have been introduced in Holland. Dogs get from six to twenty-five pounds of dog cake a month, depending on their size. Cats fare worse – they get three pounds of food a month.

Berlin August 8, 1940 24.46

This is Berlin.

The German version of attacks by motor torpedo boats and bombers on British shipping today was given in a special war communiqué issued here this evening. It claims fifteen British ships with a total tonnage of 72,000 tons sunk within twenty-four hours and further that thirty-four British fighters against only three German planes were lost in air fights this morning.

The attack by German speedboats took place last night. Out of a strongly defended convoy, three ships – an 8,000 ton tanker, and two freighters totaling 12,000 tons – were torpedoed and sunk by the little German craft, all of which, according to the High Command, returned safely to their base.

The German air force claimed a much bigger bag. The special war communiqué declared that German planes attacked a British convoy in the Channel this morning. According to it, no less than twelve British ships with a total tonnage of 55,000 tons were sunk by the German bombers, and five others damaged.

An air battle developed during the bombing, we are told, in which five British fighters were shot down. One German plane, it was added, is missing.

During further air battles during the morning, concludes the special communiqué, twenty-nine further British fighters were shot down; only two German planes were lost. Those are the German figures, and they will certainly boost faith here in the air force. Mr. Murrow's figures, perhaps, will not agree with mine.

Earlier in the day, the Supreme Command reported that German planes during the night had dropped mines before several British ports. This led afternoon papers like the *Nachtausgabe* to print large headlines saying: AIR FORCE BLOCKS SEVERAL BRITISH PORTS WITH MINES. The High Command also reported German bomber attacks on motor works at Leyland, the Vickers Armstrong works at Chester, factories at Plymouth, anti-aircraft and searchlight positions at Manchester, Cardiff, Dorchester and Plymouth.

British bombers were again over north and west Germany last night and again the High Command reported they had not caused any considerable damage. They paid a visit to Essen where the great Krupps munitions works are. They must have arrived there shortly after Herr Hitler left that city last night.

Well, from all these German communiqués it does look as if Germany's *air* war, at least, against Britain is beginning to get underway. Some people here characterized today's activity as a signal, but that may be going too far.

Berlin August 9, 1940 24.45

This is Berlin.

Yesterday the air forces of Germany and Great Britain fought it out with guns. Today, the battle continues, only with propaganda, with words.

Last night at this time I reported that the Germans claimed to have shot down thirty-four British planes with the loss of only three of their own. This noon, after a final checking up, the High Command in its daily communiqué put the figure at forty-nine British craft down against twelve German planes lost.

This evening the German press is furious at the British claim to have shot down fifty-three German planes. DIRTY LOSERS is the caption over a front page editorial in the *Börsen Zeitung*. THEY LIE, WE WIN, is the headline over the front-page editorial in the *Deutsche Allgemeine Zeitung*. CHURCHILL RECOUNTS FAIRY TALES, says the *Lokal Anzeiger*.

A spokesman for the German air force, justifying the German figures, told us at a press conference today that the shooting down of an enemy plane must be verified by two witnesses. He argued that German figures are more accurate than British because the Germans have a much more centralized system. The British, according to him, depend for their reports upon civilian eyewitnesses. I remember last year Major Schumacher, who led the coastal fighters on the North Sea, telling us that in his outfit there had to be three witnesses for every plane shot down, that is, two who were not in the plane which claimed the victim.

The air force spokesman today said he could give an exact breakdown of yesterday's losses on both sides. On the British side he claimed: thirty-three Spitfires, nine Hurricanes, three Blenheim-Bristol bombers, one Hampton and three unrecognized types. On the German side: seven Junkers 87s, three Messerschmitt 109s. Of the two German planes which had to make forced landings, one was a Messerschmitt 109, the other a Messerschmitt 110. The crew of one of these was killed in landing.

374

Berlin August 11-12, 1940 01.01

This is Berlin.

Well, it looks as if the war on Britain, at least in the air, has started in earnest. Today, judging by German reports, saw – along the English coast – the greatest air battle of the war, and probably the greatest ever fought any time, anywhere.

I realize you're going to hear both sides about these air-clashes off Britain today. This is Berlin, and I give you the German account as issued this afternoon and this evening in various special war communiqués by the High Command.

First of all, the score. Or rather the scores, because they kept coming in all afternoon and evening. The main special war communiqué which came out early this afternoon said that seventy-three British planes were shot down while only fourteen German planes were lost. But the battle was not yet over when the Germans issued these figures. The communiqué concluded: "The battle over the Channel continues." Later tonight, the number of British planes shot down was raised by six to seventy-nine. The German losses, or as the communiqué put it, "the planes which have not yet returned," remained at fourteen. When I started to jot down my notes for this talk, the score stood, as given out in Berlin, at seventy-nine to fourteen in favor of Germany.

Then a couple of hours ago, the radio in the room where I work suddenly switched off the music, and we were given a further special communiqué of the High Command. There had been two further air battles beside the main one over Portland, and the final figures stood at eighty-nine British planes shot own; seventeen German planes down. This was an all-time record.

According to the German account, there were three separate battles in the air today.

The main one over the British naval base at Portland, lying roughly half-way between Southampton and Plymouth on the south coast of England; a second over Dover; a third east of Harwich.

The first and largest air fight began when German bombing squadrons, protected by Messerschmitt fighters, began to bomb Portland. A word about the bombing attack itself, because somehow you get so interested in the air fight that you forget the main object of the flight which was to bomb the British naval base at Portland. The German High Command claims it was very successful. It says well-aimed bombs destroyed important harbor works and set oil tanks on fire. The German radio gives more details. It makes the flat statement, for instance, that most of the ships in the harbor were completely destroyed. The quays along the water-front, it says, were heavily bombed;many explosions were observed on the dam which leads to the mainland. Further, declares the German radio, a loading pier near Castletown showed several big bomb craters after the attack and warehouses were seen burning. It says all this was observed by German reconnaissance planes which radioed a running report of the attack back to German bases.

So much for the German version of the attack on Portland. 150 miles eastward along the coast, German planes attacked barrage-balloons protecting Dover. According to the German account, eight of them were shot down. British fighters came up to engage the Germans at Dover. Seven of them, says the German communiqué, were shot down. No German losses at Dover are specifically mentioned.

The third air battle took place east of Harwich, on the east coast of England. Here the Germans say they attacked a convoy of ships, sent three of them, with a total tonnage of 17,000 tons, to the bottom and scored a direct hit on a destroyer, damaging it. The convoy, say the Germans, consisted of seventy merchant ships, escorted by fourteen warships. British fighters also swarmed up here and the German communiqué goes on to say that seventeen of them were shot down. No specific German losses are mentioned here either. The communiqué then concludes that eight more British planes were shot down elsewhere.

So much for the German version of what apparently is the greatest day's air-fighting history has yet seen. It will be interesting to compare it with London's. The theory that most neutral observers had here, that Germany would try first to soften Britain by aerial attack before attempting anything more, seems to be working out in reality. From now on, I take it, aerial warfare over the English Channel will be continued on a big scale. Germany thinks it will win it because it has more planes and is on the offensive. As to when the land army will try to get a foothold on the shore of Britain, no one knows. My guess is, not so soon. It depends upon a lot of factors, of course. Besides the military hazards involved, there is the question: what is Germany's goal?

Rudolf Kircher, editor of the *Frankfurter Zeitung*, says this morning that Germany's task now is to break Britain's will to war by all means. To break Britain's will to war, he explains, by taking away from it its physical possibilities to offer further resistance. Dr. Kircher is confident that Germany has the means to this end. Does that mean that it is hoped here that the air force itself can do the job? The editor does not tell us, and I don't know.

Dr. Kircher thinks it is all too bad, because he says Germany didn't want to destroy Britain. It only wanted to induce London to play its proper role as a non-European Empire.

Dr. Kircher even tells us the price Britain would have had to pay to accept this German proposal. It would include: return of the German colonies; the freeing of Italy from its imprisonment in the Mediterranean;

and access for both Germany and Italy to the raw materials of this world. The British, he regrets, found this price too high to pay.

Dr. Walter Funk, Minister of Economics and President of the Reichsbank, speaking at the opening of the Königsberg Fair this morning, told a nation-wide audience of Germans that he agreed with Colonel Lindbergh when the American flyer stated recently, "If the rich become too rich and the poor too poor, something must be done."

"We stand at the beginning of a new epoch," said Dr. Funk, "and this opinion is gaining momentum in the whole world." Dr. Funk then made reference to his agreement with Colonel Lindbergh that something must be done.

The German radio closed its news broadcast tonight with this appeal: "Comrades, show discipline during the night air-attacks. When the danger becomes urgent, go immediately to your air-raid shelter."

Berlin August 13-14, 1940 24.46

This is Berlin.

Today was the third day of Germany's massive air attacks on Britain and, judging from German reports, there was no let-up.

There seems to have been no concentrated attack on any particular British base as on the two previous days, when Portland and Portsmouth were the objectives. The German reports tell mostly of bombing attacks on British airfields, anti-aircraft positions, ships and balloon barrages. British bombers also struck back today with daylight attacks. It looks like a bitter war to the finish in the air, with both sides claiming victory.

Latest score of today's air-fighting, as given out in Berlin, stands at sixty-nine British planes shot down against only thirteen German. Those are the official figures here. The Germans break down the figure, claiming thirty-eight British machines were shot down in the air in and around Britain, fifteen destroyed on the ground and sixteen British bombers down as a result of a surprise daylight attack on the German-occupied Danish airbase at Aalborg.

One of the main German attacks today was on the British airfield at Eastchurch where the Germans claim to have destroyed six hangars, ten Spitfires on the ground and set the oil tanks on fire. Attacks on British shipping today brought no spectacular results. Berlin reports two merchant ships damaged, two patrol boats sunk. German fighters again attacked a balloon barrage on the south-east coast of England – presumably Dover – and twelve balloons are said to have been shot down.

Last night, according to the High Command, British bombers were over northern and western Germany. No great damage was done, says the High Command, and four bombers were shot down. Final score for yesterday is given by the High Command today as ninety-two British planes shot down against twenty-four German.

Berlin has now become conscious of the fact that figures on air losses as given out here don't bear the slightest resemblance to those issued in London. So attention is being paid to the reaction to the conflicting reports abroad. Tonight the German radio quoted the *New York Times* as emphasizing that British resistance in the air is becoming weaker.

Tomorrow I plan to fly to the Channel to see if I can pick up any information on the matter.

Berlin August 18, 1940 01.01

This is Berlin.

One little item in today's war communiqué of the German High Command struck my attention tonight on my return from a brief visit to the English Channel. It mentioned four people being killed and twenty-two wounded in Brussels last night when British bombs fell on the Belgian capital.

I happened to be in Brussels last night. About midnight I was sitting in the lobby of one of the hotels there with two other American correspondents. We were just remarking how quiet it was compared to the night before there, when the German anti-aircraft batteries had pounded through most of the night, or the previous night at Calais where the German flak guns kept us awake all night, firing at British bombers.

Then without any warning – from sirens or anti-aircraft guns – there was one of those thuds, and it was very close. The British bomber must have dived from a considerable height with its motors shut off and then let loose his bomb. Later we went out to see the damage, but couldn't get near enough for close inspection because of the police cordons.

I'd like to say a few words about how the air war against Britain looks from the cliffs near Calais. But first about tonight's news.

According to a special war communiqué issued here a couple of hours ago, German bombers and fighters have again been active over Britain today. Though the German radio earlier this evening quoted the Air Force Command as saying that today's air operations were limited by the weather, the score on the fighting, as given out in Berlin late tonight, just about sets up a new record. The Germans say they shot down 138 British machines and lost thirty-four. Some twenty-three of the British machines, it is added, were destroyed on the ground.

378

Main German objectives today seem to have been British airfields around London and in Kent and Hampshire. This would seem to indicate that the Germans are concentrating more and more on trying to smash the British air force on the ground, a tactic they used very successfully in Poland. I would say offhand, though, that if the British camouflage their fields anywhere near as well as the Germans have camouflaged the ones I saw in Belgium and France, then it will be a difficult job destroying planes on the ground. Once in Belgium our German pilot couldn't find his landing field for several minutes because it looked just like all the other farms from the air. In France I constantly drove by German landing fields without recognizing them as such until some officer started counting the bombers or fighters tucked away . . . Well, it would be letting out military secrets if I said any more.

Among British airfields attacked today, according to German reports, were Croydon and Sutton, near London, where it's claimed twenty-one planes were destroyed on the ground. The German radio admits that here British fighters attempted to block the German bombers, but says they failed and lost twenty-five planes in the attempt.

So much for today's air warfare, with the Germans giving the score as 138 to 34 in their favor. Thursday and Friday I spent idling along the Channel cliffs between Calais and Boulogne watching the German bombers and fighters start out for England, twenty-one miles away. I might as well admit that I was on the wrong side of the Channel, so far as watching the fireworks was concerned. There Ed Murrow has the advantage over me. Actually, I didn't see a British plane during the two days I was on the French side of the Channel. The Germans told me that a few Spitfires came over on Thursday, the day of the big attack on London, and that three of them were shot down, but none of us American correspondents saw them. Of course, night-time is a different story in that region, judging by the German anti-aircraft fire I heard.

But during the day the French side of the Channel is dominated completely by the German air force. We spent several hours at Cap Gris Nez and Cap Blanc Nez, the two French coastal points only twenty-one miles from Dover, where the Channel swimmers like Gertrude Ederle used to hang out. All day long German torpedo boats cruised up and down, a mile or so from land, and we never saw them molested.

Incidentally, Thursday afternoon was so clear that we could see the Dover cliffs and hear quite distinctly the roar of the British anti-aircraft guns and the sounds of the bomb explosions.

One thing that impresses you is the great height at which the planes fly. Often you hear the roar of the German bombers setting out over the Channel for England, but you can't see them with the naked eye, they're flying so high. You can only follow them with strong field glasses. When they passed us on the cliffs the German bombers must have been flying between 10,000 and 12,000 feet, with the Messerschmitt fighters protecting them still higher in the air and often invisible even through glasses. Thursday, we estimated that the Germans may have used some 200 bombers and 300 fighters against London. We could see them going out in formation of twenty-five or so bombers with about twice as many Messerschmitts protecting them. I saw no Stuka dive-bombers that day. The Germans were using exclusively level bombers, mostly big Heinkels. Often, both German bombers and fighters returned more or less out of formation. But it was absolutely impossible to judge as to losses. Fred Oechsner of the U.P. and I checked fifty-three bombers out and saw less than that return, but others might easily have returned to other airfields, of which there are a large number. Those we saw took off and landed at these improvised, almost invisible landing fields which are masterpieces of camouflage. Nearby, a French peasant would be sitting behind a team of horses cutting wheat. Cows would be grazing, perfectly oblivious to these roaring air monsters of destruction.

We had no chance to speak with the German pilots when they returned from their raids on Britain. But in Brussels yesterday I had a talk with one of the Messerschmitt pilots who had been active all week. He seemed confident that the war would be over before winter. Incidentally, the German pilots think the Spitfire is as good as a Messerschmitt, but that the Hurricanes and Defiants are very much inferior.

I kept my eyes open for evidence of the expected German invasion. I saw a few interesting things which I cannot go into now, but on the whole we were shown very little that would indicate that the invasion was imminent. Maybe it was there, and we just didn't see it. But we didn't get that impression after covering more than 200 miles by car along the coast. The main impression was that the war in the air would be fought first.

Berlin August 19, 1940 24.46

This is Berlin.

Today there seems to have been a lull in Germany's air war against Britain. This evening's papers and even the early editions of tomorrow morning's newspapers are still playing up yesterday's air attack. They all headline the final score as given out today by the High Command: 147 British planes destroyed against thirty-six German machines missing.

Total number of British planes shot down in the last eight days is given in Berlin as 732. British planes last night again visited Germany, both the western and southern parts, but the High Command claims no great damage was done. When you hear the German anti-aircraft guns firing all night long, as I did in Calais and Brussels on two evenings last week, you wonder what those British bombers are doing, since no great damage is ever reported.

General Christiansen, the German military commander of the Netherlands, has issued another warning to the Dutch about committing sabotage. He points out that in spite of his first warning on July 6th, another act of sabotage has been committed in Holland. If this happens again, the general warns, not only the criminals will be punished, but the communities where the sabotage takes place and also the town in which the perpetrators live will be punished. Fines will be assessed against the communities and hostages taken. *[The preceding sentence was deleted by the censor.]*

General Christiansen also warns the Dutch about not reporting the landing of enemy flyers on Dutch soil. People in Holland, he says, who give shelter to enemy soldiers will be severely punished, even by death.

Berlin August 20, 1940 14.00

This is Berlin.

We had an air-raid alarm last night, but nothing untoward happened so far as I know.

Actually, the sirens started to sound just forty-five seconds before I went on the air last night with the evening broadcast. Even through the soundproof studio doors you could hear the siren, and someone came in to announce that there was an alarm. But the engineers all stuck to their posts and we were able to proceed with the broadcast without any trouble at all. *[This paragraph was deleted by the censor.]*

Afterward I went out to watch the excitement, but there wasn't any. A few anti-aircraft guns roared in the distance, some searchlights went into action, but that was about all. Later it was explained that two bombers came over and cruised over a suburb without dropping any bombs. Later, say the Germans, one of the planes was picked up by the searchlights at Brunswick, and shot down in flames.

So far today – its just 2 p.m. here in Berlin – we have no word about air activities over Britain. Yesterday was also a quiet day in the air war, the Germans reporting that they limited their activities to reconnaissance flights and that there were few air battles. The Germans say they shot down five British planes yesterday and lost two themselves.

The period of clear weather over the Channel and Britain is drawing to a close, but the weather experts tell me you can count on probably at least two or three more weeks of good weather before the fall mists and fogs set in. Whether the Germans think that is enough for their air force to settle accounts with the British, I don't know. One Messerschmitt pilot told me after the raid on London last Thursday, that he thought they could finish the British air force in about two weeks of good weather. But he was only speaking in his private capacity.

The German press continues to cite American newspapers to prove the great damage which the German air-raids on Britain are making. The *New York Times* is quoted in the *12-Uhr Blatt* today as saying that the suburbs of London and the airfield at Croydon were hit badly by the German bombs.

As you might expect, the German press this morning is full of irony over what the papers call the victorious British withdrawal from Somaliland. They call it the fourth victorious withdrawal of the British in this war, the others being Aandalsnes, Namsos and Dunkirk. Upon receipt of the news of the British withdrawal from Somaliland, Herr Hitler immediately sent a telegram of congratulations to Mussolini. The German papers this morning laud the exploits of the Italians in driving the British out of the African colony. Whatever the facts may be about what happened there, or why, the Italian victory has served to raise still higher the prestige of the Axis powers in Europe and the confidence of the people here in a quick and final victory.

Incidentally, I stopped off at Dunkirk a few days ago, and it's remarkable how much of the débris has been cleared up. The town was terribly smashed, but most of the streets have now been cleared. I was surprised to see so many French people still living there. These civilians in the destroyed cities are certainly a courageous lot. I talked to a French waitress in Calais, and she was not downhearted by any means. She said she felt thankful to have escaped with her life, and thankful that she had a job again.

I noticed too in northern France and Belgium, that the harvests are being taken in. This will help the food situation.

Berlin August 22, 1940 24.46

This is Berlin.

For the first time since the war began, German losses in the air were given by the High Command today as almost equalling losses of the enemy. Reporting on yesterday's air activity, the German Command stated that the British lost seven planes, the Germans six.

Of course those are low figures. As a matter of fact, the figures have been low for four days now as Germany's aerial offensive, following last Sunday's big attack, slacked up – for how long no one is saying here. Why it has slacked, I don't know. Some people think it's because of the weather. But the German war communiqués do not mention the weather. Other people think the Germans are getting ready to attempt the great knock-out blow, and that is why there's a lull. We'll just have to wait and see, I guess.

British bombers last night contented themselves with bombing spots in northern Germany, according to the High Command, which declares the damage was slight. The German press waxes indignant today at the fact that a British bomb fell 200 yards from Bismarck's tomb. Berlin newspapers accuse Mr. Churchill of deliberately trying to destroy Germany's national shrines. "The entire cultured world will be shocked at this deed," says the *Lokal Anzeiger*.

Berlin August 23, 1940 24.46

This is Berlin.

For five days now the High Command in its communiqués has used the term "armed reconnaissance" to describe the action of German planes over Britain. Yesterday's armed reconnaissance, according to the High Command, consisted of attacks on two British convoys, one off Berwick, the other off the Downs, in which four ships are claimed to have been damaged. During the night German bombers attacked airfields in Cornwall and Wales, an airplane factory at Reading and a motor-works at Rochester. Many fires were caused, it is stated.

According to the *DNB*, a German bomber attacked off Moray Firth last night a 15,000 ton ship, scored four direct hits and sank it.

But of course, after the great air battles of last week, all this is small stuff. Some of us expected that Berlin might be visited last night or tonight by our English cousins as reprisals for what they reported the Germans did to London. But there was no visit last night, and there's been nothing tonight, though it's nearly 1 a.m. here.

Incidentally, Marshal Göring has made it easier for the residents of Berlin by decreeing that they do not necessarily have to go down to the air-raid cellars when the sirens blow. They can wait, he rules, until they hear anti-aircraft fire or see the nearby searchlights swinging into action. That's a concession which will be widely appreciated because it gets you out of sorts to have to get up from your sleep in the middle of the night, when the sirens sound, and sit in the cold damp cellar when nothing really is happening overhead.

Berlin August 24, 1940 14.00

This is Berlin.

These days remind me very much of last winter. It's cold and dreary and the war seems to be at a standstill. It may very well be that it's the calm before the storm. If it is, we shall soon see.

In the meantime, the German papers, having no new victories to report, warm up the old ones. Journals like the *Börsen Zeitung*, a noon paper, tell us today again of the terrible effectiveness of the German bombings in Britain. According to this paper, the residents of the English towns on the south-coast are leaving their homes and going north to escape the bombings. They cannot stand the strain, we are told here, of the continuous German attacks and the hardships of spending day and night in the air-raid cellar. That's the picture the German papers give their readers.

As further proof of the effectiveness of Germany's air attack on Britain the papers this morning publish photographs of some of the bombed airfields. I'm afraid I'm an amateur at reading aerial photographs and I don't see in them what the experts see. However, I find these pictures interesting. One on the front page of the *Völkischer Beobachter* shows the airfield at Maidstone in England. From one corner of the field you can see smoke issuing from some buildings. The German caption explains it is the result of direct hits. Another photograph shows a railway-gun position near St. Margaret's which has been bombed. A third shows smoke issuing from some buildings on the edge of an airfield which the German caption says is south-east of London. Croyden is south-east of London. The caption explains that a Stuka bombing has just taken place. Two buildings seem to be on fire.

Incidentally, this unusual August weather we've been having over here for the last three weeks not only hampers air activity, it affects the crops. No figures are available yet of the damage, but there seems little doubt that not only the grain, so badly needed in Europe this winter, but also other crops like potatoes, are going to be adversely affected by the cold, damp weather.

The German papers today pay some attention to Albania. They quote an Albanian journal to the effect that another one of these Albanian patriots has been murdered, though it develops that the murder took place last May, and it is not specifically stated that the Greeks did it. However, the Greeks are taken to task for practically closing the border been Albania and Greece. This is said to cause hardship to Albanians. Questioned about the state of relations between Italy and Greece today, the Wilhelmstrasse advised that the situation was not critical. No ultimatums have been sent, it pointed out.

German women, as you know, are not permitted to have anything to do with Polish prisoners. Today I notice in the papers that two German women have been sentenced to three years in the penitentiary because they did. The court called them women without honor.

And here's an item from the official journal of German lawn tennis. It jibes at Germans who still use English expressions when playing the racquet game. Germans should no longer say, for example, that the score is "fifteen-thirty". They should use the German words for figures. Nor should they say "deuce" or "game" or "set point". So the journal gives the German equivalents for about thirty English tennis terms previously used by most German players. For "lob", they should say "*hochball*", literally a "high ball". For "smash", "*schmetterball*". "*Rückhand*" for "backhand". And so on. For a little time, I suppose, some people will get a little mixed up in their tennis.

Berlin August 25, 1940 01.07

This is Berlin.

We're having an air-raid alarm here at the moment. The sirens went off some time ago, about midnight, and afterward you could hear the big anti-aircraft guns going into action, and see the searchlights trying to pick up the British planes. More details are not yet available.

The news of the fight in the air over Britain today is very spotty here in Berlin tonight. The early editions of the Monday morning newspapers content themselves with headlining the German communiqués claiming big successes in the air yesterday.

64 ENEMY PLANES DESTROYED – EXTENSIVE DESTRUCTION FOLLOWING SURPRISE ATTACK ON ENGLAND – PORTSMOUTH NAVAL BASE AFLAME. Those are typical headlines here in Berlin. And they refer to yesterday's goings-on. Taking advantage of protection afforded by clouds, the Germans, it's explained here, took the British by surprise. According to the German war communiqué, the British naval yard at Portsmouth was set on fire. Other surprise daylight raids were made on Northwood, Hornchurch, Manston, Canterbury, Ramsgate and Great Yarmouth. A big army barracks near Dover, it's claimed here, received seventy bombs, the German planes escaping into the clouds before the British had time to do anything about it.

There is no news in Berlin about reports from Britain that German bombs have fallen on London itself. I can find nothing about that in the German press. Indeed, the *DNB* issues a denial that last Friday and Saturday nights the Germans bombed London suburbs. It explains that only military objectives outside the British capital were attacked. It goes on to say that the British were first to start bombing the outskirts of a capital when they attacked Babelsberg, a town lying halfway between here and Potsdam. We may hear more about that later.

At any rate, no British bombs have fallen closer than that so far as I know, and none within the city of Berlin proper – up until the moment at least. We don't know yet the results of the raid going on now.

Berlin August 26, 1940 24.46

This is Berlin.

Were having another air-raid now, or at least an air-raid alarm.

Last night's fireworks here which sent several million residents of Berlin to their cellars for three hours and prompted considerable anti-aircraft fire, gets a six-line news item in the Berlin press tonight. It merely says that several enemy planes flew over the capital last night and dropped incendiary on two suburbs. Aside from a garden shanty burning down, the statement says no damage was done. It claims one British plane was shot down on its way home. And that's all we're told.

If the newspaper could find but six lines for last night's air-raid, the inhabitants of the town certainly made it their main topic of conversation today. After all, it was the first real raid on Berlin, the first time the people had ever heard the anti-aircraft guns that dot the capital thundering away, and the first time they'd lost three hours of sleep in the air-raid cellars. And that was something to talk about. Almost everyone I ran into today could produce a handful of shrapnel picked up in the streets or in the gardens after the raid. *[The preceding sentence was deleted by the censor.]*

At least three streets were roped off today so that it was impossible to get near enough to see why. Leaflets were dropped in some parts of the city asking Berliners to wake up, warning them that "the war which Hitler started will go on" and that "it will last as long as Hitler does."

But as I say, the big story in the Berlin press today is not last night's excitement but the success of the German raids on Britain. The emphasis is put on that. Thus a typical headline in the *Börsen Zeitung*: NEW HEAVY BLOWS AGAINST ENGLAND. And the local papers are full of accounts of the terrible havoc wrought in London by the German air attacks.

I mentioned last night that it had been denied here that London itself had been bombed last Friday and Saturday by the German air force and that there was nothing in the German papers to indicate that bombs could have fallen inside London itself. But today the Berlin newspapers print eyewitness accounts from Swedish correspondents in London describing a big fire in the heart of London which resulted from a German attack.

Columbia's short-wave station, WCBS, is quoted tonight by the German short-wave radio as saying that according to American reports, one-fifth of the London area is a heap of ruins following the German bombings.

Berlin August 28, 1940 24.46

This is Berlin.

I see by the evening papers that we had an alarm here this morning. I'm afraid I slept through it – but it seems it was a false alarm, due to a technical breakdown of the sirens, the papers say.

The Germans seem to be taking more and more to night bombing. Last night's air-raids on Britain were fairly extensive, judging from the German war communiqué which says that bombs were unloaded on harborworks, factories and airplane works at Southampton, Aberdeen, Dundee, Leeds, Hull, Derby, Birmingham and Chatham. The German radio claims that buildings of the Spitfire aircraft plant near Birmingham were badly damaged.

The German headlines still concentrate on the terrific damage which is being wrought in Britain by these German attacks. FIRES FROM SCOTLAND TO SOUTHAMPTON bannerlines the *Börsen Zeitung* this evening. Again we are told today in the German war communiqué that the British night air-raids on Germany last night caused little damage. Some houses in Kiel, Germany's greatest naval base, were damaged, says the communiqué.

The German papers are full of editorials today arguing that while German airplanes only bomb military objectives, British machines are purposely going after German civilians. This is a very dangerous game, warns the *Völkischer Beobachter*. I myself know practically nothing of what is going on in Britain, but I can find nothing in the papers here to indicate that the German bombers are causing civilian casualties in Britain.

By tomorrow night at this time, the fate of Transylvania, and indeed the fate of Romania as a sizeable Balkan state, probably will be known.

Tonight the German Foreign Minister, Herr von Ribbentrop, accompanied by the Italian Foreign Minister, Count Ciano, flew to Vienna where tomorrow they will meet the foreign ministers of Romania and Hungary. As the communiqué here phrases it, the four will discuss questions of common interest.

Before leaving Salzburg, Count Ciano and Herr von Ribbentrop dined with Herr Hitler at Obersalzburg. During the afternoon the two foreign ministers were in conference with the Führer. Presumably they reached an understanding on the line to be taken tomorrow. The Wilhelmstrasse denied today that Germany would act as arbitrator. Germany, it was explained, was only offering her good offices in the unfortunate conflict between the two countries.

Some people in the Wilhelmstrasse compared tomorrow's meeting in Vienna to one held there almost two years ago between Hungary and Czechoslovakia when Germany and Italy stepped in and regulated conflicting claims about a boundary line. It's a comparison worth noting.

Berlin August 29, 1940 14.05

This is Berlin.

The bannerline over page one of Berlin's noon paper, the *Börsen Zeitung*, says: UNBROKEN HAMMERING OF OUR BOMBERS ON THE BRITISH ISLES – IMPORTANT MILITARY OBJECTIVES CONTINUALLY ATTACKED. And most of the first page is given over to the report of German air attacks on Britain.

On page five of the *Börsen Zeitung* there is a one-paragraph account of last night's air-raid alarm. It reads as follows: "Last night between 12.24 and 3.17 am., there was an air-raid alarm in Berlin. Some British planes appeared at short intervals over the metropolitan district of greater Berlin and dropped incendiary and high-explosive bombs on residential districts and suburbs. Military objectives were not attacked."

The paragraph continues: "The damage done is insignificant. At several places in the center of the city roof fires were caused but quickly extinguished by the ARP *[Air Raid Precaution]* service. Ten persons were killed and twenty-eight were wounded. None of the killed and injured had taken refuge in the air-raid cellars."

That's the official communiqué on the air-raid we had last night. I can't report much about it first hand because though it began before my broadcast last evening and continued for nearly three hours, I was permitted to view the proceedings from a window for only a few minutes. For most of the three hours that the British planes appeared over Berlin, I was not allowed to look out at the scene. I was told that it was too dangerous, and that police regulations really called for everyone repairing to the cellar. I did see, however, for a short interval how the searchlights sought to locate the planes. There seemed less anti-aircraft fire than on Sunday night, though in some districts it sounded pretty heavy.

Occasionally the British would drop flares, lighting up the sky. *[This paragraph was deleted by the censor.]*

About an hour after the raid, the Propaganda Ministry conducted the foreign correspondents around the city to observe the damage. In the Kottbusserstrasse, about a thousand yards from a railroad station in the south-east part of Berlin, two 110 pound bombs had landed in the street, torn off the leg of an air-raid warden standing at the entrance to his house, and killed four men and two women who, unwisely, were standing in the doorway.

The Propaganda Ministry also conducted the journalists to the airfield at Tempelhof, the Klingenberg electrical works and to the Siemens factory which makes armaments, where nothing untoward was observed. Most of last night's activity appeared to be to the west and north-west of the city.

According to a bulletin just issued here, German planes last night heavily bombed Liverpool, especially the docks there and at Birkenhead across the Mersey River. Other German bombs were thrown on Middlesbrough, Thameshaven and Chatham. Fuller details on these night raids are expected later.

Berlin September 1, 1940 01.09

This is Berlin.

A year ago today the great German counter-attack against Poland – as it was officially called – got under way.

I will not soon forget that gray day – Hitler in the Reichstag announcing the end of a European époque, the first news of German victories, the feeling of weariness we all had from the realization that war had come and from the lack of sleep, and yet somehow a feeling of relief that at last the terrible tension that had hung over Europe for days, yes for weeks and months – at last was over. Everyone knew where they stood, or thought they did.

And then that evening – the first night of the blackout, stumbling through the pitch-dark streets to the broadcasting studio – and later on that night, our first air-raid alarm, and how we waited, gas-masks ready, for the Poles to come over. They didn't. The Poles never came over – why, I can't tell you. Perhaps it was because Berlin's air defenses were so good.

Nobody ever came over here for almost a year – until in fact last Sunday just about this time, when the British paid Berlin their first big visit and have been repeating it almost every night since. They were over against last night, though I see by the official statement that German anti-aircraft hindered them from dropping bombs over the city itself and forced them to drop their loads outside the city. I thought last night I heard some bomb explosions very near to my hotel which lies near to the Tiergarten, and indeed I see by an official statement, released here this evening, that gardeners today did find several bomb craters in the Tiergarten, right in the middle of Berlin. For fear of possible duds or time-bombs, police today roped off part of the park.

As to today's air war against Britain, there is no news in Berlin except that the German air attacks were continued today with strong forces. Details are lacking.

As to yesterday's air activities, the German High Command tells us today that 133 British planes were destroyed, 116 in the air. Against this, it says, only thirty-two German planes were lost. Also, says the German war communiqué, seventy-four British balloons were shot down. The High Command also reports the torpedoing by a German U-boat of the British auxiliary cruiser *Dunvegan Castle* of 15,000 tons.

Well, these things appear in the headlines today. But so also does the first anniversary of the beginning of World War Number Two. How do the Germans feel today, after one year of war, you may ask.

Well, judging by the front-page editorials in such leading papers as the *Völkischer Beobachter*, the *Frankfurter Zeitung* and the *Deutsche Allgemeine Zeitung* today, they have a clear conscience that the war was forced upon them by Britain, that they have a righteous cause, that they've done pretty well in a year of fighting, and that victory stands not far off. That's the official view, to be sure, but it would be a mistake to assume that it is not also the view of the great mass of the German people.

True, the ordinary people in the street that I talk to hope the war will be over before winter – and moreover they're confident it will be. But the German people realize on this first anniversary of the war that there is now no chance of compromise – that either they or the British must win, and that the side that loses will face lean days, to put it mildly.

As for the Germans who are doing the fighting – I was up on the Channel visiting them the other day, soldiers, sailors, airmen – they were dead certain the war would be over before winter.

Well, how fare the German people, you may ask, after a year of war? Take food. On the whole, right now they are probably better fed than a year ago. Butter, bacon, and eggs imported from Denmark, and vegetables imported from Holland have helped. Also Germany's own stocks of food are still, I take it, very sizeable. Germans will not starve this winter.

The situation in occupied Holland, Belgium, and France is not so rosy. I don't know where their food is going to come from this winter. The official German standpoint is that if they suffer, it will be the fault of the British blockade.

In regard to clothing, the prospects are slightly better. This year a German gets 150 points of clothing against 100 last year. Large quantities of raw textile material in Poland have contributed to this.

The morale of the people after a year of fantastic victories is just what you would expect. And from personal observation I would say that the night air-raids – and the people in the west and north-west have been taking them nearly every night for three months – have not broken the nerves of the people. They've caused them to lose sleep and they've embittered them. But I think that's the story in all countries. It's wonderful what the human being can stand.

As to the much-talked-of invasion of Britain, we're still in the dark, and if we weren't, we couldn't tip the British off by saying so.

Berlin September 2, 1940 24.41

This is Berlin.

Last spring when the big offensive in the West started, the Propaganda Ministry set up a gigantic, illuminated map of the Western Front. Every day a German army officer, pointer in hand, would help us to follow on the map just what the German army was doing in the field.

Today that map was taken down, and an equally large one substituted. It was a map of England. And it left us all wondering, well, whether one of these days now we would be following a new campaign on this excellent map.

Dr. Goebbels yesterday, answering those who wonder when Britain is to be attempted, said: "The Führer acts when the time is ripe." Some people here conclude from that that the time for the invasion of Britain therefore is not considered here to be ripe.

At any rate, the German air force today again made a determined attack on Britain. According to a special communiqué issued here tonight by the commander-in-chief of the German air force, the objectives of today's bombing attacks were airfields in south-east England. During the air battles that accompanied the attack, says the communiqué, eighty-six British planes were shot down. Twenty-three German planes, it is added, are missing.

Note the four to one ratio there in favor of the German air force. A German radio commentator pointed out the other day that the four to one ratio has been constant in the German reports since the big war in the air began. The German figures, for example, on planes shot down between August 6th and September 1st, are 1,627 British against 415 German, almost an exact four to one ratio.

391

As to damage caused by today's German raids, the Berlin communiqué tells us that hangars and other property on British landing fields were hit by bombs.

The official version of last night's raids by the British air force on Germany, and in particular on Berlin, reads as follows: "Enemy planes again attempted last night to attack Berlin and other cities. Thanks to the strong anti-aircraft defenses, the enemy was unable to drop bombs on the metropolitan area of Greater Berlin. At other places in Germany, there was damage to houses, but no military damage."

Berlin September 3, 1940 24.46

This is Berlin.

News that the United States is to give Great Britain fifty badly needed destroyers for her war with Germany in exchange for naval and airbases in the British possessions in the western hemisphere reached Berlin too late today to enable the German press to comment. Most people here seemed to have first picked up the news from Columbia's short-wave station late this afternoon, our time.

First reaction in the Wilhelmstrasse was not to take the thing too seriously. The official line seemed to be that the transfer of the fifty destroyers has come too late to save the British and that most of the destroyers are old World War crates anyway and therefore of not much use.

At any rate, judging from initial reaction in German political circles, it seemed evident that Berlin would not make an issue of it with the United States. That has been the German policy in regard to us all along, and there is no evidence that it has changed. As I've often told you before, Berlin is confident that it can whip the British before American aid becomes really effective. And that goes for airplanes as well as naval craft.

Well now, today's news about the air offensive is meagre. A bulletin issued in Berlin at 5 p.m., that is seven hours ago, states that German bombers today attacked military objectives north of London and also in southern England. According to the German figures, thirty-nine British planes were shot down in aerial combats, and a further fifteen destroyed on the ground during attacks on airfields. Twelve German planes, says the communiqué, are missing. Note again that approximately four to one ratio in the German reports.

Now all these reports, as you might suspect, provide plenty of headlines for the German newspapers. A typical one across the front page of the *Börsen Zeitung* tonight reads: AIRFIELDS DESTROYED, HARBORS ON

FIRE. GERMAN BOMB ATTACKS NIGHT AND DAY. More than one German said to me today: "With such terrific destruction the British certainly can't hold out much longer." And I think that's what people here think.

Ten civilians killed in the British air-raid of last Thursday night were buried here today. The local newspapers commenting state that it was a cowardly and criminal thing for the British to have done.

Berlin September 3-4, 1940 04.34

This is Berlin.

There is hardly a line in the German press today recalling that a year ago Great Britain and France entered the war, thus transforming what Berlin at first thought would be a brief campaign against Poland into World War Number Two.

On that day, I remember, Herr Hitler issued a number of proclamations to his armies, his party, his people. And the burden of them all was that Great Britain was the real enemy. France was not even mentioned. England was the foe that must be beaten, the German people were told, if the German nation was to survive.

England the real enemy! Today, after the lapse of one of the most fantastic years in European history, it is still true. England is all that stands between Germany and that total victory so confidently expected by almost everyone in this country.

And so the German press today, omitting references to what took place a year ago, concentrates on the great air offensive against Britain. We, here in Berlin, are given a terrible picture of the devastating effects of mass German bombing throughout the British Isles. A German, reading his newspaper tonight, must wonder: Can those British really hold out much longer after what our air force is doing to them night and day?

Today, for instance, German reports say that their bombers attacked objectives both north of London and in southern England. Fifty-four British planes, it is claimed here, were shot down, against twelve German machines lost. Yesterday, according to the High Command, ninety-three British planes were destroyed in the air-fighting, to twenty-three German planes missing. Extensive damage to British airfields, airplane factories, munitions works and harbors is claimed.

Tonight we had another visit from the British here in Berlin. According to an official communiqué just out, they dropped no bombs on the capital and most of the British planes, it is stated here, were driven back by the defenses along the Elbe to the west of the city.

The fateful day of September 3rd, a year ago, was sunny and hot here in

393

Berlin. The tension in the Wilhelmstrasse as the deadline hour of 11 a.m. – when Britain's time-limit ran out – approached was terrific. That is, among the statesmen, the diplomats, the correspondents – their eyes bloodshot from lack of sleep and the strain.

And yet, I remember, that was not true of the people in Berlin. They were strangely phlegmatic, and indeed have remained so throughout the war. Today, as I watched them go about their work, I doubted if one out of twenty even remembered that today was the anniversary of the beginning of the new world war. In the course of today I suppose I spoke to two or three dozen Germans about this or that. Not one of them mentioned the anniversary.

Berlin September 4, 1940 24.54

This is Berlin.

Adolf Hitler made a speech here today. It contained a warning. He said that if the British dropped two or three tons of bombs on Germany, the German air force would drop ten, fifty or even a hundred times as many bombs on Britain. And that if the British attacked German cities, then the cities and towns of England would be razed to the ground.

It was a surprise speech. That is, the public and even the correspondents knew nothing about it beforehand. Newspapermen, arriving at the afternoon press conference at 4 p.m., were spirited off in buses to the Sport Palace. There, shortly after 5 p.m., our time, Herr Hitler opened the second annual war time winter relief campaign.

It was a confident, almost jaunty Hitler that we saw today on the threshold of the second year of the war. His ironic remarks about the British, accompanied by the gestures he made, had the crowd rocking with laughter. But at times, of course, he struck a grimmer note, as when earlier in his speech he said: "Come what may, England is going to be destroyed!" This remark brought vociferous applause.

Then he returned to the ironic when he came to the matter of the much-discussed attack on Britain.

"The English are wondering when the attack is going to begin. The English ask: 'Why doesn't he come?'" Hitler stepped back, raised his arms and said: "Be calm. Be calm. He's coming. He's coming. One must not be so curious." Whereupon the house exploded with laughter.

And then came the part about razing the English towns if the British continue to drop bombs on Germany. Said Hitler: "For three months the English have been sending over night bombers. I thought that in the end Herr Churchill would give it up. But now the German air force will

394

answer the British night for night. And when the British drop two or three tons of bombs, the German flyers will answer with fifty, a hundred, two hundred tons on Britain, until the cities of England are razed and until these pirates of the night are forced to desist."

Concluding, Hitler said: "The hour will come when one of the nations will break down, and it won't be Germany."

The High Command communiqué today tells us that German flyers, raiding Britain last night, bombed harbor works and armament factories at Liverpool, Avonmouth, Bristol, Portland, Poole, Rochester, and Middlesbrough. The day-time raids were restricted to attacks on British airfields.

German air attacks on Britain were renewed this afternoon, according to a Berlin communiqué, which says that the German objectives were aircraft factories in the south of England. Several hits on factories are claimed here. The score in the air fighting is given by Berlin as twenty-eight British planes shot down, six German machines not yet returned.

Berlin September 5, 1940 24.46

This is Berlin.

The German navy today steals the limelight from the air force in the Berlin reports of the war on Britain – a war which Herr Hitler assured his fellow countrymen yesterday would end in the breakdown of England.

Not that the air forces of either side are taking a rest. Berlin continues to tell us that its air attacks on Britain are proceeding with devastating effect. And last night we had a visit from the British. The official statement on last night's raid admits that the British did hit a military objective – an army supply depot in a suburb on the north-west fringe of the capital, but it adds that great damage was not done.

Well, as to the navy, according to today's official communiqué of the German High Command, the navy has sunk five British destroyers in the last few days. And a special High Command communiqué issued this afternoon adds that last night German motor-torpedo boats sank another, making a total of six. If these reports are later confirmed by the British, you can see that those fifty destroyers being turned over by the United States will certainly come in handy right now.

The names of three of the British destroyers reported sunk are given by the High Command as the *Express*, the *Esk* and the *Ivanhoe*. I seem to recall the *Ivanhoe* having been in the headlines during the Narvik battles.

The motor-torpedo engagement in which a destroyer is said to have been bagged took place last night, we're told, near the east coast of

England. Five merchant ships, including a 12,000-ton tanker, were sunk, says the German report, and another ship damaged.

As to the air war, a communiqué issued here this afternoon says that German bombing squadrons this morning attacked airdromes in the south of England. The German score in the air-fighting so far today reads: twenty British machines shot down, five German planes missing. Note that four to one ratio again. It's the same day after day.

Mr. Churchill's speech today is covered briefly by the German radio this evening. Nothing is said about his figures on the number of civilian casualties in Britain. The German radio report notes that Parliament had to be adjourned because of an air-raid alarm. "Only after the adjournment," says this German radio report – and I'm quoting, "could the war-criminal Churchill begin his speech." Commenting on Mr. Churchill's warning that even more intensive air-raids lay ahead, the German radio says: "The British Prime Minister admits therefore that two weeks ago he lied when he proclaimed through the radio and press that the danger was already over."

Commenting on Herr Hitler's speech tonight, the local radio said: "The British plutocrats must pay for their war-crime with their destruction."

Because I got interested in the shooting going on here last night, I forgot to mention an important matter. Herr Hitler remarked in his speech yesterday that though he abstained from coffee himself, he knew many Germans liked it, and it was ridiculous that Britain should be able to deprive Germans of their coffee. Simultaneously it was announced that, starting immediately, adults over eighteen living in cities which experience frequent air-raids, will get 75 grams of real coffee a month. Beginning in October, Germans who don't have to duck into their cellars at night, will get 50 grams a month.

Berlin September 7, 1940 24.51

This is Berlin.

The High Command has just announced in a special war communiqué that London has been bombed for the first time today with *strong* forces. It says it's a reprisal for the increased bombings of Germany carried out by the Royal Air Force recently.

According to the German Command, one great cloud of smoke tonight stretches from the middle of London to the mouth of the Thames as the result of the German attack.

So far, says the High Command, in a special communiqué just issued, seventy-five British planes were shot down in the day's fighting. The

Germans, it says, lost twenty-six machines – twenty-two fighters, and four bombers. That last is a surprising figure since you'd think that the bombers would fall more easily to fighter attack than the fighters themselves.

This communiqué says that great damage was inflicted upon the industrial part of eastern London as well as on the docks. The report continues: "The streets in these quarters of London are torn up, many buildings have collapsed. Some subway stretches also fell in. Two gas works blew up and a large number of warehouses were destroyed."

Unofficial reports here speak of a thousand German planes being used in this afternoon's raid, and one semi-official dispatch says that "several million pounds of iron" were dropped on London in the attack. "The Führer has struck back," concludes this dispatch.

Now, last night, by all accounts, we had the biggest raid of the war on Berlin. The anti-aircraft fire was the heaviest I've yet heard with the single exception of a night in Calais recently when the British attacked there. When I returned home at 3 a.m. this morning, after the alarm was over, the sky over the north-central part of Berlin was lit up by two great fires. One was in the freight-house of the Lehrter railroad station. It's reported that another bomb hit a railroad station in the Schussendorfstrasse. Another landed in a prominent jail, killed a prisoner and a guard, and injured some others. Several civilians are known to have been killed or injured, but for the first time no official casualty list has been published here. Well that was last night, and an exciting night it was for the citizens of this town.

Early this afternoon, the High Command in its daily war communiqué published the following statement: "The enemy again attacked the German capital last night causing some damage to persons and property as a result of his indiscriminate throwing of bombs on non-military targets in the middle of the city.

"The German air force," continued the communiqué, and I'm still quoting, "has therefore also begun to attack London with strong forces." Actually, according to an official statement on last night's bombings in Berlin, only a few British planes flew over the capital.

And so tonight, as I said a minute ago, we have the special communiqué of the High Command stating that as reprisals for these British raids, London was attacked with strong forces for the first time today.

To accurately reflect the state of mind here, I'd like to read you what the Berlin newspaper *Börsen Zeitung* told its readers in a front-page editorial this evening: "While the attack of the German air force on purely military objectives in England increases – this fact is recognized by both the British press and radio – the Royal Air Force knows nothing better to do than to continually attack non-military objectives in Germany. A perfect example of this was the criminal attack on the middle of Berlin last night. In this attack only lodging houses were hit; not a single military objective."

I talked to quite a few Germans today. Most of them seemed to sincerely believe that the German planes attack exclusively military objectives; the Royal Air Force exclusively non-military targets.

General von Schroeder, president of the German air-raid protection league, today advises the Berlin population to go earlier to bed and get some sleep before the raiders arrive. The habit of Berliners of stepping out in the evening must be given up for a time, he says. And he suggests that since the raiders usually arrive punctually shortly after midnight, that the people set their alarm clocks for twelve midnight, so that they won't feel so raw when they make for the cellar.

Berlin September 8, 1940 01.10

This is Berlin.

Judging from the editorials, the local press seems pleased with the success of yesterday's massive air-raid on London. More will follow, it tells us, unless the British give up what the German press terms the Royal Air Force's criminal night attacks on Germany.

All the newspapers in Germany that I've seen declare in headlines and editorials that yesterday's bombing of London was done as a reprisal for what they term the British bombing of non-military objectives in Germany, and especially the bombing of Berlin Friday night which, as the official German communiqué stated, was done by only a very few British planes.

The German press and radio today emphasize the terrific damage done to London yesterday by the German bombers. The High Command declares in its official communiqué today that the German bombers attacked objects of military-economic importance. The German radio, at least – I've seen no reference to the matter yet in the press – gives its listeners tonight the British estimate of civilian casualties, naming the figure of 400 civilians killed and 1,300 to 1,400 severely injured.

Another German radio report describing the scene in London yesterday concludes: "All this combined to create the impression of a blazing inferno, ghastly beyond human imagination."

A *DNB* report issued this afternoon tells us that the smoke was still so heavy over London this morning that German reconnaissance planes that hovered over the city had to return to their bases without fulfilling their tasks. They reported, we are told, that it was impossible for them to see the city through the smoke.

This, however, does not seem to have prevented the Germans from renewing their attack on London today. A bulletin here says: "Renewed reprisal attacks started again this forenoon on London." Another report says that while the smoke hindered the British planes, it helped the German planes.

The German radio tonight draws the conclusion that the British really cannot defend London from air attack. It says: "For weeks the British people have been deluded into believing that the German raids on London had been repulsed. In reality no such raids took place. They did not begin until yesterday."

The latest German bulletin says that Woolwich and the south-eastern outskirts of London were the principal targets of the German attacks today. Today's score in the fighting is given by Berlin as twelve British planes and four German machines lost. The Germans also tell us that three British planes this afternoon suddenly swooped out of the clouds and made a dive-attack on the harbor works at Ostende. One of the three, say the Germans, was shot down.

German attacks on London were also continued this evening, according to the latest reports here.

How many planes were used against London yesterday? The High Command does not tell us. Unofficial information is that at least a thousand machines were used. The High Command does say that more than a million kilograms of bombs of all calibers were dropped. That would be, if it were just a million kilos, eleven hundred tons of bombs.

The High Command also reveals that Marshal Göring has gone to the north of France to personally direct the air attacks on Britain. That's a signal, if any were needed, that the great German offensive is now on in earnest. Most neutral military observers here expect a show-down before this month of September is over. The *Frankfurter Zeitung* warns its readers today against thinking that the British will be a push-over. "The desperate energy of Churchill," it says, "is not to be underestimated. It will be a hard and difficult struggle."

For the first time in some days, the British air force failed to visit Berlin last night. Most people, I think, stayed up or woke up about midnight thinking they would; but they didn't. And so the Berliners had a good night's sleep.

Berlin September 9, 1940 24.50

This is Berlin.

A curious thing. Just when the German air force steps up its bombing of London to the point reached Saturday night and Sunday, the British air force ceases visiting Berlin.

For military reasons, I'm not allowed to say whether we have a raid on here at the moment or not. But anyway we had none last night, nor the night before. Why?

The official explanation both yesterday and today is that the British bombers tried to get through to bomb Berlin, but were turned back both nights by the German defenses, especially the German anti-aircraft. What has suddenly been done to so strengthen the German air-defenses that the British, who flew over Berlin almost every night for a fortnight without losing a plane over the capital despite intensive anti-aircraft fire, are unable now to penetrate to the city, is not known.

At any rate Hamburg, and not Berlin, was heavily bombed last night and the German press holds that it was a criminal attack, an act of terror against the German civilian population.

The *Nachtausgabe* writes that Mr. Churchill really ordered his pilots to again bomb the civil population of Berlin last night, but that the British were unable to get through.

The German newspapers today are full of stories about the terrific damage wrought on London by the German attacks of Saturday and Sunday. The press here is unanimous that the bombing of London was a justified reprisal for what the British flyers have done to Germany for three months. The German radio says tonight that London is now appealing for the world's pity. "This criminal attempt of the British to mislead public opinion," it holds, "must be sharply exposed."

No attempt is made here, it is only fair to say, to hold from the people the picture of ghastly destruction wrought in London. British casualty lists are published here, as well as details of damage to property. And it is emphasized in all official statements that the German flyers attacked only military objectives in London. Many Englishmen, observes tonight's *Deutsche Allgemeine Zeitung*, probably didn't realize how many military objectives were hidden away in London, and so the German bombers taught them something about this.

The German radio today quotes the *New York Times* to back up the German announcement that only military objectives were attacked. "The *New York Times* admits in its report," it says, and I'm quoting, "that once more the German planes attacked exclusively military objectives."

The New York press is also cited to show the manner of damage done to London. Mr. Halfeld, New York correspondent of the *Lokal Anzeiger,* cables his paper tonight that the American correspondents in London, despite a particularly sharpened British censorship, were able to get out details of the German attack, which, coupled with American press comment, lead one to believe that London cannot stand many such bombings.

German air attacks on London, it's announced here, were resumed this afternoon at 4 o'clock. "With tremendous accuracy," says a *DNB* dispatch, "the German bombers dropped their destructive loads on London. Again and again great fires and explosions were observed."

A later bulletin issued here said over three hundred German bombers attacked objectives along the Thames, scoring hits on harbor works and factories north and south of the river. The attacks, it's stated, were also renewed this evening.

According to the latest reports in Berlin, forty British planes were shot down today; sixteen German machines are missing.

And here's one just in. It says British bombers tonight attacked the German harbor of Wesermünde, near Bremen. They were met, it's added, by anti-aircraft fire, and that most of the bombs fell in fields.

A German report tells us tonight of a German air force squadron having scored its two hundredth victory over England. It says the event was celebrated by each pilot drinking a bottle of champagne over the Channel and then dropping the bottle on Buckingham Palace.

The German radio announced tonight that its broadcasts, already curtailed in the last fortnight on military grounds, will be further curtailed in the next days. This is no time, it adds, to explain further the reasons for this.

Berlin September 10, 1940 24.46

This is Berlin.

The Berlin press is exceedingly resentful today because last night a few English planes came over and dropped some bombs on the German capital.

No one, we are told, was killed. No one was injured. Several houses were damaged, and in one flat a hundred and fifty people had to be evacuated during the night because some bombs landed nearby but failed to explode. Police feared they might be time bombs.

Last night I commented on the curious fact that we'd had no air-raids here for two nights. The words were hardly out of my mouth when to the north of the city the thunder of the anti-aircraft guns began. It was some time before the sirens sounded. When they did, your correspondent was herded down into an air-raid cellar, so he cannot give you an eye-witness picture of how it looked. A statement in the papers this afternoon says that by law everyone must go to the cellar, and so to the cellar I went, muttering a few protests the while.

The *DNB* account of the raid, published in all newspapers, says that no military objectives were hit and that indeed the British purposely attacked the civil populations. This *DNB* account, which may be regarded as authoritative, concludes: "the Berlin population will endure this act of force in the knowledge that from now for every bomb dropped here, reprisal will be taken a thousand times."

Commenting on last night's bombing of Berlin, the *Lokal Anzeiger* says: "The flyers of His Britannic Majesty have given a heavy blow to the laws governing an honorable and manly conduct of war."

Speaking of the conduct of war, Berlin today accused the British air force of using what the *DNB* describes as a particularly detestable and low-down implement of warfare – a new kind of incendiary weapon.

I've heard whispers about this new secret British weapon for some time, but only today did the German military authorities release the story. At our press conference this evening, we were shown a half dozen of the new things which the Germans tell us have been dropped on Germany since August 11th.

Well, actually they look like a blank calling card, except that they're square, about two inches square. They're made of a celluloid substance which resembles the stiff paper of a calling card. Two of these celluloid sheets are pasted together and between them is a tablet of phosphorus. The British drop them in a dampened condition. When they dry, they ignite and cause a small fire that burns for two or three minutes. A few minutes of sun, or ten minutes of dry daytime air, and they go up in flames. I watched several of them ignite today in a demonstration given us after our press conference. The Germans insist that they are no good against military objectives, but that they have set fire to fields of grain and hay, as well as woods. They are difficult to find, but I judge special measures have been taken by the Germans to pick them up and render them useless. A German official told me today that one plane could carry 200,000 of them.

According to the information given out in Berlin tonight, no bombs were dropped on London today by the German air force. A bulletin issued here tonight says that German planes flew over London today in relays in order to establish the results of the previous German attacks, but that no bombs were dropped. Nevertheless, adds the bulletin, the Londoners had to seek refuge in their air-raid shelter four times during the day.

For the first time today, so far as I remember, the German High Command mentions its big guns on the French coast which are capable of firing on Dover.

It explains the reason they fired last evening was to bombard a British convoy putting out from Dover. The convoy, says the German Command, was broken up, four ships returning to Dover, two to Deal.

The German guns ceased firing at 8:40 because of darkness, but resumed during the night when long-range British guns opened fire on the Germans. For two hours, says the report, there was an artillery duel from the two coasts, and finally, says the High Command, the British battery was silenced.

The German radio tonight instructs its listeners to make for the cellar as soon as they hear anti-aircraft fire, and not to wait for the sirens to sound the alarm.

Berlin September 11, 1940 24.56

This is Berlin.

When British bombs first started falling on Berlin some two weeks ago, the local papers gave the matter a paragraph on an inside page.

Last night's bombing, probably the severest Berlin has had, is all over the first page today. And the press is very indignant about it. A headline in the *Börsen Zeitung* calls the British pilots "barbarians" and the same newspaper has this banner-line over its front page: CRIME OF BRITISH ON BERLIN. All papers call the British "criminals" for what they did to Berlin last night.

What did they do? They dropped some incendiary bombs on the Reichstag, the Brandenburg Gate, the Academy of Art, which is next door to the Munitions Ministry, a Catholic hospital, a Jewish hospital, and on numerous private houses. No serious fires, so far as I know, ensued. Explosive bombs hit other houses, killed five people and injured an unannounced number.

What seems to arouse the wrath of the Berlin press more than anything else is that one national memorial, the Brandenburg Gate, was hit by an incendiary bomb which did not damage it, as it's made of stone. Another memorial, the Victory Column in the middle of the Tiergarten, was missed by a bomb that fell a half mile away in the middle of the new East-West highway. The crater this particular bomb made in the street almost brought your correspondent to a sad end. I was speeding home after the all-clear at about forty miles an hour. You couldn't see the crater in the darkness – the police had not yet discovered it – but I missed it by twenty feet, only taking a bad skid in the débris.

The papers accuse the British of having deliberately aimed at sacred memorials like the Brandenburg Gate. If this is so, they certainly aimed well, because the gateway is a very small target in a big city.

The garden of our embassy received five incendiary bombs. Three went off immediately. Two were buried in the ground. At first, it was thought that they might be time bombs, but when the police, assisted by several U.S. army attachés, dug them up this afternoon, they turned out to be only incendiaries. A splinter from the bomb whose crater almost wrecked me last night was hurled 200 yards through the double window of the office of Mr. Donald Heath, our first secretary of embassy, and finally came to rest four inches inside a wall. Mr. Heath was not present at the time.

The latest reports in Berlin say that German bombers made a daylight attack on London today. Further hits on factories and harbor works are claimed, and it's also stated that an oil depot at Port Victoria on the Thames estuary was set on fire. The Spitfire aircraft works at Southampton was also bombed this afternoon and the Germans say they damaged several sheds. During the air-fighting that followed these bombings, Berlin says fifty-four British planes were shot down against eighteen German.

A late bulletin says that at dusk German attacks on Britain were renewed. We're also told that the long-range German guns shelled Dover this afternoon.

[On September 12 Shirer went to Geneva at the request of the CBS New York office so that he could talk by telephone with Paul White about his problems with the censors. The upshot of their talks is summarized in this letter Shirer sent White just before he returned to Berlin:

Dear Paul:

Here is a résumé of what I tried to say on the telephone this week. I would appreciate it if you would show it to Mr. Klauber *[head of CBS News]*.

Whenever during the past year events have reached a crucial stage our censorship has tightened up. But until three weeks ago when the big air-raids on London and Berlin started, I always felt that we were given enough freedom to make it worth our while to remain. For the last three weeks, however, this has not been the case. At the present we are reduced to mouthing absurd Nazi propaganda. It is no longer possible to give anything like an objective report. My own position is this:

1. I cannot even attempt to describe the air attacks on Berlin as they really are. I am not even permitted to *see* them. Until my 24:46 broadcast I am allowed to remain upstairs, but the blinds and curtains are drawn over my windows. As soon as my talk is over I'm hustled down to the air-raid cellar. I made a formal request to the High Command to be allowed to observe the raids at my own risk. This was rejected.

404

2. I am then pressured to broadcast the official account of the raids, though I know it to be incomplete when not, often, false. I am asked to believe and report the absurd official line that Germans only bomb military objectives; the British only non-military objectives. Any material discrediting this official view is not allowed in my scripts.

3. The policy of my censors now is that anything in my scripts liable to create an unfavorable impression in the United States from the Nazi view cannot be broadcast. Needless to say this covers much ground. To be sure, by careful writing I sometimes get around this. But it seems to me that this is a restriction which you who determine the policies of American radio ought to deeply ponder over before accepting. I have seen one Democracy after another undermined because they accepted just this thing.

4. The censors sometimes blue-pencil material on the ground that the BBC will pick it up and use it for propaganda purposes against Germany. From the German standpoint, there is of course some justification for this attitude. But from our standpoint it covers too much ground because recently the BBC has taken to quoting nearly all of the very few items from our talks that have not been official statements.

5. As I recently cabled you, when I protested recently against the sharpening of the censorship, the RRG *[Reichs Rundfunk Gesellschaft]* advised me that it could not be changed and suggested that if we didn't like it why didn't we draw the consequences. Also as I cabled, personally I think we should.

I realize that the next few weeks may decide the issue of the war, and that it is not the best time to threaten to pull out because of censorship. If Germany should win, you will naturally want coverage of the events to follow that victory – a coverage which would largely come from the German side. For that reason I'm going back to have another crack at the job. But if there is a stalemate this winter and the censorship is not relaxed, I personally cannot remain there, as I've already cabled you, and do Nazi propaganda. You, Paul, said on the phone that you wanted someone in Berlin even if they were restricted to reading the official communiqués and nothing else. But in that case, I could hire a pro-Nazi American student for $50 a week and no expenses to do that job. And in that case too, I think I could be more useful elsewhere.

By the time you get this Hitler will either have tried his invasion of Britain or given it up at least until spring. So I will not risk any guesses. The position at the moment is that he thinks it will succeed but some of his experts think it's too risky. They also thought the

Anschluss and especially the dizzy plan to conquer Norway were too risky. But some day they're bound to be right.

Looking out over the Channel the other day from Calais and Cap Gris Nez, those narrow waters looked to me to be rather wide and very wet for an invading army. The barges and pontoons we saw concentrated would only be good on a very calm day.

It is just a month since I was there and at that time the German airmen thought the Royal Air Force would be wiped out in two weeks. Obviously something has gone wrong in their calculations . . .]

Berlin September 18, 1940 24.46

This is Berlin.

Returning to Berlin after an absence of six days in Switzerland, I find one change in people here. They're not thinking so much about the air-raids. The reason is simple. They're not having many.

During the last six days, the British flyers have visited Berlin on only one night. People here greeted me today with the remark that they're sleeping normally again. And they don't feel any worse when after a night of uninterrupted slumber they read, as they did today, that London had ten hours of bombing again yesterday.

Not that the British have given up bombing Germany altogether. Somewhere in western Germany last night, lying in a Pullman berth, I was awakened by the distant sound of anti-aircraft fire. And I notice in the evening papers great indignation at the British bombing of Hamburg last night. As with all British bombings that I've ever read about in the German press, it's again stated here that the bombing of Hamburg last night was indiscriminating. *[The preceding sentence was deleted by the censor.]* Four apartment houses, we're told, were destroyed and several others damaged so that more than a hundred civilians had to be hurriedly evacuated. The local radio tonight says that in bombing Hamburg last night, Mr. Churchill gave his pilots orders to murder, and adds that revenge will be taken on Britain.

I notice today that both the German press and the radio give their public, without comment, the news that London's West End was hit by bombs yesterday, that big stores in Oxford Street as well as business houses in the center of the city were damaged.

The military objectives in these quarters which the Germans were aiming at, are not given in the local accounts.

Well now, as to today's news of the war in the air, the German accounts say that the weather has again been bad. This morning, according to a bulletin issued here, German bombers attacked the docks at Tilbury, scoring several hits. A switchyard nearby was also bombed, and, says the German report, badly damaged.

One attacking group, we're told, went after some big oil tanks at Port Victoria on the lower Thames and set three of them on fire. One oil tanker, taking on oil, was, say the Germans, sunk.

At least two sets of air fights followed this attack, says Berlin, one over the county of Kent, the other over the lower Thames, but they were not on a very large scale. Berlin's score on the fighting reads: fifteen British fighters shot down, three German planes missing. That's the news so far available here on the day's action.

On the political front, the big news here today is that Herr von Ribbentrop has left for Rome. The commentaries in the local press do not help us much in ascertaining why he's gone to Rome. They hint it's in connection with the German air offensive on Britain and the Italian drive on Egypt, and in political quarters here we're given to understand that it's not a pleasure trip, that something specific is expected to come out of it.

Some speak of Ribbentrop's trip in conjunction with the presence here of General Franco's brother-in-law and Minister of Interior, Senor Suñer, whom I met in, of all places, the elevator of my hotel here this evening. Senor Suñer has said Spain wants Gibraltar but, he has been careful to add, after the New Order in Europe has been established. Well, Gibraltar is one key to the Mediterranean and there are signs that this winter the war may shift chiefly to that part of the world. The weather is better there anyway for winter fighting.

Berlin September 19, 1940 24.52

This is Berlin.

Not since this war started has the German press been so indignant against the British as today.

Last night, as you probably know, British planes dropped bombs on, among other places, a well-known children's hospital at Bethel in western Germany. According to a *DNB* dispatch, three buildings of the hospital were destroyed, nine children killed and twelve wounded.

Tonight the German press tells us it was cold-blooded murder, that it was done on purpose, that this is proof that the Royal Air Force carries on war only against German women and children, and that this deed must be revenged many times over.

And indeed from more than one quarter tonight, I heard it said that the

407

Luftwaffe will now go all-out on London. As some Berlin papers put it, revenge will now be taken not only in the interests of the German people but of the whole civilized world. The civilized world, they conclude, will condone any action which the German air force may deem fit to take.

But I must read you some of the front-page headlines.

The *Börsen Zeitung* – ASSASSINS MURDER IS NO LONGER WAR, HERR WINSTON CHURCHILL – THE BRITISH ISLAND OF MURDERERS WILL HAVE TO TAKE THE CONSEQUENCES OF THEIR MALICIOUS BOMBINGS. The *Nachtausgabe* – NIGHT CRIME OF BRITISH AGAINST TWENTY-ONE GERMAN CHILDREN – THIS BLOODY ACT CRIES FOR REVENGE. The *Deutsche Allgemeine Zeitung* – THE MURDER OF CHILDREN AT BETHEL – REVOLTING CRIME. The *Börsen Zeitung*: GERMANY WILL HIT BACK HARD – BRITISH CRIME – CHILDREN MURDERED BY BOMBS ON BETHEL.

Editorial comment is in a similar vein.

The *Börsen Zeitung* tells us that there is no doubt that the British flyers knew what they were hitting. "They wished," it says, and I'm quoting, "on the orders of Churchill to simply murder." The same paper holds that Albion has shown herself to be, "a murder-hungry beast which the German sword will liquidate in the interest not only of the German people but of the whole civilized world." And the paper concludes: "The sadistic threats of the British apostles of hate will end in the smoke of their cities."

The *Deutsche Allgemeine Zeitung* tells us that the reckoning now with Britain will be frightful. In an adjoining column of this paper, there is a headline telling how German bombers penetrated right to the center of London.

The *Nachtausgabe* argues that the British have now taken so much guilt upon themselves that not the slightest consideration can henceforth be shown to them. It tells its readers that what the German *Luftwaffe* is now going to do to the British will have nothing to do with the clean sort of warfare which it says the Germans have fought up until now in bombing military objectives in London. But it concludes that such reprisals will be a punishment, "carried out under the moral laws of humanity."

In this connection the *Diplomatic Correspondence*, organ of the Foreign Office, states today: "It is a fact that Germany is waging war with clean weapons and in a chivalrous manner."

Whether the German people know that many English children have been killed and wounded by German bombers, I don't know. *[This sentence was deleted by the censor.]*

We know very little here tonight of what has gone on in the air today. A communiqué issued this afternoon said the weather was bad, but that the attacks on "military and war-important objectives in London was continued today." No further details are given.

I might say here that we had no air-raid in Berlin last night and everyone got a nice night's sleep. This afternoon I went out to one of Berlin's biggest factories in a district where in recent nights one heard most of the anti-aircraft fire. I watched thousands of workers filing out and I must say they looked very healthy and fit. Well, for one thing, they haven't had their sleep disturbed by having to go to an air-raid shelter since last Sunday evening.

There is as yet no news here in Berlin of just what Herr von Ribbentrop and the Duce discussed in Rome today. But the German radio tonight gives an interesting slant to the talks. It says the Axis powers are being supported in their struggle by the sympathy of the awaking peoples. And then it adds: "That goes especially for Spain, which is showing its solidarity with the policies of the Axis." That's the first time I've heard such a statement about Spain from official quarters here. Senor Suñer, Franco's Minister of Interior and brother-in-law, is still in Berlin.

Berlin September 20, 1940 24.46

This is Berlin.

Today's war communiqué of the German High Command, which covers yesterday's operations, is very short. One item in it must have surprised some people. It reports that yesterday one British plane was shot down. Three German planes are missing. That's three to one for the British, the first time, so far as I can remember, that Berlin's score showed the British on top.

But tonight's German reports make up for it. It tells us that in air battles over London today, the Germans shot down twelve British machines and lost only one.

The weather over the Channel improved today, the Germans report, and German bombers, escorted by fighters, again set off for London this morning. The main objectives of today's operations, we're told here, was the London area west of the great bend in the River Thames, especially railway lines in this section. Berlin says that direct hits were scored on railway facilities between Newcross Gate station, South Bermondsey station, and Queen's Road station.

It was during these operations over London, Berlin says, that air-fights developed with the result that I mentioned a moment ago.

The *12-Uhr Blatt* remarks this morning that it is well known that there are many war-important objectives in the West End shopping district of London. It says: "The shopping district of London's West End, in which, as is well known, there are many war-important objectives, is being continually hit with bombs. A bomb crashed through several stories of a West London hotel."

Again last night we had no air-raid in Berlin, but the High Command comments laconically that a few British bombers flew over western and south-western Germany during the night and dropped bombs on residential quarters. That's all the High Command tells us, but the German radio tonight announced that four persons were killed and eight seriously injured, most of them at Heidelberg.

The bombing of Heidelberg, following the one the night before at Bethel where nine children were killed, causes fresh indignation in the German press tonight. The *Lokal Anzeiger* in a front-page editorial tonight says these British pilots are "night murderers". And it continues: "It is a quite special sadism which no other people but the British can show."

A bulletin issued here a few minutes ago says that the German night-raids were continued again this evening. Chief target of the German night-raiders, it is said, was again London, especially the docks along the Thames and military objectives in the East End. The German bulletin speaks of heavy anti-aircraft fire over London tonight and the use of a great many searchlights, but says the bombings were successfully carried out. The night was clear over London, it adds, so that observers could check the results.

And the German radio remarks tonight: "Murder, only murder, is the slogan of the English war-mongers. Churchill sets his flyers against German women and children . . . The blood which Churchill makes flow in Germany, the tears of the German women and mothers, call for hard reprisals."

Incidentally, I see that someone in Berlin figured out the comparative time spent by Londoners and Berliners in air-raid cellars during the first eight days of the big air war. According to these figures, the Londoners spent the equivalent of more than three whole days in the cellar; the people of Berlin eight hours and fifteen minutes. Well, eight hours or so spread out over eight days is really not very much of a hardship.

The German press, I notice tonight, plays up New York dispatches that the British censor has forbidden foreign correspondents in London to mention air-raids while they're taking place. Here we have the same regulation. *[This paragraph was deleted by the censor.]*

Berlin September 22, 1940 01.11

This is Berlin.

The last week of September is here and yet in Berlin we know no more about the invasion of Britain than we did a month ago, or two months ago. Will it come off this fall? Will it be postponed? We don't know. One thing you can say for these totalitarian states – they keep their secrets well.

Five weeks ago I spent a few days idling around Ostende, Calais, and Boulogne, waiting for something to happen. Some people thought the invasion would begin any day. I must say we saw very little on the Channel at that time to indicate that the German army was about to attempt the difficult Channel crossing. Of course, that didn't prove very much – because modern armies can hide themselves very well from view. And besides, the German High Command is far too intelligent to permit snooping American correspondents a view of things the outside world is supposed to know nothing about. But I came away from that trip with the impression that the invasion was not very imminent. And so it proved.

But that does not mean that it has been called off. The army is there, strung along the coast. And it may be well to remember that the last man to land in Britain and conquer it 900 years ago, William the Conqueror, did it in the middle of October.

In the meantime the air-offensive on Britain continues and we were reminded in Berlin today that last night London got its fifteenth consecutive night of bombing. Quotations from American and Swedish correspondents in London appear in the German press today asking: How long can the millions of human beings cooped up in London take it? How many nights can a man, a woman, a child go without sleep?

Apparently, the answer is: Very many nights.

The Germans have had some experience with that themselves. For four months some of the towns of western Germany have been visited by the Royal Air Force – well, not every night, but nearly every night. It's true the British raids didn't last all night, but once you get up in the middle of the night, dress and go down in the cellar, wait there an hour or two, listen to anti-aircraft guns or the explosions of bombs – you don't get very much more restful sleep that night. Now I was in western Germany a few days ago, and I must say I was surprised at the way people were taking it. I think it's affected them, but not to any considerable extent.

Here in Berlin people lost a couple of weeks of sleep the first fortnight in September, but the British have not been over the German capital since a week ago tonight, so everyone has caught up on their sleep. For the moment it's not a problem.

Herr von Ribbentrop, the German Foreign Minister, is on his way back from Rome tonight, and it may be that in due course we'll know more about the future operations in this war. Berlin so far has been extremely reserved in giving out the slightest detail about what was discussed in Rome, or decided.

But today the German correspondents who accompanied their foreign

411

minister to Rome do report that what the Axis powers now believe to be the final phase of the war with Britain was decided on. They add that this phase is sure to bring victory. And that then the Duce and Ribbentrop went over plans for the future not only in Europe but in Africa.

Rudolf Kirker, probably the best informed of all German editors, writing in the *Frankfurter Zeitung* from Rome, says that the military situation is so rosy for the Axis that the problems of the "New Order" actually were at the forefront of the discussions. One gets the impression from these German correspondents that the Mediterranean and Africa loom larger and larger in the Rome-Berlin plans.

The German correspondents in Rome also raise a new problem that they say was discussed there. It's the problem of Greece. Rome, they say, is not pleased with certain goings-on in Greece. Greece is accused of acting unneutral and to be the object of British intrigues. The *Montag* says that the British admiralty is mixing into matters in Greek ports like it did earlier in Norway.

Not only Greece, but Spain then came into the Rome talks. The press here hails the new solidarity of Spain with the Axis war efforts, but just what they're referring to I do not quite know. At any rate, Senor Suñer, Franco's minister of the interior, is expected back in Berlin tomorrow to hear from Ribbentrop personally on the latter's talks in Rome.

Thirty-thousand German farmers now living in eastern Poland around Lublin are to be transferred, it's announced today, to the district around Posen. The same number of Poles now owning farms in the Posen district will be transferred to eastern Poland.

Berlin September 23, 1940 24.52

This is Berlin.

It now seems clear from a perusal of German reports that Germany's big air attacks on Britain – unlike a month ago – are recently more at night, not during the day. The High Command today calls the day flights "armed reconnaissance", the night raids "reprisal attacks".

There has been further armed reconnaissance today. According to a bulletin issued here this evening, strong formations of Heinkel bombers made an armed reconnaissance over southern England this morning. Photographs were taken, it's said, and bombs dropped. A number of air fights ensued, says the bulletin, and the score, according to the German count, was twenty-one British planes shot down; five German machines missing.

Air losses yesterday, incidentally, seem to have been almost the lowest since the air war began. The High Command reports that the shooting down of any enemy planes was not observed yesterday, while one German plane is missing. I suppose that means that the British planes which flew over Germany last night, including Berlin, got back without mishap.

According to information given us here today, the Germans used more than 150 planes in their bombing attacks on London last night. The German report says that big fires were observed at the commercial docks, in Piccadilly Circus and in the vicinity of Regent Street.

I was talking with a German airman the other day who's been making regular flights to London. He said every night he came over London, he was surprised, after the terrific amount of explosives dropped on it, to see so much of the city still standing. "It's an awfully big city," he exclaimed.

An idea of how much explosives have been dropped on Britain since the big air offensive began was given to us here today. The Germans say that 50,000,000 pounds of explosive bombs have been let loose on England in the last six weeks. There have been 200 air attacks on British harbors during which 17 million pounds of bombs were dropped. There were 700 raids on industrial works and airfields, with 30 million pounds of bombs being dumped on them.

Well, as I said, after a week of quiet, the British returned to Berlin last night and kept the populace in their cellars for two hours and twenty minutes. The High Command war communiqué says that a few single planes got through to Berlin, without doing any damage. The *DNB* communiqué on our raid last night reads as follows: "The British air force again carried out bombing attacks on German territory, especially on the capital, with the purpose of again dropping bombs on residential districts. As a result of the fire of the anti-aircraft guns and the employment of night fighters, the enemy did not succeed in causing great damage."

Later we were told that bombs fell on a suburb, but it was officially stated no military objectives were hit.

The indignation of the German press at last night's raid is again great. A typical headline is that of the *Nachtausgabe* which says in its bannerline: NEW NIGHT ACT OF THE PIRATES – ATTACK ON BERLIN FAILS. The same paper in an editorial tells us: "Winston Churchill again yesterday afternoon gave British airmen the order to drop their bombs on the German civilian population and thus continue their murder of men, women, and children."

And the *Börsen Zeitung* holds that last night, "Churchill continued the series of his criminal blows against the German civil population. Frankly, Churchill belongs to that category of criminals who in their stupid brutality are unteachable."

We learned today from the local press and radio of the British reports of the sinking of a ship in mid-Atlantic with the loss of 293 persons, including eighty-three British children. The story is the subject of front-page editorials in some of the German newspapers tonight and they all charge that Mr. Churchill is wholly responsible for what befell the children. The British Prime Minister knew, argue the German papers, that he was sending those children to death when he allowed them to proceed through dangerous waters. Many Berlin papers suggest that the ship hit a mine. The Berlin radio made this comment on the sinking tonight: "The world will see through the British agitation and will see with horror the contorted face of the murderer Churchill who has enriched his crimes by a new one."

Herr von Ribbentrop arrived back in Berlin from Rome this evening and drove immediately to the Chancellery to report to Herr Hitler, on his conversations with the Duce.

Serrano Suñer, Franco's special envoy here, returned to Berlin today from a visit to the Western Front. He will see the German Foreign Minister this morning to learn first hand of what was discussed in Rome.

Talk is more and more here that the Mediterranean is about to become a very major factor in this war, and the Berlin press does not fail to emphasize what they term Spain's new solidarity with the Axis.

Berlin September 24, 1940 24.50

This is Berlin.

This capital had its heaviest bombing of the war last night. Eleven persons were killed, fourteen injured, and several hundred people had to evacuate their homes.

The Berlin press is again extremely angry over last night's bombing. It calls it a new crime and the British airmen "murderers" acting on instructions to murder given by Mr. Churchill. It demands that revenge be taken against Britain.

The High Command in its daily communiqué tells us this evening that, as a reprisal for the British bombing of the old university town of Heidelberg, the *Luftwaffe* last night bombed Cambridge in England.

The German radio tonight declares that the English themselves admit there are so many military objectives all over London, scattered in thickly populated areas, that taken as a whole, Greater London is of the highest military importance. If the London public suffers, says the radio, then the British authorities who allowed the city to become such an armament center are responsible.

Following last night's bombing of Berlin, the radio here warned its listeners this evening to black-out their houses more carefully. The radio also emphasized again that when the alarm sounds everyone is to get off the streets immediately and head for the cellar, and not to stay in doorways or by the window.

The latest news here in Berlin of German air attacks on Britain is contained in two bulletins issued this evening.

One says that the *Luftwaffe* continued its attacks on southern England this afternoon. An aircraft factory in Southampton was heavily bombed and it's claimed that a number of direct hits were observed. In the air fighting that followed, the Germans say eighteen British planes were shot down and only one German plane lost. That's one of the biggest ratios of losses we've had here yet.

This morning, according to the other bulletin, German planes raided the London area. Hits are claimed on Waterloo Station and the India Docks. Fires in Newcastle were started, it's stated, and an ammunition dump in Great Yarmouth set on fire.

I learn on good authority – though it hasn't yet been officially announced – that Count Ciano is coming to Berlin Thursday to continue the talks begun in Rome last week. Serrano Suñer, Franco's special envoy here, who incidentally last night had his first experience of a bombing of Berlin, will remain in Berlin until Friday. And it seems likely that there will be a three-cornered talk with the Spaniard sitting in with Foreign Ministers Ribbentrop and Ciano. Señor Suñer expects to leave Berlin Friday to report to General Franco.

Though the utmost secrecy is being observed here still about the Rome talks, neutral observers are pretty sure that Berlin and Rome are getting ready to throw their full weight in Africa. The Axis powers think that Spain has a role to play. At any rate, many think that the fate of the British Empire may be decided this winter in Egypt, and not along the stormy Channel coast.

The Russian Ambassador conferred with Herr von Ribbentrop today. In this connection, many people here feel that those who are counting on Russia and Germany breaking away from each other are making a mistake.

Berlin September 26, 1940 24.05

This is Berlin.

This capital had its longest air-raid alarm of the war last night. Whether it was the most extensive I couldn't tell from my observation post in a very deep and well-protected cellar, to which I was escorted as soon as I had

415

finished my broadcast last night. *[The last part of the preceding sentence was deleted by the censor.]*

Friends of mine who did manage to take a peek at things tell me there was very little activity over the center of the city, the attack being concentrated for the most part on the fringes of the capital. An official statement declares that some houses and shacks were destroyed, others damaged.

The British came earlier last night than expected. Cafés, night-clubs, and restaurants in Berlin close now at 11 p.m., the idea being that people should get home by 11:30, before the enemy planes arrive. But last night the British caught a lot of people off base. They appeared promptly at 11 p.m. – by far the earliest hour since the bombings started. Thousands of people were caught in subways, street-cars, and buses on the way home and had to take shelter in the public cellars.

The alarm lasted exactly five hours, which is a little more than an hour longer than the previous record attack of last Monday night. Five hours in a cellar meant that most people were being robbed of over half their sleeping time. And I noticed in my cellar last night that, for the first time, many people brought blankets and pillows and tried to get some sleep. The all-clear came at 4 a.m. this morning, which didn't leave the working man much sleep before going to his factory.

Incidentally, I'm told Herr Hitler's air-raid cellar in the Chancellery has now been made available to some 500 children and 100 expectant mothers, each night. It's even reported that two babies were born there last night during the bombing.

The papers again call last night's bombing a crime, and cry for revenge. The *Börsen Zeitung* has this headline all over page one this noon: GERMAN CAPITAL AGAIN ATTACKED BY PIRATES – HOUSES DESTROYED – THEREFORE THE HAIL OF BOMBS ON LONDON UNTIL ENGLAND BREAKS DOWN. The paper begins its account of the bombing: "The greatest war-monger of all times, Winston Churchill, dispatched his murderers to Berlin again last night . . ."

The German commissar for Norway, Gauleiter Terboven, has formally declared the King of Norway will never return to his throne, liquidated the Norwegian government of Prime Minister Nygaardsvold, done the same to the provisional governing committee which was set up by the Germans to carry on during an interim period, dissolved all Norwegian political parties and named a commissarial council to transact government business.

This drastic step in Norway is made public in a *DNB* dispatch from Norway this morning. Questions put by American correspondents in the Wilhelmstrasse this morning as to its full meaning, as to whether for instance Norway is to be incorporated into the Reich, brought no answers as to the future state of the country. The impression given here is that the matter, like the future of Holland and Belgium, will have to wait the ending of the war.

Berlin September 27, 1940 14.01

This is Berlin.

The Axis powers have sprung another surprise upon the world. Germany, Italy, and Japan have signed a pact – it was actually signed in Herr Hitler's Chancellery here in Berlin just one hour ago – a pact recognizing the respective leadership of each other in Asia and Europe, and agreeing to give mutual support in setting up what is called the "New Order" in the European and east Asiatic continents.

More than that – and this is of vital importance to the United States – the three powers agree to come to the aid of each other militarily, economically, and politically in case any of the three nations is attacked by a power not yet involved in either the European war or the Chinese-Japanese war.

That power, it is clear, could only be the United States.

You might think it could mean Russia too. But no, Russia is excepted by a special paragraph in this three-power military pact. Paragraph five says that the present alliance in no way affects the political status between any of the three signatory nations and the Soviet Union. Russia, I understand, was informed of the new alliance a few days ago.

Well, that's the pact which was signed here in Berlin an hour ago between Germany, Italy, and Japan. Herr von Ribbentrop and Count Ciano, who arrived by air only an hour before, signed for their respective countries, and the Japanese Ambassador in Berlin, Mr. Kurusu, signed for his. Political prophets who thought that Count Ciano's arrival meant that Spain would be joining the war, were caught off base – and not for the first time.

The object of the new tri-part alliance was stated in a preamble to be to enable the three powers to work side by side in setting up a new order in their respective spheres of interest. East Asia for Japan. Europe for the Axis. Neutral observers saw that it was clearly directed against the United States, designed perhaps as a deterrent to America interfering in either the European or the China war, and presenting us with a common front if we did.

The pact, incidentally, goes into effect today, and will last for ten years.

The setting for the surprise was evolved with that talent which the Axis powers have shown before. First, Count Ciano, making the last part of his

417

journey by air, was given a hearty reception when he landed at Tempelhof shortly before noon. Both the radio and the press late last night or early this morning advised the public of the exact route the Foreign Minister would take, so there was a considerable crowd lining the streets. The majority of them seemed to be schoolchildren. We got the first tip-off as to what was coming when we noticed that the children, besides waving German and Italian flags, were waving Japanese flags as well. We expected to see Spanish flags, but they were Japanese.

Count Ciano, accompanied by Ribbentrop, was driven through the streets lined by S.S. guards and a crowd to Bellevue Castle, and at noon he went to the Chancellery where he was received by Herr Hitler. In the meantime, the entire staffs of the Italian and Japanese embassies had gathered in the ambassadorial hall of the Chancellery. The foreign press had also been convoked. Into this stepped just before 1 p.m., Herr von Ribbentrop and Count Ciano and the Japanese ambassador. Klieg lights glared out and the photographers ground away. Broadcasts in several languages, including Japanese, described the scene. Herr Hitler was present during the latter part of the ceremony.

Earlier in the day not only the German public but the whole world had been prepared for something, when all German radio stations, both medium and short-wave, sent out announcements that an important proclamation of the German government would be read at 1 p.m.

What's happened to the Spanish problem, I don't know. Important is that Japan, Germany, and Italy have told the world that they will now proceed to set up a New Order in Europe and east Asia as they see fit. And any power that interferes will become the enemy of all three.

A bulletin just issued says that German planes this morning again renewed their attacks on Britain. No details are yet available. Berlin says that Britain, and especially London, got one of its worst bombings of the war last night. During the evening hours, it's stated here, 886,000 pounds of bombs of all calibers were dropped on Britain. London received the lion's share, or some 600,000 pounds of bombs, according to the *DNB*. Liverpool, Birkenhead, and Southampton are other places the Germans say they bombed.

In London hits are claimed along the Thames, and the West India Docks are also said to have been bombed.

Berlin was not bombed last night. After four successive nights of it, most people, I think, were certainly ready for it and several friends tell me they woke up and waited for the sirens. But they never sounded off.

Berlin September 27, 1940 24.52

This is Berlin.

There is no attempt in informed circles here tonight to disguise the fact that the military alliance signed in Berlin today between Germany, Italy, and Japan has one great country in mind. That country is the United States.

The core of this tri-part pact, signed amidst the glaring Klieg lights and clicking cameras in Herr Hitler's Chancellery at 1 p.m., Berlin time, is Article III. It reads: "Germany, Italy, and Japan undertake to assist one another with all political, economic, and military means when one of the three contracting parties is attacked by a power at present not involved in the European war, or in the Sino-Japanese conflict."

There are two great powers not yet involved in either of those wars, Russia and the United States. But Article III doesn't refer to Russia. Article V refers to Russia, and by name. It says: "Germany, Italy, and Japan affirm that the aforesaid terms do not, in any way, affect the political status which exists at present between each of the three contracting parties and Soviet Russia."

The Soviet Union is out. That leaves the United States in. The German point of view, of course, is that it leaves America in only if we go to war with Japan or the Axis powers. The Wilhelmstrasse had something to say on that point this evening.

It referred us to a passage in the speech which Herr von Ribbentrop made after the pact had been signed. He said: "The pact is directed against no other nation, but exclusively against those warmongers and those irresponsible elements in the rest of the world who desire a further prolongation or an extension of this war ... Should any state", Ribbentrop continued, "seek to interfere in the final stage of the solution of the problems in Europe or Eastern Asia, and attack one of the signatories of this pact, that state will have to reckon with the combined forces of three nations numbering 250 millions."

At our press conference this evening, an American correspondent asked a Wilhelmstrasse spokesman whether Berlin was in accord with a view said to have been given in the Rome newspaper, *Giornale d'Italia* today. That view was that the tri-power pact was a warning to certain warmonger groups in the United States under Mr. Roosevelt's leadership.

The spokesman, after referring us to Herr von Ribbentrop's speech, gave this reply: "It is not the business of the Axis powers to comment on the policies of the United States. But there are certain circles in the United States which are continually and increasingly acting against the spirit which motivated the three-power pact. When part of the Foreign Minister's speech refers to certain international warmongers, then

419

certainly a great part of those referred to can be found in the United States."

In one part of his remarks, the German Foreign Minister referred to "the organized warmongers of the Jewish-capitalist democracies". He said they had brought on the war.

In the pact signed today, Japan recognizes the leadership of Germany and Italy in the "establishment of a New Order in Europe". Germany and Italy recognize the same thing for Japan in what is termed "greater East Asia". The alliance is to run for ten years, as from today.

Neutral observers here were interested in a paragraph in the preamble to the treaty which states that it is the desire of the three governments to extend cooperation to such nations in other spheres of the world as may be inclined to put forth endeavors along lines similar to their own. Some observers saw in that one of the most important parts of the treaty.

The setting for today's surprise was arranged with that skill which the Axis powers have shown on similar occasions before. Count Ciano arrived almost at the last minute by air. As he drove to the Chancellery he was cheered by crowds along the streets, most of them school-children. In the reception hall of the Chancellery, blazing with lights for the cameramen, there were colorful uniforms of all sorts as the two Foreign Ministers and the Japanese Ambassador entered at exactly 1 p.m. The text of the pact was read in three languages, the signatures affixed. At this juncture there were three loud knocks on the door. It opened and in came Herr Hitler and took a seat in the middle of the table. Herr von Ribbentrop formally informed him of the signing of the treaty. Then the three signatories made brief speeches which were broadcast around the world. Afterwards, there was a general exchange of telegrams between the three rulers.

War news is off the first page in Berlin today. Briefly, it is this. After four straight nights of bombing Berlin, the British did not visit the German capital last night.

Today the Germans claim a big victory in the air. In the course of widespread bombing attacks on Britain today, Berlin says seventy-five British planes were shot down while the Germans lost twenty-three. Besides London, which Berlin says was heavily bombed, attacks were also made on Derby, Birmingham, Manchester, and Bristol. The Germans report that they met little fighter opposition today, and that most British pursuit planes encountered were old types.

Berlin September 29, 1940 02.08

This is Berlin.

We had two air-raid alarms here last night. But so far as I could see there was not a great deal of fireworks. Among the distinguished visitors who presumably had to make for the cellars like everybody else was Count Ciano, the Italian Foreign Minister, and Señor Suñer, Spain's Minister of Interior. Both of them, incidentally, left Berlin this morning in separate special trains for Rome.

I see in the newspaper *Montag* tonight that there was a technical mistake made during the first all-clear last night. This mistake resulted in the sirens sounding a new alarm when they were supposed to sound the "all-clear". It didn't make much difference because a few minutes after the all-clear came another alarm.

Strolling through a residential district near the center of Berlin today I noticed two houses badly wrecked by bombs from a previous bombing. People stood around gazing, as if it were a rare curiosity. Well, it still is in Berlin. Very few houses in the city have been hit by bombs. Last night in Cologne, four persons were killed and twelve injured in a British attack.

Today, according to a communiqué issued here this evening, the *Luftwaffe* attacked Britain in several waves. London had four alarms, we're told. Besides London, the German communiqué says, other targets were attacked on the south and east coast of England. Docks on the lower Thames were also bombed, says Berlin. German pilots reported starting fires in the docks at Tilbury. Off the east coast, it's further stated here, a convoy was attacked by bombers and scattered. During the various air fights that ensued the Germans claim to have shot down ten British fighters without losing a single German plane. Another Berlin report says that a bomber commanded by a Lieutenant von Butler, dived to a height of 150 feet over the Rolls Royce engine works at Derby and dropped heavy bombs on some of the shops.

The *Völkischer Beobachter* today reports that the wildest rumors have been circulating in Berlin about what kind of alarm is sounded if gas bombs are dropped. It says no alarm of any kind will be sounded if gas is used, but explains that the authorities will find a means of quickly informing the populace about it.

Reaction in the United States to the military alliance signed here Friday between Japan, Germany, and Italy is being closely watched by the Wilhelmstrasse. There has been no effort in well-informed circles in Berlin to disguise who the pact is directed against – hence the interest in America's reaction. Speaking of this, the *Völkischer Beobachter* says: "The clear warning to the irresponsible elements leagued with Jews who wish to spread the war has been understood." *Der Montag* speaks of New

York newspapers in the service of the "war-mongering plutocracy and the Jews". The *Deutsche Allgemeine Zeitung* tells us that *[British Ambassador]* Lord Lothian's remark to Washington correspondents after he had seen the President Saturday that Britain needed more of everything, and more rapidly, was not published in the American press.

One question that neutral observers are asking is: Would the pact have been signed if, as many here thought, the war was to end before winter? If the answer is No, then it is easy to understand why the United States is the object of the pact, for if the war is to go on until spring, then American help to Britain will be a factor that everyone would have to take into consideration. *[This paragraph was deleted by the censor.]*

Spain's position is not yet clear. Senor Suñer is now going to Rome before returning to Madrid. But experienced observers over here are still watching Spain closely.

Dr. Goebbels made a speech to the Hitler Youth today. For one thing, he touched on the danger of air-attack and its effect on the Youth Movement. In many districts liable to air attack, he said, the carrying-through of the necessary work for the Hitler Youth had become impossible.

I mentioned the other day that the German Gauleiter in Norway had announced that the King would never return, had dissolved the Norwegian political parties and appointed a commissarial government to carry on.

Last night another German Gauleiter, speaking in Luxemburg, said: "Luxemburg is German. And Germany has taken over the New Order in Luxemburg."

With the incorporation of Luxemburg into the Third Reich, the whole of western Europe, with the exception of neutral Switzerland and Sweden, was now under the domination of Nazi Germany or the fascist régimes in Spain and Italy. By the end of the year, German forces would be poised to invade Yugoslavia and Greece, and though in September Hitler had secretly postponed Operation Sea Lion – the invasion of England – he would soon issue Directive Number 21: "The German armed forces must be prepared to crush Soviet Russia in a quick campaign before the end of the war against England . . ."

By then, however, Shirer had left Berlin for good. His wife and daughter had returned to America in October, and Shirer was naturally anxious to rejoin them. He had been living outside his home country for almost sixteen years, his health was poor, he was blind in one eye, and he was approaching middle age. He would have stayed on in Europe if need be, but felt that the knowledge and experience he had gained could be better employed as a news commentator; and indeed this was what he did for the next few years before going on to another career as a writer.

422

Soon after his return, in December, 1940, Shirer met with Ed Klauber, head of CBS News, to discuss his future assignments. After the meeting, Shirer made this summary of what he had said:

My usefulness in Germany is over. What I was getting by with, by innuendo, by use of Americanisms or American slang, has now been so fully reported by the German Embassy and German agents over here that that possibility is no longer open. A new censor at my side who scans my script as I read it, noting down voice inflection, irony, pauses, etc. At the end I am reduced to telling official lies or nothing.

For some time the Germans determined to get rid of or to muzzle the independent correspondents in Berlin. Among Americans, there were five: Tolischus of the *New York Times*, Barnes of the *Herald-Tribune*, Deuel of the *Chicago Daily News*, Sigrid Schultz of the *Chicago Tribune*, and myself.

Barnes was expelled in July, and is now dead.

Tolischus was sent out of Germany through a deal between the *Times* and the Nazis. He was supposed to remain away only six weeks but the Germans never again gave him a visa.

Deuel came out with me, feeling his usefulness was over, and warned that it would be wise for him to get out while he still could.

Miss Schultz is coming home this month. She will be the last of the independent correspondents.

Another consideration: My own relations with the Wilhelmstrasse are "correct", with the German radio and the German army they are friendly. But for a long time I've been under the suspicion of the Gestapo, which is the real power in the country, over-riding the ministries and radio whenever it chooses. For instance, the German Foreign Office tried to get me a return visa good for three months. The Gestapo refused it. They are suspicious of my frequent visits to Switzerland where, though I have always refused to see or communicate with the British, I have filled in my friend, Leland Harrison, our minister at Berne. The Gestapo accuses me of working for the American intelligence service . . .

For all these reasons, I've decided not to go back to Berlin.

There remains the rest of the continent, and if the situation there hadn't completely changed in the last few months, I would certainly go back there and try to carry on. But the rest of Europe is now completely dominated by Germany. It is no longer possible to do even faintly objective broadcasts from the few outlets left, notably Switzerland. Ed [Murrow] and I saw in Portugal that even harmless broadcasts are not permitted. Same is true of Vichy, Geneva, Budapest and Stockholm. Also, it's impossible to get around – chaos of communications, no railroads, or must go through Germany or German-controlled nations like Spain, Hungary, etc.

Therefore there is no continent of Europe to go back to for my kind of reporting.

INDEX

426

431

High Command communiqués 77,
79-81, 83, 144, 156, 206, 281,
293-4, 346-7
see also relative subjects
Naval Command, sinking of *Repulse*
113
Official News Agency *see DNB*
German Peace 43
Germany 34, 107, 131, 136, 312, 414
"Action in the Spring" 180, 187
Admiralty 81, 160
Graf Spee 166
aggression 50
air, defense 76
air force *see Luftwaffe*
Air Force Command 378
Air Ministry, technical and supply
department 179
air-raids
alarms 162, 359
protection league 398
shelters 377, 403
Allied army 277-8
Ambassadors 120-1
anti-aircraft, fire 150, 166, 227-8, 290,
378-81, 389-90, 392, 400
anti-semitism 122, 181
appeasement 47
armaments 199, 258, 372, 374, 389
arms 259
army 16, 78, 84, 93, 173, 199, 209,
246, 253, 274, 284, 293-4, 402-3
artillery 91-2, 182
chiefs *see* Göring; Keitel; Raeder;
von Brauchitsch
engineers 269, 331
Field Marshals 355-6
generals 187
infantry 91
moves in West 267
official communiqués 70, 76
Ascension Day (May 2, 1940) 258
auxiliary police 83
babies rations 81
bases 304, 350, 371
beer 206, 236
Berchtesgaden 23, 54-5

blackouts 206, 389
thefts 136, 162, 193, 201, 359
blockade 42-3, 158, 187, 204
bombs (gas or bacteria) 105
books 116-17, 163
Britain and France, terror of 204
Britain, hatred of 131
British
airplanes, over 369
bombers 23, 70-1, 80, 165-7, 297,
344, 352, 359, 362, 373, 379,
383, 386, 396, 410, 413
cities 394-5
military objectives 395
non-military objectives 397-8
Western area 281, 297, 302
night bombings 288-9, 306, 314-15,
348, 365, 387, 389-91, 394-5,
408
prisoners 289, 359
victorious withdrawals 382
broadcast, *sound* of war 79
cars 82, 231-2
casualty figures 93
Catholics 217
censorship 48, 152, 191, 193, 200-1,
211, 249, 302, 337, 381, 404-6,
408, 410, 416, 423
Christmas
(1939) 158, 163, 168-71, 212
clothes and textiles rationing 95,
133-4, 191, 233, 391
coal, shortage 166, 182-3, 192, 224,
232-3
coastal air battles 160-1, 165, 175
coffee ration 235, 396
cold winter (1940) 134-5
colonies 184, 206, 253, 347, 376
communications 424
concentration camps 158-9
continental empire 357-8
currency 200
death penalties 81
Defense Council, youth of Germany
214
defense forces, heads of 41, *see also*
Göring; Keitel; Raeder

438

439

440

441

442

443

445

446

447